A PASSION FOR LEARNING

The History of Christian Thought on Education

D. BRUCE LOCKERBIE

MOODY PRESS

CHICAGO

© 1994 by
D. BRUCE LOCKERBIE

ISBN: 0-8024-6581-1

1 3 5 7 9 10 8 6 4 2

Printed in the United States of America

LINCOLN CHRISTIAN COLLEGE AND SEMINARY

A
PASSION
FOR
LEARNING

*The History
of Christian
Thought on
Education*

*To those who have covenanted with me
for excellence in Christian schooling,
especially Jim Adare, Mike Beane,
Mike Beidel, Rob Davis, Bill Graf,
David Greenhalgh, Ron Grosh, Chuck Hall,
Don Kirkwood, and Herb Luxon*

All studies, philosophy, rhetoric are followed for this one object, that we may know Christ and honor him. This is the end of all learning and eloquence.

Desiderius Erasmus
Ciceronianus, 1528

CONTENTS

*Quotation marks surrounding a reading indicate a creed, essay, letter, or treatise; italics indicate a book excerpt.

PART 5
The Roots of Modern
Universal Schooling

PART 6
The American Experience: 1620–1750

PART 7
American Reformers: 1750–1900

FOREWORD

"History," said someone long ago, "is for the race what memory is for the individual." Without its precious reminders we would scarcely be able to function. Yet with what regularity well-meaning thinkers ignore the lessons of the past. We glance about us, dazzled by the neon nonsense of current fads, then we marry the spirit of an age and find ourselves widowed in the next.

One might think educators are immune to such irresponsible behavior. After all, to them has been committed the key of knowledge, the authority to determine grave matters of learning and value. But we educators also lean so noticeably to the pragmatic. Like Italy's famous tower in Pisa, we need strengthening of ancient structures so that those who visit our halls may again be permitted to climb and view.

A Passion for Learning represents part of that scaffolding intended to reinforce the tower of knowledge. Leading his readers through ten eras of "a history of Christian thought on education," Bruce Lockerbie allows us, indeed, forces us to attend primary sources, a behavior prized by serious teachers everywhere. To be sure, in many cases, perhaps most, we read translations of autographs into English; but apart from the collector's editorial introductions, the sages of the past speak for themselves without interposition of a modern hermeneutic.

Few will read through these pages from beginning to end, but many will do as I, keeping such a volume as ready reference for educational studies and documentation. It is, to be sure, a reference work, a verbal video of where pedagogical procedure has been for over 2,000 years.

Some of the selections offer no surprise—what would such a volume be without samples from Origen, Augustine, Calvin, and Luther. Other excerpts introduce us to new friends, names not common to most graduate students in Christian education—Hannah More, Anthony Benezet, and Peter Haile.

Considering the editor's expertise and eloquence, readers are well advised *not* to hurry through his introductory segments. They serve as both summary and entrance into the main body of each section and prepare our minds to absorb the wisdom that follows.

11

So we issue thanks and a collective affirmation to the compiler for allowing these shining documents of the past to illumine our all-too-troubled and harried present.

KENNETH O. GANGEL
Vice President of Academic
Affairs and Academic Dean
Dallas Theological Seminary

PREFACE

Among the foibles of human nature, one of the most discouraging is our refusal to learn from our own history. Instead, we display cycles of interest—periods of ebb and flow, waning and waxing—in those matters that ultimately ought to mean most to us. We seem unable to sustain our sometimes high regard for principles, and we throw away that which we ought to value most.

We scarcely need to look beyond our own community's public schools to find telling instances of this constantly swinging pendulum. Secular educational theory is never static, always swinging from one extreme to the other—from "kids' power" to "back-to-basics," from "open classroom" to "outcomes-based education." Whatever was true a decade ago, the opposite probably prevails today. If a decade ago our citizens voted down the budget and eliminated any presumed "frills" of instruction in art and music, today's curriculum brags about its compulsory courses in the fine arts, while the marching band prepares for an appearance at the Tournament of Roses Parade. If the last high school principal chose to be known to every student by his chummy first name, the current principal has reverted to a formal and austere relationship. If the absence of any standards for appropriate attire resulted in a costume of T-shirts and jeans, its subsequent deterioration into slovenliness and careless attitudes toward learning now demands a dress code.

Current causes seldom survive the passing of even one complete student generation—say, ten or twelve years; usually, long before that span of time elapses, the cause is abandoned. Within those years, everyone concerned seems to have forgotten the last revolution and how earnestly its champions struggled. The leaders have now grown weary of the fight, or have switched allegiances, or no longer have children of their own in school and so no longer care. When the battle cry goes up from a new band of enthusiasts, nobody seems to bother looking for anyone with a knowledge of history, someone who could inform or remind the new reformers that their cause has been debated before. So it goes, in tedious and seemingly endless endeavors that fail to find the point of balance.

Sadly, this tendency toward wild careening away from a balanced perspective is not restricted to secular society nor to secular education.

13

Among professing Christians—especially when the topic in dispute is Christian education—this same instability may be evident. We too have our periodic fascinations with fad and fancy, our temporary blind spots, our wholesale discarding of the worthwhile along with the trashy. We too have reason to repent for our own or our preceding generation's wrongheadedness, our disobedience in failing to observe the commandment of God, "Do not move an ancient boundary stone set up by your forefathers" (Proverbs 22:28).

One of these ancient landmarks of godly experience has been the provision by parents of a godly education for their children. Until recently, this ancient landmark, called *Christian schooling*, has seemed buried under brush and debris; but a new era may be upon us. This book, then, is not so much about Christian *education* in general as it is about one aspect of Christian education, namely, Christian *schooling*.

I believe in Christian education for everyone, beginning with a parent's cooing words of Scripture and gospel songs into an infant's ear, moving on to the discipline of family and personal Bible reading and prayer in the home; from there, to informal studies in lay-groups.

It costs nothing but time to establish the foundations of Christian *education* within a family. But Christian *schooling* is something else: Christian schooling does not come cheaply; it is for those willing to sacrifice to make it possible not only for their own children but also for the children of others unable—in spite of their sacrifices—to afford such schooling. Whether Christian schooling occurs in an institutional setting or at home, parents must pay for the buildings, resources, and time of the instructors who provide that schooling.

Sacrifice is necessary because anything as precious as a child's mind—as well as a child's heart, soul, and strength—requires the support of parents for whom no cost is too dear.

If, then, Christian education in the form of Christian schooling is so important, why have we sometimes lost its significance? Once having learned the merits of an ideal, why do we allow its worth to lapse from memory? What can we in this generation do to save posterity—if the Lord tarry—from repeating this folly of forgetfulness?

To begin, we must agree on terminology. *Christian schooling* is a phrase that requires careful definition and delineation, which it receives throughout this book. Here it may be used as a convenient shorthand to describe formal pedagogical instruction—whether institutionalized or at home—for children usually grouped in elementary and secondary grades, kindergarten through grade 12, intended by those who found and maintain them to be places where the principles of biblical Christian doctrine are manifest in both teaching and living. Another way of describing these schools is to say that their entire curriculum exemplifies a biblical world-and-life view, a understanding of reality from a perspective framed by the Bible's revelation of truth.

On the surface, one might expect that every earnest Christian parent, and especially every pastor and professor of Christian education in college and seminary, would support such a school environment favorable to Christian formation and discipleship. Such is not the case. Kenneth O. Gangel estimates that as many as four of every five evangelical families have never availed themselves of a Christian school for their children.[1] A survey of evangelical pastors discloses that as many as 40 percent believe that Christian schools do not merit the attendance of their own children.[2] The reasons for such negative opinion need careful research and, where possible, careful attention to correct.

Nonetheless, since the mid-1970s, more and more Christians— fundamentalist, evangelical, charismatic, and Reformed—in North America are becoming aware of the importance of placing their children in a school environment compatible with their Christian faith and practice.[3] Our ancestors, of course, knew this necessity. The Roman Catholic Church used to boast, "Give me a child until the age of seven, and I care not who instructs him thereafter." Heroes of the Protestant Reformation—Martin Luther and Philipp Melanchthon, John Calvin, and John Knox—understood the essential need for schooling that would teach a child the Lordship of Jesus Christ. The early colonists in North America brought with them this same recognition and made it the cornerstone of their society by establishing schools and colleges to fulfill that purpose. Although over the years many of these institutions abdicated their commitment to an orthodox and biblically grounded Christian education, the evangelical church never lost faith in its vision for a Christian higher education. In the closing decade of this century, more than eighty colleges—many of them founded as academies in the nineteenth century— representing some two dozen Protestant denominations and enrolling almost 100,000 students, belong to the Christian College Coalition.[4]

Yet, throughout the twentieth century, this same passion for educating college students in the fear of the Lord seemed hardly to move most North American Christians to desire similar teaching for their school-age children. Instead, most Christians either ignored the importance of a full-orbed Christian elementary and secondary schooling or fell into a comfortable complacency that readily identified the state with the kingdom of God and the democratic political system with Christian virtue.

15

Thus, most Christians have substituted a tax-supported public school education for Christian schooling. Public schooling will always have a place for those who must for a variety of reasons have a portion of their education in the public setting; yet what used to be a free Christian education with taxpayers' funds now has been converted into a largely amoral, "value-free" education that trains children to ignore the existence of God and values founded on the Judeo-Christian ethic. But every student deserves to have at least part of his education occur through Christian schooling.

Today only a few isolated communities in the United States and Canada retain their cultural identity as primarily Christian and so reflect Christian distinctives in their local public schools; Orange City, Iowa, for instance, has been a notable example of this phenomenon. But such is scarcely the case in the public schools of Long Island, New York, where my wife teaches; nor is it the norm in most other public school districts on this continent.

More often, overcautious legal decisions and bureaucratic policies designed to implement those opinions have fostered within the public schools hostility toward any attempt at breaching Thomas Jefferson's wall of separation between church and state. Generally speaking, the teaching of a Christian view of reality—a Christian epistemology that begins with the existence of a supernatural and personal God who becomes known to us, His creatures, in the person of Jesus of Nazareth and in the revealed truth of Scripture—is as unlikely as advocating a flat-earth theory.

Such conflict between approved and disapproved attitudes toward religion reflects the ongoing struggle between secularism and the gospel, accelerates the incursion of godlessness upon public schooling—the overt teaching of human autonomy and freedom from responsibility to any divinity; the erosion of moral standards based upon Scripture and the substitution of ethical choices through "values clarification"; the rise of "outcomes-based education," with politically correct social outcomes prescribed.

As a result, some Christian parents and pastors have only recently had their eyes opened to their mistaken assumptions about the nature of elementary and secondary schooling, both public and Christian. These parents and pastors now see that the public school can no longer be assumed to be an environment supportive of Christian virtues; in fact, in many public schools, substantial animosity toward Christian faith has overtaken former professions of objective neutrality. Furthermore, even where civil religion and pious patriotism once existed, enlightened eyes perceive that they were never the same as authentic Christian belief.

But as the twentieth century ends, it appears that parental and pastoral—if not yet widespread congregational—support for Christian schools is growing on account of negative pressures, from the banning of Bibles from most public school classrooms (even as a literary work) to the purging of prayers from school ceremonies. Advocates of Christian schooling would prefer parents to enroll their children for positive reasons: because parents recognize that "the fear of the Lord is the beginning of knowledge" (Proverbs 1:7); because "in [Jesus Christ] are hidden all the treasures of wisdom and knowledge" (Colossians 2:3). Far too many parents, when asked why their children attend a Christian school, respond in terms of personal safety, protection from adverse secular values, and a caring faculty—as if to suggest that Christian school teachers have a monopoly on caring for children. Far fewer answer with reference to a rigorous academic curriculum consciously and competently taught to instill a biblical framework for understanding reality.

But while the number of Christian schools is still small (the total enrollment seldom reaches 10 percent of all school-age children in any region) and some of the reasons for existence seem more related to narcotics than nurture, nonetheless the political bureaucracy that oversees public schooling and its funding has been compelled to take notice. The influence of Christian schools and their constituents continues to grow. The most telling feature of the burgeoning Christian school movement is the willingness of parents to commit themselves to the financial burden of supporting their children's education with tuition and fees, while at the same time continuing to pay taxes levied on behalf of public schooling.

Enthusiasm is vital to the continuing existence and growth of Christian schools, but more important is godly *enlightenment*—wisdom derived from God's own revealed truth in Scripture, knowledge based upon fact illumined by the Spirit of Truth, and a godly understanding that gives every member of the Christian community a grasp of the purpose, program, and promise that belong to Christian schooling.

Wisdom, knowledge, and understanding: This book offers an overview of how to find godly enlightenment in those three areas. First, we find godly wisdom by looking at biblical instruction, which informs believing Christians of their mission to teach God's truth. Second, we find godly knowledge by reviewing the historical facts, which tie together the work of Christians from the Church Fathers to our own times. Third, we find godly understanding in those texts that spell out the philosophy and practice of a Christian education, which integrate all learning under the reality of the Lordship of Jesus Christ.

A word about the shape this book takes: This collection is primarily intended for students rather than scholars. It does not purport to represent the whole canon of documents concerning Christian education in schools; it presents selected readings, some of which, by necessity, have been cut. But in each chronological period, I have placed at least one major document to serve as a touchstone for the thinking and development of the Christian mind of that era. This method will be of particular use to students; scholars of Christian schooling already know where to find the full documents. In addition, many, but not all, primary documents have endnotes; this reflects my desire to please the student—not the scholar—with references to books that students should be able to find in general university libraries rather than at the specialists' libraries. Thus books published prior to the early twentieth century typically are not listed for the reader in the endnotes (even though the studious academic may have access to such works).

Finally, after Part 4, "Christian Humanism and the Protestant Reformation," I have made no attempt at balancing subsequent and divergent religious perspectives; instead, there is a clear choice to highlight the English-speaking Protestant movement in founding schools, particularly those in the United States. I have not excluded all other nonevangelical or even anti-Christian voices; for instance, you will read the ideas of such leaders as Horace Mann and John Dewey. My reasoning is that their very opposition to an evangelical world-and-life view has weighed heavily upon the history of Christian schooling. Although Mann, Dewey, and others disputed Christian thought on education, we cannot ignore their influence.

I invite you to read this history and learn, or be reminded, how Christian thought has affected—and can continue to affect—Western education for the good.

ACKNOWLEDGMENTS

The publication of this book coincides with the fortieth anniversary of the most influential book on Christian schooling published in this century, *The Pattern of God's Truth* by Frank E. Gaebelein, founding headmaster of The Stony Brook School. The material was first delivered as the W. H. Griffith Thomas Lectures at Dallas Theological Seminary before being published by Oxford University Press in 1954 and later by Moody Press.

For six years, 1957–1963, I was privileged to work under Frank Gaebelein's leadership at Stony Brook. From him I learned to struggle toward wholeness in preparing and teaching my classes, seeking to live out my faith in a community of teenagers and adults, learning to discover the centrality of God's presence as the final test of truth. Frank Gaebelein nurtured in me whatever gifts he perceived. As a result, I acknowledge the debt I owe him for encouraging me in my vocation as a Christian schoolman.

I acknowledge those who assisted me in the compiling of this book: Phyllis Akins, Emma Clark Library, Setauket, New York; Warren E. Benson, Trinity Evangelical Divinity School, Deerfield, Illinois; Kenneth O. Gangel, Dallas Theological Seminary; Dorothie L. Goldberg, The Stony Brook School, New York; and David L. Zercher, University of North Carolina, whose editorial assistance has been invaluable.

I thank God for the support of my wife, Lory, whose never-failing love inspires me.

PART I
THE BIBLICAL
FOUNDATION

"*I am the Alpha and the Omega,*" *says the Lord God, "who is, and who was, and who is to come, the Almighty.*"

Revelation 1:8

THE BIBLICAL
FOUNDATION

F rom the time that Moses received the Law of God, the people of Israel had known their responsibility to teach their children: "These commandments that I give you today are to be on your hearts. Impress them upon your children. Talk about them when you sit at home and when you walk along the road, when you lie down and when you get up" (Deuteronomy 6:6–7).

In short, the religious instruction of children was to be an all-encompassing enterprise. Evidently each father was to be responsible for the instruction of his own household, a duty by which a father's effectiveness would be measured and his name honored or dishonored.

After Moses, Joshua affirmed his intention, both for himself and his family: "Choose for yourselves this day whom you will serve . . . but as for me and my house, we will serve the Lord" (Joshua 24:15). Yet without a systematic means of instructing all youths beyond the home, irresponsibility within individual families inevitably led to national apostasy. To the mass of people, God's commandments to Israel became largely unknown. Only those whose fathers were as faithful as Joshua or who, like the child Samuel, were singled out for priestly instruction, learned the Law.

Even among them, the record points to a shameful succession of fathers who failed to teach their children the ways of obedience to the Lord. Eli, the priest to whom Hannah entrusted her son Samuel, had two corrupt sons of his own, Hophni and Phineas. When Phineas died, his wife named their newborn son Ichabod, which means "the glory has departed from Israel" (1 Samuel 2:12–4:22). Samuel, however, was equally unsuccessful as a father of faithful sons. His offspring, Joel and Abijah, were so notoriously corrupt in their perversion of justice that the leaders of Israel rejected them as Samuel's successors and demanded a king instead (1 Samuel 8:1–6).

Most sadly stands the case of King David. His eldest sons, Absalom and Adonijah, both rebelled against him and usurped his throne. At Absalom's death, David lamented, "O my son Absalom! My son, my son Absalom! If only I had died instead of you— O Absalom, my son, my son!" (2 Samuel 18:33). The reason for David's sorrow—as well as his sons' rebellious behavior—is explained to us in the story of Adonijah's insurrection. The chronicler writes that "his father [David] had never interfered with him by asking, 'Why do you behave as you do?'" (1 Kings 1:6).

In those homes where God was still honored, the law of God was memorized and so passed on to succeeding generations. But before the end of the seventh century B.C., oral tradition had been augmented by the written word. So the five books of Moses —the Pentateuch or Torah—became available in written form, as were the Psalms; the history of Israel was being compiled; the Word of the Lord through prophets such as Habakkuk was being transcribed.

But with the example of faithless fathers in high positions— including kings who did that which was evil in the sight of the Lord—the law and its teaching fell into discard. By 621 B.C., during the reign of the godly king Josiah, the discovery of the Torah and its public reading at Josiah's orders excited a national reform (2 Kings 22:1–23:30). However, immediately upon Josiah's death, his son Jehoahaz and then another son Jehoiakim reversed their father's example, so that once again the teaching of the Law was ignored.

Then came God's judgment in the form of captivity in Babylon (588–538 B.C.). During these years of bondage by the rivers of Babylon, remorse that the Scriptures had been ignored led to a particular mission on the part of Ezra, sometime during the latter part of the fifth century B.C. At the same time that Sophocles was writing his Oedipus trilogy in Athens, Ezra is described as "a teacher well versed in the law of Moses" (Ezra 7:6), which means that he had been schooled in the skill of writing down and interpreting the Law. When he returned to the rebuilt city of Jerusalem, Ezra "devoted himself to the study and observance of the law of the Lord, and to teaching its decrees and laws in Israel" (Ezra 7:10).

Ezra's opportunity to fulfill his mission began auspiciously enough with a public reading of the Book of the Law, probably Deuteronomy (Nehemiah 7:73b–8:18). Because many of the returned exiles no longer understood Hebrew, the language in which the Law had been written, Ezra had translators stationed among the people to give them a simultaneous translation—an instant understanding in Aramaic—of the words being read. With this translation, it may be supposed, also went interpretation; thus we read, "They read from the Book of the Law of God, making it clear and giving the meaning so that the people could understand what was being read" (Nehemiah 8:8).

Upon returning from captivity, the Hebrew people recognized the need to institutionalize, for the first time, the teaching that one generation would pass along to the next. So, during the period following the Exile, a professional class of teachers developed, generally known as "scribes." Along with them arose a synagogue in every village. Children came to the synagogue for instruction, at first only boys from ages six or seven. This system is sometimes credited to one of the first great teachers, Joshua ben Gamala or Gamaliel, under whose system a youth named Saul of Tarsus was taught.

A student addressed his synagogue teacher as "Rabbi," meaning "my master" or "my teacher." From the local synagogue school, a student could advance to higher forms of schooling, similar to our modern progression from primary and secondary school to university. There a student met teachers whose credentials qualified them to be called "sages" or "doctors of the law," such as those with whom the child Jesus was found in the temple (Luke 2:41 ff.).

Although these teachers could both read and write, they taught largely by requiring rote recitation; their students, sitting around them, repeated the prescribed answer to each dictated question over and over until the obligatory response came with automatic precision. Much the same method of instruction still prevails throughout Middle and Far East schooling today, as well as in those religions which catechize or drill into new converts the teaching of doctrine by this same means: Ask a series of questions to which the approved answers must be given.

To this system of teaching and learning—no doubt—came a young child in the village of Nazareth, ostensibly the son of a carpenter named Joseph and his wife Mary. But by the time of His bar mitzvah, a half-dozen years later, this boy passing through the rites to Jewish manhood had already departed from the conventional education process. Instead of parroting the memorized answers His teachers had compelled Him to learn and repeat, this youth dared to ask questions of His own. As a result, "everyone who heard him was amazed at his understanding and his answers" (Luke 2:47).

When His own time came to be hailed as "Rabbi" by Andrew, son of Zebedee, and his companion (John 1:35 ff.), Jesus of Nazareth welcomed their question, "Rabbi, where are you staying?" According to Alfred Edersheim, the reply of Jesus, "Come and you will see," signifies more than an invitation to view His dwelling-place; it also completes a formula recognized as a request for admission to the Rabbi's tutelage.

Here, of course, is the great distinction between the teaching of Jesus Christ and that of His predecessors or contemporaries. The teaching of Jewish scribes, rabbis, or doctors of the law depended largely upon their quoting acknowledged commentators on the law, much the same as so-called teaching by literary critics today, who refer continually to each other's writings more often than to the texts of literature they presume to be teaching. But Jesus' teaching was different, "because he taught them as one who had authority, not as the teachers of the law" (Mark 1:22). That authority—that prerogative or privilege of manifest power—derived from the Person of the Teacher himself and from His example. Jesus of Nazareth taught not only what He knew but also who He is.

Some four hundred years before Jesus of Nazareth taught in the synagogues of Galilee and Judaea, the Greek philosopher Plato had written, "If you ask what is the good in general of education, the answer is easy: Education produces good men, and good men act nobly." Thus the classical Greco-Roman ideal for education was established; its purpose was the engendering of good and noble citizens.

The teacher of Nazareth also called for faithful citizenship, but He pointed to a source of goodness different from Plato's. Jesus returned to the commands of God given to Moses, compressed into two statements, on which, He said, "all the Law and the Prophets hang: 'Love the Lord your God with all your heart and with all your soul and with all your mind.' This is the first and greatest commandment. And the second is like it: 'Love your neighbor as yourself'" (Matthew 22:37–40).

Jesus Christ taught that love for God must be expressed in love for one's neighbor; so all His teaching condemned mere pious performance of religious rites as a means of pleasing God and commended acts of service and self-sacrifice on behalf of others.

The selections from Scriptures that follow explain and in some cases even define true wisdom, a wisdom that comes from God alone and which He reveals through His holy Word. As we will see, the superiority of such wisdom does not preclude the need for knowledge, but makes knowledge subordinate to it. Wisdom is found through understanding of truth, as the following parts will show.

THE OLD TESTAMENT

The following twelve passages from the Old Testament begin at the beginning, the point of all origination: the creation itself. The creation narrative unfolds from the very mind and will of God. Here we find God's purpose for creating the universe, with mankind at the pinnacle of that creation, made in the *imago dei*, the very image and likeness of God.

From this creation narrative through the story of the Fall and beyond to the giving of the law and the words of the prophets, we trace God's revelation of divine *wisdom*, always surpassing human *knowledge* yet mediated through *understanding*.

Genesis 1:1-2:3

In the beginning God created the heavens and the earth. Now the earth was formless and empty, darkness was over the surface of the deep, and the Spirit of God was hovering over the waters.

And God said, "Let there be light," and there was light. God saw that the light was good, and he separated the light from the darkness. God called the light "day" and the darkness he called "night." And there was evening, and there was morning—the first day.

And God said, "Let there be an expanse between the waters to separate water from water." So God made the expanse and separated the water under the expanse from the water above it. And it was so. God called the expanse "sky." And there was evening, and there was morning—the second day.

And God said, "Let the water under the sky be gathered to one place, and let dry ground appear." And it was so. God called the dry ground "land," and the gathered waters he called "seas." And God saw that it was good.

Then God said, "Let the land produce vegetation: seed-bearing plants and trees on the land that bear fruit with seed in it, according to their various kinds." And it was so. The land produced vegetation: plants bearing seed according to their kinds and trees bearing fruit with seed in it according to their kinds. And God saw that it was good. And there was evening, and there was morning—the third day.

And God said, "Let there be lights in the expanse of the sky to separate the day from the night, and let them serve as signs to mark seasons and days and years, and let them be lights in the expanse of the sky to give light on the earth." And it was so. God made two great lights—the greater light to govern the day and the lesser light to govern the night. He also made the stars. God set them in the expanse of the sky to give light on the earth, to govern the day and the night, and to separate light from darkness. And God saw that it was good. And there was evening, and there was morning—the fourth day.

And God said, "Let the water teem with living creatures, and let birds fly above the earth across the expanse of the sky." So God created the great creatures of the sea and every living and moving thing with which the water teems, according to their kinds, and every winged bird according to its kind. And God saw that it was good. God blessed them and said, "Be fruitful and increase in number and fill the water in the seas, and let the birds increase on the earth." And there was evening, and there was morning—the fifth day.

And God said, "Let the land produce living creatures according to their kinds: livestock, creatures that move along the ground, and wild animals, each according to its kind." And it was so. God made the wild animals according to their kinds, the livestock according to their kinds, and all the creatures that move along the ground according to their kinds. And God saw that it was good.

Then God said, "Let us make man in our image, in our likeness, and let them rule over the fish of the sea and the birds of the air, over the livestock, over all the earth, and over all the creatures that move along the ground."

So God created man in his own image
in the image of God he created him;
male and female he created them.

God blessed them and said to them, "Be fruitful and increase in the number; fill the earth and subdue it. Rule over the fish of the sea and the birds of the air and over every living creature that moves on the ground."

Then God said, "I give you every seed-bearing plant on the face of the whole earth and every tree that has fruit with seed in it. They will be yours for food. And to all the beasts of the earth and all the birds of the air and all the creatures that move on the ground—everything that has the breath of life in it—I give every green plant for food." And it was so.

God saw all that he had made, and it was very good. And there was evening, and there was morning—the sixth day.

Thus the heavens and the earth were completed in all their vast array.

By the seventh day God had finished the work he had been doing; so on the seventh day he rested from all his work. And God blessed the seventh day and made it holy, because on it he rested from all the work of creating that he had done.

Genesis 2:4–10, 15–25

This is the account of the heavens and the earth when they were created.

When the Lord God made the earth and the heavens, no shrub of the field had yet appeared on the earth and no plant of the field had yet sprung up; the Lord God had not sent rain on the earth and there was no man to work the ground, but streams came up from the earth and watered the whole surface of the ground. And the Lord God formed man from the dust of the ground and breathed into his nostrils the breath of life, and man became a living being.

Now the Lord God had planted a garden in the east, in Eden; and there he put the man he had formed. And the Lord God made all kinds of trees grow out of the ground—trees that were pleasing to the eye and good for food. In the middle of the garden were the tree of life and the tree of the knowledge of good and evil.

A river watering the garden flowed from Eden, and from there it divided; it had four headstreams. . . .

The Lord God took the man and put him in the Garden of Eden to work it and take care of it. And the Lord God commanded the man, "You are free to eat from any tree in the garden; but you must not eat from the tree of the knowledge of good and evil, for when you eat of it you will surely die."

The Lord God said, "It is not good for the man to be alone. I will make a helper suitable for him."

Now the Lord God had formed out of the ground all the beasts of the field and all the birds of the air. He brought them to the man to see what he would name them; and whatever the man called each living creature, that was its name. So the man gave names to all the livestock, the birds of the air and all the beasts of the field.

But for Adam no suitable helper was found. So the Lord God caused the man to fall into a deep sleep; and while he was sleeping, he took one of the man's ribs and closed up the place with flesh. Then the Lord God made a woman from the rib he had taken out of the man, and he brought her to the man.

The man said,
"This is now bone of my bones
and flesh of my flesh;
she shall be called 'woman,'
for she was taken out of man."

For this reason a man will leave his father and mother and be united to his wife, and they will become one flesh.

The man and his wife were both naked, and they felt no shame.

Genesis 3:1–24

Now the serpent was more crafty than any of the wild animals the Lord God had made. He said to the woman, "Did God really say, 'You must not eat from any tree in the garden'?"

The woman said to the serpent, "We may eat fruit from the trees in the garden, but God did say, 'You must not eat fruit from the tree that is in the middle of the garden, and you must not touch it, or you will die.'"

31

"You will not surely die," the serpent said to the woman. "For God knows that when you eat of it your eyes will be opened, and you will be like God, knowing good and evil."

When the woman saw that the fruit of the tree was good for food and pleasing to the eye, and also desirable for gaining wisdom, she took some and ate it. She also gave some to her husband, who was with her, and he ate it. Then the eyes of both of them were opened, and they realized they were naked; so they sewed fig leaves together and made coverings for themselves.

Then the man and his wife heard the sound of the Lord God as he was walking in the garden in the cool of the day, and they hid from the Lord God among the trees of the garden. But the Lord God called to the man, "Where are you?"

He answered, "I heard you in the garden, and I was afraid because I was naked; so I hid."

And he said, "Who told you that you were naked? Have you eaten from the tree that I commanded you not to eat from?"

The man said, "The woman you put here with me—she gave me some fruit from the tree, and I ate it."

The Lord God said to the woman, "What is this you have done?"

The woman said, "The serpent deceived me, and I ate."

So the Lord God said to the serpent, "Because you have done this,

> "Cursed are you above all the livestock
>> and all the wild animals!
> You will crawl on your belly
>> and you will eat dust
>> all the days of your life.
> And I will put enmity
>> between you and the woman,
>> and between your offspring and hers;
> he will crush your head,
>> and you will strike his heel."

To the woman he said,

> "I will greatly increase your pains in childbearing;
>> with pain you will give birth to children.
> Your desire will be for your husband,
>> and he will rule over you."

To Adam he said, "Because you listened to your wife and ate from the tree about which I commanded you, 'You must not eat of it,'

> "Cursed is the ground because of you;
> through painful toil you will eat of it
> all the days of your life.
> It will produce thorns and thistles for you,
> and you will eat the plants of the field.
> By the sweat of your brow
> you will eat your food
> until you return to the ground,
> since from it you were taken;
> for dust you are
> and to dust you will return."

Adam named his wife Eve, because she would become the mother of all the living.

The Lord God made garments of skin for Adam and his wife and clothed them. And the Lord God said, "The man has now become like one of us, knowing good and evil. He must not be allowed to reach out his hand and take also from the tree of life and eat, and live forever." So the Lord God banished him from the Garden of Eden to work the ground from which he had been taken. After he drove the man out, he placed on the east side of the Garden of Eden cherubim and a flaming sword flashing back and forth to guard the way to the tree of life.

Exodus 20:1–17

And God spoke all these words:

"I am the Lord your God, who brought you out of Egypt, out of the land of slavery.

"You shall have no other gods before me.

"You shall not make for yourself an idol in the form of anything in heaven above or on the earth beneath or in the waters below. You shall not bow down to them or worship them; for I, the Lord your God, am a jealous God, punishing the children for the sin of the fathers to the third and fourth generation of those who hate me, but showing love to thousands who love me and keep my commandments.

"You shall not misuse the name of the Lord your God, for the Lord will not hold anyone guiltless who misuses his name.

"Remember the Sabbath day by keeping it holy. Six days you shall labor and do all your work, but the seventh day is a Sabbath to the Lord your God. On it you shall not do any work, neither you, nor your son or daughter, nor your manservant or maidservant, nor your animals, nor the alien within your gates. For in six days the Lord made the heavens and the earth, the sea, and all that is in them, but he rested on the seventh day. Therefore the Lord blessed the Sabbath day and made it holy.

"Honor your father and your mother, so that you may live long in the land the Lord your God is giving you.

"You shall not murder.

"You shall not commit adultery.

"You shall not steal.

"You shall not give false testimony against your neighbor.

"You shall not covet your neighbor's house. You shall not covet your neighbor's wife, or his manservant or maidservant, his ox or donkey, or anything that belongs to your neighbor."

Deuteronomy 6:1–25

These are the commands, decrees and laws the Lord your God directed me to teach you to observe in the land that you are crossing the Jordan to possess, so that you, your children and their children after them may fear the Lord your God as long as you live by keeping all his decrees and commands that I give you, and so that you may enjoy long life. Hear, O Israel, and be careful to obey so that it may go well with you and that you may increase greatly in a land flowing with milk and honey, just as the Lord, the God of your fathers, promised you.

Hear, O Israel: The Lord our God, the Lord is one. Love the Lord your God with all your heart and with all your soul and with all your strength. These commandments that I give you today are to be upon your hearts. Impress them on your children. Talk about them when you sit at home and when you walk along the road, when you lie down and when you get up. Tie them as symbols on your hands and bind them on your foreheads. Write them on the doorframes of your houses and on your gates.

When the Lord your God brings you into the land he swore to your fathers, to Abraham, Isaac and Jacob, to give you—a land with large, flourishing cities you did not build, houses filled with all kinds of good things you did not provide, wells you did not dig, and vineyards and olive groves you did not plant—then when you eat and are satisfied, be careful that you do not forget the Lord, who brought you out of Egypt, out of the land of slavery.

Fear the Lord your God, serve him only and take your oaths in his name. Do not follow other gods, the gods of the peoples around you; for the Lord your God, who is among you, is a jealous God and his anger will burn against you, and he will destroy you from the face of the land. Do not test the Lord your God as you did at Massah. Be sure to keep the commands of the Lord your God and the stipulations and decrees he has given you. Do what is right and good in the Lord's sight, so that it may go well with you and you may go in and take over the good land that the Lord promised on oath to your forefathers, thrusting out all your enemies before you, as the Lord said.

In the future, when your son asks you, "What is the meaning of the stipulations, decrees and laws the Lord our God has commanded you?" tell him: "We were slaves of Pharaoh in Egypt, but the Lord brought us out of Egypt with a mighty hand. Before our eyes the Lord sent miraculous signs and wonders—great and terrible—upon Egypt and Pharaoh and his whole household. But he brought us out from there to bring us in and give us the land that he promised on oath to our forefathers. The Lord commanded us to obey all these decrees and to fear the Lord our God, so that we might always prosper and be kept alive, as is the case today. And if we are careful to obey all this law before the Lord our God, as he has commanded us, that will be our righteousness."

Psalm 111:1–10

Praise the Lord.
I will extol the Lord with all my heart
   in the council of the upright and in the assembly.
Great are the works of the Lord;
   they are pondered by all who delight in them.

Glorious and majestic are his deeds,
and his righteousness endures forever.
He has caused his wonders to be remembered;
the Lord is gracious and compassionate.
He provides food for those who fear him;
he remembers his covenant forever.
He has shown his people the power of his works,
giving them the lands of other nations.

The works of his hands are faithful and just;
all his precepts are trustworthy.
They are steadfast for ever and ever,
done in faithfulness and uprightness.
He provided redemption for his people;
he ordained his covenant forever—
holy and awesome is his name.
The fear of the Lord is the beginning of wisdom;
all who follow his precepts have good understanding.
To him belongs eternal praise.

Proverbs 1:1–9

The proverbs of Solomon son of David, king of Israel:
for attaining wisdom and discipline;
for understanding words of insight;
for acquiring a disciplined and prudent life,
doing what is right and just and fair;
for giving prudence to the simple,
knowledge and discretion to the young—
let the wise listen and add to their learning,
and let the discerning get guidance—
for understanding proverbs and parables,
the sayings and riddles of the wise.
The fear of the Lord is the beginning of knowledge,
but fools despise wisdom and discipline.
Listen, my son, to your father's instruction
and do not forsake your mother's teaching.
They will be a garland to grace your head
and a chain to adorn your neck.

Proverbs 3:1–6

My son, do not forget my teaching,
    but keep my commands in your heart,
    for they will prolong your life many years
    and bring you prosperity.
Let love and faithfulness never leave you;
    bind them around your neck,
    write them on the tablet of your heart.
Then you will win favor and a good name
    in the sight of God and man.
Trust in the Lord with all your heart
    and lean not on your own understanding;
    in all your ways acknowledge him,
    and he will make your paths straight.

Proverbs 4:1–7

Listen, my sons, to a father's instruction;
    pay attention and gain understanding.
I give you sound learning,
    so do not forsake my teaching.
When I was a boy in my father's house,
    still tender, and an only child of my mother,
he taught me and said,
    "Lay hold of my words with all your heart;
    keep my commands and you will live.
Get wisdom, get understanding;
    do not forget my words or swerve from them.
Do not forsake wisdom, and she will protect you;
    love her, and she will watch over you.
Wisdom is supreme; therefore get wisdom.

Proverbs 8:1–26, 30–36

Does not wisdom call out?
Does not understanding raise her voice?
On the heights along the way,
    where the paths meet, she takes her stand;
beside the gates leading into the city,

at the entrances, she cries aloud:
"To you, O men, I call out;
   I raise my voice to all mankind.
You who are simple, gain prudence;
   you who are foolish, gain understanding.
Listen, for I have worthy things to say;
   I open my lips to speak what is right.
My mouth speaks what is true,
   for my lips detest wickedness.
All the words of my mouth are just;
   none of them is crooked or perverse.
To the discerning all of them are right;
   they are faultless to those who have knowledge.
   Choose my instruction instead of silver,
   knowledge rather than choice gold,
for wisdom is more precious than rubies,
   and nothing you desire can compare with her.

"I, wisdom, dwell together with prudence;
   I possess knowledge and discretion.
To fear the Lord is to hate evil;
   I hate pride and arrogance,
   evil behavior and perverse speech.
Counsel and sound judgment are mine;
   I have understanding and power.
By me kings reign
   and rulers make laws that are just;
   by me princes govern,
   and all nobles who rule on earth.
I love those who love me,
   and those who seek me find me.
With me are riches and honor,
   enduring wealth and prosperity.
My fruit is better than fine gold;
   what I yield surpasses choice silver.
I walk in the way of righteousness,
   along the paths of justice,
   bestowing wealth on those who love me
   and making their treasuries full.

"The Lord possessed me at the beginning of his work,
    before his deeds of old;
I was appointed from eternity,
    from the beginning, before the world began.
    When there were no oceans, I was given birth,
    when there were no springs abounding with water;
before the mountains were settled in place,
    before the hills, I was given birth,
before he made the earth or its fields
    or any of the dust of the world. . . .
"Now then, my sons, listen to me;
    blessed are those who keep my ways.
Listen to my instruction and be wise;
    do not ignore it.
Blessed is the man who listens to me,
    watching daily at my doors,
    waiting at my doorway.
For whoever finds me finds life
    and receives favor from the Lord.
But whoever fails to find me harms himself;
    all who hate me love death."

Proverbs 9:1–12

Wisdom has built her house;
    she has hewn out its seven pillars.
She has prepared her meat and mixed her wine;
    she has also set her table.
She has sent out her maids, and she calls
    from the highest point of the city.
"Let all who are simple come in here!"
    she says to those who lack judgment.
"Come, eat my food
    and drink the wine I have mixed.
Leave your simple ways and you will live;
    walk in the way of understanding.

"Whoever corrects a mocker brings on insult;
    whoever rebukes a wicked man incurs abuse.

Do not rebuke a mocker or he will hate you;
 rebuke a wise man and he will love you.
Instruct a wise man and he will be wiser still;
 teach a righteous man and he will add to his learning.
"The fear of the Lord is the beginning of wisdom,
 and knowledge of the Holy One is understanding.
For through me your days will be many,
 and years will be added to your life.
If you are wise, your wisdom will reward you;
 if you are a mocker, you alone will suffer."

Proverbs 22:6

Train a child in the way he should go,
 and when he is old he will not turn from it.

THE NEW TESTAMENT

The following selections from the New Testament show how the incarnate Lord Himself fulfilled the law's demand. In all aspects of His humanity, Jesus Christ loved the Lord God: with His heart emotionally, with His soul devoutly, with His body physically, with His mind intellectually.

We begin by noticing how Jesus commissioned His disciples to teach what they had learned from Him. Christ's teaching, found in the Gospels as well as the writings of Paul the apostle, sets forth both the simplicity and rigor of the gospel: simple enough for a youth like Timothy to believe yet rigorous enough to demand the best use of Timothy's intellectual training for proclaiming the message and persuading his audience.

Thus the gospel appeals to both emotion and reason—the heart and the mind—of every person. It is a rational and heartfelt faith capable of winning even the most hostile skeptic to faith in Jesus Christ.

Matthew 28:16–20

Then the eleven disciples went to Galilee, to the mountain where Jesus had told them to go. When they saw him, they worshiped him; but some doubted. Then Jesus came to them and said, "All authority in heaven and on earth has been given to me. Therefore go and make disciples of all nations, baptizing them in the name of the Father and of the Son and of the Holy Spirit, and teaching them to obey everything I have commanded you. And surely I will be with you always, to the very end of the age."

Luke 2:40–52

And the child grew and became strong; he was filled with wisdom, and the grace of God was upon him.

Every year his parents went to Jerusalem for the Feast of the Passover. When he was twelve years old, they went up to the

Feast, according to the custom. After the Feast was over, while his parents were returning home, the boy Jesus stayed behind in Jerusalem, but they were unaware of it. Thinking he was in their company, they traveled on for a day. Then they began looking for him among their relatives and friends. When they did not find him, they went back to Jerusalem to look for him. After three days they found him in the temple courts, sitting among the teachers, listening to them and asking them questions. Everyone who heard him was amazed at his understanding and his answers. When his parents saw him, they were astonished. His mother said to him, "Son, why have you treated us like this? Your father and I have been anxiously searching for you."

"Why were you searching for me?" he asked. "Didn't you know I had to be in my Father's house?" But they did not understand what he was saying to them.

Then he went down to Nazareth with them and was obedient to them. But his mother treasured all these things in her heart. And Jesus grew in wisdom and stature, and in favor with God and men.

Colossians 1:9–2:15

For this reason, since the day we heard about you, we have not stopped praying for you and asking God to fill you with the knowledge of his will through all spiritual wisdom and understanding. And we pray this in order that you may live a life worthy of the Lord and may please him in every way: bearing fruit in every good work, growing in the knowledge of God, being strengthened with all power according to his glorious might so that you may have great endurance and patience, and joyfully giving thanks to the Father, who has qualified you to share in the inheritance of the saints in the kingdom of light. For he has rescued us from the dominion of darkness and brought us into the kingdom of the Son he loves, in whom we have redemption, the forgiveness of sins.

He is the image of the invisible God, the firstborn over all creation. For by him all things were created: things in heaven and on earth, visible and invisible, whether thrones or powers or rulers or authorities; all things were created by him and for him. He is before all things, and in him all things hold together. And he is the head of the body, the church; he is the beginning and the firstborn from among the dead, so that in everything he might have the supremacy. For God was pleased to have all his fullness dwell in him, and through him to reconcile to himself all things, whether things on earth or things in heaven, by making peace through his blood, shed on the cross.

Once you were alienated from God and were enemies in your minds because of your evil behavior. But now he has reconciled you by Christ's physical body through death to present you holy in his sight, without blemish and free from accusation—if you continue in your faith, established and firm, not moved from the hope held out in the gospel. This is the gospel that you heard and that has been proclaimed to every creature under heaven, and of which I, Paul, have become a servant.

Now I rejoice in what was suffered for you, and I fill up in my flesh what is still lacking in regard to Christ's afflictions, for the sake of his body, which is the church. I have become its servant by the commission God gave me to present to you the word of God in its fullness—the mystery that has been kept hidden for ages and generations, but is now disclosed to the saints. To them God has chosen to make known among the Gentiles the glorious riches of this mystery, which is Christ in you, the hope of glory.

We proclaim him, admonishing and reaching everyone with all wisdom, so that we may present everyone perfect in Christ. To this end I labor, struggling with all his energy, which so powerfully works in me.

I want you to know how much I am struggling for your and for those at Laodicea, and for all who have not met me personally. My purpose is that they may be encouraged in heart and united in love, so that they may have the full riches of complete understanding, in order that they may know the mystery of God, namely, Christ, in whom are hidden all the treasures of wisdom and knowledge. I tell you this so that no one may deceive you by fine-sounding arguments. For though I am absent from you in body, I am present with you in spirit and delight to see how orderly you are and how firm your faith in Christ is.

43

So then, just as you received Christ Jesus as Lord, continue to live in him, rooted and built up in him, strengthened in the faith as you were taught, and overflowing with thankfulness.

See to it that no one takes you captive through hollow and deceptive philosophy, which depends on human tradition and the basic principles of this world rather than on Christ.

For in Christ all the fullness of the Deity lives in bodily form, and you have been given fullness in Christ, who is the head over every power and authority. In him you were also circumcised, in the putting off of the sinful nature, not with a circumcision done by the hands of men but with the circumcision done by Christ, having been buried with him in baptism and raised with him through your faith in the power of God, who raised him from the dead.

When you were dead in your sins and in the uncircumcision of your sinful nature, God made you alive with Christ. He forgave us all our sins, having canceled the written code, with its regulations, that was against us and that stood opposed to us; he took it away, nailing it to the cross. And having disarmed the power and authorities, he made a public spectacle of them, triumphing over them by the cross.

1 Timothy 4:12–16

Don't let anyone look down on you because you are young, but set an example for the believers in speech, in life, in love, in faith and in purity. Until I come, devote yourself to the public reading of Scripture, to preaching and to teaching. Do not neglect your gift, which was given you through a prophetic message when the body of elders laid their hands on you.

2 Timothy 1:1–5

Paul, an apostle of Christ Jesus by the will of God, according to the promise of life that is in Christ Jesus,

To Timothy, my dear son:

Grace, mercy and peace from God the Father and Christ Jesus our Lord.

I thank God, whom I serve, as my forefathers did, with a clear conscience, as night and day I constantly remember you in my prayers. Recalling your tears, I long to see you, so that I may be filled with joy. I have been reminded of your sincere faith, which first lived in your grandmother Lois and in your mother Eunice and, I am persuaded, now lives in you also.

2 Timothy 2:1–2

You then, my son, be strong in the grace that is in Christ Jesus. And the things you have heard me say in the presence of many witnesses entrust to reliable men who will also be qualified to teach others.

2 Timothy 2:14–17a; 22–26

Keep reminding them of these things. Warn them before God against quarreling about words; it is of no value, and only ruins those who listen. Do your best to present yourself to God as one approved, a workman who does not need to be ashamed and who correctly handles the word of truth. Avoid godless chatter, because those who indulge in it will become more and more ungodly. Their teaching will spread like gangrene.

Flee the evil desires of youth, and pursue righteousness, faith, love and peace, along with those who call on the Lord out of a pure heart. Don't have anything to do with foolish and stupid arguments, because you know they produce quarrels. And the Lord's servant must not quarrel; instead, he must be kind to everyone, able to teach, not resentful. Those who oppose him he must gently instruct, in the hope that God will grant them repentance leading them to a knowledge of the truth, and that they will come to their senses and escape from the trap of the devil, who has taken them captive to do his will.

2 Timothy 3:14–4:5

But as for you, continue in what you have learned and have become convinced of, because you know those from whom you learned it, and how from infancy you have known the holy Scriptures, which are able to make you wise for salvation through faith

PART II
THE FIRST
FIVE CENTURIES

*I*f the Apostles had not left us the Scriptures, would it not be necessary to follow the order of tradition which they handed down to those to whom they committed the churches?

Irenaeus
"Against the False Gnosis," ca. 190

THE FIRST
FIVE CENTURIES

Jesus of Nazareth taught that God must be loved with the whole being, including the mind. Accordingly, Paul of Tarsus, himself a scholar educated in the school of Gamaliel, encouraged his own protégé Timothy to use his intellectual powers and the classical education he had received—as well as the example of his teachers—to reason with and persuade his audience. So Paul seemed to be commending the pagan curriculum of rhetoric and oratory, geometry, music, and physical training for Christians as well.

But among Christians of the next few centuries, controversy sprang up as to whether believers in Jesus Christ could bother to learn—or should be prevented from corruption by learning—the course of study taught in pagan schools.

Justin Martyr, born around 100 A.D., had been a wandering teacher of philosophy before coming to faith in Christ. At first, his profession and his new faith seemed in conflict; yet the more he studied the Scriptures, the more he came to believe that the Logos, the Word made Flesh, was the very seed of truth; that knowing the one who is truth complemented the truth of literature and philosophy. So Justin Martyr chose to remain a teacher until his death, about 165 A.D.

In his school in Rome and in his public defenses before the Senate, Justin Martyr may have been the first Christian to express what we today sometimes call "the integration of faith and learning." He wrote in *The Second Apology*, "Whatever has been uttered aright by any man in any place belongs to us Christians; for, next to God, we worship and love the Logos which is from the unbegotten and ineffable God."[1]

Others followed Justin Martyr's example. In Alexandria, Clement's and Origen's catechetical school became a model for others throughout the Near East and North Africa. New believers came to the school to receive not only doctrinal instruction prior to baptism but also a fresh understanding of science, literature, and philosophy from a Christian perspective. The purpose of their school was to show, through the breadth and diversity of learning, the unity of knowledge revealed in Jesus Christ.

But their North African contemporary, Tertullian from Carthage, disapproved of the synthesis these Alexandrians sought. About 200 A.D., in his "Prescription Against Heretics," Tertullian wrote, "What, indeed, has Athens to do with Jerusalem? What concord is there between the Academy and the Church? What between heretics and Christians?" By his rhetorical questions, Tertullian implied a negative response: None whatsoever! For any reader who missed his implied point, however, Tertullian spelled it out plainly, seeming to shut the door forever on a fundamental method of learning and teaching, the art of asking leading questions popularized by Socrates. "We have no need," Tertullian declared, "for curiosity since Jesus Christ, nor for inquiry since the Gospel."[2]

The value of education for a Christian was reasserted during the fourth century by the so-called Cappadocian Fathers: Basil the Great, his brother Gregory of Nyassa, and Gregory of Nazianzus. These learned and powerful bishops of the Eastern Church taught that every Christian must know what is best in pagan education, the better to learn how to love and serve God. One of Basil's famous sermons, "Address to the Youth," is sometimes called "the honeybee sermon" because it urges Christian young people to choose selectively, like a bee, what is good and reject what is bad.

At Basil's funeral in 379, Gregory of Nazianzus argued in support of his former schoolmate in Athens, that "the first of our advantages [as Christians] is education."[3] He went on to contend against those who disparage learning as "treacherous and dangerous, and keeping us afar from God." Instead, Gregory called upon Christians to "reap what advantage we can" from learning and reminded his listeners of the apostle Paul's desire to "take captive every thought to make it obedient to Christ" (2 Corinthians 10:5).

A generation later, another African, Augustine of Hippo, taught that knowledge of pagan culture and learning is worthwhile for the Christian, provided that such knowledge finds its proper place. For Augustine, wisdom is superior to knowledge, and faith is superior to both. Indeed, faith must precede wisdom and knowledge, since it is belief alone that makes understanding possible. *"Credo ut intelligam"*: "I believe in order that I may understand." Thus spoke Augustine, thereby setting the priorities for a godly epistemology.[4]

According to Augustine, Christians learn only by believing that Jesus Christ is the *magister interior*, the inward teacher, who reveals truth as we learn from Him. With this foundation of faith as his base for wisdom, knowledge, and understanding, Augustine could nurture an intellect of breadth and discriminating taste. He did not have to exclude learning in any form or from any human source. In a document intended to be a handbook for teachers of rhetoric, "On Christian Doctrine," he wrote that "every good and true Christian should understand that wherever he may find truth, it is his Lord's."[5]

From Augustine, therefore, at the start of the fifth century, we hear a restatement of Justin Martyr's 250-year old claim: "Whatever has been uttered aright by any man in any place belongs to us Christians." From both Justin Martyr and Augustine of Hippo, we have derived an echoing phrase in our own time, boldly enunciated by Frank E. Gaebelein in *The Pattern of God's Truth*, where he wrote, "All truth is God's truth."[6]

EARLY HYMNS AND PRAYERS

E very culture teaches the oral traditions and incantations of that culture; so new Christians, both children and adult believers, were instructed in what the apostle Paul called "the teachings [or traditions] we passed on to you, whether by word of mouth or by letter" (2 Thessalonians 2:15). These teachings or traditions eventually found expression as the canon of the New Testament and became accepted and distributed. But even before the Scriptures, both Old and New Testaments, received their authority in the Christian Church, other expressions of praise and tests of orthodoxy were in use; some of these continue to our own time.

As Christian educators began establishing a curriculum to be taught and learned, these hymns, prayers, catechisms, and creeds became part of the genuine Christian and apostolic tradition. Memorized and rehearsed, these expressions of faith prepared those who learned them to participate in worship wherever the church met to praise God. So too, these hymns, prayers, catechisms, and creeds served as the first textbooks in Christian schools.

Hymns

The first Christians—those 120 fugitives upon whom the Holy Spirit fell on Pentecost—were all Jews; so too were their first 3,000 converts. Not unexpectedly, therefore, the songs of praise to God they sang were the Psalms and other songs familiar to Jewish worship. For instance, the threefold *Sanctus*, "Holy, Holy, Holy," derives from Isaiah 6, and was part of Jewish worship long before the Christian era. The fact that Clement of Rome alludes to the *Sanctus* at the end of the first century confirms that it had already been adopted in Christian worship.[7]

But the young church did not confine itself to those ancient texts and tunes. Twice in his letters, Paul refers to the practice of singing "psalms, hymns, and spiritual songs" (Ephesians 5:19; Colossians 3:16). In both instances, it is worth noting, such sing-

ing was to be an act of praise in which the entire assembly participated. Music in the early church was not restricted to those who
could perform as artists.

Church historians and musicologists continue to debate the
differences among "psalms, hymns, and spiritual songs."[8] Here it is
enough to note that Paul himself appears to have cited all three in
various letters. Indeed, Paul may be the author of several such
works familiar to his readers and cited in his letters. Scholars have
often noted that these early hymns were also formal confessions of
faith; in other words, early creeds. A prime example is Paul's most
extended and beautiful hymn, Philippians 2:5–11. Another is
Ephesians 4:4–6. Two creeds from 1 Timothy also became early
hymns:

> Now to the King eternal, immortal, invisible, the only God,
>   be honor and glory for ever and ever. Amen. (1:17)

> Beyond all question, the mystery of godliness is great:
> He appeared in a body, was vindicated by the Spirit, was
> seen by angels, was preached among the nations, was be-
> lieved on in the world, was taken up in glory. (3:16)

Other early songs would include the canticles of Mary, Zech-
ariah, the angelic host, and Simeon, recorded in Luke 1 and 2; so
too the Lord's Prayer and the announcement of John the Baptist.
These are known respectively by the Latin phrase with which each
begins: *Magnificat, Benedictus, Gloria in excelsis, Nunc dimittis, Pater
noster, and Agnus dei.* The singing of these and other canticles,
such as *Kyrie eleison* ("Lord, have mercy") was known to be an
element of Christian worship by the end of the first century. Etheria, a woman who made a pilgrimage to Jerusalem in the fourth
century carefully recorded the worship she observed then and
heard the canticles sung.[9] Many churches continue singing them
in worship today. Here is the ancient text of the *Gloria,* as found
in the 1979 Book of Common Prayer of the Episcopal Church:

> Glory be to God on high,
> and on earth peace, good will towards men.
> We praise thee, we bless thee, we worship thee,
> we glorify thee, we give thanks to thee for thy great glory,

Lord God, heavenly King, God the Father Almighty.
O Lord, the only-begotten Son, Jesus Christ;
O Lord God, Lamb of God, Son of the Father,
that takest away the sins of the world,
    have mercy upon us.
Thou that takest away the sins of the world,
    receive our prayer.
Thou that sittest at the right hand of God the Father,
    have mercy upon us.
For thou only art holy, thou only art the Lord;
thou only, O Christ, with the Holy Ghost,
art most high in the glory of God the Father. Amen. [10]

The *Gloria* is also known as the Greater Doxology, distinct from the song familiar to Protestants as "Praise God from Whom All Blessings Flow," published in 1695 by its author, Thomas Ken, and often sung to a tune known as Old Hundredth.

Clement of Alexandria, teacher and head of the famous school there, was both a theologian and a hymnwriter. He appears to have used his poetic gift as a rhetorical means of persuading readers of his theological arguments by inserting a hymn-poem in his essays. The contrast is strikingly effective. Theological argument, often ponderous and difficult to comprehend, is quickened by the poem's vivid imagery, appealing to the senses and warming the heart.

Perhaps the most familiar of Clement's poems, "Hymn to the Savior Christ," serves as an appendix to his essay on pedagogy, "The Instructor," written around 200. Addressed to Jesus Christ, Clement's hymn weaves a fabric of metaphors showing the Lord's various relationships to young Christians. Its first four lines, literally translated, read,

> *O bridle of colts untamed,*
> *Wing of the hovering birds,*
> *Steady helm of the ships,*
> *Shepherd of royal lambs.* [11]

Contemporary hymnals contain paraphrases, such as this written in the nineteenth century by Henry M. Dexter:

Shepherd of tender youth,
Guiding in love and truth,
Through devious ways;
Christ our triumphant King,
We come thy name to sing,
Hither our children bring
To shout thy praise. [12]

To Ambrose (ca. 339–397), bishop of Milan, belongs much of the credit for bringing into the Western church a custom long popular in the Eastern church, congregational singing.[13] According to Augustine of Hippo, whom Ambrose baptized in 387, Ambrose fled persecution and lived in the sanctuary of a church with other refugees. Their communal singing was a means of encouraging each other. Addressing God in his *Confessions*, Augustine writes,

> The pious people kept guard in the church, prepared to die with their bishop, thy servant. . . . At this time it was instituted that, after the manner of the Eastern Church, hymns and psalms should be sung, lest the people should pine away in the tediousness of sorrow; which custom, retained from then till now, is imitated by many, yea, by almost all of thy congregation throughout the rest of the world.[14]

Tradition holds that Ambrose and Augustine are jointly responsible for the great canticle, *Te Deum laudamus*, "We Praise Thee, O God." Immediately after Ambrose had baptized Augustine, the story goes, they stood together singing spontaneously and alternately, improvising the composition of a hymn. Other evidence suggests that the text came from a variety of sources. Whatever its origins, the *Te Deum* remains one of the great confessional hymns.

We praise thee, O God; we acknowledge thee to be the
  Lord.
All the earth doth worship thee, the Father everlasting.
To thee all Angels cry aloud; the Heavens and all the
  Powers therein;
To thee Cherubim and Seraphim continually do cry,
Holy, Holy, Holy, Lord God of Sabaoth;
Heaven and earth are full of the Majesty of thy glory.

The glorious company of the Apostles praise thee.
The goodly fellowship of the Prophets praise thee.
The noble army of Martyrs praise thee.
The holy Church throughout all the world doth
   acknowledge thee;
The Father of an infinite Majesty;
Thine adorable, true, and only Son;
Also the Holy Ghost, the Comforter.
Thou art the King of Glory, O Christ.
Thou are the everlasting Son of the Father.
When thou tookest upon thee to deliver man, thou didst
   humble thyself to be born of a Virgin.
When thou hadst overcome the sharpness of death, thou
   didst open the Kingdom of Heaven to all believers.
Thou sittest at the right hand of God, in the glory of the
   Father.
We believe that thou shalt come to be our Judge.
We therefore pray thee, help thy servants, whom thou
   hast redeemed with thy precious blood.
Make them to be numbered with thy Saints, in glory
   everlasting.[15]

A near contemporary of Ambrose, the Spaniard Marcus Aurelius Clemens Prudentius (348–ca. 410), did not become a Christian until late in life; nonetheless, he produced a sufficiently large number of poems and books reflecting his faith to earn for him the nickname of "the Christian Pindar." His Christmas hymn, dating from 405, translated by Henry W. Baker, reveals his understanding of the mystery of the Incarnation. The first stanza reads,

> *Of the Father's love begotten*
> *Ere the worlds began to be,*
> *He is Alpha and Omega,*
> *He the source, the ending he;*
> *Of the things that are, that have been,*
> *And that future years shall see,*
> *Evermore and evermore!*[16]

Venantius Honorius Fortunatus (ca. 530–ca. 610) published hymns written for special celebrations, seasonal or for a specific baptism. His great hymn *Salve festa dies,* "Hail Thee, Festival Day," was written about 582 and dedicated to Felix, bishop of Nantes, on the occasion of the Easter baptisms.

> *Hail thee, festival day!*
> *Blest day that art hallowed forever;*
> *Day whereon Christ arose,*
> *Breaking the kingdom of death.* [17]*fn*

Prayers

The earliest prayer common to Christians, of course, is the Lord's Prayer, whether sung as the *Pater noster* or recited, "Our Father in heaven, hallowed be your name" (Matthew 6:9 ff.). But after the dispersion of the apostles from Jerusalem, instructions to new believers forming new local branches of the church began to be written. The most familiar of these documents we know, of course, as the letters of Paul, Peter, and others. But there were also documents of encouragement and instruction which, while not received into the canon of Holy Scripture, were nonetheless highly regarded throughout the early centuries.

One of these is the *Didache,* or "The Teaching of the Twelve Apostles." This ancient record may date from as early as 100; it was discovered in 1873, in a monastery library in Constantinople. Its origin seems to be in Syria, where an unknown writer compiled the teachings and customs of the Church as he knew them. Sections IX and X of the *Didache* record three prayers apparently used during the celebration of the Eucharist, or Holy Communion. The first prayer represents one of the earliest post-Apostolic texts and contains obvious echoes of the Lord's Prayer. The repeated phrase, "To thee be the glory forever," may signify a liturgical response by the congregation, following the leader's petition. [18]

> Now concerning the Eucharist, thus give thanks: First, concerning the cup: We thank thee, our Father, for the holy wine of David thy servant, which thou hast made known to us through Jesus thy servant. To thee be the glory forever.

And concerning the broken bread: We thank thee, our Father, for the life and knowledge which thou hast made known to us through Jesus thy servant. To thee be the glory forever. Just as this broken bread was scattered over the hills and having been gathered together became one, so let thy Church be gathered together from the ends of the earth into thy Kingdom; for thine is the glory and the power through Jesus Christ forever. But let no one eat or drink of thy Eucharist except those baptized into the name of the Lord, for in regard to this the Lord hath said: Give not that which is holy to the dogs.

And after ye are filled, thus give thanks: We thank thee, holy Father, for thy holy name, which thou hast caused to dwell in our hearts, and for the knowledge and faith and immortality which thou hast made known to us through Jesus thy servant. To thee be the glory forever. Thou, almighty Master, didst create all things for thy name's sake; both food and drink thou didst give to men for enjoyment, in order that they might give thanks to thee; but to us thou hast graciously given spiritual food and drink and eternal life through thy servant. Before all things we thank thee that thou art mighty. To thee be the glory forever. Remember, Lord, thy Church, to deliver it from every evil and to make it perfect in thy love, and gather it from the four winds, it, the sanctified, into thy Kingdom, which thou hast prepared for it; for thine is the power and glory forever. Let grace come and this world pass away.

Another ancient prayer, *Sursum corda*, "Lift up your hearts," dates from before 220, when it was included in a work by Hippolytus.

Leader: The Lord be with you.
People: And with thy spirit.
Leader: Lift up your hearts.
People: We lift them up to the Lord.
Leader: Let us give thanks unto our Lord God.
People: It is meet [fit] and right so to do.
Leader: It is very meet, right, and our bounden duty, that we should at all times, and in all places, give thanks unto thee, O Lord, holy Father, almighty, everlasting God.

At this point, the leader inserted a sentence or two, called the proper, regarding the season or celebration. For instance, during the season celebrating the Incarnation, the following would be added:

Leader: Because thou didst give Jesus Christ, thine only Son, born for us; who, by the mighty power of the Holy Ghost, was made very Man of the substance of the Virgin Mary his mother; that we might be delivered from the bondage of sin, and receive power to become thy children.

Then the celebrant continued,

Leader: Therefore, with Angels and Archangels, and with all the company of heaven, we laud and magnify thy glorious Name, evermore praising thee and saying:
People: Holy, holy, holy, Lord God of Hosts:
Heaven and earth are full of thy glory.
Glory be to thee, O Lord Most High.
Blessed is he that cometh in the Name of the Lord.
Hosanna in the highest.[19]

One of the most beautiful prayers comes from the Eastern church father, John Chrysostom, a nickname meaning "golden-tongued." John was born about 347, in Antioch, the son of a Greek military officer; his mother was one of the most devout women in Antioch. At an early age, John made his reputation as an orator, studying with a pagan tutor Libanius. When asked upon his deathbed which of his students might best succeed him, Libanius replied, "John, if only the Christians had not stolen him from us!" John Chrysostom's prayer that follows, dating from around 400, is often used at the close of worship.

> Almighty God, who has given us grace at this time
> with one accord to make our common supplication
> unto thee, and has promised through thy well-
> beloved Son that when two or three are gathered
> together in his Name thou wilt be in the midst of
> them: Fulfill now, O Lord, the desires and petitions
> of thy servants as may be best for us; granting us
> in this world knowledge of thy truth, and in the
> world to come life everlasting. Amen.[20]

CATECHISMS AND CREEDS

Christianity is by nature a confessional faith; it demands of those who would claim its power that they not only believe but also confess (Romans 10:9). Other religions may have allowed for private, unuttered devotion, but Christianity demands a willingness to declare boldly and publicly, by both words and acts, the faith professed.

To this end, the church very early established catechisms—as both a means of uniform declaration and a test of orthodoxy. Catechisms take the form of a series of questions and prescribed answers; creeds are formalized statements of belief.

Jesus Christ set the pattern for catechizing at Caesarea Philippi, when he asked his disciples the absolutely essential questions: "Who do people say the Son of Man is? . . . But what about you? Who do you say I am?" Simon Peter's response, "You are the Christ, the Son of the living God" (Matthew 16:13, 15–16) completed the question with the best possible answer. This incident established the precedent for challenging one's beliefs by question-and-answer.

Initially the first Christians found that one phrase in Greek could sum up their faith: *Kyrios Iesous Christos*, meaning "Jesus Christ is Lord." This same phrase appears in the hymn Paul quotes to the Philippians, when he says that "every knee should bow . . . and every tongue confess that Jesus Christ is Lord" (Philippians 2:10–11).

But as doctrinal differences and heretical interpretations began to afflict the Church, the single phrase needed further development; for instance, a doctrinal confession as a means of instructing candidates for baptism. Because their instruction was by question-and-answer, these new believers were called "catechumens." They were considered to be on probation until qualified for baptism—a period that, in some regions, lasted as long as three years. When the appointed time came—often on the Saturday evening before Easter—the catechumens were examined by this baptismal catechism known throughout the church from a very early date:

Do you believe in God the Father?
Do you believe in Jesus Christ, the Son of God?
Do you believe in God the Holy Spirit?

These questions had their prescribed answers, slightly different in their various forms from place to place but all affirming the Father's power as creator; affirming the incarnation, atonement, resurrection, and ascension of the Son; and affirming the work of the Holy Spirit in the church. To each question the catechumen replied, "I believe."

These words in English translate the single Latin word, *credo*, from which comes our word *creed*. The relationship between the ancient baptismal catechisms and the formulation of the various creeds is too complicated a story for this context. In brief, no one knows the exact origins of the earliest extended creeds. As early as 105 or so, when Ignatius wrote his letters to the churches at Ephesus, Magnesia, and Tralles, we find elements recognizable in latter creeds.[21] In the Apology of Justin Martyr, written to the Roman emperor Antoninus Pius around 155, the same elements appear.[22] Later in the second century, Irenaeus (ca. 130–ca. 200), bishop of Lyons, wrote a treatise against heretics, in which he refers to "the Rule of Truth" which "the Church, though dispersed through the whole world to the ends of the earth, has received from the Apostles and their disciples."[23] Then Irenaeus states that Rule in language later to be heard in the formal creeds. The same can be found in later writings of Tertullian and Origen.

The first creed to be formalized and required throughout Christendom is the so-called Nicene Creed.[24] In 325, the emperor Constantine summoned the bishops throughout the world to a council at Nicaea in Bithynia, now northwestern Turkey. His purpose was to assert his authority as emperor over both East and West. At the same time, Constantine hoped to resolve the schism within the church, brought by the teachings of Arius, that Jesus the Son could not be equal with God the Father. Perhaps as many as 300 bishops or their delegates attended the Council of Nicaea, at which Arius and his heresy called Arianism were discredited. Heretics were exiled and declared anathema, accursed.

The text of the creed derived from this council was revised at subsequent councils and finally set in 451, at the Council of Chalcedon. Still known as the Nicene Creed, this is the creed held in common by Christians of both East and West:

The Nicene Creed

I believe in one God,
    the Father Almighty,
    maker of heaven and earth,
    and of all things visible and invisible.
And in one Lord Jesus Christ,
    the only-begotten Son of God,

begotten of his Father before all worlds,
God of God, Light of Light,
very God of very God,
begotten, not made,
being of one substance with the Father;
by whom all things were made;
who, for us men and for our salvation
   came down from heaven,
and was incarnate by the Holy Ghost of the
   Virgin Mary,
and was made man;
and was crucified also for us under Pontius Pilate;
he suffered and was buried;
and the third day he rose again according to the
   Scriptures,
and ascended into heaven,
and sitteth on the right hand of the Father;
and he shall come again, with glory,
   to judge both the quick and the dead;
whose kingdom shall have no end.
And I believe in the Holy Ghost, the Lord,
   and Giver of Life,
who proceedeth from the Father and the Son;
who with the Father and the Son together is
   worshiped and glorified;
who spake by the Prophets.
And I believe one holy Catholic and Apostolic Church;
I acknowledge one baptism for the remission of sins;
   and I look for the Resurrection of the dead,
   and the life of the world to come. Amen.[25]

Another creed familiar only in Western churches is the so-called Apostles' Creed.[26] There is no validity to the tradition that, following the ascension, each of the apostles contributed a single clause. Rather, this text was known from 390 on as the *Symbolorum Apostolorum,* a "symbol" or passport, warrant, or seal of approval for the orthodoxy of those who professed it. The Apostles' Creed, ratified by Charlemagne sometime around 800, became the official creed of the West.

The Apostles' Creed

I believe in God, the Father almighty,
　maker of heaven and earth;
And in Jesus Christ his only Son our Lord:
　who was conceived by the Holy Ghost,
　born of the Virgin Mary,
　suffered under Pontius Pilate,
　was crucified, dead, and buried.
　He descended into hell;
　The third day he rose again from the dead.
　He ascended into heaven,
　and sitteth on the right hand of God the Father
　　almighty.
　From thence he shall come to judge the quick and
　　the dead.
I believe in the Holy Ghost;
　the holy catholic Church,
　the communion of saints,
　the forgiveness of sins,
　the resurrection of the body,
　and the life everlasting. Amen.[27]

These, then, are some of the texts—hymns and prayers, catechisms and creeds—that served as primers and lesson materials for students in the earliest Christian schools. Learning these and other similar texts—as well as memorizing passages of Scripture—might well be commended to both students and teachers in all Christian schools today.

JUSTIN MARTYR

After the apostle Paul, Justin Martyr (ca. 100–ca. 165) ranks as the greatest apologist of the Early Christian era and a strong advocate of a Christian recognition that all truth has its source in God.

Justin was born at Flavia Neapolis, now called Nablus, on the Jordan River's west bank, the site of Jacob's Well, where Jesus encountered the Samaritan woman. Justin's education qualified him to become an itinerant teacher of philosophy, in token of which he wore the distinctive bluish robe, or *pallium*.

But upon his conversion in Ephesus, about 130, Justin questioned whether his profession as a philosopher and teacher was compatible with his new faith in Christ. Could he continue to wear the philosopher's robe?

His studies brought him to believe that philosophy is indeed compatible with the gospel. He came to see that his pagan quest to know and understand the *logos* of philosophy had, in fact, prepared him to meet the Logos, the Word-made-Flesh, and the revelation of truth in Jesus Christ. So Justin retained his robe and, in Rome, conducted his own school.

About 150 A.D., he was denounced for the first time to the Roman authorities; again, a dozen years later he was accused. For each appearance before the Roman senate, Justin wrote an *apologia*, or argument, addressed to his detractors. In the excerpt that follows from his "First Apology," Justin defends himself and other Christians against the false charges that they are immoral and atheistic, not to mention dangerous to the Empire, by explaining Christian practices in faith and worship.

His second defense went unheeded, and Justin became a martyr in 165 or so, at the orders of Emperor Marcus Aurelius.

"The First Apology"[28] (Excerpt)

To the Emperor Titus Aelius Adrianus Antoninus Pius Augustus Caesar, and to his son Verissimus the Philosopher, and to Lucius the Philosopher, the natural son of Caesar, and the adopted son of Pius, a lover of learning, and to the sacred Senate, with the whole People of the Romans, I, Justin, the son of Priscus and grandson of Bacchius, natives of Flavia Neapolis in Palestine, present this address and petition in behalf of those of all nations who are unjustly hated and wantonly abused, myself being one of them.

. . . Do you, then, since ye are called pious and philosophers, guardians of justice and lovers of learning, give good heed, and hearken to my address; and if ye are indeed such, it will be manifested. For we have come, not to flatter you by this writing, nor please you by our address, but to beg that you pass judgment, after an accurate and searching investigation. . . . As for us, we reckon that no evil can be done us, unless we be convicted as evildoers, or be proved to be wicked men; and you, you can kill but not hurt us.

. . . It is in our power, when we are examined, to deny that we are Christians; but we would not live by telling a lie. For impelled by the desire of the eternal and pure life, we seek the abode that is with God, the Father and Creator of all, and hasten to confess our faith, persuaded and convinced as we are that they who have proved to God by their works that they followed Him and loved to abide with Him where there is no sin to cause disturbance, can obtain these things. This, then, to speak shortly, is what we expect and have learned from Christ, and teach.

. . . That all these things should come to pass, I say, our Teacher foretold, He who is both Son and Apostle of God the Father of all and the Ruler, Jesus Christ; from whom also we have the name of Christians. . . . It were possible to pause here and add no more, reckoning that we demand what is just and true; but because we are well aware that it is not easy suddenly to change a mind possessed by ignorance, we intend to add a few things, for the sake of persuading those who love the truth, knowing that it is not impossible to put ignorance to flight by presenting the truth.

What soberminded man, then, will not acknowledge that we are not atheists, worshipping as we do the Maker of this universe, and declaring, as we have been taught, that He has no need of streams of blood and libations and incense; whom we praise to the utmost of our power by the exercise of prayer and thanksgiving for all things wherewith we are supplied, as we have been taught that the only honor that is worthy of Him is not to consume by fire what He has brought into being for our sustenance, but to use it for ourselves and for those who need, and with gratitude to Him to offer thanks by invocations and hymns for our creation, . . . and to present before Him petitions for our existing again in incorruption through faith in Him.

Our teacher of these things is Jesus Christ, who also was born for this purpose, was crucified under Pontius Pilate, procurator of Judaea, in the times of Tiberius Caesar; and that we reasonably worship Him, having learned that He is the Son of the true God Himself.

. . . And if these things seem to you to be reasonable and true, honor them; but if they seem nonsensical, despise them as nonsense, and do not decree death against those who have done no wrong, as you would against enemies. For we forewarn you, that you shall not escape the coming judgment of God, if you continue in your injustice; and we ourselves will invite you to do that which is pleasing to God.

CLEMENT OF ALEXANDRIA

Titus Flavius Clemens (ca. 150–ca. 215), better known as Clement of Alexandria, was born in Athens at about the same time that Justin Martyr, in Rome, was issuing his "First Apology."

His search for knowledge carried Clement far. In Alexandria, Egypt, a principal center of learning, he came under the teaching of Pantaenus, a Christian conducting his own catechetical school. In such a school both pagan inquirers and catechumens awaiting baptism could receive instruction, not only in Christian doctrine but also in the standard disciplines of the ancient curriculum, yet from a Christian teacher's understanding of truth.

Clement became a believer, and as his eager mind soaked up the Scriptures and doctrines of the Church, he—like Justin Martyr before him—found that his classical learning was not contradicted but fulfilled by his newfound knowledge of Christ. As he later wrote in a collection of sayings called *Stromateis*, Greek philosophy is "a schoolmaster to bring the Hellenic mind—as the Law, the Hebrews—to Christ."[29]

But such latitude in learning did not prevent Clement from observing strictly the authority of both the apostles and the Scriptures. Pantaenus had stressed fidelity to the teachings of the apostles, and when, around 190, Clement succeeded his mentor as head of the Alexandria school, he was equally firm in instructing his pupils.

In his *Paedagogus*, or "The Instructor," Clement laid down precise rules not only for learning but also for behavior and dress by those who claimed to be Christians. In effect, this was a student handbook for a Christian school.

The Instructor[30] (Excerpt)

. . . Since, then, we have shown that all of us are by Scripture called children; and not only so, but that we who have followed Christ are figuratively called babes; and that the Father of all alone is perfect, for the Son is in Him, and the Father is in the Son; it is time for us in due course to say who our Instructor is.

He is called Jesus. Sometimes He calls Himself a shepherd, and says, "I am the good Shepherd." [From] a metaphor drawn from shepherds, who lead the sheep, is hereby understood the Instructor, who leads the children—the Shepherd who tends the babes. For the babes are simple, being figuratively described as sheep. "And they shall all," it is said, "be one flock, and one shepherd." The Word, then, who leads the children to salvation, is appropriately called the Instructor, the Pedagogue.

With the greatest clearness, accordingly, the Word has spoken respecting Himself by Hosea: "I am your Instructor." Now piety is instruction, being the learning of the service of God, and training in the knowledge of the truth, and right guidance which leads to heaven. And the word "instruction" is employed variously. For there is the instruction of him who is led and learns, and that of him who leads and teaches; and there is, thirdly, the guidance itself; and fourthly, what is taught, as the commandments enjoined.

Now the instruction which is of God is the right direction of truth to the contemplation of God, and the exhibition of holy deeds in everlasting perseverance.

. . . With all His power, therefore, the Instructor of humanity, the Divine Word, using all the resources of wisdom, devotes Himself to the saving of the children, admonishing, up-braiding, blaming, chiding, reproving, threatening, healing, promising, favoring; and as it were, by many reins, curbing the irrational impulses of humanity. To speak briefly, therefore, the Lord acts towards us as we do towards our children. . . . It is not immediate pleasure but future enjoyment, that the Lord has in view.

. . . Sick, we truly stand in need of the Savior; having wandered, of one to guide us; blind, of one to lead us to the light; thirsty, of the fountain of life, of which whosoever partakes, shall no longer thirst; dead, we need life; sheep, we need a shepherd; we who are children need a tutor, while universal humanity stands in need of Jesus.

. . . Generous, therefore, is He who gives for us the greatest of all gifts, His own life; and beneficent exceedingly, and loving to men, in that, when He might have been Lord, He wishes to be a brother man; and so good was He that He died for us.

. . . So that from this it is clear, that one alone, true, good, just, in the image and likeness of the Father, His son Jesus, the Word of God, is our Instructor; to whom God hath entrusted us, as an affectionate father commits his children to a worthy tutor, expressly charging us, "This is my beloved Son; hear Him." The divine Instructor is trustworthy, adorned as He is with three of the fairest ornaments—knowledge, benevolence, and authority of utterance. With knowledge, for He is the paternal wisdom. With authority of utterance, for He is God and Creator. And with benevolence, for He alone gave Himself a sacrifice for us.

TERTULLIAN

Quintus Septimus Florens Tertullian (ca. 160–225) was born in Carthage, North Africa. He was educated there to become a lawyer and may have spent time in Rome. In his thirties, Tertullian came face to face with the reality of the Christian faith, expressed in the example of martyrs under persecution. His conversion occurred around 195.

Returning to Carthage, Tertullian took upon himself the task of defending Christianity by writing apologetics. Skilled in the rhetorical use of language, Tertullian became known as one of the great phrase-makers in the Church. For instance, among his sayings is this aphorism: "The seed [of the Church] is the blood of Christians."[31]

Around 200, he published his "Prescription Against Heretics," in which he rejected the claims of those like Justin Martyr, Clement of Alexandria, and Origen, who held that knowledge of pagan literature was beneficial for Christians. Tertullian strongly disagreed, as the excerpt below makes clear.

Yet Tertullian also recognized that Christians could not live in ignorance or without cultivating their critical powers of reasoning. He saw the value of what he called "secular studies," but only as a necessary introduction to "divine studies." Nonetheless, by his voluminous writings and challenging argument, Tertullian summoned all Christians to a literate understanding of truth.

His enormous body of literature included tracts for catechumens, treatises on marriage (he was among those church fathers who regarded any second marriage as verging on adultery), and a defense of the literal resurrection of the body. His blunt language and his use of sarcasm—for example, his ironic suggestion that Jesus chose unwisely in selecting fishermen, rather than philosophers, to carry the gospel—give his rhetoric a modern ring. In all his writings the influence of his legal training and powerful gifts in argumentation make Tertullian a most effective defender of the faith as he perceived it.

"Prescription Against Heretics"[32] (Excerpt)

Chapter 3

. . .Would to God that no "heresies" had ever been neces-sary, in order that they which are approved may be made manifest! We should then never be required to try our strength in contests about the soul with philosophers, those patriarchs of heretics, as they may be fairly called. The apostle, so far back as his own time, foresaw, indeed, that philospohy would do violent injury to the truth. This admonition *about false doctrine* he was induced to offer after he had been at Athens . . . and had there a taste of its huck-stering wiseacres and talkers.

Chapter 7

. . . Philosophy . . . is the material of the world's wisdom, the rash interpreter of the nature and dispensation of God. In-deed, heresies are themselves instigated by philosophy.

From this source came the Aeons, and I know not what infi-nite forms, and the trinity of man in the system of Valentinus, who was of Plato's school. From the same source came Marcion's better god, with all his tranquility; he came of the Stoics. Then, again, the opinion that the soul dies is held by the Epicureans; while the denial of the restoration of the body is taken from the aggregate school of all the philosophers; also, when matter is made equal to God, then you have the teaching of Zeno; and when any doctrine is alleged touching a god of fire, then Heraclitus comes in.

The same subject-matter is discussed over and over again by the heretics and the philosophers; the same arguments are in-volved. Whence comes evil? Why is it permitted? What is the origin of man? and in what way does he come? Besides the ques-tion which Valentinus has very lately proposed—Whence comes God? Which he settles with the answer: From *enthymesis* and *ec-troma* ["thoughtful reflection" and "premature expelling"]. Un-happy Aristotle! who invented for these men dialectics, the art of building up and pulling down; an art so evasive in its propositions, so far-fetched in its conjectures, so harsh in its arguments, so pro-ductive of contentions—embarrassing even to itself, retracting every-thing, and really treating of nothing!

Whence spring those "fables and endless genealogies," and "unprofitable questions," and "words which spread like a cancer"? From all these, when the apostle would restrain us, he expressly names philosophy as that which he would have us be on our guard against. Writing to the Colossians, he says, "See that no one beguile you through philosophy and vain deceit, after the tradition of men, and contrary to the wisdom of the Holy Ghost." He had been at Athens, and had in his interview with its philosophers become acquainted with that human wisdom which pretends to know the truth, whilst it only corrupts it, and is itself divided into its own manifold heresies, by the variety of its mutually repugnant sects.

What indeed has Athens to do with Jerusalem? What concord is there between the Academy and the Church? What between heretics and Christians? Our instruction comes from "the porch of Solomon," who had himself taught that "the Lord should be sought in simplicity of heart." Away with all attempts to produce a mottled Christianity of Stoic, Platonic, and dialectic composition! We want no curious disputation after possessing Christ Jesus, no inquisition after enjoying the gospel! With our faith, we desire no further belief.

For this is our palmary faith, that there is nothing which we ought to believe besides.

Origen and Gregory Thaumaturgus

Born in Alexandria, Origen (ca. 185–254) lived up to the characteristics suggested by his second name, Adamantius. He was rock-like in his beliefs, as in his temperament.

Christian parents—his father Leonides died a martyr in 202—gave Origen an early beginning in his study of the Scriptures and the writings of the church fathers.

According to the historian Eusebius, writing about 300, Origen studied under Clement of Alexandria; then Origen eventually succeeded Clement as head of the school, with Heracles teaching the elementary levels and Origen the advanced pupils. About 230, Origen traveled to Greece by way of Caesarea in Palestine, where Simon Peter had preached to Cornelius (Acts 10). Thereafter Caesarea became Origen's home and teaching center.

Among his pupils was Gregory Thaumaturgus (213–ca. 270), whose nickname means "the wonder-worker." Converted by Origen's teaching in 233, Gregory Thaumaturgus became one of the leading missionaries of his day.

Here follow excerpts from a letter sent by Origen to his pupil, written perhaps from Tyre, where Origen was to die. Next is a tribute, or panegyric, delivered by Gregory Thaumaturgus concerning his teacher on the occasion of Gregory's leaving Origen's school, around 238. For us, Gregory's essay resembles a valedictorian's appreciative address at commencement exercises, when the school's highest ranking student expresses gratitude to the faculty for their commitment to teaching and their personal concern for students. Gregory's tribute shows the importance of a teacher's enthusiasm and the benefits of friendship in influencing a pupil to devote himself to learning and to a love for "the Holy Word, " as Gregory calls the Scriptures.

A Letter from Origen to Gregory Thaumaturgus[33] (Excerpt)

Greeting in God, my most excellent sir, and venerable son Gregory, from Origen.

A natural readiness of comprehension, as you well know, may, if practice be added, contribute somewhat to the contingent end, if I may so call it, of that which any one wishes to practise. Thus, your natural good parts might make of you a finished Roman lawyer or a Greek philosopher, so to speak, of one of the schools in high reputation.

But I am anxious that you should devote all the strength of your natural good parts to Christianity for your end; and in order to this, I wish to ask you to extract from the philosophy of the Greeks what may serve as a course of study or a preparation for Christianity, and from geometry and astronomy what will serve to explain the sacred Scriptures, in order that all that the sons of the philosophers are wont to say about geometry and music, grammar, rhetoric, and astronomy, as fellow-helpers to philosophy, we may say about philosophy itself, in relation to Christianity.

. . . Do you then, my son, diligently apply yourself to the reading of the sacred Scriptures. Apply yourself, I say. For we who read the things of God need much application, lest we should say or think anything too rashly about them. And applying yourself thus to the study of the things of God, with faithful prejudgments such as are well pleasing to God, knock at its locked door, and it will be opened to you by the porter, of whom Jesus says, "To him the porter opens."

And applying yourself thus to the divine study, seek aright, and with unwavering trust in God, the meaning of the holy Scriptures, which so many have missed. Be not satisfied with knocking and seeking; for prayer is of all things indispensable to the knowledge of the things of God. For to this the Savior exhorted and said not only, "Knock, and it shall be opened unto you; and seek, and ye shall find," but also "Ask, and it shall be given unto you."

My fatherly love to you has made me thus bold; but whether my boldness be good, God will know, and His Christ, and all partakers of the Spirit of God and the Spirit of Christ. May you also be a partaker, and be ever increasing your inheritance, that you may say not only, "We are become partakers of Christ," but also partakers of God.

Panegyric Addressed to Origen by Gregory Thaumaturgus[34] (Excerpt)

. . . My earliest upbringing from the time of my birth on-wards was under the hand of my parents; and the manner of life in my father's house was one of error, and of a kind from which no one, I imagine, expected that we should be delivered. . . . Then followed the loss of my father, and my orphanhood, which per-chance was also the beginning of the knowledge of the truth to me. For then it was that I was brought over first to the Word of salvation and truth, in what manner I cannot tell, by constraint rather than by voluntary choice. For what power of decision had I then, who was but fourteen years of age?

. . . It seemed good to my mother that, being already under instruction in those other branches in which boys not ignobly born and nurtured are usually trained I should attend also a teach-er of public speaking. . . . Putting the idea, therefore, into this teacher's mind, he set me to learn in a thorough way the laws of the Romans by his help. And that man took up this charge zeal-ously with me; and I, on my side, gave myself to it—more, how-ever, to gratify the man, than as being myself an admirer of the study. And when he got me as his pupil, he began to teach me with all enthusiasm.

. . . Moreover, the stimulus of friendship was also brought to bear upon us, a stimulus, indeed, not easily withstood, but keen and most effective—the argument of a kind and affectionate dispo-sition, which showed itself benignantly in his words when he spoke to us and associated with us. For he did not aim merely at getting round us by any kind of reasoning; but his desire was, with a benignant and affectionate and most benevolent mind, to save us and make us partakers in the blessings that flow from philoso-phy, and most especially also in those other gifts which the Deity has bestowed on him above most men, or, as we may perhaps say, above all men of our own time.

. . . And thus, like some spark lighting upon our inmost soul, love was kindled and burst into flame within us—a love at once to the Holy Word, the most lovely object of all, who attracts all irre-sistibly towards Himself by His unutterable beauty, and to this man, His friend and advocate.

AUGUSTINE OF HIPPO

The conversion of Aurelius Augustinus (354–430) is one of the notable events in the history of Christianity.

Born in what is now Algeria, the young Augustine knew both the paganism of his father Patricius and the Christian faith of his mother Monica. His intellectual promise was such that he received the best education available in Carthage. These youthful years, he records in his *Confessions*, were spent in the fulfillment of sexual lust as much as in the pursuit of knowledge.

After the completion of his formal studies, Augustine became a teacher of rhetoric and an adherent to the cult of Manicheanism, which taught a duality between soul and body, light and darkness. But in his late twenties, Augustine grew weary of his life in Carthage and left for Rome and its greater pleasures. Soon after arriving in Rome, he received an appointment to teach in Milan, then the place of residence for the Roman emperor Valentinian. There in Milan, Augustine heard of the bishop Ambrose and went to listen to him preach. Never before had the young North African intellectual encountered the Christian gospel so presented.

Prompted by Ambrose's preaching, Augustine began his own search. One day in a garden, he had a mystical experience: He heard a child's voice saying to him, "Take up and read." He opened a copy of Paul's Letter to the Romans, where his eyes fell on this passage: "Let us behave decently, as in the daytime, not in orgies and drunkenness, not in sexual immorality and debauchery . . . Rather, clothe yourselves with the Lord Jesus Christ" (Romans 13:13–14).

A few months later, in the spring of 387, Augustine was baptized by Ambrose. With his mother, Augustine set out to return to Africa, but Monica died on the journey. Augustine continued on alone to live his new life of faith. Ordained in 391, he was appointed bishop of Hippo in 396.

The Church into which Augustine was baptized and ordained was deeply divided over how far Christians might indulge themselves in the pagan culture. One contemporary document, called "Constitutions of the Holy Apostles," dating from around 380, argues on Tertullian's side against any influence of pagan philosophy and literature, taking serious issue with the contrary position of someone like Basil the Great. A generation earlier, Basil had preached a sermon "To the Youth, How They Can Read Heathen Authors to Their Profit."

"Abstain from all the heathen books," says the "Constitutions of the Holy Apostles,"

> For what hast thou to do with such foreign discourses, or laws, or false prophets, which subvert the faith of the unstable? For what defect dost thou find in the law of God, that thou shouldst have recourse to those heathenish fables? For if thou hast a mind to read history, thou hast the books of the Kings; if books of wisdom or poetry, thou hast those of the prophets, of Job, and Proverbs, in which thou wilt find greater depth of sagacity than in all the heathen poets and sophisters because these are the words of the Lord, the only wise God.[35]

How was the worldly intellectual Augustine to react to such teaching? How was he to preach as a pastor and teach as a bishop? We have his answer in his preaching (some five hundred of his sermons are extant) and teaching, which resonates with wit and vivid imagery.

For instance, when a deacon in Carthage named Deogratias inquired how best to instruct the unlearned, Augustine wrote a treatise called "On the Catechising of the Uninstructed." With commendable common sense and grace, Augustine warns his reader not to bore his heretofore uninstructed students by attempting to tell too much at once nor require them to "repeat by memory the entire Pentateuch." Instead, "what we ought to do is to give a comprehensive statement of all things, summarily and generally, so that certain of the more wonderful facts may be selected which are listened to with superior gratification."[36]

When someone else, "who has cultivated the field of liberal studies . . . [and] who has already made up his mind to be a Christian," comes for catechetical instruction, Augustine urges the deacon to "develop a brief method of procedure . . . so as not to inculcate on them, in an odious fashion, things which they know already."[37]

The deacon may also encounter graduates of grammar schools who have studied not the liberal arts but public speaking—perhaps like today's college students who major in "communications" but learn very little content to communicate! Of such students Augustine writes,

> When such persons approach you, it will be your duty. . . to make it plain that they are to be diligently admonished to clothe themselves with Christian humility, and learn not to

despise individuals whom they may discover keeping themselves free from vices of conduct more carefully than from
faults of language.[38]

On Christian Doctrine was begun around 396, set aside, then completed in 426. While its title suggests a theological discourse, On Christian Doctrine is really a manual for teachers of the Scriptures. Even if a
modern reader is not familiar with classical rhetoric's technical terms,
the rich store of truth contained in this work is too precious to ignore,
especially for those who presume to teach the Bible in a Christian
school.

On Christian Doctrine[39] (Excerpt)

There are certain rules for the interpretation of Scripture
which I think might with great advantage be taught to earnest
students of the Word, that they may profit not only from reading
the works of others who have laid open the secrets of the sacred
writings, but also from themselves opening such secrets to others.
These rules I propose to teach to those who are able and willing to
learn.

. . . There are two things on which all interpretation of
Scripture depends: the mode of ascertaining the proper meaning,
and the mode of making known the meaning when it is ascer-
tained.

. . . First of all, then, it is necessary that we should be led by
the *fear of God* to seek the knowledge of His will, what He commands us to desire and what to avoid. Now this fear will of necessity excite in us the thought of our mortality and of the death that
is before us, and crucify all the motions of pride as if our flesh were
nailed to the tree.

Next it is necessary to have our hearts subdued by *piety,* and
not to run in the face of Holy Scripture, whether when understood
it strikes at some of our sins, or, when not understood, we feel as if
we could be wiser and give better commands ourselves. We must
rather think and believe that whatever is there written, even
though it be hidden, is better and truer than anything we could
devise by our own wisdom.

After these two steps of fear and piety, we have come to the
third stop, *knowledge,* of which I have now undertaken to treat.

For in this every earnest student of the Holy Scriptures exercises himself, to find nothing else in them but that God is to be loved for His own sake, and our neighbor for God's sake; and that God is to be loved with all the heart, and with all the soul, and with all the mind, and one's neighbor as one's self . . .

And in this frame of mind he gradually comes to the fourth step, that is *strength* and *resolution,* in which he hungers and thirsts after righteousness. . . .

And when, to the extent of his power, he has gazed upon this object shining from afar, and has felt that owing to the weakness of his sight he cannot endure that matchless light, then in the fifth step—that is, in the *counsel of compassion*—he cleanses his soul . . . from the filth it has contracted.

At this stage he exercises himself diligently in the love of his neighbor; and when he has reached the point of loving his enemy, full of hopes and unbroken in strength, he mounts to the sixth step, in which he *purifies the eye itself which can see God.*

. . . Such a son ascends to *wisdom,* which is the seventh and last step, and which he enjoys in peace and tranquility. For the fear of God is the beginning of wisdom. From that beginning, then, till we reach wisdom itself, our way is by the steps now described.

. . . Not a few things, too, are closed against us and obscured by ignorance of music . . . for we must not listen to the falsities of heathen superstition, which represent the nine Muses as daughters of Jupiter and Mercury; we ought not to give up music because of the superstition of the heathen, if we can derive anything from it that is of use for the understanding of Holy Scripture. . . . For we ought not to refuse to learn letters because they say that Mercury discovered them; nor because they have dedicated temples to Justice and Virtue, and prefer to worship in the form of stones things that ought to have their place in the heart, ought we on that account to forsake justice and virtue. Nay, but let every good and true Christian understand that wherever truth may be found, it belongs to his Master.

. . . As, then, I have already said a great deal about the mode of ascertaining the meaning, and have given three books on this one part of the subject, I shall only say a few things about the mode of making known the meaning.

. . . Now, the art of rhetoric being available for the enforcing either of truth or falsehood, who will dare to say that truth in the person of its defenders is to take its stand unarmed against falsehood? For example, that those who are trying to persuade men of what is false are to know how to introduce their subject, so as to put the hearer into a friendly, or attentive, or teachable frame of mind, while the defenders of the truth shall be ignorant of that art? That the former are to tell their falsehoods briefly, clearly, and plausibly, while the latter shall tell the truth in such a way that it is tedious to listen to, hard to understand, and, in fine, not easy to believe it? That the former are to oppose the truth and defend falsehood with sophistical arguments, while the latter shall be unable either to defend what is true, or to refute what is false? That the former, while imbuing the minds of their hearers with erroneous opinions, are by their power of speech to awe, to melt, to enliven, and to rouse them, while the latter shall in defence of the truth be sluggish, and frigid, and somnolent? Who is such a fool as to think this wisdom?

Since, then, the faculty of eloquence is available for both sides, and is of very great service in the enforcing either of wrong or right, why do not good men study to engage it on the side of truth, when bad men use it to obtain the triumph of wicked and worthless causes, and to further injustice and error?

. . . It is the duty, then, of the interpreter and teacher of Holy Scripture, the defender of the true faith and the opponent of error, both to teach what is right and to refute what is wrong, and in the performance of this task to conciliate the hostile, to rouse the careless, and to tell the ignorant both what is occurring at present and what is probable in the future.

But once his hearers are friendly, attentive, and ready to learn, whether he has found them so, or has himself made them so, the remaining objects are to be carried out in whatever way the case requires. If the hearers need teaching, the matter treated of must be made fully known by means of narrative. On the other hand, to clear up points that are doubtful requires reasoning and the exhibition of proofs. If, however, the hearers require to be roused rather than instructed, in order that they may be diligent to do what they already know, and to bring their feelings into harmony with the truths they admit, greater vigor of speech is needed. Here entreaties and reproaches, exhortations and upbraidings, and all the other means of rousing the emotions, are necessary.

And all the methods I have mentioned are constantly used by nearly everyone in cases where speech is the agency employed.

But as some men employ these coarsely, inelegantly, and frigidly, while others use them with acuteness, elegance, and spirit, the work that I am speaking of ought to be undertaken by one who can argue and speak with wisdom, if not with eloquence, and with profit to his hearers, even though he profit them less that he would if he could speak with eloquence too.

But we must beware of the man who abounds in eloquent nonsense, and so much the more if the hearer is pleased with what is not worth listening to, and thinks that because the speaker is eloquent what he says must be true. . . .

Now a man speaks with more or less wisdom just as he has made more or less progress in the knowledge of Scripture; I do not mean by reading them much and committing them to memory, but by understanding them aright and carefully searching into their meaning. For there are those who read and yet neglect them; they read to remember the words, but are careless about knowing the meaning. It is plain we must set far above these the men who are not so retentive of the words, but see with the eyes of the heart into the heart of Scripture. Better than either of these, however, is the man who, when he wishes, can repeat the words, and at the same time correctly apprehend their meaning.

. . . For teaching, of course, true eloquence consists not in making people like what they disliked, nor in making them do what they shrank from, but in making clear what was obscure; yet if this be done without grace of style, the benefit does not extend beyond the few eager students who are anxious to know whatever is to be learned, however rude and unpolished the form in which it is put; and who, when they have succeeded in their object, find the plain truth pleasant food enough.

. . . He, then, who speaks with the purpose of teaching should not suppose that he has said what he has to say as long as he is not understood; for although what he has said be intelligible to himself, it is not said at all to the man who does not understand it. If, however, he is understood, he has said his say, whatever may have been the manner of saying it.

But if he wishes to delight or persuade his hearer as well, he will not accomplish that end by putting his thought in any shape no matter what, but for that purpose the style of speaking is a matter of importance. And as the hearer must be pleased in order to secure his attention, so he must be persuaded in order to move him to action. . . . I need not go over all the other things that can be done by powerful eloquence to move the minds of the hearers, not telling them what they ought to do, but urging them to do what they already know ought to be done.

. . . And it is needful when people, knowing what they ought to do, do it not. Therefore, to teach is a necessity. For what men know, it is in their own hands either to do or not to do. But who would say that it is their duty to do what they do not know?

. . . And so our Christian orator, while he says what is just, and holy, and good (and he ought never to say anything else), does all he can to be heard with intelligence, with pleasure, and with obedience; and he need not doubt that if he succeed in this object, and so far as he succeeds, he will succeed more by piety in prayer than by gifts of oratory; and so he ought to pray for himself, and for those he is about to address, before he attempts to speak.

And when the hour is come that he must speak, he ought, before he opens his mouth, to lift up his thirsty soul to God, to drink in what he is about to pour forth, and to be himself filled with what he is about to distribute. For, as in regard to every matter of faith and love there are many things that may be said, and many ways of saying them, who knows what is expedient at a given moment for us to say, or to be heard saying, except God who knows the hearts of all? And who can make us say what we ought, and in the way we ought, except Him in whose hand both we and our speeches are?

Accordingly, he who is anxious both to know and to teach should learn all that is to be taught, and acquire such a faculty of speech as is suitable for a divine. But when the hour for speech arrives, let him reflect upon that saying of our Lord's, as better suited to the wants of a pious mind: "Take no thought how or what ye shall speak; for it shall be given you in that same hour what ye shall speak. For it is not ye that speak, but the Spirit of your Father which speaketh in you." The Holy Spirit, then, speaks thus in those who for Christ's sake are delivered to the persecutors; why not also in those who deliver Christ's message to those who are willing to learn?

Now if any one says that we need not direct men how or what they should teach, since the Holy Spirit makes them teachers, he may as well say that we need not pray, since our Lord says, "Your Father knoweth what things ye have need of before ye ask Him". . .

What then are we to think? Does the apostle in any way contradict himself, when, though he says that men are made teachers by the operation of the Holy Spirit, he yet himself gives them directions how and what they should teach?

. . . The same apostle says to Timothy, speaking of course as teacher to disciple: "But continue thou in the things which thou has learned, and hast been assured of, knowing of whom thou hast learned them." For as the medicines which men apply to the bodies of their fellow-men are of no avail except God gives them virtue (who can heal without their aid, though they cannot without His), and yet they are applied . . . ; so the aids of teaching, applied through the instrumentality of man, are of advantage to the soul only when God works to make them of advantage, who could give the gospel to man even without the help or agency of man.

. . . But whatever may be the majesty of the style, the life of the speaker will count for more in securing the hearer's compliance. The man who speaks wisely and eloquently, but lives wickedly, may, it is true, instruct many who are anxious to learn; . . . therefore it is that men who themselves lead unprofitable lives are heard with profit by others. . . . Now these men do good to many by preaching what they themselves do not perform; but they would do good to very many more if they lived as they preach.

. . . Such a teacher as is here described may, to secure compliance, speak not only quietly and temperately, but even vehemently, without any breach of modesty, because his life protects him against contempt. For while he pursues an upright life, he takes care to maintain a good reputation as well, providing things honest in the sight of God and men, fearing God, and caring for men.

. . . To speak eloquently, then, and wisely as well, is just to express truths which it is expedient to teach in fit and proper words—words which in the subdued style are adequate, in the temperate, elegant, and in the majestic, forcible. But the man who cannot speak both eloquently and wisely should speak wisely without eloquence, rather than eloquently without wisdom.

If, however, he cannot do even this, let his life be such as shall not only secure a reward for himself, but afford an example to others; and let his manner of living be an eloquent sermon in itself.

. . . But whether a man is going to address the people or to dictate what others will deliver or read to the people, he ought to pray God to put into his mouth a suitable discourse. For if Queen Esther prayed, when she was about to speak to the king touching the temporal welfare of her race, that God would put fit words into her mouth, how much more ought he to pray for the same blessing who labors in word and doctrine for the eternal welfare of men?

. . . This book has extended to a greater length than I expected or desired. . . . I, however, give thanks to God that with what little ability I possess I have in these four books striven to depict, not the sort of man I am myself (for my defects are very many), but the sort of man he ought to be who desires to labor in sound, that is, in Christian doctrine, not for his own instruction only, but for that of others also.

JEROME

His Latin name was Eusebius Hieronymus, but he is known as Jerome, translator of the Bible into Latin, a version called the Vulgate. A native of the region near Trieste, in what we formerly called Yugoslavia, Jerome (ca. 345–420) studied in Rome and was baptized there as a young man. He traveled to Syria and was ordained at Antioch, then returned to Rome to serve as secretary to Pope Damasus.

In 383, Damasus commissioned Jerome to produce a new version of the Bible, drawing upon Old Latin manuscripts and the Greek translation of the Old Testament known as the Septuagint. Jerome completed this enormous task in 404, by which time he had also completed many volumes of commentaries on the Scriptures, as well as a vast number of treatises and argumentative letters.

In Rome, he also conducted Bible classes for a group of wealthy widows and their daughters. One of the widows, Paula, accompanied by her daughter Julia Eustochium, helped to finance Jerome's pilgrimage to the Holy Land in 385. The following year found Jerome in Bethlehem; by 389, Paula had paid for the establishing of a monastery there under Jerome's leadership. He remained in Bethlehem until his death.

In 403, Jerome wrote to Paula's daughter Laeta concerning a granddaughter, also named Paula. Portions of this letter follow. Laeta accepted Jerome's advice and sent her daughter to study and live out her life in the religious community founded by her grandmother, headed by her Aunt Eustochium, and subsequently headed by the younger Paula herself.

"Letter CVII, to Laeta"[40] (Excerpt)

The apostle Paul writing to the Corinthians and instructing in sacred discipline a church still untaught in Christ has among other commandments laid down also this: "The woman which hath an husband that believeth not, and if he be pleased to dwell with her, let her not leave him. For the unbelieving husband is sanctified by the believing wife, and the unbelieving wife is sanctified by the believing husband; else were your children unclean but now are they holy.". . .

You yourself are the offspring of a mixed marriage; but the parents of Paula—you and my friend Toxotius—are both Christians. Who could have believed that to the heathen pontiff Albinus should be born—in answer to a mother's vows—a Christian granddaughter; that a delighted grandfather should hear from the little one's faltering lips Christ's Alleluia, and that in his old age he should nurse in his bosom one of God's own virgins? Our expectations have been fully gratified. The one unbeliever is sanctified by his holy and believing family. For, when a man is surrounded by a believing crowd of children and grandchildren, he is as good as a candidate for the faith.

I for my part think that, had he possessed so many Christian kinsfolk when he was a young man, he might then have been brought to believe in Christ. For though he may spit upon my letter and laugh at it, and though he may call me a fool or a madman, his son-in-law did the same before he came to believe. Christians are not born but made.

. . . I speak thus to you, Laeta my most devout daughter in Christ, to teach you not to despair of your father's salvation.

. . . You know the Lord's promise: "The things which are impossible with men are possible with God." It is never too late to mend.

. . . I have nearly wandered into a new subject, . . . for in answer to your prayers and those of the saintly Marcella, I wish to address you as a mother and to instruct you how to bring up our dear Paula, who has been consecrated to Christ before her birth and vowed to his service before her conception. . . . As then Paula has been born in answer to a promise, her parents should give her a training suitable to her birth.

. . . Thus must a soul be educated which is to be a temple of God. It must learn to hear nothing and to say nothing but what belongs to the fear of God. It must have no understanding of unclean words, and no knowledge of the world's songs. Its tongue must be steeped while still tender in the sweetness of the Psalms. Boys with their thoughts must be kept from Paula: even her maids and female servants must be separated from worldly associates. For if they have learned some mischief they may teach more.

Get for her a set of letters made of boxwood or ivory and called each by its proper name. Let her play with these, so that even her play may teach her something. And not only make her grasp the right order of the letters and see that she forms their names into rhyme, but constantly disarrange their order and put the last letters in the middle and the middle ones at the beginning that she may know them all by sight as well as by sound.

Moreover, so soon as she begins to use the stylus upon the wax, and her hand is still faltering, either guide her soft fingers by laying your hand upon hers, or else have simple copies cut upon a tablet; so that her efforts confined within these limits may keep to the lines traced for her and not stray outside these. Offer prizes for good spelling and draw her onwards with little gifts such as children her age delight in.

And let her have companions in her lessons to excite emulation in her, that she may be stimulated when she sees them praised. You must not scold her if she is slow to learn, but must employ praise to excite her mind, so that she may be glad when she excels others and sorry when she is excelled by them. Above all you must take care not to make her lessons distasteful to her, lest a dislike for them conceived in childhood may continue into her maturer years.

. . . Again, you must choose for her a master of approved years, life, and learning. A man of culture will not, I think, blush to do for a kinswoman of a high-born virgin what Aristotle did for Philip's son when, descending to the level of an usher, he consented to teach him his letters.

. . . She ought to rise at night to recite prayers and psalms; to sing hymns in the morning; at the third, sixth, and ninth hours to take her place in the line to do battle for Christ; and lastly, to kindle her lamp and to offer her evening sacrifice. In these occupations let her pass the day, and when night comes let it find her still engaged in them. Let reading follow prayer with her, and prayer again succeed to reading. Time will seem short when employed on tasks so many and so varied.

. . . You will answer, "How shall I, a woman of the world, living at Rome, surrounded by a crowd, be able to observe all these injunctions?" In that case, do not undertake a burden to which you are not equal. When you have weaned Paula as Isaac was weaned, and when you have clothed her as Samuel was clothed, send her to her grandmother and aunt; give up this most precious of gems, to be placed in Mary's chamber and to rest in the cradle where the infant Jesus cried. Let her be brought up in a monastery, let her be one amid companies of virgins, let her learn to avoid swearing, let her regard lying as sacrilege, let her be ignorant of the world, let her live the angelic life, while in the flesh let her be without the flesh, and let her suppose that all human beings are like herself.

PART III
POPES, PRINCES, AND PEDAGOGUES: 500–1400

All this must be ensued lest humility be wanting when office is assumed, the way of life be at variance with the office accepted, teaching divest life of rectitude, and presumption overrate teaching.

Gregory the Great
Pastoral Care, ca. 591

POPES, PRINCES,
AND PEDAGOGUES:

Augustine's vision had included the possibility that Rome might become a foretaste of the City of God. What Augustine did not foresee was the collapse of Rome and its influence when, in 410, the Visigoth chieftain Alaric conquered the capital of the empire. A few decades later, the entire Roman Empire lay shattered; the "barbarians" had been victorious, bringing with them little or no appreciation for the civilities of learning. During the next three centuries, formal education all but ended; even the pagan schools were closed. Ignorant of Latin, the conquerors corrupted the language, leading to its almost total decline into disuse. Roman civilization decayed; the light of Roman culture seemed all but extinguished.

Furthermore, the new culture that swept away Rome was not accustomed to resolving its controversies by closely reasoned argument but by bloodshed. Some of these tribes had been evangelized and had made nominal conversion to Christianity; yet they possessed no passion for peace, no apparent desire for tranquility. They loved to fight, and their code elevated killing for a cause to the pinnacle of honor.

Even so, all was not lost. Throughout this period, one light continued to gleam, however dimly, from the monasteries. In the middle of the third century, when persecution had fallen upon the church, many Christians had fled for refuge to the deserts of Egypt, the Sinai peninsula, Judaea, or Syria. There they had formed communities called monasteries; there too they had found places for the safekeeping of important manuscripts, such as early versions of the New Testament and writings of the Church Fathers. From such storehouses, copies could be sent for wider distribution.

Although persecution had ended by the Emperor Constantine's Edict of Milan in 313, many of these monastic communities, such as Jerome's in Bethlehem, continued to provide opportunity for a life of service and devotion. So the monastic movement thrived, spreading westward from the Nile and Palestine to Italy, France, and the British Isles.

But many of those who took up the monastic life apparently were illiterate upon arrival. Thus began the teaching of reading and writing to novices in the monastery, the better to equip them to serve as manuscript copyists. At the heart of such instruction the art of dialectic—discussion and dispute between teacher and pupils—developed as the lasting legacy of Western teaching and learning.

Over the next nine hundred years, the pall of the so-called Dark Ages gradually gave way to a rebirth of learning—a renaissance of culture. Throughout the first half of this period, the influence of popes such as Gregory the Great, princes such as Alfred and Charlemagne, and pedagogues such as Alcuin and Rabanus Maurus led the way toward such renewal.

The years from the death of King Alfred the Great to the death of the English poet Geoffrey Chaucer, spanning five centuries from 900 to 1400, bridge a turbulent period in European history, known as the Middle Ages. Chiefly responsible for much of the turmoil was the rise of Islam, the spread of its prophet Muhammad's teachings throughout Europe, the desecration of Christian shrines in Palestine, and the resulting Crusades, whose bitter consequences still gnaw in the memory of devout Muslims a millennium later.

Certain aspects of this period have been romanticized—uncritically and mostly undeservedly—in the legends of Camelot, the novels of Sir Walter Scott, the poetry of Alfred, Lord Tennyson, and the illustrations by N. C. Wyeth; even the romantic songs of Lerner and Loewe glamorize the period. But it was a period ruinously wasteful of human life; a period in which brutalizing combat in tournaments, like the earlier Roman spectacles in the Colosseum, served as public sport; a period that led eventually to the religious sham called the Crusades. In all this, the church participated wholly, particularly in the secularizing of what little training was offered as part of instruction in "chivalry."

This age of chivalry purported to train a young man for an honorable career as a nobleman. More accurately, it prepared him for a life of debauchery, bloodthirstiness, and foolish pride. The typical "knight in shining armor" was less than the heroic image passed on to us in novels and films. He was, more often, semi-literate at best, having been schooled in formal manners and in the etiquette of the times. What piety he may have possessed had largely been diluted by his degenerate upbringing from boyhood as the consort of ladies fair and their dissolute companions.

Yet, the church conferred on this twenty-one-year-old man its blessing in an impressive ceremony, dubbing him a knight and swearing him in allegiance to the cross. Some truly noble knights may have gone off in quest of the Holy Grail and may have rescued damsels in distress. Most, however, settled down to a fore-shortened life of coarse behavior, carousing and jousting, emulating their sexually indiscriminate troubadour and paragon, King Richard the Lion-Hearted.

But as always seems to be true of history, even out of these adversities came certain benefits. In spite of opposition from professing Christian kings and knights, Islam's expansion—from Arabia across North Africa and the Straits of Gibraltar to Spain, across the Bosporus from Turkey to the Balkan Peninsula and on to Greece—contributed a new culture to Europe.

As Muslim invaders moved westward, they drove out before them Eastern Christians, who fled with whole libraries of Byzantine manuscripts and caravans of Byzantine art. Muslim scholars who followed brought with them not only the Qur'an, Muhammad's allegedly sacred text, but also their knowledge of pre-Christian Greek philosophers, particularly Aristotle, long forgotten in the West. For instance, it was to the Spanish Muslim scholar Averroës (1126–98) that Europe owed a debt for his commentaries on Aristotle, which in turn became standard texts in European universities.

During the centuries of the Middle Ages, monastery and palace schools such as those of Charlemagne and Alfred the Great expanded to cathedral schools, at Canterbury and Winchester, for instance. But groups of monks and their pupils wished for more. Seeking to broaden their curriculum, they sought a higher level of education; so they formed themselves into communities of teachers and students called *universitas magistrorum et scholarium.*

The earliest such universities, founded in the tenth century, were at Salerno and Bologna, where, respectively, medicine and law were taught. The University of Paris was founded after 1150. By 1168, members of the clergy specifically called to be scholars, known as "clerks," were in residence at Oxford; Cambridge followed around 1225. In 1387, Chaucer described one of these clerks and his earnestness in the Prologue to *The Canterbury Tales*: "And gladly would he learn, and gladly teach."

The method of learning and teaching with which Chaucer's "Clerk of Oxenford"—as well as every other student and master of the time—would be acquainted is called *scholasticism*. This was the traditional means by which medieval education was dispensed, based on the dialectics of logical reasoning: argument, refutation, and resolution.

Augustine of Hippo had taught that belief and understanding are intertwined. Anselm, archbishop of Canterbury around 1100, reiterated Augustine's famous phrase, *Credo ut intelligam* ("I believe in order that I may understand") and, along with other scholars of the Middle Ages—Peter Abelard, John of Salisbury, Thomas Aquinas—stood on this foundation, which became known as "scholasticism," seeking to build a superstructure by means of logical reasoning to support the church's teachings.

But out of even this commendable desire to wed faith to reason came the conventional human desire to force a system upon those who would search for truth. Formal lists of questions and their prescribed, complicated answers comprised these theological disputations. In time, achieving the approved answer seemed more important than understanding that faith and reason have a common source.

Yet for those who believe that God's providence overrules in history, eventually alternatives to scholasticism arose in groups such as the Brothers (and, later, also Sisters) of the Common Life. Even John Wyclif's call to translate the Bible into English can be seen as breaking with the method of teaching and learning by recitation. In time, with the advent of Christian humanism—the "New Learning" of the fifteenth and sixteenth centuries—scholasticism came under increasing criticism for its elevation of rationalism over faith and its dependence upon commentaries and argument rather than reliance upon the text of Scripture as its own primary authority. So cold logic yielded to warmer inquiry and even doubt as a means of access to truth.

The power of the reasoning mind to illumine the mysteries of Scripture lay in its imagination; thus the question *Why?* became the cornerstone of late medieval and early Renaissance and Reformation teaching.

GREGORY THE GREAT

Among the "doctors of the church," Gregory (ca. 540–604) is remembered for his personal character and his missionary zeal. Born to a noble Roman family—his father was a senator—Gregory rose to become a prefect of the city in 573. But soon after, he sold his possessions and entered one of the seven monasteries he had founded, called St. Andrew's.

He was not to remain in the cloistered life for long, being chosen first as one of Rome's regional deacons, then as ambassador to the court at Constantinople and the Eastern Church there. By 585, he was back in Rome as abbot of St. Andrew's monastery.

In 590, he was chosen to be pope, but only after deep personal struggle with that calling. His papacy faced internal and external threats, including treachery from the Eastern Church. But Pope Gregory possessed not only moral strength of character but also political skill, which he exercised by appointing local authorities loyal to him and the Roman papacy rather than Constantinople's intrigues.

He also recognized a need to blend politics and evangelism; so, as much to assert the authority of Rome over Western Europe as to save souls, Gregory sent missionaries abroad. Among these was another Augustine who, in 597, established a church in Canterbury, England.

Among Gregory's writings, his book called *Pastoral Care* merits being cited here. Written about 591 to be a handbook for bishops on the care of souls in their charge, it had lasting influence upon those most responsible for the education of that time. In 796, Alcuin recommended it to Eanbald, the archbishop of York; in 901, King Alfred the Great had it translated from Greek into Old English and renamed it *The Shepherd's Book.*

Gregory's other contributions include the favor he gave to the development of a new musical form for worship called the plainsong, or Gregorian chant.

Unlike too many ecclesiastical authorities, Pope Gregory the Great lived out the meaning of his title, "Servant of the servants of God," with humility and grace.

Pastoral Care[1] (Excerpt)

Gregory to His Most Reverend and Most Holy Brother, John, Fellow Bishop:

Most dear brother, you reprove me with kind and humble regard for having wished to escape by concealment from the burdens of the pastoral care. Now, lest these burdens might appear light to some, I am explaining, by writing this book, how onerous I regard them, so that he who is free from them may not imprudently seek to have them, and he who has been so imprudent as to seek them may feel apprehension in having them.

. . . The nature of the case requires that one should carefully consider the way in which the position of supreme rule ought to be approached, and when it is duly reached, how life should be spent in it; how, in a life of rectitude, one should teach others; and, in the proper performance of his teaching office, with what vigilance one should realize each day one's weakness. All this must be [pursued] lest humility be wanting when the office is assumed, the way of life be at variance with the office accepted, teaching divest life of rectitude, and presumption overrate teaching.

. . . No one ventures to teach any art unless he has learned it after deep thought. With what rashness, then, would the pastoral office be undertaken by the unfit, seeing that the government of souls is the art of arts! For who does not realize that the wounds of the mind are more hidden than the internal wounds of the body? Yet, although those who have no knowledge of the powers of drugs shrink from giving themselves out as physicians of the flesh, people who are utterly ignorant of spiritual precepts are often not afraid of professing themselves to be physicians of the heart, and though, by divine ordinance, those now in the highest positions are disposed to show a regard for religion, some there are who aspire to glory and esteem by an outward show of authority within the holy Church. They crave to appear as teachers and covet ascendancy over others. . . .

. . . Yet everyone who is unworthy would flee from the burden of such great guilt if with the attentive ear of the heart he pondered on that saying: "He that shall scandalize one of these little ones that believe in me, it were better for him that a millstone should be hanged about his neck, and that he should be drowned in the depth of the sea."

THE VENERABLE BEDE

The first English historian, Bede spent most of his life (ca. 670–735) in the monasteries of Jarrow and Wearmouth, near Durham. Most of what is known about Bede personally comes from an autobiographical note in his great work, *Ecclesiastical History of the English Nation,* written in 731:

> I, Bede, a servant of Christ and priest of the monastery of the blessed apostles St. Peter and St. Paul, which is at Wearmouth and at Jarrow, . . . was born in the territory of the said monastery, and at the age of seven I was, by the care of my relations, given to the reverend Abbot Benedict Biscop, and afterwards to Ceolfrid, to be educated. From that time I have spent the whole of my life within the monastery devoting all my pains to the study of the Scriptures; and amid the observance of monastic discipline, and the daily charge of singing in the church, it has ever been my delight to learn or teach or write.[2]

Bede's influence as a teacher might well be compared with that of Socrates—who taught Plato, who taught Aristotle, who taught Alexander the Great. Bede taught Egbert, later archbishop of York and founder of the famous school there. At Egbert's school Alcuin came to study and eventually, in 778, was appointed its head; but in 781, Alcuin accepted the invitation of the Emperor Charlemagne to found a school at his court in Aachen, where one of those in attendance was the emperor himself. Thus, like Socrates, the influence of Bede swept through the vast realm.

The excerpt that follows describes the work of Theodore, first archbishop of Canterbury to head the entire English church. Appointed in 668, this native of Tarsus founded a school at Canterbury, whose work Bede relates.

"Ecclesiastical History of the English Church"[3] (Excerpt)

. . . Theodore then arrived at his church in the second year after his consecration, on Sunday 27 May (670 A.D.), and lived in it twenty-one years, three months, and twenty-six days. He soon travelled through the whole island, wherever it was inhabited by the English race. For he was willingly received and listened to by every one, and everywhere in the company and with the assistance of Hadrian, he sowed the right rule of life, the canonical rite for the celebration of Easter. And he was the first of the archbishops to whom the whole English church consented to do fealty.

And because, as we have said, both were abundantly learned both in sacred and profane literature, rivers of saving knowledge daily flowed from them to irrigate the hearts of the band of pupils whom they brought together, insomuch that they passed on to their hearers the knowledge even of the art of meter, of astronomy and of ecclesiastical arithmetic, together with volumes of the sacred text.

A proof of this is that even today, some of their pupils are still living who know the Latin and Greek languages as well as their native tongue. Never since the English came to Britain were there happier times than these, in which, under brave and Christian kings, they were a terror to all barbarian tribes, when the aspirations of all hung on the lately revealed joys of the kingdom of heaven, and every one who wished to become learned in Holy Writ, had masters at hand to teach him.

ALCUIN AND CHARLEMAGNE

Alcuin (732–814) enrolled at Archbishop Egbert's school as a child. He stayed in York until he was almost fifty years old, becoming a teacher and finally master of studies.

Meanwhile, the Frankish kingdom was being consolidated by Charles the Great, or Charlemagne, into the Holy Roman Empire. As king and emperor, Charlemagne showed concern for the education and advancement of culture among his subjects. To further this end, he founded a school at his palace in Aachen. In 782, Charlemagne chose as his first schoolmaster the most renowned educator in Europe, Alcuin of York.

Just before leaving York to take up his duties in Aachen, Alcuin wrote a long poem, celebrating the accomplishments of York's most renowned men. In the prose adaptation that follows, Alcuin speaks of Aelbert, his own teacher and the master of studies whom Alcuin had succeeded.

Upon arriving at the court of Charlemagne, Alcuin obtained the nickname Albinus. He found that the emperor's sixteen-year-old son Pepin was to be one of his pupils. For Pepin, the master invented a pedagogical catechism as a device for teaching, calling it *The Disputation of Pepin, the Most Noble and Royal Youth, with Albinus the Scholastic* (an excerpt appears on page 103).

But Charlemagne's concern for education extended beyond his own family and court. He also recognized the need for literacy among his subjects, especially those in the monasteries who presumed to teach and preach to others. In 787, presumably under Alcuin's guidance—and perhaps written by Alcuin—Charlemagne sent out a proclamation to all abbots of monasteries throughout the Holy Roman Empire. This proclamation condemned the abbots for tolerating illiteracy and summoned them to add to godly living the teaching of correct speaking and writing, "so that those who desire to please God by living rightly should not neglect to please him also by speaking correctly." The text of Charlemagne's summons that follows is addressed specifically to the Abbot Baugulf of Fulda, a Benedictine abbey northeast of Frankfurt am Main, a monastery eventually famous for its missionary zeal and theological studies.

Evidence abounds that Charlemagne obviously understood what Christians in every age need to remember: that orthodox belief and biblical doctrine need clear, careful, and precise expression. Good intentions, no matter how spiritual, are hardly sufficient in themselves to overcome ignorance, confused and confusing speech, inaccurate and inappropriate choice of words, clichés and trite phrases.

Two years after his *Proclamation*, in 789, Charlemagne issued a second directive, in which he wrote, "Let schools be established in which boys may learn to read."[4] So the mightiest ruler in Europe showed his concern for elementary education.

In 796, Alcuin left Charlemagne's palace school at Aachen, having been appointed by Charlemagne to become abbot of the monastery of St. Martin's at Tours in France. There Alcuin remained until his death in 804, creating eventually the most famous school in the Empire. From Tours, Alcuin wrote a personal letter to Charlemagne, revealing by his use of Scripture a fuller sense of Alcuin's vocation and mission as a teacher. In it, Alcuin reminds the king of the Bible's edict to learn wisdom:

> . . . This is a matter which has not escaped your most noble notice, how through all the pages of Holy Scripture we are urged to learn wisdom. In toiling toward the happy life, nothing is more lofty, nothing more pleasant, nothing bolder against vices, nothing more praiseworthy in every place of dignity; and moreover, according to the words of philosophers, nothing is more essential to government, nothing more helpful in leading a moral life, than the beauty of wisdom, the praise of learning, and the advantages of scholarship.
>
> . . . O Lord King, exhort the youths who are in your excellency's palace to learn wisdom with all their might, and to gain it by daily toil while they are yet in the flush of youth, so that they may be deemed worthy to grow grey in honor, and by the help of wisdom may reach everlasting happiness.[5]

"On the Saints of the Church at York"[6]

Bide with me for a while, I pray you, youth of York, while I proceed with poetic steps to treat of him, because here he often drenched your senses with nectar, pouring forth sweet juices from his honey-flowing bosom.

Fairest Philosophy took him from his very cradle and bore him to the topmost towers of learning, opening to him the hidden things of wisdom. He was born of ancestors of sufficient note, by whose care he was soon sent to kindly school, and entered at the Minster in his early years, that his tender age might grow up with holy understanding. Nor was his parents' hope in vain; even as a boy as he grew in body so he became proficient in the understanding of books.

Then pious and wise, teacher at once and priest, he was made a colleague of Bishop Egbert, to whom he was nearly allied by right of blood. By him he is made advocate of the clergy, and at the same time is preferrèd as master in the city of York.

There he moistened thirsty hearts with diverse streams of teaching and the varied dews of learning, giving to these the art of the science of grammar, pouring on those the rivers of rhetoric. Some he polished on the whetstone of law, some he taught to sing together in Aeonian chant, making others play on the flute of Castaly and run with the feet of lyric poets over the hills of Parnassus. Others the said master made to know the harmony of heaven, the labors of the sun and moon, the five belts of the sky, the seven planets, the laws of the fixed stars, their rising and setting, the movements of the air, the quaking of the sea and earth, the nature of men, cattle, birds and beasts, the divers kind of numbers and various shapes. He gave certainty to the solemnity of Easter's return; above all, opening the mysteries of Holy Writ and disclosing the abysses of the rude and ancient law.

Whatever youths he saw of conspicuous intelligence, those he joined to himself, he taught, he fed, he loved; and so the teacher had many disciples in the sacred volumes, advanced in various arts.

Soon he went in triumph abroad, led by the love of wisdom, to see if he could in other lands find anything novel in books or schools, which he could bring home with him. He went also devoutly to the city of Romulus [Rome], rich in God's love, wandering far and wide through the holy places. Then returning home, he was received everywhere by kings and princes as a prince of doctors, whom great kings tried to keep that he might irrigate their lands with learning. But the master, hurrying to his appointed work, returned home to his fatherland by God's ordinance.

"The Disputation of Pepin . . ."[7] (Excerpt)

1. General Questions and Answers

PEPIN	ALBINUS
What is writing?	The custodian of history.
What is speech?	The interpreter of the soul.
What produces speech?	The tongue.
What is the tongue?	The whip of the air.
What is air?	The guardian of life.
What is life?	The joy of the good, the sorrow of the evil, the expectation of death.
What is death?	An inevitable event, an uncertain journey, a subject of weeping to the living, the fulfillment of wills, the thief of men.
What is man?	The slave of death, a transient traveller, a host in his dwelling.
What is man like?	Like a fruit tree.
How is man placed?	Like a lantern exposed to the wind.
Where is he placed?	Between six walls.
Which are they?	Above, below; before, behind; right, left.
To how many changes is he liable?	To six.
Which are they?	Hunger and satiety; rest and work; waking and sleeping.
What is the liberty of man?	Innocence.
What is the head?	The top of the body.
What is the body?	The domicile of the soul.

Charlemagne's "Proclamation of 787"[8]

Charles, by the grace of God, King of the Franks and Lombards and Patrician of the Romans, to Abbot Baugulf and to all the congregation, also the faithful committed to you, we have directed a loving greeting by our ambassadors in the name of omnipotent God.

Be it known, therefore, to your devotion pleasing to God, that we, together with our faithful, have considered it to be useful that the bishoprics and monasteries entrusted by the favor of Christ to our control, in addition to the order of monastic life and the intercourse of holy religion, in the culture of letters also ought

103

to be zealous in teaching those who by the gift of God are able to learn, according to the capacity of each individual, so that just as the observance of the rule imparts order and grace to honesty of morals, so also zeal in teaching and learning may do the same for sentences, so that those who desire to please God by living rightly should not neglect to please him also by speaking correctly.

For it is written: "For by your words you will be acquitted, and by your words you will be condemned" (Matthew 12:37). For although correct conduct may be better than knowledge, nevertheless knowledge precedes conduct. Therefore, each one ought to study what he desires to accomplish, so that so much the more fully the mind may know what ought to be done, as the tongue hastens in the praises of omnipotent God without the hindrances of errors. For since errors should be shunned by all men, so much the more ought they to be avoided as far as possible by those who are chosen for this very purpose alone, so that they ought to be the especial servants of truth.

For when in the years just passed letters were often written to us from several monasteries in which it was stated that the brethren who dwelt there offered up in our behalf sacred and pious prayers, we have recognized in most of these letters correct thoughts and uncouth expressions; because what pious devotion dictated faithfully to the mind, the tongue, uneducated on account of the neglect of study, was not able to express in the letter without error.

When it happened that we began to fear lest perchance, as the skill in writing was less, so also the wisdom for understanding the Holy Scriptures might be much less than it rightly ought to be. And we all know well that, though errors of speech are dangerous, far more dangerous are errors of the understanding.

Therefore, we exhort you not only not to neglect the study of letters, but also with most humble mind, pleasing to God, to study earnestly in order that you may be able more easily and more correctly to penetrate the mysteries of the divine Scriptures. Since, moreover, images, tropes, and similar figures are found in the sacred pages, no one doubts that each one in reading these will understand the spiritual sense more quickly if previously he shall have been fully instructed in the mastery of letters.

Such men truly are to be chosen for this work as have the will and the ability to learn and a desire to instruct others. And may this be done with a zeal as great as the earnestness with which we commend it. For we desire you to be, as fitting that soldiers of the church should be, devout in mind, learned in discourse, chaste in conduct and eloquent in speech, so that whosoever shall seek to see you out of reverence for God, or on account of your reputation for holy conduct, just as he is edified by your appearance, may also be instructed by your wisdom, which he has learned from your reading or singing, and may go away joyfully giving thanks to omnipotent God.

Do not neglect, therefore, if you wish to have our favor, to send copies of this letter to all your suffragans and fellow-bishops and to all the monasteries. (And let no monk hold courts outside of his monastery or go to the judicial and other public assemblies.) Farewell.

RABANUS MAURUS

Rabanus (ca. 776–856) was schooled first at the abbey in Fulda, Germany, where Baugulf was abbot; then at Tours, where his teacher was Alcuin. In 818, he returned to Fulda as *scholasticus,* or master of studies; in 822, Rabanus was appointed abbot of Fulda. He served for twenty years, resigning in 842. Five years later he was elected archbishop of Mainz, which post he held for nine years until his death.

His principal writings include "On the Education of the Clergy," written in 819. The following excerpt gives some indication of the medieval search for an integration of academic learning and biblical truth. But it also clearly shows how well Abbot Baugulf took to heart Charlemagne's Proclamation of 787 and how much his pupil Rabanus remembered its import.

"On the Education of the Clergy"[9] (Excerpt)

. . . The first of the liberal arts is Grammar, the second Rhetoric, the third Dialectic, the fourth Arithmetic, the fifth Geometry, the sixth Music, the seventh Astronomy.

(a) *Grammar.* Grammar takes its name from the written character, as the derivation of the word indicates. The definition of grammar is this: Grammar is the science which teaches us to explain the poets and historians; it is the art which qualifies us to write and speak correctly. Grammar is the source and foundation of the liberal arts. It should be taught in every Christian school, since the art of writing and speaking correctly is attained through it. . . .

All the forms of speech, of which secular science makes use in its writings, are found repeatedly employed in the Holy Scriptures. Every one, who reads the sacred Scriptures with care, will discover that our biblical authors have used derivative forms of speech in greater and more manifold abundance than would have been supposed and believed. There are in the Scriptures not only examples of all kinds of figurative expressions, but the designations of some of them by name; as allegory, riddle, parable. A knowledge of these things is proved to be necessary in relation to the interpretation of those passages of Holy Scripture which admit of a two-fold sense; an interpretation strictly literal would lead to absurdities. Everywhere we are to consider whether that, which we do not at once understand, is to be apprehended as a figurative expression in some sense. . . .

(b) *Rhetoric.* According to the statements of teachers, rhetoric is the art of using secular discourse effectively in the circumstances of daily life. From this definition rhetoric seems indeed to have reference merely to secular wisdom. Yet it is not foreign to ecclesiastical instruction. Whatever the preacher and herald of the divine law, in his instruction, brings forth in an eloquent and becoming manner; whatever in his written exposition he knows how to clothe in adequate and impressive language, he owes to his acquaintance with this art. Whoever at the proper time makes himself familiar with this art, and faithfully follows its rules in speaking and writing, needs not count it as something blameworthy. On the contrary, whoever thoroughly learns it so that he acquires the ability to proclaim God's word, performs a true work. . . .

(c) *Dialectic.* Dialectic is the science of the understanding, which fits us for investigations and definitions, for explanations, and for distinguishing the true from the false. It is the science of sciences. . . . Therefore the clergy must understand this excellent art and constantly reflect upon its laws, in order that they may be able keenly to pierce the craftiness of errorists, and to refute their fatal fallacies.

(d) *Arithmetic.* Arithmetic is the science of pure extension determinable by number; it is the science of numbers. . . . The holy Fathers were right in advising those eager for knowledge to cultivate arithmetic, because in large measure it turns the mind from fleshly desires, and furthermore awakens the wish to comprehend what with God's help we can merely receive with the heart. . . .

(e) *Geometry.* We come now to the discussion of geometry. It is an exposition of form proceeding from observation; it is also a very common means of demonstration among philosophers. . . . When this in a proper manner is transferred to God, the Almighty Creator, this assumption may perhaps come near the truth. If this statement seems admissible, the Holy Trinity makes use of geometry in so far as it bestows manifold forms and images upon the creatures which up to the present day it has called into being, as in its adorable omnipotence it further determines the course of the stars. . . .

This science found realization also at the building of the tabernacle and the temple; the same measuring rod, circles, spheres, hemispheres, quadrangles, and other figures were employed. The knowledge of all this brings to him, who is occupied with it, no small gain for his spiritual culture.

(f) *Music.* Music is the science of time intervals as they are perceived in tones. This science is as eminent as it is useful. He who is a stranger to it is not able to fulfill the duties of an ecclesiastical officer in a suitable manner. A proper delivery in reading and a lovely rendering of the Psalms in the church are regulated by a knowledge of this science. Yet it is not only good reading and beautiful psalmody that we owe to music; through it alone do we become capable of celebrating in the most solemn manner every divine service.

Music penetrates all the activities of our life, in this sense namely, that we above all carry out the commands of the Creator and bow with a pure heart to his commands; all that we speak, all that makes our hearts beat faster, is shown through the rhythm of music united with the excellence of harmony; for music is the science which teaches us agreeably to change tones in duration and pitch.

When we employ ourselves with good pursuits in life, we show ourselves thereby disciples of this art; so long as we do what is wrong, we do not feel ourselves drawn to music. Even heaven and earth, as everything that happens here through the arrangement of the Most High, is nothing but music, as Pythagoras testifies that this world was created by music and can be ruled by it. Even with the Christian religion music is most intimately united; thus it is possible that to him, who does not know even a little music, many things remain closed and hidden.

(g) *Astronomy.* There remains yet astronomy which, as some one has said, is a weighty means of demonstration to the pious, and to the curious a grievous torment. . . . Astronomy, of which we now speak, teaches the laws of the stellar world. The stars can take their place or carry out their motion only in the manner established by the Creator, unless by the will of the Creator a miraculous change takes place. Thus we read that Joshua commanded the sun to stand still in Gibeon, that in the days of King Josiah the sun went backward ten degrees, and that at the death of the Lord the sun was darkened for three hours. We call such occurrences miracles, because they contradict the usual course of things and therefore excite wonder. . . .

The seven liberal arts of the philosophers, which Christians should learn for their utility and advantage, we have, as I think, sufficiently discussed. We have this yet to add. When those, who are called philosophers, have in their expositions or in their writings, uttered perchance some truth, which agrees with our faith, we should not handle it timidly, but rather take it as from its unlawful possessors and apply it to our own use.

ALFRED THE GREAT

An Anglo-Saxon prince, Alfred (849–899) spent some of his childhood in Rome, which afforded him an opportunity for education considerably broader than that of most of his contemporaries in England. Throughout his youth, Alfred and his older brothers fought off repeated invasions by the Danes. These Viking ravages had done much to curtail schooling in England, but after 871, when Alfred became king of Wessex, he labored to restore education to his kingdom. His goal was to achieve the same sense of value granted to education during the previous century, when Egbert, Aelbert, and Alcuin were teachers at York.

Alfred set a personal example of scholarship by translating the works of some of the Church Fathers into English. He also employed leading scholars to help him rebuild schools throughout his kingdom. The king's own children received their schooling along with "the children of almost all the nobility of the country, and many also who were not noble." So writes Asser, Alfred's friend and biographer, in the decade just after Alfred's death. Asser goes on: "Books in both languages, namely Latin and Saxon, were read in the school. They also learned to write, so that before they were of an age to practice manly arts, namely hunting and such pursuits as befit noblemen, they became studious and clever in the liberal arts." The biographer also noted that these students "have carefully learned the Psalms and Saxon books, especially the Saxon poems, and are continually in the habit of making use of books."[10]

The "Letter to Waerferth," dating from about 890, shows further Alfred's concern for education in his realm. In it he offers a plan for elementary studies in the English language, to be followed by more advanced instruction in Latin. Eventually this became the pattern for formal schooling, with a Latin school providing the necessary preparation for university admission.

In 1899, for the one-thousandth anniversary of his death, a statue was erected at Winchester, bearing this inscription:

Alfred found learning dead, and he restored it;
Education neglected, and he revived it;
The laws powerless, and he gave them force;
The Church debased, and he raised it;
The land ravaged by a fearful enemy, from which he
delivered it. [11]

"Letter to Waerferth" [12]

King Alfred bids greet Bishop Waerferth with loving words and with friendship; and I let it be known to thee that it has very often come into my mind what wise men there formerly were throughout England, both of sacred and secular orders; and what happy times there were then; and how the kings who had power over the nation in those days obeyed God and his ministers; how they preserved peace, morality, and order at home, and at the same time enlarged their territory abroad; and how they prospered both in war and in wisdom; and also the sacred orders, how zealous they were both in teaching and learning, and in all the services they owed to God; and how foreigners came to this land in search of wisdom and instruction, the which we should now have to get from abroad if we were to have them.

So general became the decay of learning in England that there were very few on this side of the Humber who could understand the rituals in English, or translate a letter from Latin into English; and I believe that there were not many beyond the Humber. There were so few, in fact, that I cannot remember a single person south of the Thames when I came to the throne. Thanks be to God Almighty that we now have some teachers among us. And therefore I command thee to disengage thyself, as I believe thou art willing, from worldly matters as often as thou art able, that thou mayst apply the wisdom which God has given thee wherever thou canst. Consider what punishments would come upon us if we neither loved wisdom ourselves nor suffered other men to obtain it: we should love the name only of Christian, and very few of the Christian virtues.

When I thought of all this, I remembered also how I saw the country before it had been ravaged and burned; how the churches throughout the whole of England stood filled with treasures and

111

books. There was also a great multitude of God's servants, but they had very little knowledge of the books, for they could not understand anything of them because they were not written in their own language. As if they had said, "Our forefathers, who formerly held these places, loved wisdom, and through it they obtained wealth and bequeathed it to us. In this we can still see their traces, but we cannot follow them, and therefore we have lost both the wealth and the wisdom, because we would not incline our hearts after their example."

When I remembered all this, I wondered extremely that the good and wise men who were formerly all over England, and had learned perfectly all the books, did not wish to translate them into their own language. But again I soon answered myself and said, "Their own desire for learning was so great that they did not suppose that men would ever be so careless, and that learning would so decay; and they wished, moreover, that the wisdom in this land might increase with our knowledge of languages." Then I remembered how the law was first known in Hebrew, and when the Greeks had learned it how they translated the whole of it, through learned interpreters, into their own language. And also all other Christian nations translated a part of it into their own language.

Therefore it seems better to me, if you agree, for us also to translate some of the books into the language which we can all understand; and for you to see to it, as can easily be done if we have tranquillity enough, that all the free-born youth now in England, who are rich enough to be able to devote themselves to it, be set to learn as long as they are not fit for any other occupation, until that they are well able to read English writing; and let those afterwards be taught more in the Latin language who are to continue learning, and be promoted to a higher rank.

ANSELM OF CANTERBURY

Born into the family of a Lombard landowner, Anselm (ca. 1033–1109) did not have a disciplined youth. At age twenty-three he left Italy for France and, in 1059, entered a Norman monastery at Bec, studying under Lanfranc. By 1063, he had been appointed prior of the monastery.

His early written works included an introduction to scholasticism's method of pedagogy, *De Grammatico*, or *On Dialectics*. But Anselm's reputation for godliness and intellect grew as he wrote not only scholarly treatises but also letters of encouragement to other monks.

When the abbot of Bec, Herluin, died in 1078, Anselm was named to succeed him. By this time, the Norman invasion of England in 1066 under William the Conqueror had settled into its occupation. Normans moved back and forth across the English Channel with regularity. Anselm made several such journeys, visiting his mentor Lanfranc, now archbishop of Canterbury.

Upon Lanfranc's death in 1089, the seat remained empty until 1093, when William II appointed Anselm archbishop of Canterbury. Thereafter followed several years of dispute with the king over control of lands and tenants, over the extent of the archbishop's authority, and even over his desire to visit Pope Urban II in Rome.

In Rome, Anselm participated in the Vatican Council of 1099, at which he took a position against the power of the king to invade the archbishop's powers, especially to promote clergy by their consecration as bishops. Returning to England in 1100, he found his last decade to be a constant struggle against the new King Henry I and his attempted usurpation of ecclesiastical rule. At the same time, Anselm contended against the claims of the archbishop of York to primacy over Canterbury.

But for all his political and ecclesiastical battling, Anselm remains a dominant figure in medieval scholasticism. He was regarded as the keenest intellect of his period. His "Proslogion" demonstrates a devout medieval mind at work, struggling to discover rational arguments for the existence of God and discovering that faith comes first. So Anselm presents himself as one "seeking to understand what he believes."

"Proslogion"[13] (Excerpt)

Preface

Upon the insistent adjurations of certain brothers, I wrote a short work—as an example of meditating about the rational basis of faith—in the role of someone who, by arguing with himself, investigates what he does not yet know. Afterwards, considering this work to be composed of a chain of many arguments, I began to ask myself whether perhaps a single argument could be found which would constitute an independent proof and would suffice by itself to demonstrate that (1) God truly exists, that (2) He is the Supreme Good, needing no one else yet needed by all else in order to exist and to fare well, and that (3) He is, whatever else we believe about the Divine Substance.

I often and earnestly turned my attention to this goal. At times what I was in quest of seemed to me to be apprehensible; at other times it completely eluded my mental powers. At last, despairing, I wanted to give up my pursuit of an argument which I supposed could not be found. But when I wanted to shut out the very thought, lest by engaging my mind in vain, it would keep me from other projects in which I could make headway—just then this argument began more and more to force itself insistently upon me, unwilling and resisting as I was.

Then one day, when I was tired as a result of vigorously resisting its entreaties, what I had despaired of finding appeared in my strife-torn mind in such way that I eagerly embraced the reasoning I had been anxiously warding off. Supposing, then, that to record what I had joyously discovered would please its readers, I wrote the following short work on this subject (and on various others) in the role of someone endeavoring to elevate his mind toward contemplating God and seeking to understand what he believes.

And although I deemed neither this present writing nor the former one as worthy to be called a treatise or to bear the name of an author, nevertheless I thought that they should not be circulated without titles which in some way would issue to anyone coming across them an invitation to read them. Hence I gave a title to each—calling the first *An Example of Meditating About the Rational Basis of Faith* and calling the present work *Faith Seeking Understanding*. But after a number of people had already copied both works under these respective titles, I was urged by several readers to prefix my name to these writings—urged especially by Hugh, the revered archbishop of Lyons and apostolic legate in Gaul, who on the basis of his apostolic authority directed me to do this. To make the affixing of my name less inappropriate, I retitled the first writing *Monologion*, i.e., a soliloquy, and the present writing *Proslogion*, i.e., an address.

Chapter 1:
"Arousing the Mind for Contemplating God"

Come now, insignificant man, leave behind for a time your pre-occupations; seclude yourself for a while from your disquieting thoughts. Turn aside now from heavy cares and disregard your wearisome tasks. Attend for a while to God and rest for a time in Him. Enter the inner chamber of your mind; shut out all else except God and whatever is of aid to you in seeking Him; after closing the chamber door, think upon your God. . . .

O Lord, You are my God and my Lord; yet never have I seen You. You have created me and created me anew, and have bestowed upon me whatever goods I have; but not yet do I know You. Indeed, I was made for seeing You; but not yet have I done that for which I was made. . . .

Teach me to seek You, and reveal Yourself to me as I seek; for unless You instruct me I cannot seek You, and unless You reveal Yourself I cannot find You. Let me seek You in desiring You; let me desire You in seeking You. Let me find You in loving You; let me love You in finding You.

O Lord, I acknowledge and give thanks that You created me in Your image so that I may remember, contemplate, and love You. But this image has been so effaced by the abrasion of transgressions, so hidden from sight by the dark billows of sin, that unless You renew and refashion it, it cannot do what it was created to do. Lord, I do not attempt to comprehend Your sublimity, because my intellect is not at all equal to such a task. But I yearn to understand some measure of Your truth, which my heart believes and loves. For I do not seek to understand in order to believe but I believe in order to understand. For I believe even this: that I shall not understand unless I believe.

PETER ABELARD

The development we recognize as the founding of medieval universities received its impetus from two great factors: a rising spirit of inquiry among the people and the availability—however limited —of teachers whose intellectual gifts could help to satisfy such a spirit.

Among such teachers the name of Peter Abelard (ca. 1079–1144) stands so high that his subsequent lapse is that much the more lamentable. Born in Brittany to a noble family, he declined the rights of first-born son, gave up his inheritance, and chose the life of the mind rather than military exploits. As Abelard himself wrote, "I preferred the arms of logic . . . and preferred the conflicts of debate to the trophies of war."[14]

Arriving in Paris about 1100, Abelard studied under William of Champeaux, then master of the cathedral school of Notre Dame and the most famous teacher of logic in France. But William of Champeaux had never encountered a student like Peter Abelard, whose own reasoning exposed the weakness of his teacher's method. By 1117, William of Champeaux had been removed and Peter Abelard appointed to replace him.

Soon thereafter occurred the event that overshadows Abelard's contribution to scholarship and pedagogy. Fulbert, the canon of Notre Dame, had a niece named Heloise to whom Abelard became romantically attracted. She conceived and gave birth to a child; a secret marriage followed. Outraged at the violation of his niece's honor and Abelard's integrity as a teacher, Fulbert had him emasculated. Heloise became a nun, Abelard a monk in 1118. Years later, Abelard founded a devout community dedicated to the Paraclete, which he gave to Heloise and her sisterhood of nuns.

Abelard survived his shame and found employment at a school called Mont St. Genevieve. There Abelard attracted crowds of students and curious listeners to his lectures. In fact, no hall could hold the numbers, who spilled out into the cloisters and quadrangle. What was the secret of his teaching powers? One biographer, comparing Abelard to other teachers of his day, says that "he was as a butterfly to an elephant."[15] Where others were plodding and dull, Abelard brought freshness, vivacity, and human warmth, as well as a towering mind and retentive memory, to his lessons.

Furthermore, Abelard was an innovator among the scholastics: He believed in the efficacy of inquiry, even of doubt. He differed from Augustine of Hippo and Anselm, who had urged that reason justify faith. Rather, said Abelard, "By doubting we are led to inquiry, and by inquiry we attain the truth." Abelard held that all men possessed the capacity for understanding, if not comprehending, the truth of God. He also believed that God might choose to reveal truth beyond the limits of revelation in Scripture, the Incarnation, or the church. Thus, he taught, even pagan philosophers might have been able to understand the Trinity.

The working out of this pedagogical innovation took the form of setting out a statement and its contradiction, a thesis and its antithesis. Abelard called this *Sic et Non*, "Yes and No." In its written form, published about 1123, Abelard offered 158 instances of debatable topics, followed by deliberately conflicting citations from various sources to provoke debate. Both in his lectures and in his book, Abelard never stated his own opinion but allowed his student or reader to come to his own decision.

Two facts seem remarkable: First, that in an era of mandatory orthodoxy, Abelard dared to consider these topics debatable at all is a tribute to his courage. Second, that he found it possible not to impose his own opinions on those he taught is a tribute to his wisdom.

The popularity of Abelard drew thousands of students to Paris, which fact, perhaps, led to the founding of the University later in the twelfth century.

"Sic et Non" (Excerpt)

1. That faith is based upon reason, *et contra* [and the opposite].
8. That in the Trinity it is not to be stated that there is more than one Eternal being, *et contra*.
13. That God the Father is the cause of the Son, *et contra*.
14. That the Son is without beginning, *et contra*.
28. That the providence of God is the cause of things happening, *et non* [or not].
32. That to God all things are possible, *et non* [and not].
36. That God does whatever he wishes, *et non*.
37. That nothing happens contrary to the will of God, *et contra*.
38. That God knows all things, *et non*.

116. That the sins of the fathers are visited upon the children, *et contra.*

122. That everybody should be allowed to marry, *et contra.*

153. That a lie is never permissible, *et contra.*

156. That it is unlawful to kill a man, *et non.*

Anselm then gives the opposite thesis to 156:

Jerome on Isaiah, Book V: He who cuts the throat of a man of blood, is not a man of blood.

Cyprian, in the Ninth Kind of Abuse: The King ought to restrain theft, punish deeds of adultery, cause the wicked to perish from off the face of the earth, refuse to allow parricides and perjurers to live.

Augustine: Although it is manslaughter to slaughter a man, a person may sometimes be slain without sin. For both a soldier in the case of an enemy and a judge or his official in the case of a criminal, and the man from whose hand, perhaps without his will or knowledge, a weapon has flown, do not seem to me to sin, but merely to kill a man.

Augustine, Book I of The City of God: Thou shalt not kill, except in the case of those whose death God orders, or else when a law hath been passed to suit the needs of the time and express command hath been laid upon a person. . . .

JOHN OF SALISBURY

John of Salisbury was a twelfth-century (ca. 1120–80) scholar and teacher who earned a reputation as the best-read man of his time; he occupied the very center of learning in England. Unlike many of his contemporaries, whose formal schooling was local and almost ephemeral in its brevity, John of Salisbury was not content with the schools available to him in England. Moving on to France, he spent a dozen years, from 1136 to 1148, enrolled at Paris and Chartres.

Around 1159, John of Salisbury published an account of his schooling, *Metalogicus*, which affords a critical, first-hand account of the education available to peripatetic students like him. In Paris, at Mont St. Genevieve, John's first teacher was Peter Abelard, whom he described as "the subject of admiration of all men."

John of Salisbury was not equally complimentary of all his teachers, one of whom he caricatured as "Cornificus." John's description of this unfortunate object of contempt includes such phrases as "the shamelessness of his looks, the rapacity of his hands, the frivolousness of his bearing, the foulness of his manners (which the whole neighborhood spews out), the obscenity of his lust, the ugliness of his body, the baseness of his life, his spotted reputation, I would lay bare and thrust into the face of the public, did not my respect for his Christian name restrain me. For being mindful of my profession, and of the fraternal communion which we have in the Lord, I have believed that indulgence should be given to his person while, nevertheless, indulgence is not given to his sin."[16]

Reading such a diatribe, one wonders what John might have written if he had not been so courteous as to "restrain" himself! Still, however *ad hominem* (an attack on the person) his critique, John's observations about medieval pedagogy offer historical insight and contemporary application.

John of Salisbury was more appreciative of the methods of two successors to Abelard, masters named Alberic and Robert de Melun, whose contrasting methods he described, along with their effect upon his own pride and, later, humility. After two years in their school, John went on to Chartres, where his teachers were William de Conches, Richard l'Eveque, as well as Theodoric and Bernard, brothers who ran the school at Chartres.

Under these instructors, John of Salisbury became an exponent of the study of the liberal arts—not just dialectical disputation but the reading of ancient literature, as preparation for the study of philosophy and theology. As John wrote in *Metalogicus*, "The greater the number of Arts with which one is imbued, and the more fully he is imbued with them, so much the more completely will he appreciate the elegance of the authors, and the more clearly will he teach them."

In 1148, having completed his circuit of studies, John of Salisbury returned to Mont St. Genevieve, where he found—to his dismay—that his former colleagues had not advanced in manner or method of learning, as he knew he had.

In fact, John of Salisbury anticipated the movement toward a rebirth or renaissance of new learning which would sweep across Europe three centuries later. His knowledge of Aristotle, his acquaintance with Latin classical writers, his grasp of history, his deftness in political affairs, his skill in composing letters, all mark him as an early example of what was to become known as "the Renaissance man."

He returned to England, where he was employed by Theobald, archbishop of Canterbury, then by his successor Thomas Becket. John of Salisbury sided with Becket in the controversy with Henry II, and was in Canterbury when the archbishop was murdered on December 29, 1170.

In 1176, John of Salisbury was named bishop of Chartres, where he was in office when he died.

Metalogicus

. . . When first as a mere lad I went to Gaul for an education in the year after the illustrious king of the Angles, Henry, the lion of justice, departed from human affairs, I betook me to the Peripatetic of Pallet [Peter Abelard], who at that time presided at Mont St. Genevieve as a doctor celebrated and admired by all. There at his feet I received the first rudiments of the art of logic and as far as my small talents permitted I received with all the avidity of my mind whatever fell from his lips. Then after his departure, which seemed to me all too soon, I attached myself to Master Alberic, who shone forth as the dialectician most esteemed among the rest and was indeed the sharpest opponents of the nominalists. Thus, spending almost the whole two years on the hill, I had as my teachers in this art Alberic and master Robert of Melun—to use the name that he earned in the school system, although he was of English birth.

One of them, very exact in everything, found room for questioning everywhere, so that no matter how polished the surface he could find some flaw in it. . . . The other, on the other hand, very quick in his answers, never dodged any question by means of subterfuges, nay he would take either side of a contradiction, or by bringing out the manifold arguments he would teach that there was no one answer. So one was subtle and prolific in questions; the other, clear-headed, brief, and apt in his answers.

If the qualities of these two had all been combined in any one man, his equal as a disputant would not have been found in our age. For both were sharp-witted and hard students and in my opinion would have become great and famous men in physical studies, if they had built on the great foundation of literature, if they had devoted as much attention to the remains of the ancients as they gave applause to their own inventions. . . .

Drilled by them for all of two years, I became so accustomed to allotting places, and to rules, and to the other elementary rudiments with which the minds of boys are instructed and in which the aforesaid doctors were most capable and expeditious, that it seemed to me that I knew all these things as well as my own nails and fingers. Evidently I had learned this: to account my knowledge with youthful levity as of more importance than it was. I thought myself an adept because I was quick in those things that I had heard.

Then coming to myself and measuring my powers, thanks to the kindness of my teachers I straightway betook me to the grammarian of Conches and heard him lecture for three years. Meanwhile I did a great deal of reading, nor shall I ever regret that time. . . .

Thus well nigh twelve years slipped by, as I was occupied with varied studies.

So I thought it would be pleasant to revisit the old classmates whom I had left and whom dialectic still detained on the Mount, to confer with them concerning the old problems, and, by comparing notes, measure our respective progress. I found the same men and just where they were, for they neither seemed to have advanced an inch towards solving the old problems, nor had they added a single new one. As teachers they drove with the same goads that drove them as students. In only one respect had they grown proficient: they had unlearned moderation, they knew no modesty, to such a degree that one despaired of their reformation.

Thus I learned by experience an evident lesson, that, just as dialectic facilitates other disciplines, so, if studied alone, it remains lifeless and sterile, nor does it stimulate the soul to bear fruits of Philosophy, unless it conceives elsewhere.

The medieval university was a far cry from the organized institution we know today, with its hierarchy of administration, ranking professors, graduate assistants, support staff, and undergraduate students. To begin, today's students are much older than were the boys in Europe's universities eight and nine centuries ago. They were, in fact, barely beyond childhood. Their formal schooling had been irregular at best, scant in most instances. The one prerequisite each youthful scholar brought with him to Oxford or Bologna was a reading and speaking knowledge of Latin.

His university teachers or masters also differed from today's professors. The medieval teacher was no specialist in a single discipline; he had to be equally well acquainted with theology, philosophy, natural science, mathematics, literature, and politics. Living among his students, he had little administrative support and no clerical help. He wrote his own lectures, managed the communal life of the college, attended to matters spiritual as well as intellectual, recruited students, and begged for money from the prince or duke or king in whose realm he was situated.

As boys in their adolescent years, students becoming scholars were subject to rules that reflected their ages and reminded them of the seriousness of their purpose. For instance, Robert, a priest of St. Stephen in Mons Caelius, published a set of rules for the young student at the University of Paris. We know little about Robert, but clearly he had concerns for the behavior of the lecturers and students alike. He warned each that in their meetings "there shall be no drinking," and they could have visits from "only a few" friends during the school term. He also cautioned students that "no one shall be a scholar at Paris who has no definite master."

THOMAS AQUINAS

H e remains one of the towering figures in Christian education. The writings of Thomas Aquinas include commentaries, disputations, analyses, philosophy, and systematic theology. Aquinas (ca. 1225–74) wrote a handbook for missionaries to the Arabians. His monumental *Summa Theologica,* unfinished at the time of his death, is still recognized by Roman Catholics as the keystone to an understanding of Catholic theology. The *Summa Theologica* in three parts, informs about God's existence, God's relationship to man, and man's relationship to God through Jesus Christ. Though Reformed and Protestant Christians will differ profoundly with Thomas on major issues, nonetheless the *Summa* remains a worthy effort to explain the mysteries of God's existence.

Thomas of Aquino was the son of a count and countess, relatives of Italian and French royalty. At age five, Thomas was sent to a Benedictine school; at fifteen, he enrolled in Naples for university training. But in 1243, he announced his conviction of a call to join the Dominican Order; dismayed, his parents took him prisoner, holding him for more than a year to deter his intention.

Unable to break his son's will, Count Landulf finally permitted Thomas to take holy orders as a Dominican. In 1245, Thomas went to Paris, where he studied under Albertus Magnus, whom he then followed to Cologne.

In 1252, Thomas Aquinas returned to Paris to teach at the Dominican Convent of St. Jacques for seven years. He was then sent back to Italy, teaching at Anagni, Orvieto, Rome, and Viterbo. Briefly recalled to Paris in 1269, he was back in Naples in 1272, establishing a Dominican school there. He died in 1274, while travelling to the Council of Lyons.

Thomas Aquinas brought to medieval education the influence of Aristotle, a knowledge of whose philosophy had recently been reintroduced by his teacher Albertus Magnus, among others. For Thomas, the seeming conflict between faith and reason could best be bridged by revelation, whose source is the Scriptures and the teaching of the church. To accept such revelation requires an act of the will; but since everyone needs such a revelation in order to be saved, God provides it with sufficient clarity that even a plowman—who could not fairly be expected to learn philosophy in order to gain salvation—may be saved.

The work of this "Doctor of the Church" has come to be known as Thomism and forms the groundwork for much of Roman Catholic dogma; some of this dogma clearly contradicts Protestant theology. It is almost impossible to present a fragment of the work of Thomas Aquinas without doing his life and thought a disservice; yet it is equally impossible to compile a book such as this without including him.

Summa Theologica[17] (Excerpt)

Part One
Question I
The Nature and Domain of Sacred Doctrine

To place our purpose within definite limits we must first investigate the nature and domain of sacred doctrine. Concerning this there are ten points of inquiry:

(1) Whether sacred doctrine is necessary? (2) Whether it is a science? (3) Whether it is one or many? (4) Whether it is speculative or practical? (5) How it is compared with other sciences? (6) Whether it is a wisdom? (7) Whether God is its subject-matter? (8) Whether it is argumentative? (9) Whether it rightly employs metaphors and similes? (10) Whether the Sacred Scripture of this doctrine may be expounded in different senses?

First Article

Whether, Besides the Philosophical Sciences, Any Further Doctrine Is Required?

We proceed thus to the First Article:

Objection 1. It seems that, besides the philosophical sciences, we have no need of any further knowledge. For man should not seek to know what is above reason: *Seek not the things that are too high for thee*[18]. But whatever is not above reason is sufficiently considered in the philosophical sciences. Therefore any knowledge besides the philosophical sciences is superfluous.

Objection 2. Further, knowledge can be concerned only with being, for nothing can be known, save the true, which is convertible with being. But everything that is, is considered in the philo-

124

sophical sciences—even God Himself; so that there is a part of philosophy called theology, or even the divine science, as is clear from Aristotle. Therefore, besides the philosophical sciences, there is no need of any further knowledge.

On the contrary, it is written (2 Timothy iii.16): *All Scripture [is] inspired of God [and] profitable to teach, to reprove, to correct, to instruct in justice.* Now Scripture, inspired of God, is not a part of the philosophical sciences discovered by human reason. Therefore it is useful that besides the philosophical sciences there should be another science—i.e., inspired of God.

I answer that, It was necessary for man's salvation that there should be a knowledge revealed by God, besides the philosophical sciences investigated by human reason. First, because man is directed to God as an end that surpasses the grasp of his reason: *The eye hath not seen, O God, besides Thee, what things Thou hast prepared for them that wait for Thee* (Isaiah lxiv.4). But the end must first be known by men who are to direct their thoughts and actions to the end. Hence it was necessary for the salvation of man that certain truths that exceed human reason should be made known to him by divine revelation. Even as regards those truths about God that human reason can investigate, it was necessary that man be taught by a divine revelation. For the truth about God, such as reason can know it, would only be known by a few, and that after a long time, and with the admixture of many errors; whereas a man's whole salvation, which is in God, depends upon the knowledge of this truth. Therefore, in order that the salvation of men might be brought about more fitly and more surely, it was necessary that they be taught divine truths by divine revelation. It was therefore necessary that, besides the philosophical sciences investigated by reason, there should be a sacred science by way of revelation.

Reply Objection 1. Although those things which are beyond man's knowledge may not be sought for by man through his reason, nevertheless, what is revealed by God must be accepted through faith. Hence the sacred text continues, *For many things are shown to thee above the understanding of man.*[19] And in such things sacred science consists.

Reply Objection 2. Sciences are diversified according to the diverse nature of their knowable objects. For the astronomer and the physicist both prove the same conclusion—that the earth, for instance, is round; the astronomer by means of mathematics (i.e., abstracting from matter), but the physicist by means of matter itself. Hence there is no reason why those things which are treated by the philosophical sciences, so far as they can be known by the light of natural reason, may not also be treated by another science so far as they are known by the light of divine revelation. Hence the theology included in sacred doctrine differs in genus from that theology which is part of philosophy.

ROGER BACON

R oger Bacon (ca. 1214–ca. 1292) was born in England and studied at Paris, where he learned the works of Aristotle and, between 1240 and 1245, wrote some of the earliest published lectures on them. Returning to England about 1247, he studied languages, science, and mathematics under the famous Robert Grossteste.

In 1257, Bacon joined the Franciscan order and went back to Paris. There his reputation as a scholar with knowledge of arcane Greek and Arabic literature, as well as of science and mathematics, presented him with ecclesiastical opportunity. He acquainted Cardinal Guy le Gros de Foulques with certain criticisms he had of the education being given candidates for the clergy. Soon thereafter, in 1265, the cardinal became Pope Clement IV, and summoned Bacon to Rome to institute the changes he had recommended.

By 1267, this renowned scholar had completed a work in which he spelled out the impediments to learning and how to correct them. Among his reforms were a new emphasis on the importance of learning languages in order to understand the Scriptures, and the importance of mathematics and experimental science to a theological education.

But the death of Pope Clement IV, in 1268, brought Bacon's efforts to naught; in fact, in 1277, he was condemned and sent to prison by his own Franciscan Order for having propagated "dangerous doctrine" concerning "suspect novelties" in education, such as contained in his *Opus Minus* regarding the teaching of the Bible.

Unhappily—like too many other intellectuals—Bacon's sharp tongue and apparently disagreeable temperament left an impression of his inability to respect anyone who disagreed with him. That sharp tongue is evident in the several of the caustic phrases in the following excerpt from his *"Opus Minus."*

"Opus Minus"[20] (Excerpt)

. . . The fourth sin [about the study of theology] is in that one manual of a master [Thomas Aquinas's *Summa Theologica*] and

127

is given preference to the text of the Bible in the Faculty of Theology; this is the *Book of Sentences* which is the glory of the theologians and which is so weighty that it takes a horse to carry it. And the man who has lectured on it dreams that he is already a master of theology, though he has not heard lectures on one-thirtieth of the Bible. And the bachelor who lectures on the Bible gets the worse of the lecturer on the *Sentences* at Paris and elsewhere, and the latter is honored and receives honors and preferential treatment in everything. For he has the main lecture hour just as he wishes and an associate and a room at a religious house.

But the lecturer on the Bible is deprived of such benefits and goes begging for an hour to lecture, just as it pleases the lecturer of *Sentences*. And while the latter has the right to dispute and is considered master, the one who lectures on the Bible is not allowed to dispute, which is absurd.

Every other faculty uses its basic text in its classroom instruction; for it is around this text that the material of the faculty is organized since this is the end for which texts are written. This applies so much more to the Bible text since it had been given to the world by the mouth of God and by the Saints.

JOHN WYCLIF

Born near York (ca. 1330), John Wyclif (sometimes spelled Wycliffe) attended Merton College, Oxford, in 1356, and became master of Balliol College, Oxford, in 1360. He distinguished himself by achieving a doctorate in theology—rare in those days—in 1372; his reputation as one of the best teachers at Oxford, in the manner of Thomas Aquinas, added to his fame.

A parish priest for a quarter-century, John Wyclif was also a person well connected to one of the most powerful politicians of his day, the Duke of Lancaster, John of Gaunt. Among Wyclif's prolific theological arguments, two of his works, "On Divine Lordship" and "On Civil Lordship," represented Wyclif's defense of Lancaster's machinations against William Courtenay, bishop of London.

Published in 1375 and 1376, respectively, Wyclif's treatises argued that no man is lord except through God's grace; such grace turns any presumed "lordship" into "stewardship." Hence, said Wyclif, the pope must be a steward, not a master. Furthermore, any steward not living in grace is unworthy of his stewardship—surely, dangerous words for Wyclif to utter in so corrupt a time!

In another treatise, "On the Pastoral Office," published in 1378, Wyclif declared that the priest's chief responsibilities were to keep his flock from sin and to feed them on the Word. The better to make the Word available, the Bible must be translated into plain English, the vernacular of the people, said Wyclif. Interestingly, as one of the early advocates of the authority of Scripture, Wyclif was not unaware of the possibility of lapse and error in translation; but that did not deter him from his high purpose.

That same year, Wyclif published "On the Truth of the Holy Scriptures," holding that the Bible has supreme authority over the papacy or the customs of the church. "Holy Scripture," Wyclif wrote, "is the highest authority for every Christian and the standard of faith and of all human perfection." He also proposed that mere membership in the visible church—even for pope and cardinals—was no guarantee of membership in the body of Christ, the church invisible.

Pope Gregory XI retaliated by issuing papal bulls to condemn Wyclif's opinions. Intervention by the mother of Richard II saved Wyclif. But Wyclif would not be silenced: In 1379, Wyclif denied the teaching of transubstantiation, in which the church taught that the consecrated bread and wine miraculously became the very body and blood of Christ. Two years later, Wyclif called the pope the Antichrist and denied his authority.

When Wyclif's challenge to the Roman Church resulted in condemnation of his teaching and the banning of his books, he then turned his energies toward working with a small group of so-called "poor preachers," not unlike the followers of Francis of Assisi. Led by Nicholas of Hereford, these dissidents became known as Lollards and were themselves categorically condemned in 1382 for insisting upon an English version of the Bible and for preaching in English.

A series of strokes disabled Wyclif and led to his death in 1384. In 1428, Richard Fleming, bishop of Lincoln, accused the dead teacher and priest of some three hundred instances of heresy. Dead more than forty years, Wyclif was considered sufficiently dangerous so that the bishop ordered his remains exhumed and had them burned.

Of course, today, nobody remembers Richard Fleming, bishop of Lincoln; however, the Wycliffe Bible Translators carry on the work urged more than six centuries ago by John Wyclif.

"On the Pastoral Office" (Excerpt)

. . . We have touched superficially on the first part of the priestly office, holiness of life. . . . Now the second part pertaining to the pastor, that is, wholesomeness of teaching, remains to be looked at. While Jesus Christ "began to do and to teach," the curate, who ought to be his vicar, ought to shine with sanctity in his own person, and, secondly, ought to be resplendent with righteousness of doctrine before his sheep. Otherwise his preaching would be useless. . . .

The friars with their followers say that it is heresy thus to write God's law in English and make it known to ignorant men. . . . It seems first that the knowledge of God's law should be taught in that language which is best known, because this knowledge is God's Word.

. . . For this reason Saint Jerome labored and translated the

Bible from divers tongues into Latin that it might after be translated into other tongues. Thus Christ and His apostles taught the people in that tongue that was best known to them. Why should men not do so now? And for this reason the authors of the new law who were apostles of Jesus Christ wrote their Gospels in divers tongues that were better known to the people. Also the worthy kingdom of France, notwithstanding all hindrances, has translated the Bible and the Gospels with other true sentences of doctors out of Latin into French. Why should not Englishmen do so?

. . . I well know that there may be faults in unfaithful translating as there might have been many faults in turning from Hebrew into Greek and from Greek into Latin, and from one language into another. But let men live a good life, and let many study God's law, and where errors are found let them who reason well correct them.

. . . May God move lords and bishops to stand up for the knowing of His law.

PART IV
CHRISTIAN HUMANISM
AND THE
PROTESTANT REFORMATION

To be a schoolmaster is next to being a king. Do you count it lowly employment to imbue the minds of the young with the love of Christ and the best of literature, and to return them to their country honest and virtuous men? In the opinion of fools, it is a humble task, but in fact it is the noblest of occupations.

Desiderius Erasmus
Letter to Johan Witz (Sapidus), ca. 1515

CHRISTIAN HUMANISM
AND THE
PROTESTANT REFORMATION

T he Renaissance is so named because most regard it as the period of European history when a rebirth of interest took place in classical languages and the fine arts. The Renaissance can be loosely dated as beginning during the later years of the fourteenth century and lasting into the sixteenth century.

Throughout Europe were men and women of broad intellectual curiosity and artistic gifts, waiting for the legacy of Athens, Constantinople, and Jerusalem to be unveiled to them. (The fewer female leaders of the Renaissance reflects only the limited opportunities woman had for education and expression.)

The leading figures of the Renaissance are often thought to have been the Italian princely House of Medici in Florence, the writers Dante Alighieri, Petrarch, and Boccaccio, the artists Leonardo and Michelangelo. Under their genius, it is assumed, life became more closely attuned to nature; the ancient cultures of Greece and Rome were revived; and this rebirth of learning brought with it a renewed emphasis upon the worth of human experience—a new humanism to counterbalance the church's emphasis on "the Life everlasting"—the beginnings of a Christian humanism.

What finally ended the Dark Ages and ushered in a new era of light and joy was more than a rebirth or renaissance of classical learning; it was a renaissance accompanied by new yearnings for spiritual and national freedom. To these interior forces were added some advances in travel and, after 1440, the technology of printing by means of movable type, developed by Johannes Gutenberg.

During much of the Middle Ages, theology had taught that godly living meant elevating spirituality and denigrating human experience in the here-and-now. So generations of medieval Christians had attempted to please God by causing a line to be drawn between their presumed "sacred" and "secular" behavior. Such a line, of course, resulted in an overemphasis on "the life of the world to come," denigrating ordinary human responsibilities in this world. Piety seemed to exclude the possibility of godly living in *these* bodies, performing *these* tasks as faithful Christians. The possibility that God might be praised through the mundane acts of everyday experience seemed not to exist.

But some Christians saw otherwise. These were believers in whom arose the conviction called "Christian humanism," designating a responsiveness to art and the things of the spirit under a recognition of the sovereignty of God, showing an openness toward all of life and learning.[1] Held alike by pre-Reformationist believers such as the Czech Jan Hus and those who remained loyal to Roman Catholicism as well as Protestantism, scholars and artists sought to correct an imbalance they regarded as both dehumanizing and unscriptural. They were convinced that the doctrine of the Incarnation had ratified God's work in creation and deemed human experience to be "very good."

Among Christian humanists stands the towering example of Desiderius Erasmus of Rotterdam. Committed to the Roman Church, Erasmus nonetheless contributed to broadening intellectual life and thought by insisting on universal education for all social classes and for girls as much as boys. His strong affirmation of the Christ-centered purpose of education ("All studies . . . are for this one object . . .") serves as the epigraph to this book; it might well serve as the ensign for every Christian educator.

Through the scholarship of teachers and translators, through the art of poets, painters, and musicians, a new awareness of God's presence in every facet of human life became a liberating doctrine. The teaching that God "richly provides us with everything for our enjoyment" (1 Timothy 6:17) was now a freedom belonging to every Christian. Such teaching needs to be reiterated in each generation; today in certain Christian quarters the fear and reluctance to enjoy God's creation continues a schism between "sacred" and "secular" aspects of common life, which impedes many devout believers from coming to know the reality of freedom in Christ and permitting the misconception that "Christian humanism" is somehow an unholy contradiction in terms.

But while the Renaissance was highly influenced by Christian humanism, another and more compelling force must also be considered, one that ties the Renaissance inextricably to another historical phenomenon known as the Protestant Reformation.

The Protestant Reformation usually refers to those events set in motion by Martin Luther's posting of his Ninety-Five Theses on the door of Wittenberg's church. The Reformation's beginning, therefore, dates from October 31, 1517. Yet both the Renaissance and the Reformation are more mercurial, less easy to pin down, than the assigning of names, dates, and places would suppose. For both the cultural rebirth or renewal and the religious reformation began long before Lorenzo de Medici's rule or Luther's daring act on All Hallows' Eve of 1517.

Their origins lay not in some palace court or artist's studio but in the hearts of those who sought for the truth that would set them free. For them, the rebirth that changed their lives was the New Birth of Nicodemus; in turn, this New Birth led to calls for reforming the corrupt institution that had become the Roman Catholic Church.

The wealth, pomp, and political power of the Roman Church had been scandalous for centuries. At the beginning of the thirteenth century, Francis of Assisi had condemned the church's materialism and, in protest, founded his own order of devout men committed to serving Christ through vows of poverty. One of these Franciscan friars, William of Ockham, wrote a strong indictment of Pope John XXII's suppression of the New Testament's teachings on poverty; he also paved the way for subsequent denials of the pope's infallibility and won the admiration of his countryman John Wyclif, as well as later Reformers like Luther.

Wyclif's influence upon a group of pre-Reformation Reformers called Lollards encouraged a movement to recognize the authority of Scripture and translate the Bible into national languages. The Lollards spread from England to Scotland, then to the European continent. In Bohemia, Jan Hus became an adherent. As rector of Prague University, Hus had come to know of Wyclif's writings about 1400; he translated some of Wyclif's work into Czech. For a time, Hus received favor from church authorities in Prague, but as his own attacks on ecclesiastical corruption increased, Hus was accused of being Wyclif's disciple; he was excommunicated and eventually burned at the stake.

More than a century before Martin Luther's Ninety-Five Theses, the fires of reformation and rebirth had already been lighted. In the Netherlands, for instance, Gerhard de Groote, a priest from Utrecht, was instrumental in founding the Brothers of the Common Life (*Fratres Communis Vitae*, in Latin), a community located at Deventer. Without burdening themselves with the vows or rituals of monastic orders, these Brothers—whether clergy or laymen—sought to emulate the early church, as reported in Acts 4:32 ff.: "All the believers were one in heart and mind. No one claimed that any of his possessions was his own, but they shared everything they had."

The Brothers of the Common Life also committed themselves to educating boys and to caring for the poor. The schools they founded in the Netherlands and Germany were operated without tuition. To meet expenses, the Brothers produced copies of manuscripts and, eventually, engaged in printing books.

Among the pupils of the Brothers of the Common Life were such later notables as Thomas a Kempis, Nicholas of Cusa, and Desiderius Erasmus. De Groote also founded the Sisters of the Common Life, whose work included education and the production of copied manuscripts.

Every school described so far in this account came under the ultimate authority of the papacy. In these schools, therefore, could be found both the sincere and earnest piety of believers and also those doctrinal and cultural abuses of a contaminated institution such as the Roman Church had become. On October 31, 1517, the young monk Martin Luther challenged the teachings and traditions of Rome with his ninety-five points of argument nailed to the cathedral door at Wittenberg. The revolt that followed from Luther's act was primarily a theological schism between Luther and the authority of the pope and the doctrines of the Roman Church. But it could not be contained as an ecclesiastical controversy alone; it was also, by the nature of the church's power, a political and cultural revolt.

Even the term "Protestant" derives from a political document drawn up in 1529, the *Protestation* of German princes now identified with Luther's movement. These rulers had seen their right to determine matters of religious freedom curtailed by the Diet of Speyer in that same year. Rejecting this intrusion upon their territorial domain, these first Protestants declared that "in matters which concern God's honor and salvation and the eternal life of our souls, everyone must stand and give an account before God himself."[2] At the heart of Protestantism, therefore, lies the fundamental political concept of an individual's personal relationship with God; Luther's theology showed that such a relationship was made possible only through grace.

What fueled the Protestant Reformation? Luther and his followers awoke the European consciousness with several similarly astonishing realizations. For instance, Luther had opposed vehemently the Roman Church's prohibition against translating the Bible into the common languages of Europe. Now, standing upon the basic premise of individual accountability before God, Luther could also argue that (1) the Word of God can be read and understood by any reasoning person; and (2) such a person, upon reading the Bible, will discover for himself or herself what the Scriptures teach: salvation by grace alone through faith.

To give each person an opportunity to judge for himself what the Scriptures teach, two conditions were necessary: (1) the Bible must be translated into the various national languages; and (2) people must learn to read in their own languages so that a literate populace might read the Bible when it became available to them. To both these tasks Luther committed himself.

In 1525, he accepted a commission from the Duke of Mansfield to establish both a primary and a secondary school in Eisleben. In collaboration with his protégé Philipp Melanchthon, in 1528 they devised a comprehensive plan for education throughout Saxony; the following year, Luther completed two catechisms for the instruction of clergy and laity. All this while, at the same time, he worked on his German translation of the Bible, published in 1534. So two important historical developments go hand-in-hand: translation of the Scriptures into indigenous languages, and the formal instruction of all youths for the purpose of making them competent to read and understand the Bible in their own tongues.

By no means was Luther a solitary voice in calling for an enlightened Christianity. But it was Luther's personal force and dynamism that gave impetus to the Protestant school movement throughout Europe. By the commitment of his prodigious energies, as well as the power of his sometimes vitriolic tongue and pen, Martin Luther encouraged or cajoled his countrymen to achieve educational reform.

Foremost among Luther's associates was the precocious Philipp Melanchthon, who carried out as teacher what Luther spoke in theory. A scholar and translator by age sixteen, Melanchthon gained respect among Christian humanists throughout Europe, including Erasmus. Arriving in Wittenberg the year after Luther's public act, Melanchthon became strongly attached to Luther and his cause. In 1528, he proposed the plan—later revised by Luther—for a German school system, eventually adopted in nearly sixty German cities. He conducted a school in his own house in Wittenberg, wrote textbooks in German, and was responsible for organizing schools and universities, such as those at Marburg, Königsberg, Jena, and Helmstedt. Luther was the Great Reformer, but to Melanchthon belongs the title, "the Teacher of Germany."

From Germany, Lutheranism and its manifestation in the raising up of new schools spread quickly to Switzerland, France, and Scotland. In Zurich, Huldrych Zwingli led the Swiss Reformation of 1522, one of whose earliest results was the publication of the first book on education from the Protestant point of view, *The Christian Education of Boys.*

In Paris, meanwhile, a young scholar named John Calvin came under the influence, first, of Christian humanism, then of Lutheran teaching. His 1534 preface to a translation of the Bible into French declared him an "evangelical," as the Reformers were then being called. For this Calvin was exiled and fled to Geneva, where he helped to found an elementary school in 1537. In the prospectus Calvin wrote for this school, he showed his continuing concern for balancing both the evangelical regard for the Bible and the Christian humanist regard for a full curriculum of studies. "The Word of God is indeed the fountain of all learning," wrote Calvin, "but the liberal arts are aids to the full knowledge of the Word and not to be despised."[3]

At St. Andrews, the fiery Scot John Knox became the spokesman for the Reformation. After years of exile in Switzerland, Knox returned to Scotland and, in 1560, published *The First Book of Discipline* for Presbyterians. In this work, Knox laid out the details for a compulsory and free education for all children, with special provisions to insure that children of the poor would also receive an education. Knox's plan called for each church to appoint a schoolmaster. Even in the remote Highlands, where there were no schools, the minister himself was to take responsibility for educating the youth of his parish, making certain that they could read and understand the principles of religion.

So the flame of the Reformation, ignited in Wittenberg, blazed across Europe, from the Alps in Switzerland to the lochs of Scotland. With its message of justification by grace alone on the authority of Holy Scripture went the need to prepare succeeding generations of enlightened believers, capable of reading the Bible and reasoning for themselves the truth therein contained.

To provide such enlightenment, there must be schools.

VITTORINO DA FELTRE

In the history of education, Vittorino da Feltre (1378–1446) is generally identified as the founder of the boarding school. By 1423, when he accepted on his own terms the offer of the ruler of Mantua, Gianfrancisco Gonzaga, to begin a palace school, Vittorino adopted a custom already familiar in the early universities: students and their masters living and studying together in a single house. In Mantua, Vittorino merely extended this same custom to the younger children he was to teach.

But Vittorino da Feltre is significant for more than his innovation of residential education. He was also a pioneer in Christian humanism.

Born in the northern Italian city of Feltre, Vittorino went to university at Padua in 1396. This was the same year in which Manuel Chrysoloras of Constantinople was invited by the university at Florence to become the first professor of Greek in Western Europe. Many historians regard this event and date—1396—as the beginning point of the revival of learning, the Renaissance.

At Padua, Vittorino first won his reputation as a master teacher, paying for his own studies by teaching elementary grammar to boys not yet qualified for advanced university work. After receiving his doctoral degree, or laurea, Vittorino continued to teach and study at Padua for more than twenty years. During all this time he declined to wear any visible evidence—the gown or ring to which he was entitled—marking his status as a professor.

A man of devout piety, Vittorino saw his university becoming corrupted by the decadence of Padua. The immoral influences of the town upon its youth, presumably sent to prepare for service as Christian noblemen, were sufficiently detrimental to cause Vittorino to set up his own house with student residents. But by 1422, Vittorino no longer felt able to combat the evil rife in Padua. He resigned as professor of rhetoric and went to Venice, where under his own auspices, he conducted a school with boarders in his own house.

All this time, Vittorino's reputation as a man of great learning and superb teaching gifts continued to increase. He represented the finest ideal of Christian faith blended with the New Learning, the humanism of the burgeoning Renaissance. So it is no wonder that, in 1423, Gonzaga invited Vittorino to begin a school in Mantua. But Vittorino saw the likelihood of pitfalls in trying to establish a school in the decadent environment of an Italian palace, so he set down certain demands to be met before he would accept the appointment.

His terms were bold: He would tolerate no intrusion upon his authority as teacher; he alone would be responsible for the conduct and discipline of his students; and to make these conditions feasible, he would remove his students from their homes to live together with him in a residential institution—in effect, creating the first boarding school.

Surprisingly, Gonzaga agreed to Vittorino's plan. To accommodate the new school, an abandoned brothel formerly known as "the House of Pleasure" was transformed into Vittorino's school and renamed *La Giocosa,* "the House of Joy." The prince's three sons, ages three to nine, were to be Vittorino's primary concern; but he was permitted to welcome other noblemen's sons. To these he added impoverished but intellectually promising boys at no fee; the tuition paid by the wealthy subsidized the sons of poorer families. More than sixty boys enrolled.

His curriculum consisted of the classical course of study, but physical exercise was integral to Vittorino's curriculum, along with the conventional studies of Latin language and literature, mathematics, and music. But by far the most important contribution to education made at "the House of Joy" was the enduring personal example of the Christian teacher. Devotions became a daily part of his instruction.

Thus came into being the model for the residential Christian school, where young people might live and learn from the example of Christians in residence with them. While few in number in North America, such schools continue to influence students to a depth that day schools rarely can.

The school flourished for years after Vittorino's death in 1446. Included among his many scholars was Lorenzo Valla, a controversial theologian whose views later influenced both Erasmus and Luther.

The anthology in Part 4 consists of selections by, rather than about, educators whose work has had an effect upon Christian schooling. The entry for Vittorino da Feltre, however, must be the exception because the master teacher left no tracts or treatises on his work. Only a few letters to Paola, wife of his patron Gonzaga, survive. These brief letters report to a mother on the welfare and progress of her children.

In place of the usual excerpt, therefore, here are passages from the first book in English to deal with him: William H. Woodward's *Vittorino da Feltre and Other Humanist Educators,* published in 1897.

Vittorino da Feltre and
Other Humanist Educators[4] (Excerpt)

. . . The picture which we are enabled to form of Vittorino at this juncture is both clear and attractive. In person he was slight and in appearance frail. But by dint of rigorous self-discipline and of active habits he had built up a constitution capable of sustaining the gravest exertions. For the greater part of his life he never admitted a day's illness. The careful practice of gymnastic had given him a peculiar suppleness and grace of movement. His expression was grave though not austere. Sympathy and affection, we are told, readily beamed from his face, though his eye had a penetrating quality before which conscious wrong-doing stood confessed and ashamed.

. . . Vittorino was before all else a Christian imbued with the spirit and doctrine of his faith. This indeed is the dominating note of his personality. It was this which preserved him from exaggerations and moral perversities which disfigured some of his contemporaries and gave an evil name to a certain type of Humanist. It was Vittorino's aim to graft ancient learning upon the stock of Christian training; and we shall see that within the next five-and-twenty years this had become his achievement.

. . . But permeating and controlling this humanist enthusiasm the Christian spirit retained its supreme place. With Vittorino this was the result both of rational conviction and of devoutness of temper. Amidst the temptations of life at Padua or Venice, amidst the distractions of Pagan ideals, to which so many scholars succumbed, he had always lived up to a high standard of Christian faith and conduct. So that he brought with him to Mantua a desire to combine the spirit of the Christian life with the educational apparatus of classical literature, whilst uniting with both something of the Greek passion for bodily culture and for dignity of the outer life.

It has been said that Vittorino was the first to conceive and to carry out a system of education framed on this ideal. . . .

But we must again remind ourselves of the depth of religious conviction upon which his own educational ideal ultimately rested. Reverence, piety, and religious observance formed the dominant note of Vittorino's personal life. The dignity of human life was with him based upon its relation to the Divine. Hence the transparent sincerity of his religious teaching; the insistence upon attendance at the ordinances of the Church; the inculcation of forgiveness and humility. He himself accompanied the boys to Mass; he set the example of regular Confession. Part of the religious instruction he himself took every day.

Apart from the light that is thus thrown upon his personality, what is of chief interest in this aspect of Vittorino is its relation to his Humanism. This was with him no nominal reconciliation between the new and the old. Christianity and Humanism were the two coordinate factors necessary to the development of complete manhood. There is no reason to suppose that Vittorino was embarrassed by a sense of contradiction between the classical and the Christian ideals of life. . . .

THOMAS À KEMPIS

Born ca. 1380 at Kempen, near Cologne, of impoverished parents, Thomas Hemerken was admitted to the school at Deventer founded by the Brothers of the Common Life. From there, in 1399, he entered a monastery dedicated to St. Agnes, founded by his older brother John. In 1406, Thomas became a monk and lived the rest of his life in devotion and service through his own writing and copying of manuscripts.

The Imitation of Christ was published in 1441. Presumably it reflects the training he had first received from Florentius Radewijns and other successors to Gerhard de Groote at Deventer. One does not need to read far before discovering a certain tone of dismay about the contemporary education most widely available in other schools and universities, whose objective seemed to be learning for learning's sake. Thomas à Kempis was clearly opposed to such sheer acquisition of data—rote memorization of the "sentences" and sayings of earlier philosophers.

The Imitation of Christ remains one of the most well-known and beloved devotional guides ever written. All evidence points to a man who lived by what he believed and wrote, a man of exemplary faith blended with exemplary humility.

The Imitation of Christ[5] (Excerpt)

Chapter 1
Of the Imitation of Christ

"Anyone who follows me shall not walk in darkness," says the Lord. These are the words of Christ, and by them we are reminded that we must imitate his life and his ways if we are to be truly enlightened and set free from the darkness of our own hearts. Let it be the most important thing we do, to reflect on the life of Jesus Christ.

Christ's teaching surpasses all the teachings of the saints, and the person who has his spirit will find hidden nourishment in his words. Yet many people, even after hearing scripture read so often, lack a deep longing for it, for they do not have the spirit of Christ. Anyone who wishes to understand Christ's words and to savor them fully should strive to become like him in every way.

What good does it do, then, to debate about the Trinity, if by a lack of humility you are displeasing to the Trinity? In truth, lofty words do not make a person holy and just, but a virtuous life makes one dear to God. I would much rather feel profound sorrow for my sins than to be able to define the theological term for it. If you knew the whole Bible by heart and the sayings of all the philosophers, what good would it all be without God's love and grace? Vanity of vanities and all is vanity, except to love God and to serve only him. This is the highest wisdom: to see the world as it truly is, fallen and fleeting; to love the world not for its own sake but for God's; and to direct all your effort toward achieving the kingdom of heaven. . . .

Make every effort, then, to shift your affections from the things that you can see to the things you cannot see, for people who live in the world on its terms instead of on God's stain their conscience and lose God's grace.

Chapter 2
Of Having a Humble Opinion About Yourself

Everyone naturally wishes to have knowledge, but what good is great learning unless it is accompanied by a feeling of deep awe and profound reverence toward God? . . . If I knew everything in the world and did not have love, what good would it do me before God, who will judge me by what I have done?

Calm that excessive thirst for knowledge, for there is great discord and deception in it. People who have great learning are often eager to appear wise, and they often wish others to recognize them as wise people. There are many things that you can know about, though, that are of little or no use to the soul, and a person is exceedingly foolish who reaches for anything that does not lead toward salvation. Endless reading and talk do not satisfy the soul, but a good life puts the mind at rest, and a clean conscience brings great confidence in God. The more you know and the better you know it, the greater is your responsibility for using your knowledge wisely.

147

So, do not think highly of yourself because of what you know about any art or science, but rather respect the knowledge that has been entrusted to you. If it seems to you that you know many things and that you are an expert in them, recognize nevertheless that there are many things that you do not know. Do not be high-minded, but admit your great ignorance. . . . If you want to learn something that will really help you, learn to see yourself as God sees you and not as you see yourself in the distorted mirror of your own self importance. This is the greatest and most useful lesson we can learn: to know ourselves for what we truly are, to admit freely our weaknesses and failings, and to hold a humble opinion of ourselves because of them. Not to dwell on ourselves and always to think well and highly of others is great wisdom and perfection. . . .

Chapter 3
Of the Teaching of Truth

Happy is that person whom Truth itself teaches, not by figures of speech and eloquent language, but as it is itself. Our opinions and our understanding often lead us astray and offer us very little insight. What good is a brilliant argument about hidden and obscure matters when God does not judge us by our knowledge of such things? It is a great mistake for us to neglect useful and necessary things and to direct our thoughts to curious and harmful ones. Having eyes, we do not see. Why should we bother about clever arguments and subtle reasoning?

When the eternal Word speaks we are set free from countless theories and conjectures. All things spring from this one Word and all things speak of one Word, and this Word is the beginning, which also speaks to us. Without the Word, no one understands correctly or draws the right conclusions about anything. . . .

Surely, when the day of judgment comes we shall not be asked what we have read but what we have done, not how well we have spoken but how devoutly we have lived. Tell me, where are those professors and teachers today whom you knew so well while they were living and flourishing in their learning? Now other people hold their positions, and I do not know whether they ever think of them. While they lived they seemed to be important, and now no one mentions them. Oh, how swiftly the glory of the world passes away! If only their lives had been in harmony with their learning, then all their studying and reading would have been worthwhile. How many people perish in a generation through empty learning, caring little for the service of God? And because they prefer to be famous rather than humble, they perish with their own thoughts.

That person is truly great who has great love. He is truly great who is small in his own eyes and who regards every pinnacle of honor as nothing in itself. He is truly wise who regards all earthly ambitions as supremely unimportant, if they stand in the way of gaining Christ. And he is very learned indeed who knows God's will and who makes it his own.

Thomas à Kempis, *The Imitation of Christ*, trans. William C. Creasy.
Excerpt reprinted with permission by Mercer University Press,
1400 Coleman Avenue, Macon, Ga. 31207.

NICHOLAS OF CUSA

Nicholas (1401–64) was born in Cues, Germany, on the Moselle River, to a notoriously ill-tempered father, a prosperous landholder and merchant. Nicholas displeased his father by his early studious interests, and eventually escaped his father's influence by entering a school operated by the Brothers of the Common Life at Deventer. By age twenty-two, he had earned from Cologne a doctorate in canon law. He served Cardinal Giordano Orsini as secretary, then legate in Germany, where following his ordination in 1430, he became dean of the cathedral at Coblenz.

Throughout his vocation in the Roman Church, Nicholas was an activist in church affairs, entering into political disputes without hesitation and taking strong positions on controversial issues. For instance, as early as 1433, he wrote an argument in favor of reforming both the Roman Church and the empire. His advocacy of reuniting the Eastern and Western branches of the church under the Roman papacy won the favor of two popes, Eugenius IV and Nicholas V, who named him cardinal in 1448.

In 1450, the pope named Nicholas of Cusa bishop of Brixen, with particular responsibilities for German-speaking peoples. Opposition from the Hapsburg ruler, Duke Sigismund, compelled Nicholas to return to Rome, where Pope Pius II welcomed him as vicar-general, with authority over Rome and the resources of St. Peter's basilica.

Nicholas of Cusa's reputation in intellectual history derives largely from his major work, *Of Learned Ignorance*, published about 1440. Relying on paradox to make his point, Nicholas showed how divine wisdom can be apprehended only through divinely granted intuition. Since ultimate truth is too simple to be known by human reason, it must be perceived by its opposite, which is *docta ignorantia*, learned ignorance.

Such an apparent oxymoron indicates the playful-minded manner in which Nicholas of Cusa sought to water the arid deserts of scholastic thought. Like Thomas à Kempis—who rebuked scholastic theologians for disputing the nature of the Trinity without concern as to whether their work and witness might be honoring to the Trinity—Nicholas of Cusa looked to paradox to expose the vainglory of human presumption at knowing and understanding God.

Of Learned Ignorance[6] (Excerpt)

. . . Our ancient writers are at one in asserting that faith lies at the root of all understanding. In every science certain things must be accepted as first principles if the subject matter is to be understood; and these first postulates rest only upon faith. He who wishes to rise to knowledge must first believe those things without which knowledge is impossible. Says Isaiah: "Unless you believe you shall not understand." Faith, therefore, embraces every intelligible thing. Understanding is the unfolding of what was wrapped up in faith. The intelligence is therefore directed by faith; and faith is extended by understanding. Without sound faith, then, there is no true understanding. There is no mistaking the kinds of conclusions that are reached from faulty principles and from a weak foundation; and on the other hand, there is no faith more perfect than that which is founded upon the truth itself, which is Jesus.

Everyone knows that a right faith is the most excellent gift of God. The Apostle John tells us that faith in the Incarnation of the Word of God leads us into truth, that we may become the sons of God. He first sets forth this faith simply and only then narrates many works of Christ in accordance with this faith, that the intelligence may be enlightened in faith. And at the end he suggests the conclusion: "These things are written that you may believe that Jesus is the Son of God."

Now this most wholesome faith in Christ, constantly strengthened in simplicity, can, in our accepted doctrine of ignorance, be extended and unfolded. The greatest and profoundest mysteries of God, though hidden from the wise, may be revealed to little ones and humble folk living in the world by their faith in Jesus; for in Jesus are hidden all the treasures of wisdom and of knowledge, so that without Him no man can do anything. For He is the Word, and the power by whom God made the world, He the most high having alone power over everything in heaven and on earth. He cannot be apprehended within the context of this world.

Here we are led by reason, opinion, or doctrine from the better known to the less known by symbols; whereas He is grasped only when movement ceases and faith takes its place. By this faith we are caught up into simplicity above all reason and intelligence to the third heaven of most pure simple intellectuality; that in the body we may contemplate Him incorporeally, because in spirit, and on the earth in an entirely unearthly fashion and rather in a heavenly and incomprehensible manner, whereby we perceive that He cannot be comprehended because of the immensity of His excellence. And this none other than that every learned ignorance—by which the blessed Paul himself, raised higher and into a closer knowledge, perceived that the Christ with whom he was at one time acquainted, he never really knew.

We, then, believers in Christ, are led in learned ignorance to the mountain that is Christ, which our animal nature is forbidden to touch; and when we endeavor to gaze upon Him with the eye of the mind, we fall into darkness, knowing that in that very darkness is the mount in which He is pleased to dwell for the sake of all those who live a life of the spirit. But if, in the constancy of a firmer faith we approach Him, we are snatched away from the eyes of them that live by sensuality, to perceive with interior hearing the voices and the thunder and the dread signs of His majesty. We are given to realize that He alone is the Lord whom all things obey. And step by step we come close even to certain incorruptible foot-prints of Him (as to most divine characters) in which, hearing the voice not of mortal creatures but of God Himself in His holy organs and in the words of His prophets and saints, we come, as in a cloud of more transparent quality, to perceive Him more clearly.

. . . God be praised that he has by his Son redeemed us from the darkness of such ignorance and has taught us that all is false and a lie, howsoever produced, that comes to us from any other mediator than Christ who is the truth, and from any other faith but that of Jesus. There is but one Lord Jesus, the master of all things, who fills us with every blessing and who alone makes ample satisfaction for all our deficiencies.

Of Learned Ignorance, by Nicholas Cusanus, translated by Germain Heron. Copyright 1954 and reprinted by permission of Routledge and Kegan Paul; London, England.

DESIDERIUS ERASMUS

He may have been the greatest scholar in Europe—an indefatigable writer and translator. As a Christian humanist *nonpareil*, Erasmus of Rotterdam (ca. 1455–1536) mastered Greek and Latin and translated the New Testament into both languages, among his many accomplishments.

He received his early schooling from the Brothers of the Common Life at Deventer, but he left at about age eighteen, after both his parents died. By 1486, under pressure to find a future place for himself, he had entered an Augustinian monastery and was eventually ordained a priest in 1492.

But Erasmus was never cut out to be a typical parish priest. Instead, he obtained permission from his superiors to leave the monastery and set upon his life's work as a roving scholar. Already Erasmus was expressing distaste for the traditional methods of study governed by the church's commitment to the scholasticism of Thomas Aquinas. Erasmus believed that true knowledge could not be found in the third-hand ideas of men who had borrowed those same ideas from a second-hand source but who had no first-hand knowledge of the original text. So he set out to master Greek, adding this language to his already acclaimed knowledge of Latin.

Erasmus found a comfortable environment for this new way of approaching scholarship at both Oxford and Cambridge. At Oxford, he became friendly with John Colet and Thomas More. Colet had amazed the scholarly world with his 1496 lectures on the Pauline epistles, Romans and 1 Corinthians. Colet's daring innovation was to abandon allegory and treat the text of these letters as though they had been composed by a real writer as real letters to real readers. Colet did not choose to subordinate the original intent of these letters to prove theological points or to construct complex allegories. In Colet, who went on to found St. Paul's School in London around 1509, Erasmus found a worthy exemplar of educational theories Erasmus had himself been harboring.

More, a scholar of the classics and author of *Utopia*, was renowned not only for his own learning but for that of his three daughters, whom he taught along with his son. More was to become chancellor of England, King Henry VIII's most trusted advisor. But More alienated himself from the king when, first, he opposed Henry on the Act of Supremacy, which declared the king sovereign in all things, including ecclesiastical matters, then refused to commend the king's wish to divorce his first wife, Catherine of Aragon, in order to marry Anne Boleyn. Beheaded in 1535, More is regarded as a Roman Catholic martyr and saint.

During the years that Erasmus and More were companions, More promoted Erasmus' career, defending him against charges that Christian humanism was godless; instead, More praised Erasmus for his work of pointing the way to theology by means of philosophy and the liberal arts. More contended that while a knowledge of Greek or Latin—or, for that matter, any formal learning—is unnecessary for salvation, education in matters outside theology does instill discipline and other virtues. This, of course, continues to be the whole point of a Christian liberal arts education.

At Cambridge for three years, 1511–14, Erasmus produced some of his greatest accomplishments, including a Greek New Testament and its translation into Latin; he also worked on fresh translations of the writings of several Church Fathers, among them Irenaeus, Jerome, Ambrose, Augustine, and John Chrysostom. At the same time, he compiled textbooks for use in Colet's St. Paul's School, and a host of other works. All this time he was serving as Lady Margaret Professor of Greek and theology, while living in a small room at Queens College, overlooking the River Cam.

But Erasmus was not to be confined to any place for long. He consistently declined invitations from kings and dukes to serve in their courts, preferring to spend the last twenty years of his life near the famous printing house of Froeben in Basel, Switzerland, from which he issued another vast array of publications.

By now, Martin Luther's revolt against the papacy was underway. Although Erasmus himself had criticized and even satirized the abuses and excesses of the Roman Church, he was unable to reconcile criticism with rebellion against the pope's authority. He quarreled with his fellow Augustinian monk Martin, who heaped scorn upon Erasmus for what Luther considered to be his cowardice. In return, Erasmus said of Luther that he had thrown "the apple of discord into the world."[7]

But if Erasmus lacked Luther's political courage, he nonetheless brought to the Renaissance—and thereby also to the Reformation—new devotion to the Scriptures and to the orthodox teaching of the apostles and fathers; he also contributed to a reaffirmation of the centrality of the lordship of Jesus Christ—the Word-made-Flesh—over all thought, all discourse, all means of expression: ". . . that we may know Christ and honor Him." In 1529, Erasmus addressed a treatise on the liberal education of children to William, Duke of Cleves, a prince of the Netherlands royal family with whom Henry VIII would later ally himself by marrying Anne of Cleves. In this treatise, which follows, Erasmus makes his case for the instruction of children in an atmosphere free from fear of physical punishment and offered by a person worthy of emulation.

"On the Liberal Education of the Young"[8]

Addressed to
William, Duke of Cleves, 1529

Par. 1. The Argument at Large.

I desire to urge upon you, Illustrious Duke, to take into your early and serious consideration the future nurture and training of the son lately born to you. For, with Chrysippus, I contend that the young child must be led to sound learning whilst his wit is yet unwarped, his age tender, his mind flexible and tenacious. In manhood we remember nothing so well as the truths which we imbibed in our youth. Wherefore I beg you to put aside all idle chatter which would persuade you that this early childhood is [unfit] for the discipline and the effort of studies.

The arguments which I shall enlarge upon are the following. First, the beginnings of learning are the work of memory, which in young children is most tenacious. Next, as nature has implanted in us the instinct to seek for knowledge, can we be too early in obeying her behest? Thirdly, there are not a few things which it imports greatly that we should know well, and which we can learn far more readily in our tender years. I speak of the elements of Letters, Grammar, and the fables and stories found in the ancient Poets. Fourthly, since children, as all agree, are fit to acquire manners, why may they not acquire the rudiments of learning? And seeing that they must needs be busy about something, what else can be better approved? For how much wiser to amuse their hours with Letters, than to see them frittered away in aimless trifling!

It is, however, objected, first, that such knowledge as can be thus early got is of slight value. But even so, why despise it, if so be it serve as the foundation for much greater things? For if in early

155

childhood a boy acquire such useful elements he will be free to apply his youth to higher knowledge, to the saving of his time. Moreover, whilst he is thus occupied in sound learning he will perforce be kept from some of the temptations which befall youth, seeing that nothing engages the whole mind more than studies. And this I count a high gain in such times as ours.

Next, it is urged that by such application health may be somewhat endangered. Supposing this to be true, still the compensation is great, for by discipline the mind gains far more in alertness and in vigour than the body is ever likely to lose. Watchfulness, however, will prevent any such risk as is imagined. Also, for this tender age you will employ a teacher who will win and not drive, just as you will choose such subjects as are pleasant and attractive, in which the young mind will find recreation rather than toil.

Furthermore, I bid you remember that a man ignorant of Letters is no man at all, that human life is a fleeting thing, that youth is easily enticed into sin, that early manhood is absorbed by clashing interests, that old age is unproductive, and that few reach it. How then can you allow your child, in whom you yourself live again, to lose even one of those precious years in which he may begin to acquire those means whereby he may elevate his whole life and keep at arm's length temptation and evil? . . .

Par. 4. The Supreme Importance of Education to Human Well-being.

To dumb creatures Mother Nature has given an innate power or instinct, whereby they may in great part attain to their right capacities. But Providence in granting to man alone the privilege of reason has thrown the burden of development of the human being upon training. Well, therefore, has it been said that the first means, the second, and the third means to happiness is right training or education. Sound education is the condition of real wisdom. And if an education which is soundly planned and carefully carried out is the very fount of all human excellence, so, on the other hand, careless and unworthy training is the true source of folly and vice. . . .

7. Reason the true mark of Man.

Now it is the possession of Reason which constitutes a Man. If trees or wild beasts grow, men, believe me, are fashioned. Men in olden time who led their life in forests, driven by the mere needs and desires of their natures, guided by no laws, with no ordering in communities, are to be judged rather as savage beasts than as men. For Reason, the mark of humanity, has no place where all is determined by appetite. . . . Nature, in giving you a son, presents you, let me say, a rude, unformed creature, which it is your part of fashion so that it may become indeed a man. If this fashioning be neglected you have but an animal still: if it be contrived earnestly and wisely, you have, I had almost said, what may prove a being not far from a God.

8. Education of their children is a Duty owed by parents to the Commonwealth and to God.

Straightway from the child's birth it is meet that he should begin to learn the things which properly belong to his well-being. Therefore, bestow especial pains upon his tenderest years, as Vergil teaches. Handle the wax whilst it is soft, mould the clay whilst it is moist, dye the fleece before it gather stains. It is no light task to educate our children aright. . . . God will straitly charge the parents with their children's faults; therefore, except they bring up their little ones from the very first to live aright, they themselves will share the penalty. For a child rightly educated is a comfort and a joy to his parents, but a foolish child brings upon them shame, it may be poverty, and old age before their time. . . .

9. Vicious Habits in which parents encourage their children.

But there is an education which is worse than none at all. For how shall we describe those who go about to imbue the tender mind with wickedness, before it be able to know what wickedness is? For example, how can a child grow up to modesty and humility who in his very infancy totters in the purple? He cannot yet sound his letters, but he knows what cramoisie is, and brocade: he craves for dainty dishes and disdainfully pushes away simple food. The tailor contrives some new marvel in cap or tunic; straightway we must dress up the child therein; we tickle his vanity, and then we wonder that he develops irritation and self-conceit! The serving-women teach him evil words, and for their amusement tempt him to repeat them. He is brought up to sit through long feastings; he hears the noise of jesters, minstrels, and dancers. The guests, nay, his own father, sprawl drunkenly in his presence. And yet you pray that he may grow up honest, temperate, and pure. I would also denounce those who bring up their sons to a love of war. Straight from their mother's arms they are bidden to finger swords and shields, to thrust and strike. With such tastes, already deeply rooted with years, they are handed over to a master, who is blamed for their indifference to worthy interests. . . . For no one can exaggerate the importance of these years for character, nor the difficulty which such enervating, debasing up-bringing at this stage creates for the teachers who then take over the task. Menander and Paul were perfectly right: such "evil communications corrupt good manners." . . .

12. The Error of those who think that Experience gives all the Education that Men need.

They err, therefore, who affirm that wisdom is won by handling affairs and by contact with life, without aid from the teaching of philosophy. Tell me, can a man run his best in the dark? Or, can a gladiator conquer if he be blindfold? The precepts of philosophy—which is knowledge applied to life—are, as it were, the eyes of the mind, and lighten us to the consciousness of what we may do and may not do. . . . For example, you educate your son to the mystery of medicine. Do you allow him to rely on the method of "experience" in order that he may learn to distinguish between poisons and healing drugs? Or, do you send him to the treatises? It is an unhappy education which teaches the master mariner the rudiments of navigation by shipwrecks: or the Prince the true way of kingship by revolutions, invasions or slaughter. Is it not the wise part to learn beforehand how to avoid mischiefs rather than with the pains of experience to remedy them? Thus Philip of Macedon put his son Alexander to school with Aristotle that he might learn philosophy of him, to the end that when a king he should be saved from doing things which must be repented of. Thus education shews us in brief what we should follow, what avoid; she does not wait till we have suffered the evil results of our mistakes, but warns us in advance against courses which will lead to failure and misery. Let us, therefore, firmly knit up this threefold cord: let Nature be by Training guided to wise ends, let Nature and Training, thus united, be made perfect by right Practice. . . .

Par. 15. The Tutor and his Relation to the Parents.

But the most important of the forces that mould the development of the child is the influence of the tutor. In choosing him we cannot show too great diligence, enquire too carefully, or apply too rigorous tests. The right person once secured, we are not to conclude that all is done. Two cautions, indeed, seem necessary. First, that masters, like doctors, must not be changed except for serious cause. The repeated beginnings-afresh are as the weaving and unweaving of Penelope's web. I have known children who have, by the folly of their parents, had as many as a dozen masters before they were as many years of age. Secondly, the responsibility of parents for the education of their children in no way ceases with the appointment of the master. Let the father often visit the schoolroom and note the progress made. . . . I speak, however, now of young children: as they grow up it is wiser to remove them somewhat more from their parents' eye. . . .

Par. 20. The Importance of this Early Training ought to lead Parents to ask themselves how far they can follow the example of the Ancients in becoming themselves the Instructors of their Children.

But we may not forget that children are prone to follow the allurement of the senses rather than the rule of reason; to store up in mind what is trivial or bad rather than what is of enduring worth. This fact of human nature sorely puzzled the ancient philosophers, but has its key in the Christian doctrine of Original Sin. True as this explanation is, we are not to forget the part played by faulty training, particularly in the first and most impressionable stage. . . . In old days careful parents trained up a slave specially fit in learning that he might act as a tutor, or they bought one already skilled. But it were wiser that the parents should qualify themselves to this task. If it be objected that time is lacking, I point to the flagrant waste of leisure in play and entertainments, and in the stupid social "duties of our station." He has but lukewarm love for his son who grudges the time for teaching him. . . . But, in spite of drawbacks in our own day, certain parents of distinction have undertaken the duty of training their own children. Amongst these I name Thomas More. He, although deeply occupied in affairs of the State, devoted his leisure to the instruction of his wife, his son, and his daughters, both in the uprightness of life and in the liberal studies of Greek and Latin. The common tongue of the people may be left to be picked up in the ordinary intercourse of life.

Should, however, neither parent be a suitable instructor to the child, then, I admit, we must secure the services of an able and experienced teacher. But the father should hesitate to take an untried man. In many things, perhaps, negligence may find its pardon; but here the eyes of Argus himself are wanted. There is a proverb that teaches us that in war a general may not make two mistakes. In planning his son's education a father dare hardly make one. . . .

22. The Disposition of the Teacher.

Seeing, then, that children in the earliest stage must be beguiled and not driven to learning, the first requisite in the Master is a gentle sympathetic manner, the second a knowledge of wise and attractive methods. Possessing these two important qualifications he will be able to win the pupil to find pleasure in his task. . . .

Fear is of no real avail in education: not even parents can train their children by this motive. Love must be the first influence; followed and completed by a trustful and affectionate respect, which compels obedience far more surely than dread can ever do. . . .

Par. 25. The Permissible Instruments of Discipline.

Teaching by beating, therefore, is not a liberal education. Nor should the schoolmaster indulge in too strong and too frequent *language* of blame. Medicine constantly repeated loses its force. . . . Let us watch, let us encourage, let us press and yet again press, that by learning, by repeating, by diligent listening, the boy may feel himself carried onward towards his goal. Let him learn to respect and to love integrity and knowledge, to hate ignorance and dishonour. Bid him regard those who are lauded for their virtues, be warned by those who are denounced for their ill-doing. Set before him the example of men to whom learning has brought high praise, dignity, repute and position. Warn him of the fate of those who by the neglect of high wisdom have sunk into contempt, poverty, disgrace and evil life. These are your instruments of discipline, my Christian teacher, worthy of your calling and of your flock. But should none of these avail, then, if it must be so, let the rod be used with due regard to self-respect in the manner of it. . . .

Par. 37. Conclusion.

Now I have done. I make my appeal to that practical wisdom which you have always exhibited in affairs. Consider how dear a possession is your son; how many-sided is learning; how exacting its pursuit, and how honourable! Think how instinctive is the child's wish to learn, how plastic his mind, how responsive to judicious training, if only he be entrusted to instructors at once sympathetic and skilled to ease the first steps in knowledge. Let me recall to you the durability of early impressions, made upon the unformed mind, as compared with those acquired in later life. You know also how hard it is to overtake time lost; how wise, in all things, to begin our tasks in season; how great is the power of *persistence* in accumulating what we prize; how fleeting a thing is the life of man, how busy is youth, how inapt for learning is age. In face, then, of all these serious facts you will not suffer . . . but three days even of your son's life to pass, before you take into earnest consideration his nurture and future education.

Reprinted by permission of the publisher from William H. Woodward, ed., *Desiderius Erasmus Concerning the Aim and Method of Education* (New York: Teachers College Press, © 1964 by Teachers College, Columbia University. All rights reserved.)

MARTIN LUTHER

Precisely speaking, Protestant schooling began with Martin Luther and the Reformation; but neither Luther nor his movement burst full-grown upon Europe in 1517. The evangelical Christian schools that spring from the sixteenth century Reformation are also connected, like Luther himself, to the history and tradition of the fifteen previous centuries and to "the New Learning," or Renaissance. Martin Luther (1483–1546) was part of that Renaissance.

Luther's early interest in learning caused his parents to send him at age fourteen to school at Magdeburg, Germany; a year later, he enrolled at Eisenach. In both instances, poverty compelled him to beg for his food from townsfolk; his father was a diligent but poor miner.

In 1501, Luther enrolled at the University of Erfurt, where he excelled in scholarship. His father, Hans, had hoped that Martin would become a lawyer, and in 1505, having earned his master's degree, Luther began to study law. But two years earlier, while reading in the university library, Luther had come upon a copy of the Bible, the first he had ever seen. His reading of the Bible—and a harrowing experience during a thunderstorm—compelled him to abandon his legal studies to enter a monastery of hermits in the Augustinian order. There he continued his personal Bible reading and study. In 1507, he was ordained a priest. Luther's biographers believe the terror of the storm and his increasing acquaintance with the text of Scripture itself prepared the monk for his conversion, which certainly became public with his nailing of the Ninety-Five Theses on the Wittenberg Door ten years later.

Luther received a temporary appointment to the faculty of the University of Wittenberg in 1508, where he taught not in the typical manner of scholasticism but in a manner that paralleled other Christian humanists' inquiry into the Scriptures themselves as the primary source of truth. Like other young scholars of his time, he owed much to the work of Desiderius Erasmus, whom Luther acknowledged by using Erasmus' new version of the New Testament in his lectures on Romans, given in the fall of 1516. Later, Luther would use Erasmus' New Testament in making his own German translation; still later, of course, Luther would denounce Erasmus and all his work.

Luther's antipathy for the Church of Rome had begun to develop after 1510, when he made a visit to Rome. What he saw there astonished him, shattering his confidence in the papacy for allowing such corruption and decadence. Luther was particularly offended by the sale of indulgences, monetary payment aimed at reducing the length of time one's soul might spend in purgatory. He returned from Rome to his teaching, now fully appointed as professor of biblical theology, and to his close study of the Scriptures. The more he read, the more Luther became convinced that justification is by faith alone, a gift of God's grace not to be earned by works or paid for by money. His teaching reflected more and more the progress of his mind through personal study.

In 1513, Pope Leo X revived the sale of indulgences as a means of raising funds for the renovation of St. Peter's Basilica in Rome. Three years later, to the region near Wittenberg came a Dominican friar named Johann Tetzel, a plain-speaking man of the people whose market oratory made him an effective salesman of eternal fire insurance. By the end of the summer of 1517, Luther had heard enough. He carefully chose his time, and on October 31, 1517, the eve of the great feast of All Saints' Day—when relics of the saints were customarily on display in All Saints' Church in Wittenberg—Luther posted his ninety-five opinions, or theses, on the church door.

A century before, such an act might well have received only local notoriety for its brazen opposition to church authority. But in the middle of the previous century, a new technology called printing with movable type had come into being. Johannes Gutenberg's invention made possible the almost immediate and wider distribution of every written word. Luther's Ninety-Five Theses were soon published throughout Germany and the rest of Europe.

The story of the Reformation that ensued is better traced in books such as Roland Bainton's *Here I Stand* or Heinrich Boehmer's *Martin Luther: Road to Reformation*. For purposes here, it is sufficient to say that, in all the furor he created as Luther the Reformer, the man himself never lost sight of his vocation as Luther the Educator. No wonder, then, that among his earliest concerns—while his very freedom and safety were still threatened—was the establishing of Christian schools and the responsibility of politicians and parents to maintain and send their children to such schools. Certainly, Luther's greatest gift to the education of children in Germany was his translation of the Bible into their own language.

The excerpted letter that follows reveals the passion with which Luther lived. He was not concerned about tactful disagreements or polite exchanges of views with his opponents. For Luther, the very souls of children were at stake, and so no weapon was too strong to use against those who would deprive such children of salvation. His 1524 letter addressed to mayors and aldermen throughout Germany suggests the forceful tone he almost always adopted.

To be sure, Luther's argument needed all the strength he could muster. The case for schools was not simple to make, especially in the face of opposition from crass materialism. Not to be about the business of making money was to be a laggard. In an age when ships from European ports might circumnavigate the globe or exchange with the New World its riches for the Old World's treasures, commerce thrived in Europe.

So, as in our own times, education-for-learning's-sake had few advocates. In defense of education, the question always to be answered was, "What use is schooling to the future employment and productivity of this citizen?" For only a few privileged youths whose parents intended for them one of the professions—medicine, law, or theology—could time spent in school be justified.

Furthermore, as the revolt against Rome swelled, schools once sponsored by monastic orders found themselves without teachers or pupils. In substantial numbers, converts to the evangelical gospel of Luther left their monasteries and schools; governing authorities took over abandoned institutions and co-opted their financial resources.

In response to Luther's call, some converts carried their reaction too far, blaming the schools they had left for propagating Rome's false doctrine, thereby accusing education in general for being the handmaiden of the Antichrist. Others now held that any formal education was superfluous to the enlightenment of the Holy Spirit.

Such, then, was the emotional context in which Luther framed his argument, offering both philosophical reasons and practical counsel for his readers to consider. Authorities in several cities heeded Luther's advice; within two years, schools were reopened in Eisleben, Gotha, Halberstadt, Magdeburg, Nordhausen, and Nurnberg. But Luther was far from satisfied. Too many parents were ignoring their moral obligation to send their children to school. By 1529, he was threatening to "really go after the shameful, despicable, damnable parents who are no parents at all but despicable hogs and venomous beasts, devouring their own young."[9]

The following year, Luther prepared a sermon intended for preachers, "On the Duty of Sending Children to School," which was printed in Wittenberg and distributed throughout Germany. Luther began with a note to the pastors in his reading audience:

> You see plainly how Satan is now attacking us on all sides.
> . . . Among his various crafty devices, one of the greatest, if
> not the greatest, is to delude the common people into withholding their children from school and instruction, while he

suggests to them such hurtful thoughts as these: "Since there is no hope for the cloisters and priesthood as formerly, we do not need learned men and study, but must consider how we may obtain food and wealth."

He ended with a call for generous support of Christian schooling.

Luther's persuasion won wide support for Christian schooling, not only in Germany but everywhere else the Reformation reached.

"Letter to the Mayors and Aldermen of All the Cities of Germany in Behalf of Christian Schools"[10] (Excerpt)

Grace and peace from God our Father and the Lord Jesus Christ. Honored and dear Sirs: Having three years ago been put under the ban and outlawed, I should have kept silent, had I regarded the command of men more than that of God. Many persons in Germany both of high and low estate assail my discourses and writings on that account, and shed much blood over them. But God who has opened my mouth and bidden me speak, stands firmly by me, and without any counsel or effort of mine strengthens and extends my cause the more . . . .

Therefore, as Isaiah says, I will not hold my peace . . . and I wish to declare to you frankly and confidently that if you hear me, you hear not me but Christ; and whoever will not hear me, despises not me but Christ. For I know the truth of what I declare and teach; and every one who rightly considers my doctrine will realize its truth for himself.

First of all we see how the schools are deteriorating throughout Germany. . . . For through the word of God the unchristian and sensual character of these institutions is becoming known. . . .

Therefore I beg you all, in the name of God and of our neglected youth, not to think of this subject lightly, as many do who see not what the prince of this world intends. For the right instruction of youth is a matter in which Christ and all the world are concerned. Thereby are we all aided. . . .

Let this, then, be the first consideration to move you—that in this work we are fighting against the devil, the most artful and dangerous enemy of men.

Another consideration is found in the fact that we should not, as St. Paul says, receive the grace of God in vain, and neglect the present favorable time. For Almighty God has truly granted us Germans a gracious visitation, and favored us with a golden opportunity. We now have excellent and learned young men, adorned with every science and art, who, if they were employed, could be of great service as teachers. . . .

I should prefer, it is true, that our youth be ignorant and dumb rather than that the universities and convents should remain as the only sources of instruction open to them. For it is my earnest intention, prayer and desire that these schools of Satan either be destroyed or changed into Christian schools. But since God has so richly favored us, and given us a great number of persons who are competent thoroughly to instruct and train our young people, it is truly needful that we should not disregard His grace and let Him knock in vain. He stands at the door; happy are we if we open to Him. He calls us; happy is the man who answers Him. If we disregard His call, so that He passes by, who will bring Him back? . . .

For know this, that the word and grace of God are like a passing shower, which does not return where it has once been. The Divine favor once rested upon the Jews, but it has departed. Paul brought the Gospel into Greece; but now they have the Turks. Rome and Italy once enjoyed its blessings; but now they have the Pope. And the German people should not think that they will always have it; for ingratitude and neglect will banish it. Therefore seize it and hold it fast, whoever can; idle hands will have an evil year.

The third consideration is the highest of all, namely, God's command, which through Moses so often urges and enjoins that parents instruct their children, that the seventy-eighth Psalm says: "He established a testimony in Jacob and appointed a law in Israel, which he commended our fathers that they should make them known to their children." And the fourth commandment also shows this, where he has so strictly enjoined children to obey their parents, that disobedient children were to be put to death. . . .

It is indeed a sin and shame that we must be aroused and incited to the duty of educating our children and of considering their highest interests, whereas nature itself should move us thereto, and the example of the heathen affords us varied instruction. . . .

But all that, you say, is addressed to parents; what does it concern the members of the council and the mayors? That is true; but how, if parents neglect it? Who shall attend to it then? Shall we therefore let it alone, and suffer the children to be neglected? How will the mayors and council excuse themselves, and prove that such a duty does not belong to them?

Parents neglect this duty from various causes.

In the first place, there are some who are so lacking in piety and uprightness that they would not do it if they could, but like the ostrich, harden themselves against their own offspring, and do nothing for them. Nevertheless these children must live among us and with us. How then can reason and, above all, Christian charity, suffer them to grow up ill-bred, and to infect other children, till at last the whole city be destroyed, like Sodom, Gomorrah, and some other cities?

In the second place, the great majority of parents are unqualified for it, and do not understand how children should be brought up and taught. For they have learned nothing but to provide for their bodily wants; and in order to teach and train children thoroughly, a separate class is needed.

In the third place, even if parents were qualified and willing to do it themselves, yet on account of other employments and household duties they have no time for it, so that necessity requires us to have teachers for public schools, unless each parent employ a private instructor. But that would be too expensive for persons of ordinary means, and many a bright boy, on account of poverty, would be neglected. Besides, many parents die and leave orphans; and how they are usually cared for by guardians, we might learn, even if observation were not enough, from the sixty-eighth Psalm, where God calls himself the "Father of the fatherless," as of those who are neglected by all others. Also there are some who have no children, and therefore feel no interest in them.

Therefore it will be the duty of the mayors and council to exercise the greatest care over the young. For since the happiness, honor, and life of the city are committed to their hands, they would be held recreant before God and the world, if they did not, day and night, with all their power, seek its welfare and improvement.

But, you say again, if we shall and must have schools, what is the use to teach Latin, Greek, Hebrew, and the other liberal arts? Is it not enough to teach the Scriptures, which are necessary to salvation, in the mother tongue? To which I answer. . . .

Let this be kept in mind, that we will not preserve the Gospel without the languages. The languages are the scabbard in which the Word of God is sheathed. They are the casket in which this jewel is enshrined; the cask in which this wine is kept; the chamber in which this food is stored. And, to borrow a figure from the Gospel itself, they are the baskets in which this bread, and fish, and fragments are preserved. . . .

Since, then, it behooves Christians at all times to use the Bible as their only book and to be thoroughly acquainted with it, especially is it a disgrace and sin at the present day not to learn the languages, when God provides every facility, incites us to study, and wishes to have His word known. O how glad the honored fathers would have been, if they could have learned the languages, and had such access to the Holy Scriptures! With what pain and toil they scarcely obtained crumbs, while almost without effort we are able to secure the whole loaf! O how their industry shames our idleness, yea, how severely will God punish our neglect and ingratitude! . . .

So much for the utility and necessity of the languages, and of Christian schools for our spiritual interests and the salvation of the soul. Let us now consider the body and inquire: though there were no soul, nor heaven, nor hell, but only the civil government, would not this require good schools and learned men more than do our spiritual interests? . . .

It is not necessary to say here that civil government is a divine institution; of that I have elsewhere said so much, that I hope no one has any doubts on the subject. The question is, how are we to get able and skillful rulers? And here we are put to shame by the heathen, who in ancient times, especially the Greeks and Romans, without knowing that civil government is a divine ordinance, yet instructed the boys and girls with such earnestness and industry that, when I think of it, I am ashamed of Christians, and especially of our Germans, who are such blockheads and brutes that they can say: "Pray, what is the use of schools, if one is not to become a priest?" Yet we know, or ought to know, how necessary and useful a thing it is, and how acceptable to God, when a prince, lord, counselor, or other ruler, is well-trained and skillful in discharging, in a Christian way, the functions of his office. . . .

Now such men are to come from boys, and such women from girls; hence it is necessary that boys and girls be properly taught and brought up. . . . Therefore, honored members of the city councils, this work must remain in your hands; you have more time and better opportunity for it than princes and lords. . . .

There is consequently an urgent necessity, not only for the sake of the young, but also for the maintenance of Christianity and of civil government, that this matter be immediately and earnestly taken hold of, lest afterwards, although we would gladly attend to it, we shall find it impossible to do so, and be obliged to feel in vain the pains of remorse forever. For God is now graciously present, and offers His aid. . . .

Finally, this must be taken into consideration by all who earnestly desire to see such schools established and the languages preserved in the German states: that no cost nor pains should be spared to procure good libraries in suitable buildings, especially in the large cities, which are able to afford it. For if a knowledge of the Gospel and of every kind of learning is to be preserved, it must be embodied in books, as the prophets and apostles did, as I have already shown. This should be done, not only that our spiritual and civil leaders may have something to read and study, but also that good books may not be lost, and that the arts and languages may be preserved, with which God has graciously favored us. St. Paul was diligent in this matter, since he lays the injunction upon Timothy: "Give attendance to reading"; and directs him to bring the books, but especially the parchments left at Troas. . . .

In the first place, a library should contain the Holy Scriptures in Latin, Greek, Hebrew, German, and other languages. Then the best and most ancient commentators in Greek, Hebrew, and Latin.

Secondly, such books as are useful in acquiring the languages, as the poets and orators, without considering whether they are heathen or Christian, Greek or Latin. For it is from such works that grammar must be learned.

Thirdly, books treating of all the arts and sciences.

Lastly, books on jurisprudence and medicine, though here discrimination is necessary.

A prominent place should be given to chronicles and histories, in whatever languages they may be obtained; for they are wonderfully useful in understanding and regulating the course of the world, and in disclosing the marvelous works of God. . . .

Herewith I commend you all to the grace of God. May He soften your hearts, and kindle therein a deep interest in behalf of the poor, wretched, and neglected youth; and through the blessing of God may you so counsel and aid them as to attain to a happy Christian social order in respect to both body and soul, with all fullness and abounding plenty, to the praise and honor of God the Father, through Jesus Christ our Saviour. Amen.

Wittenberg, 1524.

PHILIPP MELANCHTHON

Luther's protégé and mainstay, Philipp Melanchthon, was born in 1497 at Bretten. After completing his education at Heidelberg and Tubingen, he arrived at Wittenberg in 1518—the year following Luther's protest—to become professor of Greek at age twenty-one.

As a youth, he had earlier gained such a reputation as a classics scholar, his mother's relative Johann Reuchlin, himself a renowned humanist educator, had honored Philipp by renaming him, changing his family name Schwarzerd, meaning "black earth," to its Greek equivalent. Erasmus had also taken note of the young Melanchthon.

From the outset of his teaching at Wittenberg, Melanchthon made it clear that, like other Christian humanists, he would seek for the meanings to be found in the Scriptures themselves, rather than in the commentaries. This openness to the primary importance of what the Bible says naturally attracted Luther to his younger colleague. That attraction was mutual.

As the aftershocks from Luther's revolt reverberated through Wittenberg, Melanchthon became Luther's principal supporter, almost his alter ego. During the period, in 1521, when Luther was confined to Wartburg castle, Melanchthon was his spokesman and catalyst for the still-fledgling Reformation.

When Luther's cause had been established, Melanchthon emerged as a guiding intellectual spirit in the ongoing Reformation. His work in 1528, in developing a public educational plan for the Reformed states in Germany, called *The Book of Visitation*, and his contribution to the writing of the 1530 Augsburg Confession—the historic Lutheran creed—were two of his most significant accomplishments. In addition to these must be reckoned his influence as an organizer of schools, author of textbooks, and intermediary between the often tactless Luther and those, like Erasmus, whom Melanchthon wished to retain as friends and brothers in the work of Christian education.

The Book of Visitation[17]

School Plan

Preachers also should exhort the people of their charge to send their children to school, so that they may be trained up to teach sound doctrine in the church, and to serve the state in a wise and able manner. Some imagine that it is enough for a teacher to understand German. But this is a misguided fancy. For he, who is to teach others, must have great practice and special aptitude; to gain this, he must have studied much, and from his youth up. . . .

In our day there are many abuses in children's schools. And it is that these abuses may be corrected, and that the young may have good instruction, that we have prepared this plan. In the first place, the teachers must be careful to teach the children Latin only, not German, nor Greek, nor Hebrew, as some have heretofore done, burdening the poor children with such a multiplicity of pursuits that are not only unproductive, but positively injurious. Such schoolmasters, we plainly see, do not think of the improvement of the children at all, but undertake so many languages solely to increase their own reputation. In the second place, teachers should not burden the children with too many books, but should rather avoid a needless variety. Thirdly, it is indispensable that the children be classified into distinct groups.

The First Group. The first group shall consist of those children who are learning to read. With these the following method is to be adopted: They are first to be taught the child's-manual, containing the alphabet, the creed, the Lord's prayer, and other prayers. When they have learned this, Donatus and Cato may both be given them; Donatus for a reading-book, and Cato they may explain after the following manner: The schoolmaster must give them the explanation of a verse or two, and then in a few hours call upon them to repeat what he has thus said; and in this way they will learn a great number of Latin words, and lay up a full store of phrases to use in speech. In this they should be exercised until they can read well. Neither do we consider it time lost, if the feebler children, who are not especially quick-witted, should read Cato and Donatus not once only, but a second time. With this they should be taught to write, and be required to show their writing to the schoolmaster every day. Another mode of enlarging their knowledge of Latin words is to give them every afternoon some words to commit to memory, as has been the custom in schools hitherto. These children must likewise be kept at music, and be made to sing with the others, as we shall show, God willing, further on.

The Second Group. The second group consists of children who have learned to read, and are now ready to go into grammar. With these the following regulations should be observed: The first hour after noon every day all the children, large and small, should be practiced in music. Then the schoolmaster must interpret to the second group the fables of Aesop. After vespers, he should explain to them the Paedology of Mosellanus; and, when this is finished, he should select from the Colloquies of Erasmus some that may conduce to their improvement and discipline. This should be repeated on the next evening also. When the children are about to go home for the night, some short sentence may be given them, taken perhaps from a poet, which they are to repeat the next morning, such as—*A true friend becomes manifest in adversity.* Or— *Fortune, if she fondles a man too much, makes him a fool.*—*The rabble value friendships by the profit they yield.*

In the morning the children are again to explain Aesop's fables. With this the teacher should decline some nouns or verbs, many or few, easy or difficult, according to the progress of the children, and then ask them the rules and the reasons for such inflection. And at the same time when they shall have learned the rules of construction, they should be required to *construe*, (parse) as it is called; this is a very useful exercise, and yet there are not many who employ it. . . .

The hour before mid-day must be invariably and exclusively devoted to instruction in grammar: first etymology, then syntax, and lastly prosody. And when the teacher has gone thus far through with the grammar, he should begin it again, and so on continually, that the children may understand it to perfection. For if there is negligence here, there is neither certainty nor stability in whatever is learned beside. And the children should learn by heart and repeat all the rules, so that they may be driven and forced, as it were, to learn the grammar well.

If such labor is irksome to the schoolmaster, as we often see, then we should dismiss him, and get another in his place,—one who will not shrink from the duty of keeping his pupils constantly in the grammar. For no greater injury can befall learning and the arts, than for youth to grow up in ignorance of grammar. . . .

The Third Group. Now, when these children have been well trained in grammar, those among them who have made the greatest proficiency should be taken out, and formed into a third group. The hour after mid-day they, together with the rest, are to devote to music. After this the teacher is to give an explanation of Vergil. When he has finished this, he may take up Ovid's "Metamorphoses," and the latter part of the afternoon Cicero's "offices," or "Letters to Friends." In the morning, Vergil may be reviewed, and the teacher, to keep up practice in the grammar, may call for constructions and inflections, and point out the prominent figures of speech.

The hour before mid-day, grammar should still be kept up, that the scholars may be thoroughly versed therein. And when they are perfectly familiar with etymology and syntax, then prosody *(metrica)* should be opened to them, so that they can thereby become accustomed to make verses. For this exercise is a very great help toward understanding the writings of others; and it likewise gives the boys a rich fund of words, and renders them accomplished in many ways. In course of time, after they have been sufficiently practiced in the grammar, this same hour is to be given to logic and rhetoric. The boys in the second and third groups are to be required every week to write compositions, either in the form of letters or of verses. They should also be rigidly confined to Latin conversation, and to this end the teachers themselves must, as far as possible, speak nothing but Latin with the boys; thus they will acquire the practice by use, and the more rapidly for the incentives held out to them.

JOHN CALVIN

A mong the Protestant Reformers, no name except for Martin Luther stands higher than that of John Calvin. Born in the French province of Picardy in 1509, Calvin first studied theology, then law, proving himself to be a man of great scholarly capacity. As a student at Paris, then later at Orleans, he met French "evangelicals," as supporters of Luther's movement were known. By 1534, he had experienced a personal conversion and announced himself to be one of them.

King Francis I of France was persecuting evangelicals, and so Calvin fled to Basel, Switzerland. There, in 1536, he published a defense of the evangelicals against charges of treason and argued that evangelicals were being punished without trial. All this was in a preface addressed to "the Most Mighty and Illustrious Monarch, Francis, Most Christian King of the French."

Then followed Calvin's masterpiece, *Institutes of the Christian Religion,* a systematic argument beginning with the knowledge of God and moving through an explanation of justification through faith in Jesus Christ. Calvin was to issue enlarged versions of the *Institutes,* the fifth and final edition appearing in 1559.

While awaiting publication of the *Institutes,* Calvin visited Geneva, where another earnest Reformer, Guillaume Farel, persuaded Calvin to remain as a teacher and later pastor. Thereafter, except for a three-year period of exile, Calvin's work centered in Geneva, where today a plaza and grand memorial recall his presence in that city. He set about creating a theocracy ruled by ministers, whose powers exceeded those of civil authorities. Under Calvin's governance, all citizens of Geneva were compelled to confess faith in Christ or face expulsion from the city. As one might expect, this rigorous legislation sometimes led to violent excesses, including the burning at the stake of Michael Servetus in 1553.

In 1558, Calvin called his friend Theodore Beza from his professorship in Greek at nearby Lausanne to assist him in founding an academy, the College de la Rive, in Geneva. Beza served as rector of the Geneva school, and later established himself as one of the principal New Testament scholars and translators of his time. Both Calvin and Beza had been educated in the scholastic tradition, from which they had been won, first, to the "New Learning," then to the evangelical and biblical faith Christian humanism espoused and demonstrated. Their conversion did nothing to discredit the importance of classical learning, and the academy Calvin founded and Beza administered became a thoroughgoing center of intellectual inquiry, governed by the Reformation's high view of Scripture.

An outline of the course of study shows the value Calvin placed upon knowledge as part of God's gift of common grace. The curriculum begins with the Class VII learning and writing of the alphabet, using a Latin-French reading book and concludes with the Class I learning of logic from an "approved compendium (such as Melanchthon's); the elements of rhetoric in connection with it, and elocution. . . . Once a week an Epistle of St. Paul or other apostle is read in Greek."[12]

Although strict and severe in his thought, Calvin was known by his friends and associates to be honest and loyal, humorous and loving— not at all the caricature drawn by those who have chosen to paint Calvin and Calvinism in brooding colors. His death was marked by no pomp whatever. He died as he had lived, a plain and simple servant of Jesus Christ.

Institutes of the Christian Religion[13] (Excerpt)

Book Two

The Knowledge of God the Redeemer in Christ, First Disclosed to the Fathers Under the Law, and Then to Us in the Gospel

Chapter 1

1. Wrong and right knowledge of self.

With good reason the ancient proverb strongly recommended knowledge of self to man. For if it is considered disgraceful for us not to know all that pertains to the business of human life, even more detestable is our ignorance of ourselves, by which, when making decisions in necessary matters, we miserably deceive and even blind ourselves!

But since this precept is so valuable, we ought more diligently to avoid applying it perversely. This, we observe, has happened to certain philosophers, who, while urging man to know himself, propose the goal of recognizing his own worth and excellence.

And they would have him contemplate in himself nothing but what swells him with empty assurance and puffs him up with pride (Genesis 1:27). . . .

But that primal worthiness cannot come to mind without the sorry spectacle of our foulness and dishonor presenting itself by way of contrast, since in the person of the first man we have fallen from our original condition. From this source arise abhorrence and displeasure with ourselves, as well as true humility; and thence is kindled a new zeal to seek God, in whom each of us may recover those good things which we have utterly and completely lost. . . .

Chapter 2

14. Understanding as regards art and science

Then follow the arts, both liberal and manual. The power of human acuteness also appears in learning these because all of us have a certain aptitude. But although not all the arts are suitable for everyone to learn, yet it is a certain enough indication of the common energy that hardly anyone is to be found who does not manifest talent in some art. There are at hand energy and ability not only to learn but also to devise something new in each art or to perfect and polish what one has learned from a predecessor. This prompted Plato to teach wrongly that such apprehension is nothing but recollection. Hence, with good reason we are compelled to confess that its beginning is inborn in human nature. Therefore this evidence clearly testifies to a universal apprehension of reason and understanding by nature implanted in men. Yet so universal is this good that every man ought to recognize for himself in it the peculiar grace of God. . . . Now the discovery of systematic transmission of the arts, or the inner and more excellent knowledge of them, which is characteristic of few, is not a sufficient proof of common discernment. Yet because it is bestowed indiscriminately upon pious and impious, it is rightly counted among natural gifts.

15. Science as God's gift

Whenever we come upon these matters in secular writers, let that admirable light of truth shining in them teach us that the mind of man, though fallen and perverted from its wholeness, is nevertheless clothed and ornamented with God's excellent gifts. If we regard the Spirit of God as the sole fountain of truth, we shall neither reject the truth itself, nor despise it wherever it shall appear, unless we wish to dishonor the Spirit of God. For by holding the gifts of the Spirit in slight esteem, we condemn and reproach the Spirit himself. What then? Shall we deny that the truth shone upon the ancient jurists who established civic order and discipline with such great equity? Shall we say that the philosophers were blind in their fine observation and artful description of nature? Shall we say that those men were devoid of understanding who conceived the art of disputation and taught us to speak reasonably? Shall we say that they are insane who developed medicine, devoting their labor to our benefit? What shall we say of all the mathematical sciences? Shall we consider them the ravings of madmen? No, we cannot read the writings of the ancients on these subjects without great admiration. We marvel at them because we are compelled to recognize how preeminent they are. But shall we count anything praiseworthy or noble without recognizing at the same time that it comes from God? Let us be ashamed of such ingratitude, into which not even the pagan poets fell, for they confessed that the gods had invented philosophy, laws, and all useful arts. Those men whom Scripture (I Corinthians 2:14) calls "natural men" were, indeed, sharp and penetrating in their investigation of inferior things. Let us, accordingly, learn by their example how many gifts the Lord left to human nature even after it was despoiled of its true good.

16. *Human competence in art and science also derives from the Spirit of God.*

Meanwhile, we ought not to forget those most excellent benefits of the divine Spirit, which he distributes to whomever he wills, for the common good of mankind. The understanding and knowledge of Bezalel and Oholiab, needed to construct the Tabernacle, had to be instilled in them by the Spirit of God (Exodus 31:2–11; 35:30–35). It is no wonder, then, that the knowledge of all that is most excellent in human life is said to be communicated to us through the Spirit of God. Nor is there reason for anyone to ask, What have the impious, who are utterly estranged from God, to do with his Spirit? We ought to understand the statement that the Spirit of God dwells only in believers (Romans 8:9) as referring to the Spirit of sanctification through whom we are consecrated as temples to God (1 Corinthians 3:16). Nonetheless he fills, moves, and quickens all things by the power of the same Spirit, and does so according to the character that he bestowed upon each kind by the law of creation. But if the Lord has willed that we be helped in physics, dialectic, mathematics, and other like disciplines, by the work and ministry of the ungodly, let us use this assistance. For if we neglect God's gift freely offered in these arts, we ought to suffer just punishment for our sloths. But lest anyone think a man truly blessed when he is credited with possessing great power to comprehend truth under the elements of this world (cf. Colossians 2:8), we should at once add that all this capacity to understand, with the understanding that follows upon it, is an unstable and transitory thing in God's sight, when a solid foundation of truth does not underlie it. . . .

17. Summary of 12–16

To sum up: We see among all mankind that reason is proper to our nature; it distinguishes us from brute beasts, just as they by possessing feeling differ from inanimate things. Now, because some are born fools or stupid, that defect does not obscure the general grace of God. Rather, we are warned by that spectacle that we ought to ascribe what is left in us to God's kindness. For if he had not spared us, our fall would have entailed the destruction of our whole nature. Some men excel in keenness; others are superior in judgment; still others have a readier wit to learn this or that art. In this variety God commends his grace to us, lest anyone should claim as his own what flowed from the sheer bounty of God. For why is one person more excellent than another? Is it not to display in common nature God's special grace, which, in passing many by, declares itself bound to none? Besides this, God inspires special activities, in accordance with each man's calling. . . .

PART V
THE ROOTS OF
MODERN UNIVERSAL
SCHOOLING

The end, then, of learning is to repair the ruins of our first parents by regaining to know God aright . . .

John Milton
"Of Education," 1644

THE ROOTS OF
MODERN UNIVERSAL
SCHOOLING

I n England the dominant influences upon the English Reformation in the sixteenth and seventeenth centuries were the reigning monarchs of the period: Henry VIII, his son Edward VI, daughters Mary and Elizabeth I, and the latter's successor, James I. Each of these sovereigns, for better or for worse, influenced education. But there were others less regal who also contributed significantly to educational reform, especially in the cause of universal and compulsory schooling for all. Some were still pioneering for fundamental education reforms well into the nineteenth century.

Throughout the sixteenth century, as the Reformation overtook Europe, England's rulers played tug-of-war with religious freedom, now granting, now withdrawing the right of private judgment and decisions regarding faith and practice in the Tudor realm. Meanwhile on the European continent, especially in those parts of Europe outside the spheres controlled by Luther and Calvin, established religion succumbed to counter-Reformation excesses. But no imperial power could stifle the inevitable movement toward intellectual freedom that had accompanied the outcry against a tyrannical papacy.

The attitude that ultimately revealed itself as a state-sponsored approval of educational opportunity for all, without regard to class or even gender, had begun in those small details regarding the education of the landed gentry, the members of court, and of royalty themselves. Such matters as whether or not beatings administered by schoolmasters were appropriate; disputes as to whether instruction should be carried on primarily in Latin or in the nation's vernacular could not have become significant if, first, the whole question of the significance of formal schooling had not been met and resolved.

Furthermore, as we shall see, in both Europe and America, the eventual development of formal schooling—from a governess in the nursery and a tutor in the home to a schoolmaster in a "public" school such as Eton, Harrow, or Winchester, and on to the "common" or state-sponsored school—was assisted by allied forces in the Christian church.

First, leaders realized that an open Bible was of no use unless it could be read by everyone; thus the church recognized an obligation to provide such instruction in literacy to all. Here the Canons of Dordt set a precedent; soon thereafter, the name of John Amos Comenius, "The Father of Modern Education," became identified with the cause of schooling for purposes of discipleship. While the American colonists were making their first attempts at formal schooling, this exiled bishop of the Moravian Church was writing the most influential treatise on education since Plato's *Republic*. Like other Christian leaders before him, Comenius called for a literate society so as to insure a believing church capable of reading the Scriptures. But in *The Great Didactic*, completed in 1632, Comenius went beyond all but a few of his predecessors in calling for universal compulsory education for all, without regard for religion, girls as well as boys.

The schools Comenius envisioned, and helped to inaugurate in Poland, Sweden, and England anticipated our present system, offering an educational opportunity for all children. His plan consisted of infant or nursery schools leading to what we know as kindergarten; then a vernacular or primary school for the teaching of the native language; finally, a Latin school in preparation for university. But always, at the root of his system, was Comenius' desire that children should learn to read God's Word.

Second, the springing up of Sunday schools and other similar agencies of the Christian church made some form of free schooling available to those whose poverty disallowed them from attending tuition-charging schools. In many villages and towns, a Sunday school existed before any common or public school was founded. In fact, the purpose of the Sunday school in England, where Robert Raikes began Sunday school in 1780, and in the American imitation of his model, was not exclusively for Christian indoctrination; the intention was that rudimentary teaching of reading and writing would be enhanced by using the Bible and other religious literature. Where the Sunday school thrived, it subsequently expanded to occupy other days of the week and with a wider curriculum; so the common school grew out of the evangelical Sunday school movement.

Third, the call for equal educational opportunity for girls and women contributed to equal advancement in social, professional, and political spheres. From Hannah More in England the message was carried to America; thereafter, a Christian summons consistently reminded the male-dominated society that God's call to service and submission applies equally to both genders and without favor.

THOMAS ELYOT

An almost exact contemporary of King Henry VIII, Thomas Elyot (ca. 1490–1546) was the son of Sir Richard Elyot, a judge of common pleas whose family belonged to the social class called landed gentry. Thomas Elyot himself served in various local offices until his acquaintance with Thomas More and Thomas Cromwell, More's antagonist and eventual successor as chancellor of England, granted Elyot rapid political advancement.

Knighted in 1530, Elyot was appointed ambassador to the court of Charles V, who had claimed the throne of the Holy Roman Empire since 1516. Elyot was later elected to Parliament, representing a district near Cambridge.

In short, while not a member of royalty or the aristocracy, Elyot was nonetheless a "governor," one of the ruling class responsible for the welfare of the state. His work, *The Book Named the Governor*, published in 1531, attempts to outline the means by which a young man like himself, destined to be a public official, might be properly educated and prepared for those responsibilities.

The Book Named the Governor is notable for several reasons. First, the author was not formally educated, claiming to have been his own teacher since the age of twelve; yet he calls for a severely formal system. C. S. Lewis says of Elyot: "Like all his kind he issues rigid instructions which would be scattered to the winds by ten minutes' experience of any real child or any real nurse."[1] Then Lewis notes that, ironically, Elyot died without children of his own.

At the same time, Elyot grants considerable breadth to what he considers to be worthwhile instruction: not just grammar, rhetoric, and the classics, but also painting and sculpture, dance and sport, exercises and games, although Elyot is also firmly opposed to gambling and dangerous sport such as football or soccer.

Most important, however, is the fact that Elyot's book is written in English, the first such book on education to be published in the vernacular. Dedicated to King Henry VIII, Elyot's *The Book Named the Governor* shows its author to have been at least conventionally religious and loyal at a time when to be otherwise meant death.

The Book Named the Governor has survived for more than four centuries; its influence was markedly apparent in the British school system, as well as in those American preparatory schools patterned after the British. A few excerpts follow.

The Book Named the Governor (Excerpt)

V. The Order of Learning that a Nobleman Should Be Trained in Before He Comes to the Age of Seven Years.

Some old authors hold opinion that, before the age of seven years, a child should not be instructed in letters; but those writers were either Greeks or Latins, among whom all doctrine and sciences were in their maternal tongues, by reason whereof they saved all that long time which at this day is spent in understanding perfectly the Greek or Latin. Wherefore it requireth not a longer time to the understanding of both. Therefore that infelicity of our time and country compelleth us to encroach somewhat on the years of children, and specially of noblemen, that they may sooner attain to wisdom and gravity than private persons, considering, as I have said, their charge and example, which above all things is most to be esteemed. . . .

XVII. Exercises Whereby Should Grow Both Recreation and Profit

Wrestling is a very good exercise in the beginning of youth, so that it be with one that is equal in strength, or somewhat under, and that the place be soft, that in falling their bodies be not bruised. . . .

Also running is both a good exercise and a laudable solace. . . . There is an exercise which is right profitable in extreme danger of wars, but because there seemeth to be some peril in the learning thereof, and also it hath not been of long time much used, specially among noblemen, perchance some readers will little esteem it, I mean swimming. . . .

XXVII. That Shooting in a Long-Bow Is Principal of All Other Exercises.

. . . Tennis, seldom used, and for a little space, is a good exercise for young men, but it is more violent than shooting, by reason that two men do play. Wherefore neither of them is at his own liberty to measure the exercise. For if the one strike the ball hard, the other that intendeth to receive him is then constrained to use semblable violence if he will return the ball from whence it came to him. If it trill fast on the ground, and he intendeth to stop, or if it rebound a great distance from him, and he would [soon] return it, he cannot then keep any measure of swiftness of motion.

. . . In like wise football, wherein is nothing but beastly fury and extreme violence; whereof proceedeth hurt, and consequently rancor and malice do remain with them that be wounded; whereof it is to be put in perpetual silence. . . .

ROGER ASCHAM

A second book on education written in English appeared in 1570, two years after its author's death. Roger Ascham had been among the most respected teachers in England, so that his book *The Schoolmaster* was given wide reading and acceptance.

Born near York in 1515, Ascham received his education at St. John's College, Cambridge, where he was elected a fellow and subsequently served as a teacher of Greek at a salary of four pounds sterling per year. Unable to subsist on that pittance, he found other means of income, writing a book on archery, *Toxophilus*, published in 1545, and wisely dedicated to King Henry VIII, an avid archer himself. The king rewarded Ascham with a grant of ten pounds per year, a more nearly reasonable stipend. In 1548, Ascham was appointed private tutor to the fifteen-year-old Princess Elizabeth, whom he found to be among the brightest pupils he ever taught, excelling beyond her half-brother Edward, whom Ascham also taught.

Ascham's mastery of Latin equipped him for royal service as secretary to the English ambassador to the court of Charles V, a post he held from 1550 to 1553. While on the Continent, Ascham observed the Protestant Reformation in action and returned to England convinced, for more than nationalistic reasons, that Protestantism was a necessary corrective to papal apostasy.

But this was a dangerous time to be an avowed Protestant, because the new sovereign of England was the older daughter of Henry VIII, the Roman Catholic Mary, who in 1553, succeeded to the throne upon the death of her half-brother Edward VI.

Mary's treatment of English Protestants was to earn her the nickname "Bloody Mary." Yet Mary appointed Ascham as her Latin Secretary, which meant that he was responsible for the drawing up of royal and state correspondence. When, in 1558, his former pupil Elizabeth succeeded her half-sister, she continued Ascham's appointment as her secretary; he held this position until he died.

In 1563, Ascham records, he was present at a conversation among various courtiers during which the beating of schoolboys was discussed.

Apparently, several boys had run away from Eton, fearful of being beaten, a common practice in schools at that time. One of those courtiers, Sir Richard Sackville, asked Ascham to write a treatise on education showing how other means than beating might achieve the desired ends.

Ascham's manuscript for *The Schoolmaster* may have been completed by 1564, but it remained unpublished until his widow Margaret brought it out. The book reveals both the educator's experience and the Christian's compassion for others. Ascham knew the scriptural warnings against sparing the rod and spoiling the child; he also knew the human tendency toward cruelty and excess in corporal punishment. With manifestly divine understanding and common sense, Ascham explained "why, in mine opinion, love is fitter than fear, gentleness better than beating, to bring up a child rightly in learning."

Ascham's work bears careful reading, especially among those in Christian schooling who have appropriated to themselves the right of parents to administer corporal punishment. In certain Christian schools, it is a policy maintained as an alleged biblical distinctive; indeed, some Christian school personnel regard it as a measure of orthodoxy.

"God keep us in his fear," Ascham wrote. "God graft in us the true knowledge of his word, with a forward will to follow it." Then and only then, Ascham declared, "shall he preserve us by his grace from all manner of terrible days."

*The Schoolmaster*² (Excerpt)

In writing this book, I have had earnest respect to three special points: truth of religion, honesty in living, right order in learning. In which three ways, I pray God, my poor children may diligently walk, for whose sake, as nature moved, and reason required, and necessity also somewhat compelled, I was the willinger to take these pains.

For seeing at my death I am not like to leave them any great store of living, therefore in my lifetime I thought good to bequeath unto them in this little book, as in my will and testament, the right way to good learning, which if they follow with the fear of God, they shall very well come to sufficiency of living.

I wish also with all my heart that young Master Robert Sackville may take that fruit of this labor that his worthy grandfather purposed he should have done, and if any other do take either profit or pleasure hereby, they have cause to thank Master Robert Sackville, for whom specially this my *Schoolmaster* was provided.

And one thing I would have the reader consider in reading this book, that because no schoolmaster hath charge of any child before he enter into his school, therefore, [in] leaving all former care of their good bringing-up to wise and good parents as a matter not belonging to the schoolmaster, I do appoint this my schoolmaster then and there to begin where his office and charge beginneth. Which charge lasteth not long, but until the scholar be made able to go to the university, to proceed in logic, rhetoric, and other kinds of learning. . . .

Farewell in Christ.

. . . With the common use of teaching and beating in common schools of England I will not greatly contend; which if I did, it were but a small grammatical controversy neither belonging to heresy nor treason nor greatly touching God nor the prince, although, in very deed, in the end the good or ill bringing-up of children doth as much serve to the good or ill service of God, our prince, and our whole country as any one thing doth beside.

I do gladly agree with all good schoolmasters in these points: to have children brought to good perfectness in learning, to all honesty in manners; to have all faults rightly amended; to have every vice severely corrected; but for the order and way that leadeth rightly to these points we somewhat differ. For commonly many schoolmasters, some, as I have seen, more, as I have heard tell, be of so crooked nature as, when they meet with a hard-witted scholar, they rather break him than bow him, rather mar him than mend him. For when the schoolmaster is angry with some other matter, then will he soonest fall to beat his scholar, and though he himself should be punished for his folly, yet must he beat some scholar for his pleasure, though there be no cause for him to do so nor yet fault in the scholar to deserve so. These, ye will say, be fond to schoolmasters, and few they be that be found to be such. They be fond indeed, but surely overmany such be found everywhere. But this will I say, that even the wisest of your great beaters do as oft punish nature as they do correct faults. Yea, many times the better nature is sorer punished, for if one by quickness of wit take his lesson readily, another, by hardness of wit, taketh it not so speedily, the first is always commended, the other is commonly punished, when a wise schoolmaster should rather discreetly consider the right disposition of both their natures and not so much weigh what either of them is able to do now as what either of them is likely to do hereafter. For this I know, not only by reading of books in my study but also by experience of life abroad in the world, that those which be commonly the wisest, the best learned, and best men also, when they be old, were never commonly the quickest of wit when they were young. The causes why, amongst other, which be many, that move me thus to think, be these few which I will reckon. Quick wits commonly be apt to take, unapt to keep; soon hot and desirous of this and that, as cold and soon weary of the same again; more quick to enter speedily than able to pierce far, even like oversharp tools, whose edges be very soon turned. Such wits delight themselves in easy and pleasant studies and never pass far forward in high and hard sciences. And therefore the quickest wits commonly may prove the best poets but not the wisest orators—ready of tongue to speak boldly, not deep of judgment either for good counsel or wise writing. Also, for manners and life quick wits commonly be in desire newfangled, in purpose unconstant; light to promise anything, ready to forget everything, both benefit and injury, and thereby neither fast to friend nor fearful to foe; inquisitive of every trifle, not secret in greatest affairs; bold with any person, busy in every matter; soothing such as be present, nipping any that is absent; of nature, also, always flattering their betters, envying their equals, despising their inferiors; and by quickness of wit very quick and ready to like none so well as themselves.

Moreover, commonly men very quick of wit be also very light of conditions and thereby very ready of disposition to be carried overquickly by any light company to any riot and unthriftiness when they be young, and therefore seldom either honest of life or rich in living when they be old. For quick in wit and light in manners be either seldom troubled or very soon weary in carrying a very heavy purse. Quick wits also be, in most part of all their doings, overquick, hasty, rash, heady, and brainsick. These two last words, *heavy* and *brainsick*, be fit and proper words, rising naturally of the matter and termed aptly by the condition of overmuch quickness of wit. In youth also they be ready scoffers, privy mockers, and ever over light and merry. In age, soon testy, very waspish, and always overmiserable. And yet few of them come to any great age by reason of their misordered life when they were young, but a great deal fewer of them come to show any great countenance or bear any great authority abroad in the world, but either live obscurely, men know not how, or die obscurely, men mark not when. They be like trees that show forth fair blossoms and broad leaves in springtime, but bring out small and not long lasting fruit in harvest time, and that only such as fall and rot before they be ripe and so never, or seldom, come to any good at all. . . .

Some wits, moderate enough by nature, be many times marred by overmuch study and use of some sciences, namely, music, arithmetic, and geometry. These sciences, as they sharpen men's wits overmuch, so they change men's manners oversore, if they be not moderately mingled and wisely applied to some good use of life. Mark all mathematical heads which be only and wholly bent to those sciences, how solitary they be themselves, how unfit to live with others, and how unapt to serve in the world. This is not only known now by common experience, but uttered long before by wise men's judgment and sentence. Galen saith, "Much music marreth men's manners," and Plato hath a notable place of the same thing in his books *The Republic*, well marked also and excellently translated by Tully himself. . . .

Contrariwise, a wit in youth that is not overdull, heavy, knotty, and lumpish, but hard, rough, and though somewhat staffish . . . such a wit, I say, if be at first well handled by the mother and rightly smoothed and wrought as it should, not overthwartly and against the wood, by the schoolmaster, both for learning and whole course of living proveth always the best. In wood and stone, not the softest, but hardest, be always aptest for portraiture, both fairest for pleasure and most durable for profit. Hard wits be hard to receive but sure to keep, painful without weariness, heedful without wavering, constant without newfangledness; bearing heavy things, though not lightly, yet willingly; entering hard things, though not easily, yet deeply; and so come to that perfectness of learning in the end that quick wits seem in hope, but do not in deed, or else very seldom, ever attain unto. Also, for manners and life hard wits commonly are hardly carried either to desire every new thing or else to marvel at every strange thing, and therefore they be careful and diligent in their own matters, not urious and busy in other men's affairs; and so they become wise themselves and also are counted honest by others. . . .

Roger Ascham, *The Schoolmaster*, ed. Lawrence V. Ryan. Ithaca, N.Y.: Cornell Univ., 1967. Reprinted by permission of the Folger Shakespeare Library.

THE ENGLISH BIBLE:
THE KING JAMES VERSION,
1611

U ntil recent decades and the suppression of Bible reading in public schools, no other literature had so great and pervasive an
influence upon the shaping of education as had the English Bible, the King James Version in particular.

Today, when biblical ignorance seems so rife, words and phrases—
whose origins in the text of the King James Bible may not even be recognized—slip into common conversation and public dialogue unaware.
Even in Christian schools, where the study of the Scriptures is still encouraged, modern translations may have replaced the 1611 version; so
that students and younger teachers alike are unaware of its phrasing or
history. Thus it is important here that we not ignore the development of
the text that for more than three hundred years *was* the Word of God in
English.

From the time of John Wyclif, as we have seen, Christians in England had struggled to produce a Bible in their own language. The first
to do so, William Tyndale, fled from England in 1524, under threat of
death if he persisted in his plan to publish a Bible in the vernacular. In
1525, his English translation was published in Germany and, the next
year, smuggled back to England, where both the book and its translator
were condemned. Expeditions were sent from England to Belgium,
where Tyndale lived in exile, attempting to bring him back for trial.
Eventually Tyndale was betrayed, arrested, held in prison near Brussels,
and in October 1536, he was strangled and his body burned.

Yet Tyndale's work was not in vain, for its influence is most apparent upon the translation of Miles Coverdale, which Coverdale published
in 1535. This translation received the sponsorship of Thomas Cromwell,
ecclesiastical adviser to King Henry VIII. Copies were distributed without threat of violence; even the queen, Anne Boleyn, accepted a personal copy. Her husband, Henry VIII, however, was no friend of the
English Bible. Perhaps Henry felt that Coverdale and his Bibles had a
corrupting effect on his realm—especially on Queen Anne, whom he
had beheaded in 1536.

Intolerant of any threat to his sovereign ego, the king's position was that the Bible in the common language of the people constituted a subversion to his authority. Such a Bible, able to be read by anyone literate in English, would produce unending disputes; it would encourage the opposition of those who found in its pages points of difference from official doctrine. In short, taken seriously, the Bible in English—or any other popular language—could only be a source of probable hostility between those in and those out of power.

Nonetheless, in 1539, Coverdale produced a revised translation known as "The Great Bible" because of its oversized pages. The psalms in this translation were subsequently incorporated into the 1549 *Book of Common Prayer*. By 1543, the king had became so desperate, he instituted an act of Parliament forbidding the reading of the Bible by any man below the rank of gentleman and by any woman. The penalty for violating this law seemed unusually fearsome: death by hanging.

During the brief reign of "Bloody Mary," which lasted from 1553 until 1558, English Protestants who had escaped to the safety of John Calvin's Geneva decided to issue a genuinely Protestant Bible. Coverdale was among them. The Geneva Bible, published in 1560, was of smaller size and for the first time offered verse numbers. This version remained popular well after the so-called "Authorized Version" of 1611 had appeared. Indeed, it was the Geneva Bible, not the King James Version, that was familiar to the great English writers of the late sixteenth and early seventeenth centuries—Shakespeare, Marlowe, Bunyan, Milton, and the rest.

As a leading spokesman for English Puritanism, Coverdale refused to align himself with the bishops of the Church of England, who in 1568, brought out their approved edition. In 1571, it officially replaced any other version in the Anglican church, but this so-called "Bishops' Bible" never received the popular acceptance already accorded the Geneva Bible.

Meanwhile, English Roman Catholics, dissatisfied with previous versions because of their prefaces and marginal notes, sought to produce their own translation. Exiled by Queen Elizabeth I through her edicts against Roman Catholicism, English scholars fled to Flanders, where colleges were established at Douai. There a new translation of the New Testament from the Vulgate of Jerome was begun around 1578; but the work was completed at Reims, France, in 1582. The Old Testament, published in 1609, finished the project thereafter known as the Douai-Reims Bible, sanctioned for use by English-speaking Roman Catholics.

But at this very time, yet another English version was underway. In 1604, general dissatisfaction with the "Bishops' Bible" and the presence of a new and lively monarch, James I, prompted John Reynolds, a Puritan scholar at Oxford, to propose a new revision of the Bible. Under King James' orders, a group of some fifty scholars was appointed to take the best from all previous versions—including Tyndale's—and create an "authorized version." Their work, begun in 1607, resulted in the 1611 text, never actually authorized by an official royal decree, though known universally as the highest achievement in the English language, the King James Version.

Its preface, probably written by one Miles Smith, who had supervised the printing of the Bible, may seem like only an over-flowery tribute to the king; but it also contains important references to the many previous suppressions of the English Bible and to the risks undertaken by those who had done this work, in hopes that the king's approval will protect them and their work from "the censures of illmeaning and discontented persons," as well as from "Popish Persons at home or abroad, who therefore will malign us, because we are poor instruments to make God's holy Truth to be yet more and more known unto the people, whom they desire to keep in ignorance and darkness."

The preface merits close reading because it also speaks of the exact nature of this revision: Not precisely a new translation but a compilation of the best texts available, based on "the Original Sacred Tongues, together with comparing of the labours, both in our own, and other foreign Languages, of many worthy men who went before us." Reading the preface in its entirety might have the further salutary effect of reminding some earnest and devout Christians that, however precious and divinely guarded the King James Version may be, it is still a human work, not the autographed manuscripts of God's Word in His own handwriting.

An excerpt from the preface follows.

"Preface to the 1611 version of the English Bible" (Excerpt)

To the most high and mighty prince
James,
by the grace of God,
king of Great Britain, France, and Ireland, defender of the faith,
The translators of the Bible wish Grace, Mercy, and Peace,
through Jesus Christ our Lord.

Great and manifold were the blessings, most dread Sovereign, which Almighty God, the Father of all mercies, bestowed upon us the people of England when first he sent Your Majesty's Royal Person to rule and reign over us. . . .

But among all our joys, there was no one that more filled our hearts, than the blessed continuance of the preaching of God's sacred Word among us; which is that inestimable treasure, which excelleth all the riches of the earth; because the fruit thereof extendeth itself, not only to the time spent in this transitory world, but directeth and disposeth men unto that eternal happiness which is above in heaven. . . .

. . . And this their contentment doth not diminish or decay, but every day increaseth and taketh strength, when they observe, that the zeal of Your Majesty toward the house of God doth not slack or go backward, but is more and more kindled, manifesting itself abroad in the farthest parts of Christendom, by writing a defence of the Truth, (which hath given such a blow unto that man of sin, as will not be healed,) and every day at home, by religious and learned discourse by frequenting the house of God, by hearing the Word preached, by cherishing the Teachers thereof, by caring for the Church, as a most tender and loving nursing Father.

There are infinite arguments of this right Christian and religious affection in Your Majesty; but none is more forcible to declare it to others than the vehement and perpetuated desire of accomplishing and publishing this work, which now with all humility we present unto Your Majesty. . . .

And now at last, by the mercy of God, and the continuance of our labours, it being brought unto such a conclusion, as that we have great hopes that the Church of England shall reap good fruit thereby; we hold it our duty to offer it to your Majesty, not only as our King and Sovereign, but as to the principal Mover and Author of the work; humbly craving of Your most Sacred Majesty, that since things of this quality have ever been subject to the censures of illmeaning and discontented persons, it may receive approbation and patronage from so learned and judicious a Prince as Your Highness is, whose allowance and acceptance of our labours shall more honor and encourage us, than all the calumniations and hard interpretations of other men shall dismay us. . . .

LEADERS OF THE
DUTCH REFORMED CHURCH

I n the Netherlands, the Dutch Reformed Church struggled into existence under dire persecution. Holland belonged to the empire ruled by the Holy Roman Emperor Charles V, a defender of the papacy and archenemy of Luther and Calvin. Imperial edicts and their violation led to much bloodshed in the 1520s and 1530s. Still the Reformation grew, and with it Holland's desire to be free from Spain.

In 1559, the year in which Calvin published the final edition of his *Institutes,* Holland's Prince William I called for the cessation of Spanish rule. Further violence followed, including William's assassination in 1584; yet by that time, a Protestant church in Holland was certain.

During the period of strife, Dutch leaders had convened synods, or church councils, in exile as early as 1568. But the great synod of Dordt, held at Dordrecht from November 1618 to May 1619, established the ecclesiastical law and convictions of the Dutch Reformed Church. Among these canons were several having to do specifically with education. These are the famous Canons of Dordt, still observed in large measure, especially by the Christian Reformed Church.

Canons of Dordt (Excerpt)

In order that the Christian youth may be diligently instructed in the principles of religion, and be trained in piety, three modes of catechising should be employed.

I. In the House, by Parents.
II. In the Schools, by Schoolmasters.
III. In the Churches, by Ministers, Elders, and Catechists, especially appointed for the purpose.

That these may diligently employ their trust, the Christian magistrates shall be requested to promote, by their authority, so sacred and necessary a work; and all who have the oversight of churches and schools shall be required to pay special attention to this matter.

I. Parents. The office of Parents is diligently to instruct their children and their whole household in the principles of the Christian religion, in a manner adapted to their respective capacities; earnestly and carefully to admonish them to the cultivation of true piety; to engage their punctual attendance on family worship, and take them with them to the hearing of the Word of God. They should require their children to give an account of the sermons they hear, especially those on the Catechism; assign them some chapters of Scripture to read, and certain passages to commit to memory; and then impress and illustrate the truths contained in them in a familiar manner, adapted to the tenderness of youth. Thus they are to prepare them for being catechised in the schools, and by attendance on these to encourage them and promote their edification. Parents are to be exhorted to the faithful discharge of this duty, by the public preaching of the Word; but specially at the ordinary period of family visitation, previous to the administration of the Lord's Supper; and also at other times by the minister, elders, etc. Parents who profess religion, and are negligent in this work, shall be faithfully admonished by the ministers; and, if the case requires it, they shall be censured by the Consistory, that they may be brought to the discharge of their duty.

II. Schools. Schools, in which the young shall be properly instructed in the principles of Christian doctrine, shall be instituted, not only in cities but also in towns and country places where heretofore none have existed. The Christian magistracy shall be requested that well-qualified persons may be employed and enabled to devote themselves to the service; and especially that the children of the poor may be gratuitously instructed, and not be excluded from the benefit of the schools. In this office none shall be employed but such as are members of the Reformed Church, having certificates of an upright faith and pious life, and of being well versed in the truths of the Catechism. They are to sign a document, professing their belief in the Confession of Faith and the Heidelberg Catechism, and promising that they will give catechetical instruction to the youth in the principles of Christian truth according to the same. The schoolmasters shall instruct their scholars according to their age and capacity, at least two days in the week, not only causing them to commit to memory, but also by instilling into their minds an acquaintance with the truths of the Catechism. (An elementary small Catechism, the Compendium, and the Heidelberg Catechism, are those specified to be used by the different grades of children and youth.) The schoolmasters shall take care not only that the scholars commit these Catechisms to memory, but that they shall suitably understand the doctrines contained in them. For this purpose, they shall suitably explain to every one, in a manner adapted to his capacity, and frequently inquire if they understand them. The schoolmasters shall bring every one of the pupils committed to their charge to the hearing of the preached Word, and particularly the preaching on the Catechism, and require from them an account of the same.

III. Ministerial Supervision. In order that due knowledge may be obtained of the diligence of the schoolmasters, and the improvement of the youth, it shall be the duty of the Masters, with an Elder, and, if necessary, with a magistrate, to visit all the schools, private as well as public, frequently, in order to excite the teachers to earnest diligence, to encourage and counsel them in the duty of catechising, and to furnish an example by questioning them, addressing them in a friendly and affectionate manner, and exciting them to early piety and diligence. If any of the schoolmasters should be found neglectful or perverse, they shall be earnestly admonished by the ministers, and if necessary, by the Consistory, in relation to their office. The ministers, in the discharge of their public duty in the Church, shall preach on the Catechism. These sermons shall be comparatively short, and accommodated, as far as practicable, to the comprehension of children as well as adults. . . . It shall be the duty of a minister to go, with an elder, to all capable of instruction, and collect them in their houses, the Consistory chamber, or some other suitable place (a number particularly of those more advanced in years), and explain familiarly to them, the articles of the Christian faith, and catechise them according to the circumstances of their different capacities, progress, and knowledge. They shall question them on the matter of the public sermons on the Catechism. . . . The ministers shall employ diligent care to ascertain those who give any hopeful evidence of serious concern for the salvation of their soul, and invite them to them; assembling those together who have like impressions, and encouraging to friendly intercourse and free conversation with each other. These meetings shall commence with appropriate prayer and exhortation. If all this shall be done by the ministers with that cordiality, faithfulness, zeal, and discretion that become those that must give an account of the flock committed to their charge, it is not to be doubted that in a short time abundant fruit of their labors shall be found in growth in religious knowledge, and holiness of life, to the glory of God, and the prosperity of the Church.

JOHN AMOS COMENIUS

Jan Amos Komensky (1592–1670) was born in Moravia (part of the former Czechoslovakia). He completed university studies at Heidelberg, where his name became Latinized, and returned to Moravia and became a pastor among a sect known as the *Unitas Fratrum*, or Bohemian Brethren. But the Thirty Years' War (1618–48) and its persecution of Protestants in much of Central Europe drove Comenius and his family into exile.

During his years of wandering, Comenius turned his attention to problems he saw in education. Like other Christian leaders before him, John Amos Comenius recognized that a literate society was needed to ensure a believing church capable of reading the Bible. So his educational ideal became a system of schools where such a literate and reasoning society could be formed, where the Scriptures and Christian doctrine could be taught and understood.

But Comenius differed in method from the accepted customs of instruction for his day. He put great stock, for instance, in teaching the native language first, rather than Latin or Greek; he believed in the power of the eye to teach the mind and so wrote the first illustrated primer, *The Visible World in Pictures*, published in 1658.

But his greatest achievements in writing were *The School of Infancy* and *The Great Didactic*, completed in 1632 but not published until 1657 in Poland, where Comenius was pastor to Moravian exiles. In these works, Comenius challenges parents to be their children's first teachers. He also goes beyond all but a few of his predecessors in calling for universal compulsory education for all, without regard for religion or class or gender: "Not the children of the rich or of the powerful only, but of all alike, boys and girls, noble and ignoble, rich and poor, in all cities and towns, villages and hamlets, should be sent to school."

Furthermore, while his educational reforms might seem like commonplace wisdom today—for instance, "Nothing to be memorized until it is understood"—such ideas were entirely unconventional in their time. Comenius advocated, as did Sir Francis Bacon, the acquisition of all knowledge or *pansophia*, yet not for reasons of intellectual arrogance.

"God does not call us to heaven," wrote Comenius, "asking us smart questions. It is more profitable to know things humbly than to know them proudly."[3]

Comenius was no blind idealist; he saw education as a necessity but not a panacea. His faith was in God, not in education, and he warned against the trend common in parents today who abdicate their own responsibilities for the moral instruction of their children, preferring to leave it all to the schools. As he wrote in *The School of Infancy*: "Let not parents, therefore, devolve the whole instruction of their children upon teachers of schools and ministers of the church. It is impossible to make a tree straight that has grown crooked, or produce an orchard from a forest everywhere surrounded with briers and thorns. Comenius knew that the home, church, and school working together form a triad of Christian grace, a threefold cord not quickly broken.

For most of his life, this devoted Christian suffered for his faith. In the religious persecution sweeping through Bohemia and Moravia during the Thirty Years' War, Comenius saw his wife and children murdered and all his possessions lost. Nonetheless he left his mark upon the educational systems of various European countries where he lived in exile: Poland, Sweden, and England, where his work and influence led eventually to the founding of the Royal Society. Even in distant New England, he was sought after for the presidency of Harvard College, a post he declined. Honored in England and throughout much of Europe, Comenius died regretting only that he had never had an opportunity to serve God in his own homeland, where the ravages of war and religious strife had made him an outcast.

More than three centuries after his death, the reputation of John Amos Comenius as "the Father of Modern Education" continues to flourish, even where his essential purpose for schooling—so that everyone might be able to read the Word of God—is no longer accepted as valid.

The School of Infancy (Excerpt)

. . . . To Godly Christian Parents, Teachers, Guardians and all who are charged with the care of Children

GREETINGS!

Beloved,

Since it is my purpose to speak to you all about your duty, it is necessary for me to show three things:

I. The preciousness of the treasures that God bestows on those to whom He entrusts children.

II. That He has an end and purpose to which He confers them, and a goal to which their education ought to be directed.

III. That youth demand good education so greatly that if they fail to get it they are of necessity lost.

Having established these three principles, I shall proceed to my purpose and explain in order the areas of your cares in this early age of your charges. . . . Under Thy direction, O Father! by whom every generation in heaven and on earth is ordained.

John Amos Comenius

Chapter I

Children, God's Most Precious Gift, and an Inestimable Treasure, Claim Our Most Vigilant Attention

That children are a priceless treasure God testifies, saying: "Lo, children are the heritage of the Lord; the fruit of the womb His reward; as arrows in the hand, so are children. . . ."

The Son of God when manifested in the flesh not only willed to become as a little child, but thought children a pleasure and a delight. Taking them in His arms as little brethren and sisters, He carried them about and kissed and blessed them. He severely threatened anyone who should offend them, even in the least degree, and commanded that they be respected as Himself.

If one seeks to learn why He is so delighted with little children, one will find many causes. First, if the little ones at present seem unimportant, regard them not as they now are, but as God intends they may and ought to be. You will see them not only as the future inhabitants of the world and possessors of the earth, and God's vicars amongst His creatures when we depart from this life, but also equal participants with us in the heritage of Christ: A royal priesthood, a chosen people, associates of angels, judges of devils, the delight of heaven, the terror of hell . . . heirs of eternity. . . .

Philip Melanchthon once addressed the scholars assembled in a common school with these words:

"Hail, reverend pastors, doctors, licentiates, superintendents!

"Hail, most noble, most prudent, most learned lords, consuls, praetors, judges, governors, chancellors, secretaries, magistrates, professors!"

When some of the standers-by smiled, he said, "I am not jesting. My speech is serious. I look on these little boys not as they now are, but as the Divine mind purposes, on which account they are delivered to us for instruction. Assuredly such leaders will come forth from them, though they may be mixture of chaff among them as among wheat."

Why should we not with equal confidence declare a glorious future for children of Christian parents since Christ who revealed the eternal secrets said that "of such is the Kingdom of God"?

If we consider even their present state, we see at once why children are priceless to God and ought to be so to parents. . . .

The first care therefore ought to be of the soul, which is the principal part of the man, so that it may become in the highest degree possible beautifully adorned. The next care is for the body that it may be made a habitation fit and worthy of an immortal soul.

Regard that mind rightly instructed which is truly illuminated by God's wisdom, so that man perceiving the presence of the divine image within himself may diligently guard that glory. . . .

Nevertheless, God bestows long life upon many, assigns them certain duties, and in the course of their days places them in various situations demanding prudent action. Hence parents must see that their children are exercised not only in faith and godliness but also in the moral sciences, the liberal arts, and in other necessary things. Thereby, when grown up, children may become truly men wisely managing their own affairs in the various functions of life, religious or political, civil or social, that God wills them to fulfill. Thus having wisely and righteously passed through this life they may with greater joy migrate to heaven.

In short, the purpose for which youth ought to be educated is threefold: Faith and Reverence; Uprightness in Morals; Knowledge of Language and Arts. These are to be taken, however, in the precise order in which they here appear, and not inversely. . . .

206

Chapter III
Imperatively Demand Training
and Guidance
to Be Rightly Instructed

Children do not train themselves spontaneously, but are shaped only by tireless labor. A young sapling, planned for a tree, must be planted, watered, hedged round for protection, and propped up. A piece of wood designed for a special purpose must be split, planed, carved, polished, and stained. A horse, an ox, an ass, a mule must be trained to perform their services to man.

Indeed, man himself must be trained in such bodily actions as eating, drinking, running, speaking, seizing with the hand, and laboring. How then, I pray, can those duties higher and more remote from the sense such as faith, virtue, wisdom, and knowledge come spontaneously to any one? It is altogether impossible. . . .

And inasmuch as every one ought to be competent to serve God and be useful to men, we maintain that he ought to be instructed in Piety, in Morals, in Sound Learning, and in Health. Parents should lay the foundations of these in the very earliest age of their children. During the first six years this training should extend as follows.

Piety, true and salutary, consists in these three things:

1. Our hearts should always and everywhere have regard for God and should seek Him in all that we do and say and think.
2. Having discovered the steps of Divine Providence, our hearts should follow God always and everywhere with reverence, love, and ready obedience.
3. Thus always mindful of God, and conversing with God, our hearts joining God realize peace, consolation, and joy.

This true Piety brings to man a paradise of divine pleasure. Its foundations may be so impressed upon a boy within the space of six years that he may know (1) there is a God, (2) who, being everywhere present, beholds us all. (3) He bestows abundantly food, drink, clothing, and all things upon those that obey Him,

(4) but punishes with death the stubborn and immoral. (5) Therefore God ought to be feared, always invoked and loved as a father, (6) and all things ought to be done which He commands. (7) Last, if we be good and righteous, He will take us to the heavens.

I maintain that a child may be led upward in these exercises until the sixth year of his age.

Morals and Virtues. Children ought to be instructed in Morals and Virtues, especially the following. In *temperance* they should learn to eat and drink according to the wants of nature, not greedily or to cram themselves with food and drink beyond what is sufficient. In *cleanliness* and *decorum* they should be accustomed to observe decency in food, dress, and care of the body.

In *respect* towards superiors, they should learn consideration for their actions, conversations, and instructions. In *complaisance* they should be prompt to execute all things immediately at the nod and voice of their superiors.

It is especially necessary that they be accustomed to speak *truth*, so that all their words may accord with the teaching of Christ. . . . They should on no account become accustomed to falsehood, or to speak of anything otherwise than it really is, either seriously or in mirth.

They must likewise be trained to *justice* so as not to touch, move stealthily, withdraw, or hide anything belonging to another, or to wrong another in any respect.

Kindness ought to be instilled in them, and a love of pleasing others so that they may be generous, and neither niggardly nor envious. It is especially profitable for them to be accustomed to *labor* and thus to acquire an aversion to indolence.

They should be taught not only to *speak* but also to be *silent* when needful, as during prayer or while others are speaking. They ought to be exercised in *patience* so that they may not expect that all things should be done at their nod; from earliest age they should gradually be taught to restrain their desires. And in infancy they should learn youth's ornament of *serving* elders with civility and readiness.

Out of all this training *courteousness* will arise, by which they may learn to show good behavior to everyone, to salute, to shake hands, to bend the knee, to give thanks for little gifts. To avoid levity or rudeness, let them at the same time learn *gravity* of deportment, so as to do all things modestly and gracefully.

A child initiated in such virtues will easily, as occurred with Christ, obtain for itself the favor of God and man.

Sound Learning admits of threefold division, for we learn to Know some things, to Do some things, and to Say some things; or rather, we learn to know, to do, and to say *all* things except such as are bad.

To Know. In its first six years a child may begin to know *natural things*, the names of fire, air, water, and earth; of rain, snow, ice, lead, iron; trees and some of the better known and more common plants, violets, clove trees, and roses; likewise, the difference between animals: what is a bird, what are cattle, what is a horse; finally, the outward members of its own body, how they ought to be named, for what use designed. . . .

Of *Optics* it will suffice for children to know what is darkness, what light, the difference between the more common colors. In *Astronomy*, to discern between the sun, moon, and stars. In *Geography*, to know whether the place of birth and where they live be a village, a city, a town, or a citadel. What is a field, a mountain, a forest, a meadow, a river.

The child's first instruction in *Chronology* will be to know what is an hour, a day, a week, a month, a year; what is spring, what summer. The beginning of *History* will be for it to remember what was done yesterday, what recently, what a year ago. This, however, is puerile, and the remembrance of such things is obscure and as it were through a cloud. In *Household affairs* they will easily distinguish who belongs to the family and who does not.

In *Politics* they can know that there is in the state a chief ruler, ministers, and legislators; and that there are occasional assemblies of the nation.

To Do. As to Actions, some have respect to the mind and the tongue, as dialectics, arithmetic, geometry, and music. Some have to do with the mind and hand, such as labors and bodily actions.

The principles of *Dialectics* may be so far imbibed that a child may know what is a question, what an answer, and be able to reply to a question proposed, not talking about onions when the question is about garlic.

The foundations of *Arithmetic* will be to know that something is much or little, to be able to count to twenty, or even all the way to sixty . . . and to understand that three are more than two, that three and one make four, and other such simple matters.

Geometry's beginnings will be to know what is small or large, short or long, narrow or broad, thin or thick; likewise what is a span, an ell, and a fathom, and other little measures.

In *Music* the child will be to be able to sing from memory some little verses from the Psalms or hymns.

So much for the mind and tongue. For the mind and hand, the beginning of every labor or work of art is to cut, to split, to carve, to strew, to arrange, to tie, to untie, to roll up, and to unroll—such things being familiar to all children.

To Say. Propriety in language is obtained by grammar, rhetoric, and poetry. The *Grammar* of the first six years is that the child be able to express so much as it knows of things. Though it speak imperfectly, yet let it be to the point and so articulated that it may be understood. Children's *Rhetoric* will be to use natural actions and in case they understand to repeat a trope or figure. Their rudiments in *Poetry* will be to commit to memory certain verses or rhymes.

Parents must take care as to the method adopted with infants in these several things. Instruction should not be apportioned precisely to certain years and months (as afterwards in other schools) but generally only. The child's education cannot follow a fixed pattern because all parents cannot observe the Order in their homes that is obtained in public schools where no external matters disturb the regular course of things. Furthermore, in this early age all children do not develop at the same time, some beginning to speak in the first year, some in the second, and some in the third. In the following chapters I will therefore show only in the general way how infants should be instructed during the first six years . . . .

JOHN MILTON

Though he is known for such works as the great epic *Paradise Lost* and many sonnets, including "On His Blindness," which encourages every doubtful worker for Christ, John Milton (1608–74) was also a powerful writer of prose arguments.

Educated at Cambridge, Milton declined to enter the ministry because of what he considered the Church of England's "tyranny." Instead he devoted himself to writing poetry: "L'Allegro," "Il Penseroso," "Lycidas," the sonnets, along with *Paradise Lost* and *Paradise Regained.*

Alienated from the Anglican Church, Milton became a Presbyterian and wrote an attack on ecclesiastical hierarchy, preferring local church government. But an unhappy marriage, in 1643, resulted in his wife's leaving him; whereupon Milton wrote an argument favoring divorce on grounds of incompatibility. This essay estranged him also from the Presbyterians.

Milton also faced civil threats for having published his divorce treatise without approval of the royal censor. This action, in 1644, caused him to write his famous *Areopagitica*, subtitled "A Speech for the Liberty of Uncensored Printing." It stands as one of the great arguments on behalf of freedom of the press. Ironically, Milton's wife returned to him after three years and bore three daughters and a son, who died in infancy, before her own death in 1652.

In 1651, Milton had lost his eyesight totally; nonetheless, in spite of this double loss, he dictated his poetry to his daughters, completing the epics, *Paradise Lost, Paradise Regained,* and *Samson Agonistes,* between 1658 and 1671. Milton's colossal achievement stands among the most incredibly heroic in the arts.

His essay "Of Education," which follows, was written in 1644, a few months before the *Areopagitica.* Samuel Hartlib, to whom Milton addressed his treatise, was an educational reformer who had met John Amos Comenius three years earlier and published some of the Moravian's work.

Wishing to extend the influence of Comenius in England, Hartlib solicited a piece of writing from Milton, setting out his own ideas for a proper education, which Hartlib hoped would parallel those of Comenius.

Instead, Milton offered his own model, complete with a detailed and rigorous curriculum. Still, as Hartlib expected, Milton retained the same high purpose for schooling known to Christians throughout the ages.

"Of Education"[4] (Excerpt)

To Master Samuel Hartlib

Master Hartlib,

I am long since persuaded that to say and do aught worth memory and imitation, no purpose or respect should sooner move us than simply the love of God and of mankind. Nevertheless, to write now the reforming of education, though it be one of the greatest and noblest designs that can be thought on, and for the want whereof this nation perishes, I had not yet at this time been induced but by your earnest entreaties and serious conjurements; as having my mind for the present half diverted in the pursuance of some other assertions, the knowledge and the use of which cannot but be a great furtherance both to the enlargement of truth, and honest living with much more peace. . . .

The end, then, of learning is to repair the ruins of our first parents by regaining to know God aright, and out of that knowledge to love him, to imitate him, to be like him, as we may the nearest, by possessing our souls of true virtue, which, being united to the heavenly grace of faith, makes up the highest perfection. But because our understanding cannot in this body found itself but on sensible things, nor arrive so clearly to the knowledge of God and things invisible as by orderly conning over the visible and inferior creature, the same method is necessarily to be followed in all discreet teaching. . . .

First, to find out a spacious house and ground about it fit for an Academy, and big enough to lodge a hundred and fifty persons, whereof twenty or thereabout may be attendants, all under the government of one who shall be thought of [as sufficiently deserving] and [capable] either to do all, or wisely to direct and oversee it done. This place should be at once both school and university, not needing to remove to any other house of scholarship, except it be some peculiar college of law or physic, where they mean to be practitioners, but as for those general studies which take up all our time from Lilly to the commencing, as they term it, master of art, it should be absolute. After this pattern, as many edifices may be converted to this use as shall be needful in every city throughout this land, which would tend much to the increase of learning and civility everywhere. This number, less or more, thus collected, to the convenience of a foot-company or interchangeably two troops of cavalry, should divide their day's work into three parts as it lies orderly—their studies, their exercise, and their diet.

For their studies first, they should begin with the chief and necessary rules of some good grammar, either that now used, or any better, and while this is doing, their speech is to be fashioned to a distinct and clear pronunciation, as near as may be to the Italian, especially in the vowels. For we Englishmen, being far northerly, do not open our mouths in the cold air wide enough to grace a southern tongue, but are observed by all other nations to speak exceeding close and inward; so that to smatter Latin with an English mouth is as ill as hearing a law [in] French. . . .

Sundays also and every evening may now be understandingly spent in the highest matters of theology and church history ancient and modern: and ere this time the Hebrew tongue at a set hour might have been gained, that the Scriptures may be now read in their own original, whereto it would be no impossibility to add the Chaldee and the Syrian dialect.

When all these employments are well conquered, then will the choice histories, heroic poems, and Attic tragedies of stateliest and most regal argument, with all the famous political orations, offer themselves; which, if they were not only read, but some of them got by memory, and solemnly pronounced with right accent and grace, as might be taught, would endue them even with the spirit and vigour of Demosthenes or Cicero, Euripides or Sophocles.

And now, lastly, will be the time to read with them those organic arts which enable men to discourse and write perspicuously, elegantly, and according to the fitted style of lofty, mean or lowly. Logic, therefore, so much as is useful, is to be referred to this due place, with all her well-couched heads and topics, until it be time to open her contracted palm into a graceful and ornate rhetoric taught out of the rule of Plato, Aristotle, Phalereus, Cicero, Hermogenes, Longinus. . . .

The course of study hitherto briefly described is, what I can guess by reading, likest to those ancient and famous schools of Pythagoras, Plato, Socrates, Aristotle, and such others, out of which were bred up such a number of renowned philosophers, orators, historians, poets, and princes all over Greece, Italy, and Asia, besides the flourishing studies of Cyrene and Alexandria. But herein it shall exceed them, and supply a defect as great as that which Plato noted in the commonwealth of Sparta. Whereas that city trained up their youth most for war, and these in their Academies and Lycaeum all for the gown, this institution of breeding which I here delineate shall be equally good both for peace and war. Therefore, about an hour and a half ere they eat at noon should be allowed them for exercise, and due rest afterwards; but the time for this may be enlarged at pleasure, according as their rising in the morning shall be early. The exercise which I commend first is the exact use of their weapon, to guard, and to strike safely with edge or point. This will keep them healthy, nimble, strong and well in breath; is also the likeliest means to make them grow large and tall, and to inspire them with a gallant and fearless courage; which, being tempered with seasonable lectures and precepts to make them of true fortitude and patience, will turn into a native and heroic valour, and make them hate the cowardice of doing wrong. They must be also practised in all the locks and grips of wrestling, wherein Englishmen are wont to excel, as need may often be in fight to tug, to grapple, and to close. And this, perhaps, will be enough wherein to prove and heat their single strength.

The interim of unsweating themselves regularly, and convenient rest before meat, may both with profit and delight be taken up in recreating and composing their travailed spirits with the solemn and divine harmonies of music heard or learned either whilst the skilful organist plies his grave and fancied descant in lofty fugues, or the whole symphony with artful and unimaginable touches adorn and grace the well-studied chords of some choice composer; sometimes the lute or soft organ-stop, waiting on elegant voices either to religious, martial, or civil ditties, which, if wise men and prophets be not extremely out, have a great power over dispositions and manners to smooth and make them gentle from rustic harshness and distempered passions. . . .

These ways would try all their peculiar gifts of nature, and if there were any secret excellence among them, would fetch it out and give it fair opportunities to advance itself by, which could not but mightily redound to the good of this nation, and bring into fashion again those old admired virtues and excellencies, with far more advantage now in this purity of Christian knowledge.

Nor shall we then need the monsieurs of Paris to take our hopeful youth into their slight and prodigal custodies, and send them over back again transformed into mimics, apes, and kick-shaws. But if they desire to see other countries at three or four and twenty years of age, not to learn principles, but to enlarge experience and make wise observation, they will by that time be such as shall deserve the regard and honour of all men where they pass, and the society and friendship of those in all places who are best and most eminent. And perhaps then other nations will be glad to visit us for their breeding, or else to imitate us in their own country.

Now, lastly, for their diet there cannot be much to say, save only that it would be best in the same house; for much time else would be lost abroad, and many ill habits got; and that it should be plain, healthful, and moderate, I suppose is out of controversy. . . .

JOHN LOCKE

A principal figure in the "Enlightenment" or "Age of Reason," John Locke (1632–1704) is sometimes portrayed as having been hostile to Christianity. The facts are quite to the contrary.

Born near Bristol, Locke enjoyed a wise father's upbringing, which included his father's habit of discussing matters of importance with his son. So, at an early age, Locke learned the virtue of tolerance of other people's views.

After receiving his master's degree at Oxford, he became secretary to the first Earl of Shaftesbury and with him drafted the first constitution for the American colony called Carolina. While one of the tenets of this constitution granted freedom of worship to all colonists, its tolerance did not extend to atheists, who were specifically excluded from settling there.

When Shaftesbury and his Whig Party fell into disfavor with King Charles II, Locke fled to Holland with his patron, where he wrote political tracts later published as "Letters Concerning Toleration." The "Glorious Revolution" of 1688 toppled the Roman Catholic King James II and brought to England's throne the Protestant William of Orange, crowned William III. The resulting change in religious climate enabled Locke to return to England early in 1689.

The next year saw the publishing of his great work, "Essay Concerning Human Understanding," on which he had been laboring for eighteen years. In it he argued for empiricism, knowledge whose validity could be proved by experience and in the crucible of experiment. He denied the existence of innate knowledge and upheld reason gained through observation and intuition. This essay, written in strong, plain English, achieved a new level for English philosophy.

Yet, while Locke was being hailed for his rationalism and empiricism, he had not departed from holding to the Christian faith. Indeed, his last significant books before his death were *The Reasonableness of Christianity as Delivered in the Scriptures*, *A Paraphrase and Notes on the Epistles of St. Paul*, and *A Discourse on Miracles*. In each of these, Locke showed his continuing belief in the specific revelation of God in Christ and the necessity of one's living by the principles taught in Scripture. These, said Locke, were the essentials of any claim to be a Christian— hardly an unorthodox position!

Some years earlier, Locke's friend Edward Clarke had asked him for a plan to follow in educating Clarke's son. Locke's response was put together and published in 1693 as "Some Thoughts Concerning Education." As with everything else he wrote, this document of educational theory shines with practical common sense. For example, in the excerpt below, Locke discusses the appropriateness of teaching certain parts of the Bible at certain ages of maturity.

"Some Thoughts Concerning Education"⁵ (Excerpt)

Par. 155. . . . .'Tis better it be a Year later before he can read, than that he should this way get an aversion to Learning. If you have any contests with him, let it be in matters of moment, of truth, and good nature; but lay no task on him about ABC. Use your skill to make his will supple and pliant to reason: Teach him to love credit and commendation; to abhor being thought ill or meanly of, especially by you and his mother, and then the rest will come all easily. But I think, if you will do that, you must not shackle and tie him up with rules about indifferent matters, nor rebuke him for every little fault, or perhaps some, that to others would seem great ones: But of this I have said enough already.

Par. 156. When by these gentle ways he begins to be able to read, some easy pleasant book suited to his capacity should be put into his hands, wherein the entertainment, that he finds, might draw him on, and reward his pains in reading, and yet not such as should fill his head with perfectly useless trumpery, or lay the principles of vice and folly. To this purpose, I think, *Aesop's Fables* the best, which being stories apt to delight and entertain a child, may yet afford useful reflections to a grown Man. And if his memory retain them all his life after, he will not repent to find them there, amongst his manly thoughts, and serious business. If his *Aesop* has pictures in it, it will entertain him much the better, and encourage him to read, when it carries the increase of Knowledge with it. For such visible objects children hear talked of in vain, and without any satisfaction, whilst they have no ideas of them; those ideas being not to be had from sounds; but from the things themselves, or their pictures. And therefore I think, as soon as he begins to spell, as many pictures of animals should be got him, as can be found, with the printed names to them, which at the same time will invite him to read, and afford him matter of enquiry and knowledge. *Reynard the Fox*, is another book, I think, may be made use of to the same purpose. And if those about him will talk to him often about the stories he has read, and hear him tell them, it will, besides other advantages, add incouragement [sic], and delight to his reading, when he finds, there is some use and pleasure in it. . . .

Par. 157. The Lord's Prayer, the Creeds, and Ten Commandments, 'tis necessary he should learn perfectly by heart, but I think, not by reading them himself in his primer, but by somebody's repeating them to him, even before he can read. But learning by heart, and *learning to read*, should not, I think, be mixed, and so one made to clog the other. But his *learning to read* should be made as little trouble or business to him, as might be.

What other books there are in English of the kind of those abovementioned, fit to engage the liking of children, and tempt them to read, I do not know: but am apt to think that children, being generally delivered over to the method of schools . . . this sort of useful books amongst the number of silly ones, that are of all sorts, have yet had the fate to be neglected. . . .

Par. 158. As for the Bible, which children are usually [employed] in, to exercise and improve their talent in reading, I think, the promiscuous reading of it through, by chapters, . . . in order, is so far from being of any advantage to children, either for the perfecting their reading, or principling their religion, that perhaps a worse could not be found. For what pleasure or [encouragement] can it be to a child to exercise himself in reading those parts of a book, where he understands nothing? And how little are the Law of Moses, the Song of Solomon, the prophecies in the Old, and the Epistles and *Apocalypse* in the New Testament, suited to a child's capacity? And though the History of the Evangelists, and the Acts, have something easier; yet taken altogether, it is very disproportionate to the understanding of childhood. I grant, that the principles of religion are to be drawn from thence, and in the words of the Scripture; yet none should be propos'd to a child, but such, as are suited to a child's capacity and notions. But 'tis far from this to read through *the whole Bible,* and that for reading's sake. And what an odd jumble of thoughts must a child have in his head, if he have any at all, such as he should have concerning religion, who in his tender age, reads all the parts of the Bible indifferently as the Word of God, without any other distinction. I am apt to think, that this in some men has been the very Reason, why they never had clear and distinct thoughts of it all their life time.

Par. 159. And now I am by chance fallen on this subject, give me leave to say, that there are some parts of the Scripture, which may be proper to be put into the hands of a child [and have] him to read; such as are the story of Joseph, and his brethren, of David and Goliath, of David and Jonathan, &c. And others, that he should be made to read for his instruction, as That, *What you would have others do unto you, do you the same unto them;* and such other easy and plain moral rules, which being fitly chosen, might often be made use of, both for reading and instruction together; and so often read till they are thoroughly fixed in the memory; and then afterwards, as he grows ripe for them may in their turns, on fit occasions, be inculcated as the standing and sacred rules of his life and action. But the reading of the whole Scripture indifferently, is what I think very inconvenient for children, . . . [Children should not have systems and analogies forced] upon them. Dr. Worthington, to avoid this, has made a catechism, which has all its answers in the precise words of the Scripture, a thing of good example, and such a sound form of words, as no Christian can except against, as not fit for his child to learn; of this, as soon as he can say the Lord's Prayer, Creed, and Ten Commandments by heart, it may be fit for him to learn a Question every day, or every week, as his understanding is able to receive, and his memory to retain them. And when he has this catechism perfectly by heart, so as readily and roundly to answer to any Question in the whole book, it may be convenient to lodge in his mind the remaining moral rules scattered up and down in the Bible, as the best exercise of his memory, and that which may be always a rule to him, ready at hand in the whole conduct of his life.

ROBERT RAIKES

In the history of modern education, no one development exceeds in importance the founding of the Sunday school. It became a stronghold in the fight against illiteracy in England; and as noted in the introduction to this part, from the Sunday school grew up the common school, the genesis of tax-supported public education in America. The Sunday school movement is generally attributed to Robert Raikes (1735–1811) of Gloucester, England.

In 1757, Raikes inherited the Gloucester *Journal* from his father and became a leading citizen of that city. This was a period of dreadful labor and living conditions, with both children and youths working long hours, six days a week, for meager pay and returning to quarters of horrendous squalor. As a result, despair, injustice, and a severe judicial system created a culture of lawlessness equal to anything seen in the modern inner city. The established Church of England seemed almost callous toward such an appalling poverty; such persons simply were not welcome in those churches. Furthermore, there was no governmental social safety net to prevent young lives from falling even further into wretchedness.

Raikes' compassion initially led him to the miserable jails where he hoped to help prisoners. But from that experience he deduced that his energy and philanthropy would be better used in attempting to prevent the lawbreaking that led to incarceration. By educating the underclass— not only in the essentials of literacy but also in the gospel they had never heard in churches they had never attended—he believed that he would provide the working poor with some reason for hope for release from their moral and social imprisonment.

Thus, in 1780, he turned to helping rowdy youths and children on Sundays, their one day free from work. He established a meeting place and time for rudimentary instruction in reading, writing, and Christian doctrine. At first Raikes encountered remarkable opposition from political and social conservatives who feared the consequences of educating the outcast workers. Sadly but perhaps not unexpectedly, Raikes was also opposed by religious parties who considered his work a desecration of the Sabbath.

For three years, Raikes and his paid assistants, or monitors, labored under suspicion and adverse criticism. But in November 1783 Raikes felt confident enough that his experiment could work elsewhere to place an article in his *Journal* concerning the Sunday school in a street appropriately named Sooty Alley, which had been transformed by the new opportunities granted to the working class.

News of Raikes' Sunday school quickly spread; only six months later, Sunday schools were now to be found in Leeds, York, and elsewhere throughout England. The positive benefits were almost immediately apparent, even to those who had opposed the idea. Factory owners and other employers noticed a new pride in personal hygiene and attire had replaced the filthy appearance that had marked most urban workers. This change in appearance carried over to a demonstrable change in speech and attitudes, as swearing and fighting seemed to diminish.

Curiosity about Raikes' experiment led to many inquiries, one of which came from a Colonel Townley of Sheffield. Raikes' letter of reply appears below.

Before his death, in 1811, Robert Raikes' influence had spread to all parts of Great Britain. John Newton, the converted slave-trader who wrote "Amazing Grace," William Wilberforce, the great crusader for the abolition of slavery, and Hannah More were all supporters of the Sunday school movement, which eventually made its way across the Atlantic. The Sunday School Union, founded in 1803, led to its American counterpart in 1824, which became the foundation for a tax-supported public education in America.

Once more it may be said: At the heart of education in the Western world stands the cross.

"Letter to Colonel Townley"

Gloucester, November 25th, 1783.

Sir,—My friend, the Mayor (Mr. Colborne) has just communicated to me the letter which you have honoured him with, enquiring into the nature of Sunday Schools. The beginning of this scheme was entirely owing to accident. Some business leading me one morning into the suburbs of the city, where the lowest of the people (who are principally employed in the pin manufactory) chiefly reside, I was struck with concern at seeing a group of children, wretchedly ragged, at play in the streets. I asked an inhabitant whether those children belonged to that part of town, and lamented their misery and idleness. "Ah! sir," said the woman to whom I was speaking, "could you take a view of this part of the town on a Sunday, you would be shocked indeed; for then the street is filled with multitudes of these wretches, who, released on that day from employment, spend their time in noise and riot, playing at 'chuck,' and cursing and swearing in a manner so horrid as to convey to any serious mind an idea of hell rather than any other place. We have a worthy clergyman (said she), curate of our parish, who has put some of them to school; but on the Sabbath day they are all given up to follow their own inclinations without restraint, as their parents, totally abandoned themselves, have no idea of instilling into the minds of their children principles to which they themselves are entire strangers."

This conversation suggested to me that it would be at least a harmless attempt, if it were productive of no good, should some little plan be formed to check the deplorable profanation of the Sabbath. I then enquired of the woman, if there were any decent well-disposed women in the neighbourhood who kept schools for teaching to read. I presently was directed to four: to these I applied, and made an agreement with them to receive as many children as I should send upon the Sunday, whom they were to instruct in reading and in the Church Catechism. For this I engaged to pay them each a shilling for their day's employment. The women seemed pleased with the proposal. I then waited on the clergyman before mentioned, and imported to him my plan; he was so much satisfied with the idea, that he engaged to lend his assistance, by going round to the schools on a Sunday afternoon, to examine the progress that was made, and to enforce order and decorum among such a set of little heathens.

This, sir, was the commencement of the plan. It is now about three years since we began, and I could wish you were here to make enquiry into the effect. A woman who lives in a lane where I had fixed a school told me, some time ago, that the place was quite a heaven on Sundays, compared to what it used to be. The numbers who have learned to read and say their Catechism are so great that I am astonished at it. Upon the Sunday afternoon the mistresses take their scholars to church, a place into which neither they nor their ancestors had ever before entered, with a view of the glory of God. But what is yet more extraordinary, within this month these little ragamuffins have in great numbers taken it into their heads to frequent the early morning prayers, which are held every morning at the Cathedral at seven o'clock. I believe there were nearly fifty this morning. They assemble at the house of one of the mistresses, and walk before her to church, two and two, in as much order as a company of soldiers. I am generally at church, and after service they all come around me to make their bow; and, if any animosities have arisen, to make their complaints. The great principle I inculcate is, to be kind and good natured to each other; not to provoke one another; to be dutiful to their parents; not to offend God by cursing and swearing; and such little plain precepts as all may comprehend. As my profession is that of a printer, I have printed a little book, which I gave amongst them; and some friends of mine, subscribers to the Society for Promoting Christian Knowledge, sometimes make me a present of a parcel of Bibles, Testaments, [etc.], which I distribute as rewards to the deserving. The success that has attended this scheme has induced one or two of my friends to adopt the plan, and set up Sunday Schools in other parts of the city, and now a whole parish has taken up the object; so that I flatter myself in time the good effects will appear so conspicuous as to become generally adopted. The number of children at present thus engaged on the Sabbath are between two and three hundred, and they are increasing every week, as the benefit is universally seen. I have endeavoured to engage the clergy of my acquaintance that reside in their parishes; one has entered into the scheme with great fervour, and it was in order to excite others to follow the example that I inserted in my paper the paragraph which I suppose you saw copied into the London papers.

. . . With regard to the rules adopted, I only require that they may come to the school on Sunday as clean as possible. Many were at first deterred because they wanted decent clothing, but I could not undertake to supply this defect. I argue, therefore, if you can loiter about without shoes, and in a ragged coat, you may as well come to school and learn what may tend to your good in that garb. I reject none of that footing. All that I require are clean hands, clean face, and their hair combed; if you have no clean shirt, come in what you have on.

The want of decent apparel at first kept great numbers at a distance, but they now begin to grow wiser, and all pressing to learn. I have had the good luck to procure places for some that were deserving, which has been of great use. You will understand that these children are from six years old to twelve or fourteen. Boys and girls above this age, who have been totally undisciplined, are generally too refractory for this government. A reformation in society seems to me to be only practicable by establishing notions of duty, and practical habits of order and decorum, at an early age. . . .

I have the honour to be, Sir, yours, [etc.],

R. Raikes

HANNAH MORE

R eform in education led from such matters as the language of in-struction (from exclusively Latin to the national tongue) to the social class of those to be taught (noblemen's sons, gentlemen's sons, or the sons of commoners) and the location and nature of such schooling (whether home, "public" school, or Sunday school). Inevita-bly, the next reform was to include girls as well as boys. In this Hannah More took a leading part.

Born in Stapleton, Gloucestershire, Hannah More (1745–1833) was one of five daughters of a school teacher. The family must have been most unconventional for its time, since her older sisters established a school in which Hannah was first a pupil, then a teacher. She was also a promising writer of dramatic plays. In 1773, she took her gift for creating tragic dramas to London, where she found great success with such titles as *The Inflexible Captive* and *The Fatal Falsehood*. Among her theatrical and literary associates were David Garrick and Samuel Johnson.

But in the 1780s, she experienced a change of character, a true spiritual conversion. Under the influence of William Wilberforce and John Newton, her spiritual mentor, she advocated the Sunday school movement. While she later wrote some moralistic fiction, her principal efforts in writing were devoted to religious poetry and didactic tracts intended to appeal to the needs of the poor. In fact, her work in creating what she called "Cheap Repository Tracts" resulted in founding the Re-ligious Tract Society.

One of these Cheap Repository Tracts More titled "The Sunday School." In it, she wrote: "It is something gained to rescue children from idling away their Sabbath in the fields or the streets. It is no small thing to keep them from those tricks to which a day of leisure tempts the idle and the ignorant. It is something for them to be taught to read; it is much to be taught to read the Bible; and much, indeed, to be carried regularly to church.

"But all this is not enough," Hannah More contended. "To bring these institutions to answer their highest end, can only be effected by God's blessing on the best-directed means, and choice of able teachers, and a diligent attention to some pious gentry to visit and inspect the schools."[6]

In addition, Hannah More expected the "pious gentry" to contribute to the support of Sunday schools and also advocated "getting the help and countenance of the farmers and trades-people, whose duty and interest . . . it was, to support a plan calculated to improve the virtue and happiness of the parish." After all, she argued, "Is a poor fellow, who can read his Bible, so likely to sleep and drink away his few hours of leisure, as one who *cannot* read?"

But Hannah More's vision for education went well beyond the Sunday school. With one of her sisters, Hannah More began several schools for girls in Cheddar and surrounding communities. Her curriculum included not only academic subjects but also instruction in Christianity along with domestic skills such as spinning. Opposed at first by those who were distressed by her violation of convention, More's schools eventually received the approval of the local Anglican bishop of Bath and Wells.

Of course, gender discrimination had been opposed long before the end of the eighteenth century. Erasmus had called for the education of women, as had Luther and Melanchthon; Comenius had insisted upon compulsory universal education for girls as well as boys. But perhaps Hannah More's voice penetrated her culture more noticeably because she was supported by other reformers, including those compelling figures, Wilberforce and Newton.

Her essay, "Strictures on the Modern System of Female Education," was published in 1799.

"Strictures on the Modern System of Female Education With a View of the Principles and Conduct Prevalent Among Women of Rank and Fortune"

Introduction.

It is a singular injustice which is often exercised towards women, first to give them a very defective education, and then to expect from them the most undeviating purity of conduct—to train them in such a manner as shall lay them open to the most dangerous faults, and then to censure them for not proving faultless. Is it not unreasonable and unjust to express disappointment if our daughters should, in their subsequent lives, turn out precisely that very kind of character for which it would be evident to an unprejudiced by-stander that the whole scope and tenor of their instruction had been systematically preparing them?

Some reflections on the present erroneous system are here with great deference submitted to public consideration. The author is apprehensive that she shall be accused of betraying the interests of her sex by laying open their defects; but surely an earnest wish to turn their attention to objects calculated to promote their true dignity, is not the office of an enemy. So to expose the weakness of the land as to suggest the necessity of internal improvement, and to point out the means of effectual defence, is not treachery, but patriotism.

Again, it may be objected to this little work, that many errors are here ascribed to women which by no means belongs to them *exclusively*, and that it seems to confine to the sex those faults which are common to the species; but this is in some measure unavoidable. In speaking on the qualities of one sex, the moralist is somewhat in the situation of the geographer, who is treating on the nature of one country: the air, soil, and produce of the land which he is describing, cannot fail in many essential points to resemble those of other countries under the same parallel; yet it is his business to descant on the one without adverting to the other; and though in drawing the map he may happen to introduce some of the neighbouring coast, yet his principal attention must be confined to that country which he proposes to describe, without taking into account the resembling circumstances of the adjacent shores. . . .

Again, it may be said, that the author is less disposed to expatiate on excellence than error; but the office of the historian of human manners is delineation rather than panegyric. Were the end in view [a tribute] and not improvement, [a tribute] would have been far more gratifying, nor would just objects for praise have been difficult to find. Even in her own limited sphere of observation, the author is acquainted with much excellence in the class of which she treats—with women who, possessing learning which would be thought extensive in the other sex, set an example of deep humility to their own—women who, distinguished for wit and genius, are eminent for domestic qualities—who, excelling in the fine arts, have carefully enriched their understandings—who, enjoying great influence, devote it to the glory of God—who, possessing elevated rank, think their noblest style and title is that of a Christian.

That there is also much worth which is little known, she is persuaded; for it is the modest nature of goodness to exert itself quietly, while a few characters of the opposite case seem, by the rumour of their exploits, to fill the world; and by their noise to multiply their numbers. It often happens that a very small party of people, by occupying the foreground, by seizing the public attention and monopolizing the public talk, contrive to appear to be the great body; . . . a few disturbers of order, who have the talent of thus exciting a false idea of their multitudes by their mischiefs, actually gain strength, and swell their numbers, by this fallacious arithmetic. . . .

There are, however, multitudes of the young and the well disposed, who have as yet taken no decided part, who are just launching on the ocean of life, just about to lose their own right convictions, virtually preparing to counteract their better propensities, and unreluctantly yielding themselves to be carried down the tide of popular practices; sanguine, thoughtless, and confident of safety. To these the author would gently hint, that when once embarked, it will be no longer easy to say to their passions, or even to their principles, 'Thus far shall ye go, and no further.' Their struggles will grow fainter, their resistance will become feebler, till borne down by the confluence of example, temptation, appetite, and habit, resistance and opposition will soon be the only things of which they will learn to be ashamed.

Should any reader revolt at which is conceived to be unwarranted strictness in this little book, let it not be thrown by in disgust before the following short consideration be weighed.—If in this Christian country we are actually beginning to regard the solemn office of Baptism as merely furnishing an article to the parish register—if we are learning from our indefatigable teachers, to consider this Christian rite as a legal ceremony retained for the sole purpose of recording the age of our children;—then, indeed, the prevailing system of education and manners of which these pages presume to animadvert may be adopted with propriety, and persisted in which safety without entailing on our children or on ourselves the peril of broken promises or the guilt of violated vows But, if the obligation which Christian Baptism imposes be really binding—if the ordinance have, indeed, a meaning beyond a mere secular transaction, beyond a record of names and dates—if it be an institution by which the child is solemnly devoted to God as his Father, to Jesus Christ as his Saviour, and to the Holy Spirit as his sanctifier; if there be no definite period assigned when the obligation of fulfilling the duties it enjoins shall be superseded—if, having once dedicated our offspring to their Creator, we no longer dare to mock Him by bringing them up in ignorance of His will and neglect of His laws— . . . if, after having promised that they shall renounce the vanities of the world, we are not allowed to invalidate the engagement—if, after such a covenant we should tremble to make these renounced vanities, the supreme object of our own pursuit or of *their* instruction—if all this be really so, then the Strictures on Modern Education, and on the Habits of Polished Life, will not be found so repugnant to truth, and reason, and common sense, as may on a first view be supposed.

But if on candidly summing up the evidence, the design and scope of the author be fairly judged, not by the customs or opinions of the worldly (for every English subject has a right to object to a suspected or prejudiced jury) but by an appeal to that divine law which is the only infallible rule of judgment; if on such an appeal her views and principles shall be found censurable for their rigour, absurd in their requisitions, or preposterous in their restrictions, she will have no right to complain of such a verdict, because she will then stand condemned by that court to whose decision she implicitly submits.

Let it not be suspected that the author arrogantly conceives *herself* to be exempt from that natural corruption of the heart which it is one chief object of this slight work to exhibit; that she superciliously erects herself into the implacable censor of her sex and of the world, as if from the critic's chair she were coldly pointing out the faults and errors of another order of beings, in whose welfare she had not that lively interest which can only flow from the tender and intimate participation of fellow-feeling.

With a deep self-abasement, arising from a strong conviction of being indeed a partaker in the same corrupt nature; together with a full persuasion of the many and great defects of these pages, and a sincere consciousness of her inability to do justice to a subject which, however, a sense of duty impelled her to undertake, she commits herself to the candour of that public, which has so frequently, in her instance, accepted a right intention as a substitute for a powerful performance.

Bath, March 14, 1799.

PART VI

THE AMERICAN EXPERIENCE:
1620–1750

That all the Latin Scholars and all other of the Boys of Competent age and Capacity give the Master an account of one passage or sentence at least of the sermons the foregoing Sabbath on the 2nd day morning.

Orders of the Committee of Trustees
Hopkins Grammar School, New Haven, Conn., 1684

THE AMERICAN EXPERIENCE:

Spanish Franciscans and French Jesuits established schools in North America early in the sixteenth century along California's mission trail; at St. Augustine, Florida, before the Jamestown colony; and soon thereafter in Quebec. The arrival of English colonists would soon have a dominant influence in America. The English-speaking tradition would greatly affect education in the New World; to understand it we must undertake a brief political and religious history.

England needed no Luther to condemn the excesses of Roman Catholicism and ignite the Reformation. Publication of William Tyndale's English translation of the New Testament, in 1526, as well as the state and personal affairs of King Henry VIII were sufficient to advance the schism between Canterbury and Rome. The king had rebuffed the Catholic church after it refused to grant him a divorce from his first wife, Catherine; from that point he embraced the Church of England and largely ignored Roman Catholic jurisdiction. So the English Reformation had a distinctly more nationalistic tone to it than did the Continental Reformation throughout the rest of Europe.

An overtly anti-Roman Catholic spirit showed itself in the suppression of monasteries; but from the funds expropriated by Henry came new educational opportunities. Almost every village had its grammar school, and the progress from grammar school to one of the colleges at Cambridge or Oxford became the standard for any educated gentleman.

But for some Christians, the Church of England, backed by Parliament, still retained too much of Rome's ways. Compulsory church attendance, a common prayer book, kneeling before a robed clergy: These were anathema to those who preferred Calvin's plain churches and simple worship and who wished to purify the Church of England of its apparent excesses. An opposition party called Puritanism emerged. Their attempts at reform in worship thwarted, a splinter group within the Puritans reorganized themselves as Separatists; in 1608, they fled royal persecution to Holland.

Their story is familiar to every American schoolchild. From Holland, in 1620, a group of Separatists made arrangements to sail to the New World. Arriving off the coast of Cape Cod, they sealed their high purposes with a document called *The Mayflower Compact*, committing themselves to God and his service in a new Eden they called New England.

For more than a decade after their arrival, these New Englanders conducted school in their homes. Joined by others less strict, by 1635, the Massachusetts Bay Colony had founded the Boston Latin School to prepare boys to return to Cambridge and the university there, where most of New England's clergy and other educated men had studied. The next year, however, the General Court of Massachusetts appropriated money for the founding of a local college in a village named for that English university town, on the banks of a river named for their King Charles I.

Two years later, a dying clergyman named John Harvard bequeathed half his estate for the purpose of supporting that fledgling college, whose mission was to prevent "an illiterate Ministry to the Churches, when our present Ministers shall lie in Dust."

Harvard College's earliest teachers were all ordained clergy. Indeed, more than a hundred years would pass before the first layman was appointed to teach science. During that century, apostasy encroached upon the intentions of Harvard's founders, so that Connecticut churches would not ordain or accept as pastors Harvard graduates. In 1701, an alternative college was founded at New Haven, named for Elihu Yale, a prosperous Boston merchant who had contributed more than eight hundred pounds sterling. But only a generation later, during the Great Awakening of the 1730s and 1740s, Jonathan Edwards accused both Harvard and his own Yale College of neglecting their duty to be faithful in preparing its students to be spiritual leaders. Instead, Edwards charged, these colleges were more interested in teaching their scholars secular studies.

Such was not the original purpose of education in America. As the following documents demonstrate, education in early

America revolved wholly around a religious sphere, and truth was found within the Christian message. Edwards, saddened by the way Harvard and later Yale had strayed from their founding mission, helped found a college in New Jersey that would be true a godly mission. He was president at what was to become Princeton University, and his message "A Divine and Supernatural Light" (page 251) shows the heart of this university president.

NEW ENGLAND DOCUMENTS

The origins of the "Pilgrim Fathers," who arrived at Cape Cod in November 1620, can be briefly traced, and found linked to John Wyclif's Lollards and King Henry VIII's break with Rome. From the time of the Lollards, a reforming spirit had made itself felt throughout England and Scotland. The king's split with Rome was not in itself a liberating act, for it established the monarch as supreme head of an Anglo-Catholic, rather than Roman, church. Not until Henry was succeeded by his son, Edward VI, in 1547, was there any movement toward the use of English in services and in a new *Book of Common Prayer*. But Edward died in 1553; with him seemed to die any hope of further reform because his sister Mary was an ardent and vengeful Roman Catholic. For five years, until Mary's own death in 1558, English reformers fled to Switzerland and Germany, where they became imbued with the teachings of Calvin in particular.

When these English Calvinists returned home, upon the coronation of Elizabeth I, they brought with them ideas of plain worship, a clergy without robes, prayer without kneeling, and a new importance given to preaching. In all this the English reformers were strengthened by support from the north, where in 1557, Scots lords had signed a covenant called "The Common Band," pledging themselves to support an evangelical and anti-Roman church. Three years later, led by John Knox, these Scots Presbyterians published their *Book of Discipline*, simplifying church polity and forms of worship.

Thus encouraged, the English reformers set about to purify the Church of England, issuing their own *Admonition to Parliament* in 1572. In this document they condemned as "anti-Christian and devilish, and contrary to the Scriptures" certain terms and practices which, they said, had been "drawn from the Pope's shop."[1] From then on, these "Puritans," as they were known, remained at odds with each reigning monarch.

But the Puritans kept their opposition restrained; not so a more radical group called Separatists, centered mostly in the counties north and east of Cambridge. The Separatists saw no other course than secession from the established church, with its Act of Supremacy, giving royal authority over the church, and Act of Uniformity, mandating worship using *The Book of Common Prayer*. In bold defiance, the Separatists worshiped as they chose, ignoring both acts.

For this, they suffered persecution, leading to imprisonment for some and exile to Holland for others. By 1608, a group led by their pastor, John Robinson, had settled in Leyden. For ten years they enjoyed the relative freedom of a country rapidly becoming a Dutch Calvinist state. But fearing assimilation and the loss of their English identity, Robinson's congregation began looking for a settlement where they could preserve their distinctives, cultural and religious.

Representatives returned to England and found speculators willing to risk money by supporting an expedition to America, specifically to the vast territory named Virginia in honor of the Virgin Queen Elizabeth I. Only thirty-five of Robinson's congregation signed on. The other sixty-plus voyagers, including the hired military adviser, Captain Myles Standish, were not Separatists.

Too ill to make the journey with his people, Robinson in July 1620 preached a farewell sermon of encouragement, calling upon them to remain open to God's revelation to them: "I am verily persuaded the Lord hath more truth and light yet to break forth out of His holy Word."

From Leyden, the party set out for Southampton, where they were to embark on board two vessels, the *Speedwell* and *Mayflower*. But the first was a misnamed ship. Twice it sprang leaks, and twice the two ships returned to port. At last, it was decided to abandon the *Speedwell*, and on September 6, the tiny *Mayflower* began its lonely voyage. Nine weeks later, the *Mayflower* reached safe waters off Cape Cod.

One of the leaders of the expedition was William Bradford, later governor of the new colony. In his *History of Plymouth Plantation*, begun around 1630, Bradford recalls how some of the crew and others who were not Separatists had let it be known "that when they came ashore they would use their own liberty, for none had power to command them." Facing this potentially dangerous situation, the Separatists called upon their recollection of church covenants, begun by the Scots' "Common Band," and so determined to draw up a document by which to hold each other accountable. This they called the *Mayflower Compact*. As their first act of government, the forty-one signers of the *Mayflower Compact* elected John Carver as governor, "a man godly and well approved amongst them," writes Bradford.[2]

The keystone document of American social, political, and religious history, the *Mayflower Compact* recorded that its signers desired "for the Glory of God and advancement of the Christian Faith and Honour of

237

our King and Country," to establish a colony in northern Virginia. They declared solemnly "in the presence of God and one of another," to covenant "ourselves together into a Civil Body Politic, for our better ordering and preservation and furtherance of the ends aforesaid; and by virtue hereof to enact, constitute and frame such just and equal Laws, Ordinances, Acts, Constitutions and Offices, from time to time, as shall be thought most meet and convenient for the general good of the Colony, unto which we promise all due submission and obedience."

Meanwhile, back in England, Puritanism had taken a new tack. Neither advocating separation from nor conformity to the established Church of England, Puritanism championed the right of each congregation, hence "congregationalism." By 1629, however, a group of dissident Congregationalists, led by John Winthrop, formed the Massachusetts Bay Company; before the end of the next summer, a colony of 1,000 had been planted, first at Salem, then at Boston.

Contrary to popular inaccuracy and distortion, Massachusetts Bay was no haven for either democracy or religious freedom. John Winthrop inveighed against democracy, calling it "the meanest and worst" form of government, proving from the Bible that Israel had been ruled as a theocracy. Nor was it long before the Bay Colony was expelling those who dared to disagree theologically—Roger Williams and Anne Hutchinson, for example.

But Massachusetts did become the seedbed of education in America, with the Boston Latin School, founded in 1635, to prepare boys to return to England for university studies at Cambridge, then a Puritan stronghold. The following year, however, the Massachusetts legislature voted to begin a college within its own borders. Harvard College was about to appear and, at least in the beginning, would offer an education based on a religious and biblical foundation.

Because a significant number of Massachusetts' citizens were graduates of Cambridge, the location of the new college was named for their famed university town in England. But the college itself had no name until, in 1638, a young bachelor minister named John Harvard, from his deathbed, bequeathed all his books and half his estate to the new college. As is common today, this generous donation earned him the name of the college.

From its beginnings, Harvard College had as its sole reason-for-being the educating of men for the ministry. The "Rules of Harvard College," circulated in 1642, and a pamphlet, "New England's First Fruits," probably written by Harvard's first president, Henry Dunster (1609–59), and published in London in 1643, make clear the college's intention; excerpts from the two documents follow.

To receive a bachelor's degree from Harvard, a student had to be able to "read the originals of the Old and New Testament in the Latin tongue." A candidate for a master's degree, in addition to his translation and interpretation of Scripture, had to produce evidence of his knowledge of "Logic, Natural and Moral Philosophy, Arithmetic, Geometry, and Astronomy." In both cases, furthermore, the candidate's character had to earn "the Approbation of the Overseers and Master of the College."

"Rules of Harvard College"[3] (Excerpt)

(a) Entrance Requirements

1. When any scholar is able to understand Tully, or such like classical Latin Author *extempore*, and make and speak true Latin in verse and prose, *suo ut aiunt Marte;* and decline perfectly the Paradigms of *Nounes* and *Verbes* in the *Greek* tongue: Let him then and not before be capable of admission into the College.

(b) Rules and Precepts

2. Let every student be plainly instructed, and earnestly pressed to consider well the main end of his life and studies is *to know God and Jesus Christ which is eternal life,* Joh. 17.3. and therefore to lay *Christ* in the bottom, as the only foundation of all sound knowledge and Learning.

And seeing the Lord only giveth wisdom, Let every one seriously set himself by prayer in secret to seek it of him, *Prov.* 2, 3.

3. Every one shall so exercise himself in reading the Scriptures twice a day, that he shall be ready to give such an account of his proficiency therein, both in *theoretical* observations of the Language, and *logic*, and in *practical* and spiritual truths, as his Tutor shall require, according to his ability; seeing *the entrance of the word giveth light, it giveth understanding to the simple,* Psalm 119. 130.

4. That they eschewing all profanation of God's Name, Attributes, Word, Ordinances, and times of Worship, do study with good conscience, carefully to retain God, and the love of his truth in their minds, else let them know that (notwithstanding their learning) God may give them up *to strong delusions,* and in the end *to a reprobate mind,* 2. Thes. 2. 11, 12. Rom. 1. 28.

5. That they studiously redeem the time; observe the general hour appointed for all the students, and the special hours for their own *Classes*: and then dilligently attend the Lectures without any disturbance by word or gesture. And if in any thing they doubt, they shall enquire as of their fellows, . . . modestly of their Tutors.

6. None shall under any pretence whatsoever, frequent the company and society of such men as lead an unfit, and dissolute life.

Nor shall any without his Tutor's leave, or (in his absence) the call of Parents or Guardians, go abroad to other Towns.

7. Every Scholar shall be present in his Tutor's chamber at the 7th. hour in the morning, immediately after the sound of the Bell, at his opening the Scripture and prayer, so also at the 5th. hour at night, and then give account of his own private reading, as aforesaid in particular the third, and constantly attend Lectures in the Hall at the hours appointed. But if any (without necessary impediment) shall absent himself from prayer or Lectures, he shall be liable to Admonition, if he offend above once a week.

8. If any Scholar shall be found to transgress any of the Laws of God, or the School, after twice Admonition, he shall be liable, if not [of adult age], to correction, [if an adult] his name shall be given up to the Overseers of the College, that he may be admonished at the Public monthly Act.

"New England's First Fruits"

After God had carried us safe to *New England,* and we had builded our houses, provided necessaries for our livelihood, reared convenient places for God's worship, and settled the Civil Government: One of the next things we longed for, and looked after was to advance *Learning,* and perpetuate it to Posterity, dreading to leave an illiterate ministry to the Churches, when our present ministers shall lie in the dust. And as we were thinking and consulting how to effect this great Work; it pleased God to stir up the heart of one Mr. *Harvard* (a godly Gentleman and a lover of Learning, there living amongst us) to give the one half of his estate (it being in all about 1700£) towards the erecting of a College, and all his library. After him another gave 300£. Others after them cast in more, and the public hand of the State added the rest: the College was, by common consent, appointed to be at *Cambridge,* a place very pleasant and accommodate and is called (according to the name of the first founder) *Harvard College.*

The Edifice is very fair and comely within and without, having in it a spacious Hall; (where they daily meet at Commons, Lectures, Exercises) and a large library with some books to it, the gifts of diverse of our friends, their chambers and studies also fitted for, and possessed by the students, and all other rooms of office necessary and convenient, with all needful offices thereto belonging: And by the side of the College a fair Grammar School, for the training up of young Scholars, and fitting of them for Academical *Learning,* that still as they are judged ripe, they may be received into the College of this school. Master Corlet is the Mr., who hath very well approved himself for his abilities, dexterity and painfulness in teaching and education of the youth under him.

Over the College is Master Dunster placed, as President, a learned conscionable and industrious man, who has so trained up his pupils in the tongues and arts, and so seasoned them with the principles of divinity and Christianity that we have to our great comfort, (and in truth) beyond our hopes, beheld their progress in learning and godliness also; the former of these hath appeared in their public declamations in *Latin* and *Greek,* and disputations logical and philosophical, which they have been wonted (besides their ordinary exercises in the College-Hall) in the audience of the Magistrates, Ministers, and other Scholars, for the probation of their growth in learning, upon set days, constantly once every month to make and uphold . . . .

Over the College are twelve Overseers chosen by the general Court, six of them are of the Magistrates, the other six of the Ministers, who are to promote the best good of it, and (having a power of influence into all persons in it) are to see that every one be diligent and proficient in his proper place.

In 1642, the Massachusetts Bay colony enacted the first compulsory education law, taking note of "the great neglect of many parents and masters in training up their children in learning." Especially important, according to this law, was instruction that would enable children "to read and understand the principles of religion and the capital laws of this country." Five years later, the Act of 1647 took effect. This act was commonly known as "Ye Old Deluder, Satan" law because of its warning that "one chief project of ye old deluder, Satan [is] to keep men from the knowledge of ye Scriptures." The act required that towns with at least fifty households appoint someone within the town to teach the children, "whose wages shall be paid either by ye parents or masters of such children, or by ye inhabitants in general." Once a town has at least one hundred households, the citizens "shall set up a grammar school."

Schools began to appear throughout Massachusetts in compliance with the Acts of 1642 and 1647; in 1645, the Roxbury Grammar School, for instance. Outside Massachusetts, similar laws were being enacted.

For textbooks these schools, naturally, had the Bible. They also had *The Bay Psalm Book,* a collection of metrical versions of the Psalms published in 1640, the first bound book in the New World; a catechism called *Milk for Babes: Drawn Out of the Breasts of Both Testaments,* published in 1646 by John Cotton; and eventually, from 1690 on, many editions of *The New England Primer,* an illustrated alphabet and anthology of inspirational readings. Of course, these schools also made pedagogical use of the ministers' sermons from the previous Sunday. An excerpt from the primer follows.

The New England Primer[4] (Excerpt)

In *Adam's* Fall
We sinned all.

Heaven to find,
The *Bible* mind.

Christ crucify'd
For Sinners dy'd.

The *Deluge* drown'd
The Earth around.

Elijah hid,
By Ravens fed.

The Judgment made
Felix afraid.

242

As runs the *Glass*
Our life doth pass.

My Book and *Heart*
Must never part.

Job feels the Rod
Yet blesses GOD.

Proud *Korah's* Troop
Was swallow'd up.

Lot fled to Zoar,
Saw fiery Shower
On Sodom pour.

Moses was he
Who Israel's Host
Led thro' the Sea.

Noah did view
The old world and new.

Young *Obadias*,
David, Tobias,
All were pious.

Peter deny'd
His Lord and cry'd.

Queen Esther sues,
And saves the Jews.

Young pious *Ruth*
Left all for Truth.

Samuel dear
The Lord did fear.

Young *Timothy*
Learnt sin to fly.

Vashti for Pride
Was set aside.

Whales in the Sea
God's Voice obey.

Xerxes must die,
And so must I.

Zaccheus he
Did climb the Tree
Our Lord to see.

In Holland's outpost called New Amsterdam (later New York) the Collegiate School, founded in 1628, followed the pattern set by the *Canons of Dordt*. Across the river in Flatbush, now a section of Brooklyn, a teacher named Johannes Van Eckkelen signed a contract in 1682. It demonstrates both the goals of education at the time and the strict regime expected of teachers and students alike.

"Contract with Flatbush Consistory"

School Service. I. The School shall begin at eight o'clock, and go out at eleven; and in the afternoon shall begin at one o'clock and end at four. The bell shall be rung when the school commences.

II. When the school begins, one of the children shall read the morning prayer, as it stands in the catechism, and close with the prayer before dinner; in the afternoon it shall begin with the prayer after dinner, and end with the evening prayer. The evening school shall begin with the Lord's prayer, and close by singing a psalm.

III. He shall instruct the children on every Wednesday and Saturday, in the common prayers, and the questions and answers in the catechism, to enable them to repeat them the better on Sunday before the afternoon service, or on Monday, when they shall be catechised before the congregation. Upon all such occasions, the schoolmaster shall be present, and shall require the children to be friendly in their appearance and encourage them to answer freely and distinctly.

IV. He shall be required to keep his school nine months in succession, from September to June, in each year, in case it should be concluded upon to retain his services for a year or more, or without limitation; and he shall then be required to be regulated by these articles, and to perform the same duties which his predecessor was required to perform. In every particular therefore, he shall be required to keep school, according to this seven months agreement, and shall always be present himself.

Church Service. I. He shall keep the church clean, and ring the bell three times before the people assemble to attend the preaching and catechism. Also before the sermon is commenced, he shall read a chapter out of the Holy Scriptures, and that, between the second and third ringing of the bell. After the third ringing he shall read the ten commandments, and the twelve articles of our faith, and then take the lead in singing. In the afternoon after the third ringing of the bell, he shall read a short chapter, or one of the Psalms of David, as the congregation are assembling; and before divine service commences, shall introduce it, by the singing of a Psalm or Hymn.

II. When the minister shall preach at Brooklyn, or New-Utrecht, he shall be required to read twice before the congregation, from the book commonly used for that purpose. In the afternoon he shall also read a sermon on the explanation of the catechism, according to the usage and practice approved of by the minister. The children, as usual, shall recite their questions and answers out of the catechism, on Sunday, and he shall instruct them therein. He, as chorister, shall not be required to perform these duties, whenever divine service shall be performed in Flatlands, as it would be unsuitable, and prevent many from attending there.

III. For the administration of Holy Baptism, he shall provide a basin with water, for which he shall be entitled to receive from the parents, or witnesses, twelve styvers. He shall, at the expense of the church, provide bread and wine, for the celebration of the Holy supper. He shall be in duty bound promptly to furnish the minister with the name of the child to be baptized, and with the names of the parents and witnesses. And he shall also serve as messenger for the consistory.

IV. He shall give the funeral invitations, dig the grave, and toll the bell, for which service he shall receive for a person of fifteen years and upwards, twelve guilders, and for one under that age, eight guilders. If he should be required to give invitations beyond the limits of the town, he shall be entitled to three additional guilders, for the invitation of every other town, and if he should be required to cross the river, and go to New York, he shall receive four guilders.

School Money. He shall receive from those who attend the day school, for a speller or reader, three guilders a quarter, and for a writer four guilders. From those who attend evening school, for a speller or reader, four guilders, and for a writer, six guilders shall be given.

Salary. In addition to the above, his salary shall consist of four hundred guilders, in grain, valued in Seewant, to be delivered at Brooklyn Ferry, and for his services from October to May, as above stated, a sum of two hundred and thirty-four guilders, in the same kind, with the dwelling-house, barn, pasture lot and meadows, to the school appertaining. The same to take effect from the first day of October, instant.

Done and agreed upon in Consistory, under the inspection of the Honorable Constable and Overseers, the 8th, of October, 1682. . . .

I agree to the above articles, and promise to perform them according to the best of my ability.

Johannes Van Eckkelen.
A Mission to the Natives

Before we consider the impact during this period of the preacher, theologian, and scholar Jonathan Edwards, we should note the missionary enterprise to educate Native Americans and preserve the faith in an educational setting. Whether in New England or New Netherlands, the purpose of education was to defeat "ye old deluder, Satan." In fact, the seal of the Massachusetts Bay Company shows the figure of an American Indian speaking the words of St. Paul's visionary messenger, "Come over . . . and help us" (Acts 16:9). Education would therefore be consecrated to doing its part in fulfilling the Macedonian mission, the "errand into the wilderness," as it was called.

Missionary ventures among the native peoples began in the 1640s. By 1646, John Eliot had mastered the dialect well enough to preach in their own language to Indians in villages around Boston. By 1663, he had translated the entire Bible into the Algonkian tongue. Among the Algonkians, the first of fourteen "praying towns" had been constructed in 1651, with a meetinghouse that doubled as a school.

Similarly, Thomas Mayhew, Jr., whose father was owner of the island called Martha's Vineyard, also learned the native language and converted many Indians there. When he died on a voyage to England, his father, although an aged man, carried on his work. In turn, a grandson appropriately named Experience Mayhew produced a library of Christian literature and Bible translation in the Indian language.

By the late 1750s, missionary zeal impelled a Congregational minister, Eleazar Wheelock, to begin an Indian charity school at

Lebanon, Connecticut. His students included a Mohawk named Thayendanegea, later famous as a chief known in English as Joseph Brant. By 1770, Wheelock had moved his school to Hanover in what is now New Hampshire, where he desired to combine education for Indians with a training school for colonial missionaries to Indians. Thus Dartmouth College was founded, with its motto on the great seal of the college—"The Voice of One Crying in the Wilderness"—still on view in the library today.

But for all its missionary zeal and moral earnestness, the New England theocracy could not stave off the ravages of apostasy and secularism. In the beginning, since only church members could vote and hold office, any personal insincerity could be masked by outward shows of religiosity by "saint seeming deceivers." But by the 1680s, political events were largely determining religious character, rather than the reverse. In 1684, King James II attempted to consolidate his English colonies in America by annulling charters and imposing a royal governor. At the same time, the Congregationalists lost their exclusive rights to set religious practice; the Anglican Church was instituted, with Good Friday and Easter services, in Boston in 1687.

The political threat was turned back the following year, as James II was deposed, but the Congregational theocracy's wall of solidarity had been breached in Massachusetts and elsewhere. The Salem witch hunt and trials of 1692 were, in part, a repressive reaction in an attempt to stifle the colony's new flickers of religious freedom. Though the intent was to restore orthodoxy, the excesses at Salem simply accelerated skepticism and apostasy.

The crack in the wall widened when officials of Harvard College began to deviate from rigid ecclesiastical policies and personnel. By 1701 the new wave of liberalism had contributed to the ouster of Cotton Mather's father, Increase Mather, as president of Harvard. In 1703, Cotton Mather himself resigned his position at the college; thereafter, both Mathers devoted their energies to supporting a new educational venture already begun in Connecticut. Through their influence a wealthy Boston merchant named Elihu Yale made a major donation. By 1718, Yale College was well established as a bastion of orthodoxy against Harvard's increasing liberalism.

JONATHAN EDWARDS

In America, it has often been popular to denigrate preachers as anti-intellectual antagonists of education. Some clerics, of course, merit the charge. Not so Jonathan Edwards: scholar, natural scientist, recognized as America's first philosopher, theologian, writer, eloquent proclaimer of God's truth, and, until death claimed him, the third president of what is now Princeton University.

Edwards was born in 1703, the only son among ten sisters. His father was a pastor and his grandfather, Solomon Stoddard, was the leading clergyman in New England and pastor in Northampton, Massachusetts. Before departing East Windsor, Connecticut, for college at age thirteen, the precocious child wrote learned articles on the flying spider and the rainbow, based on observation.

Upon graduation from Yale in 1720, Edwards spent an additional two years in divinity studies, was briefly a lay-minister in New York, then returned to Yale for three years as tutor. Because there was no master or president of the College during those years, Edwards was—at age twenty-one—essentially in charge of sixty students and their teachers.

In 1727, he was ordained and married Sarah Pierrepont, about whom he had written a rhapsodic prose poem based only on the reputation her Christian character had evoked.[5] Edwards accepted his grandfather's invitation to join him at Northhampton. When Solomon Stoddard died in 1729, Edwards became pastor.

His gifts were many, but it was primarily as a preacher that Edwards was so extraordinary. At Yale, Edwards had read Sir Isaac Newton and John Locke; he was aware of the impending conflict between, on the one hand, scientific rationalism and empiricism and, on the other, the emotionalism upon which much of the clergy's representation of the gospel had depended. Edwards determined to find a method of writing and speaking that would accommodate both the thinking and the feeling elements in his preaching.

From 1726 to 1750, he preached at Northampton, then a frontier town full of young men rendered dissolute by their lack of inherited opportunity. Edwards made these rowdies his special mission, and in 1734 a great revival occurred in Northampton and throughout the Connecticut River valley. This revival spilled over and merged with "the Great Awakening" of the 1730s and 1740s, spurred by the preaching of Edwards and of George Whitefield, the English evangelist who preached four sermons in the Northampton church in the fall of 1740.

Both Whitefield and Edwards were educated men; such was not the case with many other evangelists of the Awakening. Indeed, many of them decried formal learning and, along with it, any prior study or preparation before delivering their sermons. Such is the spirit of one Connecticut preacher who is alleged to have told his congregation:

> What I insist upon, my brethren and sisters, is this: Larnin'
> ain't religion, and eddication don't give a man the power of
> the Spirit. It is grace and gifts that furnish the real live coals
> from off the altar. St. Peter was a fisherman—do you think
> he ever went to Yale College?[6]

In 1743, one critic of the Awakening, Charles Chauncy, for fifty years pastor of Boston's First Congregational Church, wrote his "Seasonable Thoughts on the State of Religion in New England." In attacking the anti-intellectualism among many evangelists, Chauncy said:

> They pleaded there was no Need of Learning in preaching, and that one of them could by the Spirit do better than the Minister by his Learning; as if the Spirit and Learning were Opposites. . . . Their depending on the Help of the Spirit as to despise Learning: To do it is owing that so many speak slightly of our Schools and Colleges . . . and to the same Cause still it must be attributed that so many Ministers preach, not only without Book, but without Study; and justify their doing so, lest, by previous Preparation they should stint the Spirit.[7]

What such enthusiasts feared had been described by Gilbert Tennent, a fiery Presbyterian, in his 1740 sermon, "The Danger of an Unconverted Ministry." Tennent allowed his followers to assume that education devitalized faith and that, consequently, most educated ministers were pious frauds. Tennent called them "Hirelings," "Letter-Learned Pharisees," and "Dead Dogs that cannot Bark." So, under the guise of spiritual enthusiasm, some well-meaning Christians led the way from the possible blight of educated apostasy to the certain famine of orthodox ignorance.

This same opposition to formal learning pervaded life throughout rural and frontier America, so much so that for a man to be a schoolmaster was tantamount to admitting his failure at a more respectable trade. So also, to be a divinity school graduate invited upon any preacher assumptions of heresy.

Edwards represented the balanced midpoint between cold liberalism and a fervid revivalism. On July 8, 1841, for instance, Edwards visited a church in Enfield, Connecticut, where he preached his most famous sermon, "Sinners in the Hands of an Angry God." Contrary to legend, Edwards was no ranter. In fact, Eleazar Wheelock, who was present, records that the sermon was delivered in a quiet and unspectacular manner; yet its effect was spectacular. Wheelock speaks of "such a breathing of distress, and weeping, that the preacher was obliged to speak to the people and desire silence, that he might be heard."[8]

But as the Awakening waned, the congregation in Northampton wearied of Edwards and his preaching; particularly offensive was his insistence that the celebration of the Lord's Supper was for believers only. Turned out in 1750, Edwards became a missionary to the Indians living near Stockbridge. There, under severely primitive conditions, he wrote *Freedom of the Will* and other philosophical works not published until after his death.

As for Yale College, Edwards came to see its apostate influence. Thus he joined Tennent and others in the Presbyterian venture to found a college that would remain true to its founders' godly intentions. When the second president of the College of New Jersey, his son-in-law, Aaron Burr, Sr., died in 1756, Edwards was elected president in 1757. He was inaugurated in January 1758, but he died one month later from the effects of a smallpox vaccination. The College of New Jersey was later named Princeton University.

Had he lived longer to shape the college at Princeton, one can only speculate what his administration and teaching might have done for Christian education in America. As it was, Christian education fell into serious decline during the next seventy years. Three wars decimated funds and personnel from without; rampant denial of the gospel—especially as expressed by deism and, eventually, Unitarianism—crippled churches, schools, and colleges from within.

Edwards left a legacy of intellectual as well as evangelistic example. His masterpiece is *Freedom of the Will*, published in 1754, while ministering to the Indians. But he also wrote an engaging *Personal Narrative*, published posthumously in 1808. One of the sermons that best combines these gifts of reason and warmth in this remarkable man is "A Divine and Supernatural Light." Edwards discerns between false and true spiritual insight, helping listeners to understand the nature of conviction and spiritual guidance in this vital message.

"A Divine and Supernatural Light"[9] (Excerpt)

That there is such a thing as a spiritual and divine light, immediately imparted to the soul by God, of a different nature from any that is obtained by natural means.

In what I say on this subject, at this time, I would,

    I. Show what this divine light is.

    II. How it is given immediately by God, and not obtained by natural means.

    III. Show the truth of the doctrine.

And then conclude with a brief improvement.

I. I would show what this spiritual and divine light is. And in order to it, would show,

First, In a few things what is not. And here.

1. Those convictions that natural men may have of their sin and misery, is not this spiritual and divine light. Men in a natural condition may have convictions of the guilt that lies upon them, and of the anger of God, and their danger of divine vengeance. . . .

2. This spiritual and divine light does not consist in any impression made upon the imagination. It is no impression upon the mind, as though one saw any thing with the bodily eyes: it is no imagination or idea of an outward light or glory, or any beauty of form or countenance, or a visible lustre or brightness of any object. The imagination may be strongly impressed with such things; but this is not spiritual light. . . .

3. This spiritual light is not the suggesting of any new truths or propositions not contained in the word of God. This suggesting of new truths or doctrines to the mind, independent of any antecedent revelation of those propositions, either in word or writing, is inspiration; such as the prophets and apostles had, and such as some enthusiasts pretend to. But this spiritual light that I am speaking of, is quite a different thing from inspiration: it reveals no new doctrine, it suggests no new proposition to the mind, it teaches no new thing of God, or Christ, or another world, not taught in the Bible, but only gives a due apprehension of those things that are taught in the word of God.

4. It is not every affecting view that men have of the things of religion that is spiritual and divine light. Men by mere principles of nature are capable of being affected with things that have a special relation to religion as well as other things. A person by mere nature, for instance, may be liable to be affected with the story of Jesus Christ, and the sufferings he underwent, as well as by any other tragical story: he may be the more affected with it from the interest he conceives mankind to have in it; yea, he may be affected with it without believing it; as well as a man may be affected with what he reads in a romance, or sees acted in a stage play. . . . A person therefore may have affecting views of the things of religion, and yet be very destitute of spiritual light. Flesh and blood may be the author of this: one man may give another an affecting view of divine things with but common assistance: but God alone can give a spiritual discovery of them.

But I proceed to show,

Secondly, Positively what this spiritual and divine light is.

And it may be thus described: a true sense of the divine excellency of the things revealed in the word of God, and a conviction of the truth and reality of them thence arising.

This spiritual light primarily consists in the former of these, viz., a real sense and apprehension of the divine excellency of things revealed in the word of God. A spiritual and saving conviction of the truth and reality of these things, arises from such a sight of their divine excellency and glory; so that this conviction of their truth is an effect and natural consequence of this sight of their divine glory. There is therefore in this spiritual light,

II. A true sense of the divine and superlative excellency of the things of religion; a real sense of the excellency of God and Jesus Christ, and of the work of redemption, and the ways and works of God revealed in the gospel. There is a divine and superlative glory in these things; an excellency that is of a vastly higher kind, and more sublime nature than in other things; a glory greatly distinguishing them from all that is earthly and temporal. He that is spiritually enlightened truly apprehends and sees it, or has a sense of it. He does not merely rationally believe that God is glorious, but he has a sense of the gloriousness of God in his heart.

There is not only a speculatively judging that God is gracious, but a sense how amiable God is upon that account, or a sense of the beauty of this divine attribute.

There is a twofold understanding or knowledge of good that God has made the mind of man capable of. The first, that which is merely speculative and notional; as when a person only speculatively judges that any thing is, which, by the agreement of mankind, is called good or excellent, viz., that which is most to general advantage, and between which and a reward there is a suitableness, and the like. And the other is, that which consists in the sense of the heart: as when there is a sense of the beauty, amiableness, or sweetness of a thing; so that the heart is sensible of pleasure and delight in the presence of the idea of it. In the former is exercised merely the speculative faculty, or the understanding, strictly so called, or as spoken of in distinction from the will or disposition of the soul. In the latter, the will, or inclination, or heart, is mainly concerned.

Thus there is a difference between having an opinion, that God is holy and gracious, and having a sense of the loveliness and beauty of that holiness and grace. There is a difference between having a rational judgment that honey is sweet, and having a sense of its sweetness. A man may have the former, that knows not how honey tastes; but a man cannot have the latter unless he has an idea of the taste of honey in his mind. So there is a difference between believing that a person is beautiful, and having a sense of his beauty. The former may be obtained by hearsay, but the latter only by seeing the countenance. There is a wide difference between mere speculative rational judging any thing to be excellent, and having a sense of its sweetness and beauty. The former rests only in the head, speculation only is concerned in it; but the heart is concerned in the latter. When the heart is sensible of the beauty and amiableness of a thing, it necessarily feels pleasure in the apprehension. It is implied in a person's being heartily sensible of the loveliness of a thing, that the idea of it is sweet and pleasant to his soul; which is a far different thing from having a rational opinion that it is excellent. . . .

I come now.

III. To show the truth of the doctrine; that is, to show that there is such a thing as that spiritual light that has been described, thus immediately let into the mind by God. And here I would show briefly, that this doctrine is both scriptural and rational.

First. It is scriptural. My text is not only full to the purpose, but it is a doctrine that the Scripture abounds in. We are there abundantly taught, that the saints differ from the ungodly in this, that they have the knowledge of God, and a sight of God, and of Jesus Christ. . . .

But this brings me to what was proposed next, viz., to show that,

Secondly, This doctrine is rational.

1. It is rational to suppose, that there is really such an excellency in divine things, that is so transcendent and exceedingly different from what is in other things, that, if it were seen, would most evidently distinguish them. We cannot rationally doubt but that things that are divine, that appertain to the Supreme Being, are vastly different from things that are human; that there is that god-like, high and glorious excellency in them, that does most remarkably difference them from the things that are of men; insomuch that if the difference were but seen, it would have a convincing, satisfying influence upon any one, that they are what they are, viz., divine. What reason can be offered against it? Unless we would argue, that God is not remarkably distinguished in glory from men. . . .

2. If there be such a distinguishing excellency in divine things; it is rational to suppose that there may be such a thing as seeing it. What should hinder but that it may be seen? It is no argument, that there is no such thing as such a distinguishing excellency, or that, if there be, that it cannot be seen, that some do not see it, though they may be discerning men in temporal matters. It is not rational to suppose, if there be any such excellency in divine things, that wicked men should see it. It is not rational to suppose, that those whose minds are full of spiritual pollution, and under the power of filthy lusts, should have any relish or sense of divine beauty or excellency; or that their minds should be susceptive of that light that is in its own nature so pure and heavenly. It need not seem at all strange, that sin should so blind the mind,

seeing that men's particular natural tempers and dispositions will so much blind them in secular matters; as when men's natural temper is melancholy, jealous, fearful, proud, or the like.

3. It is rational to suppose, that this knowledge should be given immediately by God, and not be obtained by natural means. Upon what account should it seem unreasonable, that there should be any immediate communication between God and the creature? It is strange that men should make any matter of difficulty of it. Why should not he that made all things, still have something immediately to do with the things that he has made? Where lies the great difficulty, if we own the being of a God, and that he created all things out of nothing, of allowing some immediate influence of God on the creation still? And if it be reasonable to suppose it with respect to any part of the creation, it is especially so with respect to reasonable, intelligent creatures, who are next to God in the gradation of the different orders of beings, and whose business is most immediately with God; who were made on purpose for those exercises that do respect God and wherein they have nextly to do with God; for reason teaches, that man was made to serve and glorify his Creator. And if it be rational to suppose that God immediately communicates himself to man in any affair, it is in this. It is rational to suppose that God would reserve that knowledge and wisdom, that is of such a divine and excellent nature, to be bestowed immediately by himself, and that it should not be left in the power of second causes. Spiritual wisdom and grace is the highest and most excellent gift that ever God bestows on any creature; in this the highest excellency and perfection of a rational creature consists. It is also immensely the most important of all divine gifts; it is that wherein man's happiness consists, and on which his everlasting welfare depends. How rational is it to suppose that God, however he has left meaner goods and lower gifts to second causes, and in some sort in their power, yet should reserve this most excellent, divine, and important of all divine communications, in his own hands, to be bestowed immediately by himself, as a thing too great for second causes to be concerned in! It is rational to suppose, that this blessing should be immediately from God. . . .

It is rational to suppose, that it should be beyond a man's power to obtain this knowledge and light by the mere strength of natural reason; for it is not a thing that belongs to reason, to see the beauty and loveliness of spiritual things; it is not a speculative thing, but depends on the sense of the heart. Reason indeed is necessary in order to [obtain] it, as it is by reason only that we are become the subjects of the means of it; which means I have already shown to be necessary in order to [obtain] it, though they have no proper causal in the affair. It is by reason that we become possessed of a notion of those doctrines that are the subject matter of this divine light; and reason may many ways be indirectly and remotely an advantage to it. And reason has also to do in the acts that are immediately consequent on this discovery: a seeing the truth of religion from hence, is by reason; though it be but by one step, and the inference be immediate. So reason has to do in that accepting of, and trusting in Christ, that is consequent on it . . . But it is out of reason's province to perceive the beauty of loveliness of any thing: such a perception does not belong to that faculty. Reason's work is to perceive truth and not excellency. . . .

I will conclude with a very brief improvement of what has been said.

First. This doctrine may lead us to reflect on the goodness of God, that has so ordered it, that a saving evidence of the truth of the gospel is such, as is attainable by persons of mean capacities and advantages, as well as those that are of the greatest parts and learning. If the evidence of the gospel depended only on history, and such reasonings as learned men only are capable of, it would be above the reach of far the greatest part of mankind. But persons with but an ordinary degree of knowledge, are capable, without a long and subtle train of reasoning, to see the divine excellency of the things of religion: they are capable of being taught by the Spirit of God, as well as learned men. The evidence that is this way obtained, is vastly better and more satisfying, than all that can be obtained by the arguings of those that are most learned, and greatest masters of reason. And babes are as capable of knowing these things, as the wise and prudent; and they are often hid from these when they are revealed to those. 1 Cor. i. 26, 27, "For ye see your calling, brethren, how that not many wise men, after the flesh, not many mighty, not many noble are called. But God hath chosen the foolish things of the world."

Secondly. This doctrine may well put us upon examining ourselves, whether we have ever had this divine light, that has been described, let into our souls. If there be such a thing indeed, and it be not only a notion of whimsy of persons of weak and distempered brains, then doubtless it is a thing of great importance, whether we have thus been taught by the Spirit of God; whether the light of the glorious gospel of Christ, who is the image of God, hath shined unto us, giving us the light of the knowledge of the glory of God in the face of Jesus Christ; whether we have seen the Son, and believed on him, or have that faith of gospel doctrines that arises from a spiritual sight of Christ.

Thirdly. All may hence be exhorted earnestly to seek this spiritual light. To influence and move to it, the following things may be considered.

1. This is the most excellent and divine wisdom that any creature is capable of. It is more excellent than any human learning; it is far more excellent than all the knowledge of the greatest philosophers or statesmen. Yea, the least glimpse of the glory of God in the face of Christ doth more exalt and ennoble the soul, than all the knowledge of those that have the greatest speculative understanding in divinity without grace. This knowledge has the most noble object that is or can be, viz., the divine glory or excellency of God and Christ. The knowledge of these objects is that wherein consists the most excellent knowledge of the angels, yea, of God himself.

2. This knowledge is that which is above all others sweet and joyful. Men have a great deal of pleasure in human knowledge, in studies of natural things; but this is nothing to that joy which arises from this divine light shining into the soul. This light gives a view of those things that are immensely the most exquisitely beautiful, and capable of delighting the eye of the understanding. This spiritual light is the dawning of the light of glory in the heart. There is nothing so powerful as this to support persons in affliction, and to give the mind peace and brightness in this stormy and dark world.

3. This light is such as effectually influences the inclination, and changes the nature of the soul. It assimilates the nature to the divine nature, and changes the soul into an image of the same glory that is beheld. 2 Cor. iii. 18, "But we all with open face, beholding as in a glass the glory of the Lord, are changed into the same image, from glory to glory, even as by the Spirit of the Lord." This knowledge will wean from the world, and raise the inclination to heavenly things. It will turn the heart to God as the fountain of good, and to choose him for the only portion. This light, and this only, will bring the soul to a saving close with Christ. . . .

4. This light, and this only, has its fruit in a universal holiness of life. No merely notional or speculative understanding of the doctrines of religion will ever bring to this. But this light, as it reaches the bottom of the heart, and changes the nature, so it will effectually dispose to a universal obedience. It shows God's worthiness to be obeyed and served. It draws forth the heart in a sincere love to God, which is the only principle of a true, gracious, and universal obedience; and it convinces of the reality of those glorious rewards that God has promised to them that obey Him.

PART VII

AMERICAN REFORMERS: 1750–1900

The object in educating youth ought to be to qualify young persons as ornaments, as blessings, and as comforts in the vineyard of the Lord.

Samuel Phillips, Jr., 1776

AMERICAN REFORMERS

A s the Great Awakening waned, new struggles for land and freedom combined in a reaction against piety. The French-Indian or Seven Years' War (1756–63) rewrote the map of New France on North America; soon thereafter, the Boston Tea Party and the Minutemen at Concord Bridge occupied the colonial consciousness; then came the War of 1812 to disturb domestic tranquility.

But even as materialism and the ravages of war coalesced against godliness in the newly independent United States of America, the first half of the nineteenth century brought to the fore a group of Christian educators whose work carried forward both the missionary zeal of Jonathan Edwards and David Brainerd and the social reforms of Anthony Benezet. Like Hannah More, Benezet's first cause was equal opportunity for girls to become educated; but he also had a heart for the elevation of all persons of color to equal human status through education and advancement.

Later reforms would follow: women's dignity and equality, the end of child labor abuses, temperance—more accurately, total abstinence from liquor—a free education for all, and of paramount importance, the abolition of America's most shameful evil, slavery.

Once more, may it be said, the impetus for these reforms originated not in political conventions but in Christian churches and schools; indeed, often in small groups of praying Christians who endeavored by their schools to achieve what the church could not. In the nineteenth century, among the leaders of this loosely aligned movement were several of Lyman Beecher's many and illustrious children; the Presbyterian evangelist Charles Grandison Finney; his convert Theodore Weld, his wife Angelina Grimké Weld, and her sister Sarah Grimké; the philanthropists Arthur and Lewis Tappan; and the educators William Holmes McGuffey and Mary Lyon.

The family of Lyman Beecher may have been the most re-markable household in American history. Beecher graduated from Yale in 1797, and took a church in East Hampton, Long Island, New York. There Roxanna, the first of his three wives, gave birth, in 1800, to Catharine, the first of thirteen children, nine of whom survived.

After serving as pastor in New York City; Litchfield, Con-necticut; and Boston, Massachusetts; in 1832, Lyman Beecher accepted the presidency of the newly founded Lane Theological Seminary in Cincinnati, Ohio. His daughters Catharine, whose reputation as an educational pioneer preceded her, and Harriet accompanied their father to Ohio. Lyman Beecher was also to be joined by Charles Grandison Finney, a powerful evangelist whose New York City converts included several wealthy sup-porters.

Although Charles Finney left in 1835 to join the Oberlin College faculty nearby, their joint intent was to use the devel-oping cultural resources of Cincinnati—being touted as "the Athens of the West"—to break with Eastern traditionalism and offer in that distant setting a wholly new vision for education and society. For Finney, if not for Lyman Beecher, that vision included the seeds of radical social reform that promoted ardent anti-slavery and abolitionism and provided women with an op-portunity for higher education. At Oberlin, Finney kept that vision alive. In Cincinnati, Catharine and Harriet Beecher may have been more faithful in carrying the torch than was their politically-minded father. For this shared vision also included the possibility of new relations between white and black races.

In the city of Cincinnati, on the northern side of the Ohio River, lived a large number of blacks, including escaped or emancipated former slaves. In the spring of 1834, during Lyman Beecher's absence on an Eastern tour to garner money for the seminary, Lane students, led by Theodore Weld and William Thomas Allan, the son of a Presbyterian minister in Huntsville, Alabama, stirred a debate. Weld wished to encourage his fel-low-students to associate with their black neighbors and share with them some aspects of the life of the seminary community. Seminary trustees objected and expelled the ringleader Weld.

Two students, Augustus Wattles and Marius Robinson, left the seminary to found a school for black children but found themselves teaching eager adults. Most of the others responded by joining Weld and Allan in enrolling at Oberlin under Finney.

For her part, Catharine Beecher's popular lectures a decade later sparked a movement for change among otherwise complacent Eastern women. Drawing startling word-portraits of the wretched conditions in which women and children worked, Catharine Beecher did not hesitate to point out that, while women in clothing factories might earn less than fifteen cents a day, the garments they produced made the male owners of those factories millionaires. She also described inadequate schools and called for more women to take up the vocation of teaching.

So, from a distant location in the Western Reserve, Finney and his converts lighted the flame in opposition to slavery and in favor of a gospel of freedom and dignity for all persons. Scholars now realize that the Eastern abolitionists were not led primarily by William Lloyd Garrison and his *Liberator*, published in Boston. The message of liberation was carried to the East by lesser-known voices such as Theodore Weld in his tracts "The Bible Against Slavery," published in 1837, and "American Slavery as It Is." The latter tract contained reports from Southern newspapers, compiled with his wife Angelina and sister-in-law Sarah Grimké. More than 100,000 copies of "American Slavery as It Is," published in 1839, were sold in its first year.

As for other members of Lyman Beecher's family, Edward Beecher went from Yale as part of the "Illinois Band," eleven students who responded to the Second Awakening's missionary fervor, to be one of the founders and first president of Illinois College, begun in Jacksonville in 1829. He was later pastor of Boston's historic Park Street Church, where he assisted the abolitionists by shipping arms disguised as "Beecher's Bibles."

Harriet Beecher married a member of the Lane Seminary faculty, Calvin Ellis Stowe, who had left Dartmouth College, where he was professor of Greek, to teach at the new seminary. In 1850, Stowe accepted a professorship at Bowdoin College, Brunswick, Maine. There Harriet Beecher Stowe drew upon her imagination, observation of runaway slaves, and reports published by Theodore Weld and the Grimké sisters, to write *Uncle Tom's Cabin, or Life Among the Lowly,* published in 1852. A decade later, upon being introduced to Harriet Beecher Stowe, President Abraham Lincoln said, "So you're the little woman who wrote the little book that started the big war!"

Henry Ward Beecher became the most famous preacher of the nineteenth century, an orator whose sermons drew large crowds to the Plymouth Congregational Church in Brooklyn.

ANTHONY BENEZET

As is true of all great spiritual revivals, the Great Awakening of the 1840s produced not only personal piety but acts of social reform spurred by Christian conviction. Among those who led such reforms was the Quaker Anthony Benezet (1713–84).

Born in Picardy, France, of Huguenot parents, Benezet and his parents fled persecution, moving first to Rotterdam, then London, and finally settling in Philadelphia in 1731. There his parents identified with the Moravians, while Anthony chose the Society of Friends.

As a young man, Benezet left jobs as a barrel maker and print shop proofreader to enter teaching, first in Germantown. In 1742, he applied to teach at the Friends' English School of Philadelphia. This school, founded in 1689 and now known as The William Penn Charter School, was among the earliest free schools in America. Benezet offered to augment the sparse course of study with French and German "so far as that the learner might read and perfectly understand the Bible, and talk it so as to be inabled to buy, sell & talk of common things."

Benezet's agreement with the overseers of the Friends' English Public School included provision for "his teaching fifteen poor children." He remained for twelve years, much admired for demonstrating what biographer George S. Brookes calls "a tolerant mind and an affectionate heart." Brookes adds: "He was a believer in loving-kindness, practising gentleness and love at a time when school discipline was exceedingly severe."[1] In fact, Benezet did away with both the instruments of punishment and the authoritarian style of teaching; at the same time, he was strict in insisting upon precision in writing and spelling, a carryover from his experience as a proofreader.

Eventually Benezet himself wrote primers, spelling books, and a grammar handbook for mothers living too distant from any school to use in teaching their children at home. But recalling his own early work experience, he never lost sight of the need for even a classically educated student to receive a "useful" or practical education, including knowing the essentials of business and account keeping.

In 1754, he resigned from the Friends' English School, citing poor health for his decision. But almost immediately he established a school for girls, among the first in America. The new Girls' School attracted the daughters of Philadelphia's most distinguished families, largely because Benezet is credited with being the first educator to insist that girls receive the full academic curriculum, including English grammar, heretofore unheard of as a subject necessary for female education.

His health was indeed at risk, so that again in 1755, after only one year, Benezet was forced to resign as master of Girls' School. He took on various charitable causes, such as relief for Acadian refugees expelled from Nova Scotia; he served as manager of Philadelphia Hospital. But he regretted his decision to leave Girls' School, writing to a friend, "Happy for us, when we know our service, to be willing to keep in it, and not aspire higher."

In 1757, he returned to Girls' School, adding Latin and French to the curriculum; he also provided time for exercise and recreation as part of his school day. But in 1766, Benezet once again resigned, presumably because of ill health. He and his wife, Joyce, moved to Burlington, New Jersey, where Benezet began to devote himself to the anti-slavery cause. His treatise, "A Caution and Warning to Great Britain and Her Colonies on the Calamitous State of the Enslaved Negroes," was one of the early evidences of the abolition movement in America. It is thought to have influenced John Wesley and William Wilberforce in their struggle for abolition in England.

Again he returned to Girls' School, in 1767, remaining this time until 1782, when he turned his energies fully to providing schooling for the children of African and Caribbean slaves. It was not Benezet's first such effort; since 1750, he had been holding evening sessions, tutoring black children in his own home, a practice he continued for twenty years. At a time when it was commonly assumed that blacks had no intellectual capacity, Benezet was not condescending when he wrote,

> I can with truth and sincerity declare, that I have found amongst the negroes as great a variety of talents as amongst a like number of whites; and I am bold to assert that the notion entertained by some, that the blacks are inferior in their capacities, is a vulgar prejudice, founded on the pride or ignorance of their lordly masters, who have kept their slaves at such a distance, as to be unable to form a right judgment of them.[2]

In 1770, the Philadelphia Meeting of the Society of Friends approved the construction of a free school for black children. Support for this venture came from as far away as London. For a dozen years, the school struggled to find teachers until, in 1782, Benezet once more resigned his position at Girls' School and took up the duties of schoolmaster at the Negroes' School. The following year, he wrote to Benjamin Franklin,

> After teaching the youth of this city near forty years, I have
> solicited & obtained the office of teacher of the Black chil-
> dren & others of that people, an employment which tho' not
> attended with so great pecuniary advantages as others might
> be, yet affords me much satisfaction. I know no station in life
> I should prefer before it.[3]

Before his death, Benezet could have pointed to eleven schools,
including the Negroes' School, under the sponsorship of the Philadelphia Society of Friends. His own deathbed legacy called for his estate to
go "to hire and employ a religious minded person or persons to teach a
number of negro, mulatto or Indian children," specifying further that
"special care may be had to prefer an industrious, careful person of true
piety, who may become suitably qualified and would undertake the service for a principle of charity, to one more highly learned not equally
disposed."

Benezet's example inspired not only the English Abolitionists but
also French. Brissot de Warville, founder of a society called *Les Amis des
Noirs* (Friends of the Blacks), who came to Philadelphia expressly to
visit Benezet's school, later wrote:

> There exists, then, a country where Negroes are allowed to
> have souls, and to be endowed with understanding capable of
> being formed to virtue and useful knowledge. . . . It is to
> Benezet that humanity owes this useful establish-
> ment. . . . The life of this extraordinary man merits to be
> known to such men as dare to think, who esteem more the
> benefactors of their fellow-creatures than their oppressors, so
> basely idolized during their life.

Worthy of such emulation as an example of Christian compassion,
Anthony Benezet's own summary of his life's work would deflect praise
from himself. In 1780, he wrote, "Oh the humility, the deep humility
which a proper sense of our weakness & utter dependence upon God
calls for."

In 1817, Roberts Vaux published *Memoirs of the Life of Anthony
Benezet,* from which the following letter is an excerpt.

"Letter to John Pemberton" (Excerpt)

Philadelphia
Fifth Month, 29th, 1783

Dear Friend, John Pemberton,

. . . With respect to the education of our youth, I would propose, as the fruit of forty years experience, that when they are proficient in the use of their pen, and become sufficiently acquainted with the English grammar, and the useful parts of Arithmetic, they should be taught [measurements] of superficies and solids; as it helps the mind in many necessary matters, particularly the use of the scale and compass; and will open the way for those parts of the mathematics, which their peculiar situations may afterwards make necessary.

It would be profitable for every scholar, of both sexes, to go through and understand a short but very plain set of merchants' accounts in single entry, particularly adapted to the civil uses of life. And in order to perfect their education in a useful and agreeable way, both to themselves and others, I would propose to give them a general knowledge of the mechanical powers, geography, and the elements of astronomy: the use of the microscope might also be profitably added, in discovering the minute parts of the creation. This, with the knowledge of the magnitude and courses of those mighty bodies which surround us, would tend to exalt their ideas.

Such parts of history as may tend to give them a right idea of the corruption of the human heart, the dreadful nature and effects of war, the advantage of virtue, &c. are also necessary parts of an education founded upon Christian and reasonable principles.

These several instructions should be inculcated on a religious plan, in such a way as may prove a delightful, rather than a painful labor, both to teachers and pupils.

It might also be profitable to give lads of bright genius some plain lectures upon anatomy, the wondrous frame of man, deducing therefrom the advantage of a plain, simple way of life; enforcing upon their understanding, the kind efforts of nature to maintain the human frame in a state of health with little medical help, but what abstinence and exercise will afford. These necessary parts of knowledge, so useful in directing the youthful mind in the path of virtue and wisdom, might be proposed by way of lectures, which the pupil should write down, and, when corrected, should copy in a neat bound book, to be kept for future perusal. . .

Anthony Benezet

CATHARINE ESTHER BEECHER

One of Lyman Beecher's predecessors in the East Hampton pastorate, Samuel Buell, had founded Clinton Academy in 1785, an early instance of co-education. In this environment Beecher's first-born daughter, Catharine, received her initial schooling. When her father took to another church in Litchfield, Connecticut, Catharine attended school there until age sixteen.

Catharine Esther Beecher (1800–78) spent much of her youth in caring for her many siblings, which gave her an early and lasting impression of the hardships many women of her time—but without her resources—were enduring.

Her first teaching appointment was in New London, where she became engaged to be married; but in 1823, her fiancé Alexander Fisher died. She determined to commit her life to education and founded her own school in Hartford, where she offered a curriculum considered innovative for the time. Among her pupils were both her younger sister Harriet and brother Henry Ward, the only boy enrolled.

In 1832, when Lyman Beecher left New England for Cincinnati, both Catharine and Harriet Beecher accompanied their father; for five years Catharine headed and Harriet taught in The Western Female Institute, until its financial failure in 1837. Thereafter Catharine Beecher devoted herself unstintingly to lecturing upon and raising money for the support of improved conditions for children and enhanced educational and employment opportunities for women.

By 1843, she was proposing a national organization with men as full-time agents to collect funds from supporters. Her choice as titular head of the agency was her brother-in-law, Calvin Ellis Stowe, Harriet's husband; Catharine herself would remain silently in charge, if only for the sake of appearances. By 1844, she had convinced not only Calvin Stowe to represent the cause of women and children but also her sister-in-law Sarah, the widow of another brother George Beecher, to contribute to founding a women's college in Putnam, Ohio. Sarah Beecher responded, promising that "while she lived and possessed the means," Sarah would provide "support and sympathy" for Catharine and her causes.

Catharine Beecher lectured wherever she could find an audience, delivering three standard addresses, published in 1846, in every major city in the East: "The Evils Suffered by American Women and American Children: The Causes and the Remedy," "The Duty of American Women to Their Country," and "An Address to the Protestant Clergy of the United States." Her appeal in these speeches was both rational and emotional, demonstrating her considerable power to move persons of means to support her work.

The national remedy her lectures offered actually resembled the formation of a Protestant equivalent to the Roman Catholic sisterhood of nuns. Her approach imitated the example of Elizabeth Ann Seton, the first American to be canonized by the Roman Catholic Church; in 1810, Mother Seton had founded the Sisters of Charity, among whose work was the establishing of parish schooling free to all children.

To achieve her goal, Catharine Beecher urged American women to end all class distinctions among themselves and commit themselves to self-denial; she also called for volunteers to join the ranks of female teachers across the country. Together the women of America would encourage a new national unity centered around the common interests of the schoolhouse rather than the factional and divisive interests of the church.

Everywhere she spoke, Catharine Beecher found both moral and financial support. She asked each audience for one hundred dollars to fund one teacher for one year; in Boston, for instance, she addressed the Ladies Society for Promoting Education at the West, identified by Robert Lincoln Kelly as "the most prominent and influential of the societies devoting their energies to the building of colleges." These Boston women responded by raising thousands of dollars for her cause. She was soon able to replace her reluctant brother-in-law with the former governor of Vermont, William Slade, representing what Catharine Beecher called the Central Committee for Promoting National Education.

In the spring and fall of 1847, she first taught, then sent out, seventy young women to remote locations in the West where schools had never been known. Their natural energy and exhilaration were apparently magnified by the inspiration of Beecher's training lectures. The first report, offered to donors in 1848, told of overcoming parental hostility to formal schooling in many communities but also recounted conversions among students and parents, along with the founding of Sunday schools and prayer meetings.

Catharine Beecher's major contribution, therefore, was to inspire and promote a surge in bringing education to the frontier. Like many idealists, she possessed too large an ego to share her vision with others who might carry it out to more lasting effect. For in spite of her noble aspirations for women and children and her efforts to achieve those ends, Catharine Beecher's own life was often in turmoil.

"The Evils Suffered by American Women and American Children" (Excerpt)

The Causes and the Remedy

Ladies and Friends,

The immediate object which has called us together, is an enterprise now in progress, the design of which is *to educate destitute American children, by the agency of American women.* . . .

Permit me first to present some facts in regard to the situation of an immense number of young children in this land, for whom your sympathies at this time are sought. Few are aware of the deplorable destitution of our country in regard to the education of the rising generation, or of the long train of wrongs and sufferings endured by multitudes of young children from this neglect. . . .

Look now at that great body of intelligent and benevolent persons, who are interesting themselves for patriotic and religious enterprises. We see them sustaining great organizations, and supporting men to devote their whole time to promote enterprises which draw thousands and hundreds of thousands for their support. There is one organization to send missionaries to the heathen and to educate heathen children; another to furnish the Bible; another to distribute tracts; another to educate young men to become ministers; another to send out home missionaries; another to sustain western colleges; another to promote temperance; and another to promote the observance of the sabbath. . . . All these objects are promoted by having men, *sustained by voluntary contributions*, who spend their whole time in urging these various objects on the public mind, while almost all have a regular periodical to advocate their cause.

But our two millions of *little children*, who are growing up in heathenish darkness, enchained in ignorance, and in many cases, where the cold law provides for them, enduring distress of body and mind greater than is inflicted on criminals, where is the benevolent association for their relief? Where is there a periodical supported by the charitable, to tell the tale of their wrongs? Where is there a single man sustained by Christian benevolence to operate on their behalf? Instead of spending time and money and employing agents to save the children of our country from ignorance and sin, the whole benevolent energies of the Christian world are engaged to remedy the evils that spring from this neglect. . . .

If all the labor and money spent for these objects at the West, for the last twenty years, had been employed in securing, for the generation now on the stage, six hours a day of good moral and intellectual training by well qualified teachers, who will affirm that the result would not have been better? . . .

I wish now to point out certain causes which have exerted a depressing influence upon our sex in this land; for we shall find that the very same effort, which aims to benefit the children of our country, will tend almost equally to benefit our own sex. The first cause that bears heavily on our sex is the fact that in our country, the principle of *caste*, which is one of the strongest and most inveterate in our nature, is strongly arrayed against *healthful and productive labor*. . . . The only remedy for this evil is, securing a proper education for all classes, and making productive labor honorable, by having all classes engage in it.

The next cause which bears severely on the welfare of our sex, is the *excess of female population* in the older states from the disproportionate emigration of the other sex. . . . In consequence of this, women at the East become operatives in shops and mills, and at the West, men become teachers of little children, thus exchanging the appropriate labors of the sexes, in a manner injurious to all concerned.

Meantime, capitalists at the East avail themselves of this excess of female hands. Large establishments are set up in eastern cities to manufacture clothing. Work of all kinds is got from poor women, at prices that will not keep body and soul together; and then the articles thus made are sold for prices that give monstrous profits to the capitalist, who thus grows rich on the hard labors of our sex. . . .

Another cause of depression to our sex is found in the fact that there is no profession for women of education and high position, which, like law, medicine, and theology, opens the way to competence, influence, and honor, and presents motives for exertion. . . . This is not because Providence has not provided an ample place for such professions for woman, but because custom or prejudice, or a low estimate of its honorable character, prevents her from entering it. *The educating of children, that* is the true and noble profession of a woman—*that* is what is worthy the noblest powers and affections of the noblest minds.

Another cause which deeply affects the best interests of our sex is the contempt, or utter neglect and indifference, which has befallen this only noble profession open to woman. . . . As it is, the employment of teaching children is regarded as the most wearying drudgery, and few resort to it except from necessity; and one very reasonable cause of this aversion is the utter neglect of any arrangements for *preparing* teachers for this arduous and difficult profession. . . .

Every one of the evils here portrayed, it is in the power of American women fully to remedy and remove. Nothing is wanting but a knowledge of the evils, and a well-devised plan for uniting the energies of our countrywomen in the effort, and the thing will be speedily and gloriously achieved.

It is the immediate object of this enterprise now presented, to engage American women to exert the great power and influence put into their hands, to remedy the evils which now oppress their countrywomen, and thus, at the same time, and by the same method, to secure a proper education to the vast multitude of neglected American children all over the land.

The plan is, to begin on a small scale, and to take women already qualified intellectually to teach, and possessed of missionary zeal and benevolence, and, after some further training, to send them to the most ignorant portions of our land, to raise up schools, to instruct in morals and piety, and to teach the domestic arts and virtues. . . .

If our success equals our hopes, soon, in all parts of our country, in each neglected village, or new settlement, the Christian female teacher will quietly take her station, collecting the ignorant children around her, teaching them habits of neatness, order, and thrift; opening the book of knowledge, inspiring the principles of morality, and awakening the hope of immortality. Soon her influence in the village will create a demand for new laborers, and then she will summon from among her friends at home, the nurse for the young and the sick, the seamstress . . . ; and these will prove her auxiliaries in good moral influences, and in sabbath school training. And often as the result of these labors, the Church will arise, and the minister of Christ be summoned to fill up the complement of domestic, moral, and religious blessings.

Thus, the surplus of female population will gradually be drawn westward, and in consequence the value of female labor will rise at the East, so that capitalists can no longer use the power of wealth to oppress our sex. Thus, too, the profession of a teacher will gradually increase in honor and respectability, while endowed institutions will arise to qualify woman for her profession, as freely as they are provided for the other sex. Then it will be deemed honorable and praiseworthy for every young and well-educated woman, of whatever station, to enter this profession, and remain in it till pure affection leads her to another sphere. Then a woman of large affections and developed intellect will find full scope and happy exercise for all the cultivated energies conferred by heaven, alike for her own enjoyment and the good of others.

This will prove the true remedy for all those *wrongs of women* which her mistaken champions are seeking to cure by drawing her into professions and pursuits which belong to the other sex. . . .

Permit me, before I close, to say a few words to those who profess to be the disciples and followers of Jesus Christ. Who are the *true* followers and disciples of Christ? It is those only who have his *spirit*, and follow his *example*. He gave up honors and joys, such as none of us ever possessed, and spent thirty-three years in toils and sufferings, to save the ignorant and lost. And he did it *because he loved to do it!* He so loved us, and our lost fellow-creatures, that he came not by compulsion, but gladly, by toils and sacrifices, to save us. . . .

My fellow Christians, we have far higher cultivation, far more extensive knowledge, far more abundant means than the early Christians; and does Christ say to us, "Sell all that thou hast, and give to the poor, and come and follow me"? . . . The standard of Christian character in the church at this time does not require those who have abundance *to practice self-denial*—or to make it their *chief business* to spend their time, and talents, and wealth, in saving the ignorant and lost. And I greatly fear that multitudes who now call themselves Christians, will at last hear the dreadful sentence, "Depart from me—I never knew you!"

It is in this view of the subject that I have felt a peculiar interest in efforts to bring this plan to the attention of those of my countrywomen who profess to be followers of Jesus Christ. . . .

THEODORE DWIGHT WELD

The son of a Connecticut Congregational pastor, Theodore Weld (1803–95) attended Oneida Institute, now Hamilton College, where he gained a reputation as a proficient speaker. In 1825, while a student, Weld was converted in evangelistic meetings held by Charles G. Finney. He attached himself to Finney, hoping to influence the evangelist toward some of the radical new thought Weld brought to his Christian faith. Among these ideas were equal rights for women—including their public speaking in churches—and the abolition of slavery.

Weld became an activist in the abolition movement. In New York City, he met Arthur Tappan and his brother, Lewis, and convinced both to join his cause. Natives of Northampton, Massachusetts, the Tappans had became wealthy silk importers. Under Weld's influence, the Tappans were never mere social reformers; they held firmly to the necessity of believing the gospel, which alone could transform individual lives and whole societies. Their generosity was extraordinary to a wide array of Christian ministries. For example, Arthur Tappan was among the founders of the American Tract Society and contributed funds for that society's first presses. He was also willing to engage in door-to-door tract distribution. He and his brother also supported the American Bible Society, along with various Sunday observance and temperance movements. They helped to underwrite the founding of Lane Theological Seminary, Oberlin College, and Kenyon College, all in Ohio; they were largely responsible for the construction of Finney's Broadway Tabernacle in New York City.

Lewis Tappan, in particular, was an outstanding spokesman against racial segregation, which he opposed on biblical grounds. Encouraged by the prospectus for Lane Theological Seminary at its founding in 1832, the Tappans paid for Weld to enroll. Two years later Weld was expelled for leading the debate over the seminary's role in helping Cincinnati's black populace; the Tappans aided Weld as he led a defection to Oberlin, where Finney was now installed. Later, the Tappans supported Weld's work with the American Anti-Slavery Society, for which he became a national representative.

In 1838, Weld married the dynamic abolitionist and advocate of women's rights, Angelina Grimké. Together they might have made a formidable team; but circumstances proved otherwise. Weld began to suffer vocal damage and ceased public speaking; instead, he lobbied politicians for legislative action. By 1840, he had left public life altogether for farming; his wife turned to motherhood and later joined her husband in operating a boarding school called Eagleswood.

By the time of his death, Theodore Weld had seen both the Emancipation Proclamation of 1863 and the Supreme Court's *Plessy v. Ferguson* decision, favoring "separate but equal" schooling for black children.

Weld's letter to Lewis Tappan, which follows, brims over with student enthusiasm as he recounts the exciting events at Lane Seminary and elsewhere in those spheres of activism that so consumed him. For instance, his reference to "Miss Crandall" speaks of one Prudence Crandall, a schoolmistress in Canterbury, Connecticut, who, in 1831, had enrolled a black girl in her school. William Lloyd Garrison had seized on this and encouraged Crandall to found a school for black girls. But Crandall's townspeople had urged an act through the legislature that forbade such a school; Crandall was prosecuted under that law and convicted. On appeal Prudence Crandall was vindicated, but she found too much hostility to continue such a school. Her example, though, inspired others as far away as Cincinnati to follow her lead.

Notorious incidents such as this helped to fuel the fires of passion for liberty among radical Christians in the 1830s and beyond.

"Letter to Lewis Tappan" (Excerpt)

LANE SEMINARY, March 18, 1834

Dear Brother—

You have seen by the *Evangelist* and *Emancipator* what we have done here on the subject of slavery. The preamble and constitution of our Anti-Slavery Society will be published this week. I will send you one. The Lord has done great things for us here. Eight months ago there was not a single immediate abolitionist in this seminary. Many students were from slave states, and some of them the most influential and intelligent in the institution. A large colonization society existed, and abolitionism was regarded as the climax of absurdity, fanaticism and blood.

The first change was brought about in some of the first minds in the seminary, and especially in an individual of great sway among the students, who was from Alabama: born, bred, and educated in the midst of slavery; his father an owner of slaves, and himself heir to a slave inheritance. After some weeks of inquiry, and struggling with his conscience, his noble soul broke loose from its shackles. He is now President of our Anti-Slavery Society.

Many of the students had taken right ground—deliberately and firmly—before the debate commenced; but a majority were still opposed. The result you know. Five or six of the *determined* colonizationists refused to attend the debate. Some five or six more were absent from the institution. Every student in both departments, from slave states, has come out and taken right ground, with the exception of *one*—and he was absent from the institution until the debate was nearly completed, and refused to attend during the remainder of the debate.

But I must tell you something more. We believe that faith without *works* is dead. We have formed a large and efficient organization for elevating the colored people in Cincinnati—have established a Lyceum among them, and lecture three or four evenings a week, on grammar, geography, arithmetic, natural philosophy, etc. Besides this, an evening free school, for teaching them to read, is in operation every week day evening; and we are about establishing one or two more. We are also getting up a library for circulation among those who can read, and are about establishing a reading room. In addition to this, two of our students, one theological and one literary, have felt so deeply their degradation, and have been so affected by the intense desire to acquire knowledge which they exhibit, that they have taken a dismission from the institution and commenced a school among the blacks in the city. They expect to teach a year, and then take up their course in the seminary again, when others will no doubt be ready to take their places. The first went down and opened a school, and it was *filled* the first day, and that mainly with adults, and those nearly grown. For a number of days he rejected from ten to twenty daily, because he could not teach them. This induced the other dear brother to leave his studies and join him. Both are now incessantly occupied.

Besides these two day schools, and the evening schools, and the Lyceum lectures, we have three large Sabbath schools and Bible classes among the colored people. By sections in rotation, and teaching the evening reading schools in the same way, we can perform an immense amount of labor among them, without interference with our studies.

In visiting among the blacks, and mingling with them, we have all felt the great importance of another species of instrumentality in raising them, which was not within our reach. I mean a *select female school*. We know of no female, except Miss Crandall, who has resolution and self-denial enough to engage in the enterprize. But the Lord has provided. Miss Lathrop, daughter of the late Mr. Charles Lathrop, of Norwich, Ct., and sister of the late Mrs. Winslow and the present Mrs. Hutchins, missionaries at Ceylon, and also of Mrs. Wm. A. Hallock, of your city—has had her heart moved by the Lord to enter upon the work. . . . Many of the people of Cincinnati call us fanatics, say the blacks can never be raised here, etc. And some of the most influential are striving to persuade Miss Lathrop from engaging in an effort to raise them. The colored people themselves will do all in their power to support the schools by contributing monthly, but that will not be a great deal.

Of the almost 3000 blacks in C. more than three-fourths of the adults are emancipated slaves, who worked out their own freedom. Many are now paying for themselves under large securities. Besides these, multitudes are toiling to purchase their friends, who are now in slavery.

I visited this week about 30 families, and found that some members of more than half of these families were still in bondage, and the father, mother and children were struggling to lay up money enough to purchase their freedom. I found one man who had just finished paying for his wife and five children. Another man and wife who bought themselves some years ago, and have been working night and day to purchase their children; they had just redeemed the last! and had paid for themselves and children 1400 dollars! Another woman who had recently paid the last instalment of the purchase money for her husband. She had purchased him by taking in washing, and working late at night, after going out and performing as help at hard work. But I cannot tell half, and must stop. After spending three or four hours, and getting facts, I was forced to stop from sheer heart-ache and agony.

In a single word—these poor brethren and sisters MUST BE HELPED. Brother T., do say something about them to our dear sisters in your city. I think this moment of Mrs. ____. Won't she take it in hand? If the ladies in New-York can raise $150 for purchasing books and fixtures for Miss Lathrop's school and for supporting HER, I think we shall be able to make out the rest. And if these schools can be kept up the first year they will be able to support themselves afterwards.

Three reasons to show that the free blacks of C. have peculiar claims upon the benevolence of the community. 1st. It is of immense importance that the public should see what blacks can do. The blacks here, having mostly emancipated themselves by their own efforts, are their own letters of introduction on the score of energy, decision, perseverance, and high attempt—an excellent material to work upon. 2nd. They have not BETTER opportunity for instruction than any others in the union, but these opportunities will not benefit them half as much as they might if they were aided a little at first in pecuniary matters. 3. Cincinnati is the best locality in the Union to act upon slavery by a spectacle of free black cultivation.

T. D. Weld

SARAH GRIMKÉ AND ANGELINA GRIMKÉ WELD

S arah Grimké (1792–1873) and her younger sister Angelina (1805–79) were natives of Charleston, South Carolina. Their father, a French Huguenot, had escaped persecution in France, studied at Cambridge University, and served in the American Revolution; their mother's family was prominent in Charleston politics.

These women had been brought up in a home where slaves were owned and sometimes beaten; at the same time, unpopular positions were commonly discussed on matters of peacemaking, temperance, equal rights, and other reforms. For instance, Sarah, well-educated by tutors herself, had taught slave children in a Sunday school, where she came under threat of legal action for violating the South Carolina law against teaching blacks to read.

In 1819, Sarah Grimké accompanied her father on a trip to Philadelphia where, in the course of seeking medical help, he died. His daughter met members of the Society of Friends, whose simple ways and more charitable attitude toward blacks she much admired. Upon returning home, Sarah announced that she was leaving Charleston and the Episcopal Church to become a Quaker and move to Philadelphia. Eight years later, in 1829, her sister Angelina followed.

But the Grimké sisters soon learned that not all Quakers were politically unconventional; in fact, some in the Philadelphia meeting strongly disapproved of abolitionism. In 1835, Angelina Grimké shocked even her sister by joining Philadelphia's Female Anti-Slavery Society. A letter written to William Lloyd Garrison appeared in his *Liberator*, prompting Angelina to write *An Appeal to the Christian Women of the South*, published in 1836. Angelina was warned not to return to Charleston.

Convinced by her sister's witness, Sarah Grimké joined Angelina in New York City. At a training session for abolitionist volunteers, the Grimké sisters met Theodore Weld. His powerful appeal led Sarah Grimké to write "An Epistle to the Clergy of the Southern States," her argument against any scriptural basis for slavery. Meanwhile, Angelina was finding her gift as a compelling speaker. New doors opened to her, even in churches where she was accorded the unusual privilege of addressing audiences of men as well as women. In 1838, she testified before the Massachusetts legislature, then considering an antislavery bill.

But while abolition was their foremost topic, Angelina and Sarah Grimké were also interested in women's rights, a subject even more incendiary because it affected all parts of the Union and every male who felt himself threatened by any talk of female equality. A split between one faction of abolitionists, including the movement's most distinguished writer, the Quaker poet John Greenleaf Whittier, seeking to deter the Grimkés from speaking out on women's rights, and another headed by Garrison encouraging them forward, endangered the entire abolitionist effort. Both women responded with published statements asserting their right to link abolitionism and feminism, and their public appearances in Boston attracted huge audiences.

At the height of this controversy, Angelina Grimké surprised her critics by marrying Theodore Weld in 1838. Only two days following her wedding, Angelina Grimké Weld was back on the platform addressing an antislavery rally. Outside a hostile crowd rioted and eventually set fire to the lecture hall.

Thereafter all three—Theodore and Angelina Weld and her sister Sarah, who lived with them for the rest of her life—retired from an active public role in the abolitionist movement. For all his golden-throated oratory, Weld found his speaking voice damaged by overuse. Angelina became the mother of three children, and her health suffered, so that her sister was heavily occupied with the children's care. While Garrison and other abolitionists resented Weld's having removed himself and the Grimké sisters from the frontlines of battle, Weld and the Grimkés' work continued by concentrating on publishing tracts such as "American Slavery as It Is: Testimony of a Thousand Witnesses," which served as a resource for Harriet Beecher Stowe in writing *Uncle Tom's Cabin*.

In 1848, Weld and the women began a school that relocated six years later to Perth Amboy, New Jersey, as a boarding school in cooperation with a utopian community called Raritan Bay Union. The school, called Eagleswood, continued to operate until 1862. The next year, the three moved to the Boston area, where they taught in a girls' school until 1867.

Although Angelina and Sarah were sometimes given to questionable religious pursuits, the basis for their activism was thoroughly grounded in respect for the Bible's clear teachings. Nowhere is this more clearly documented than in the fact that, at a time when feminism often attracted women of dubious personal morality, the Grimké sisters were above such reproach. Furthermore, in 1868, they proved their integrity in matters of race when they discovered that two boys had been born to their brother Henry and a slave woman. These mixed-race youths were taken in by Weld and their aunts, who provided for their education at Harvard and Princeton, respectively.

Sarah Grimké's pamphlet "The Education of Women" published in 1850, shows a more philosophical and spiritual argument than did Catharine Beecher's pragmatic scheme of the same period.

"The Education of Women"[4] (Excerpt)

. . . It is a remarkable fact that Christ made no distinction between the responsibilities of men and women. He addressed to them the same precepts, required from them the same evidence of discipleship, and called upon them in the same language to fulfil their glorious destiny. Can they fulfil it? Can they develop symmetrically their whole being, when they are deprived of the advantages so lavishly bestowed by church and state upon their brethren?

How many millions are invested in colleges, universities, Theological Seminaries for the education and exaltation of men to prepare them to fill offices of honor, trust, and emolument? Is there one million invested for such purposes for the benefit of women? Nay, they not only are not blest with such patronage, but are even deprived of property by legal enactments, so that they can do very little for themselves. . . .

Suffer me then to entreat that you will not close against woman the schools of learning and science thus shutting out the light from those whom God committed to your guardianship at the creation, by endowing you with superior physical strength. In the past you have nobly fulfilled your trust—you have shielded her in war; in seasons of peril you have thrown your bodies around her as a rampart, and sought safety for her at your own cost. But in the present how is it? The existing laws can answer that she is your slave, your bauble, the victim of your passions, the sharer willingly and unwillingly of your licentiousness. It is to save you, as well as her, from the gratification of unbridled desires, to open for you both a glorious path to happiness and usefulness, that I long to see her qualified to fill the station of wife and mother. . . .

The fellow feeling which universal education produces among a people is clearly discernible in America, and its influence in strengthening that sympathy is incalculable. When learning in all its higher branches shall become the common property of both sexes; when the girl, as well as the boy, may anticipate with earnest delight the complete course of study, which will enable her to look forward to a life of continued culture, of independence and of fulfilment of high and honorable trusts, the contemplation of such a future will raise her ideas of herself beyond the chameleon sphere of fashion, or the toilsome drudgery of that incessant manual labor, which is calculated in most cases to stultify intellect and which may be performed for a small compensation by those who have hands, but are nearly destitute of brains. . . . Think not because I thus speak, that I would withdraw woman from the duties of domestic life, far from it; let her fulfil in the circle of home all the obligations that rest upon her, but let her not waste her powers on inferior objects when higher and holier responsibilities demand her attention.

MARY LYON

Among the women who helped to reform American schooling in the nineteenth century, none is more worthy of note than Mary Lyon, the founder of what is today Mount Holyoke College in South Hadley, Massachusetts.

Born in 1797 to Aaron and Jemima Lyon, Mary was the sixth of eight children in a distinguished lineage. Her ancestors had arrived in Massachusetts as early as 1630; her father had fought in the Revolutionary War. Prior to American independence Mary's great-grandfather (on her mother's side), Chileab Smith, had campaigned on behalf of Baptists and their right to conduct worship services without paying tax to the crown.

Having only a scant education herself, at age seventeen Mary Lyon began teaching children who came to board at the farm she occupied with her older brother. In 1817, she enrolled at Sanderson Academy in Ashfield, a coeducational school where she received her first formal instruction; the following year found her at Amherst Academy, studying Latin among other advanced topics. While in Amherst, she observed the interest and energy with which local citizens planned the founding of a college in their town.

Mary Lyon alternated her years of study with time for teaching and earning enough for her next admission to her own studies. At one of these schools, she came under the teaching of the Reverend Joseph Emerson who, she recalled, "talked to ladies as if they had brains." From Emerson she also found encouragement for a growing idea, that she should found her own school for women.

In 1824, she returned to her hometown and began the Buckland Female Seminary, which flourished until 1828 when Mary Lyon fell ill with typhoid fever and had to yield its operation to less successful hands. But in the interim, she had enrolled at Amherst College and also at what is now Rensselaer Polytechnic Institute, learning laboratory science. Recovered sufficiently from her illness, she taught for five years at Ipswich Female Seminary, north of Boston.

But all these efforts at educating girls, she came to see, had been thwarted by the fact that schools for girls lacked sufficient financial undergirding to see them through the normal cycles of stress. In the summer of 1833, she set out to see what prospects might be outside of New England. She journeyed as far as Detroit, Michigan, where she was surprised to learn that her name was known. She returned to Ipswich resolved to found a school that would endure.

Carefully designing a plan for "a residential seminary to be founded and sustained by the Christian public," she found support from women in Ipswich, who contributed the first one thousand dollars. When her plan was ready, she approached several towns about accommodating her new enterprise. South Hadley's citizens raised eight thousand dollars and earned the bid.

In 1836, Mount Holyoke Female Seminary, named for a local peak, began construction of its first building. Classes opened in the fall of 1837. When she opened her Mount Holyoke Female Seminary, Mary Lyon remembered a verse of Scripture often quoted by Joseph Emerson: "That our daughters may be as cornerstones, polished after the similitude of a palace" (Psalm 144:12). This text became the motto for her new school.

For a dozen years, Miss Lyon served as principal and surrogate mother to her students, one of whom was a sensitive young girl of indeterminate spiritual state named Emily Dickinson. Miss Lyon had not professed faith herself until age twenty-five, when she was baptized. Now among her greatest concerns was that all her students might become believers, that some might commit their lives to foreign missionary service. Her only book, A Missionary Offering, published in 1843, makes this case.

The glory of her legacy is that Mount Holyoke College indeed survives; the tragedy is that it has long since ceased to promote the evangelical Christian faith and witness of its founder.

"Principles and Design of the Mount Holyoke Female Seminary" (Excerpt)

This institution is established at South Hadley, Massachusetts. It is to be principally devoted to the preparing of female teachers. At the same time, it will qualify ladies for other spheres of usefulness. The design is to give a solid, extensive, and well-balanced English education, connected with that general improvement, that moral culture, and those enlarged views of duty, which will prepare ladies to be educators of their children and youth, rather than to fit them to be mere teachers, as the term has been technically applied. Such an education is needed by every female who takes the charge of a school, and sustains the responsibility of guiding the whole course and of forming the entire character of those committed to her care. And when she has done with the business of teaching in a regular school, she will not give up her profession; she will still need the same well-balanced education at the head of her own family and in guiding her own household.

1. This institution professes to be founded on the high principle of enlarged Christian benevolence. In its plans and in its appeals it seeks no support from local or private interest. It is designed entirely for the public good, and the trustees would adopt no measures not in accordance with this design. It is sacredly consecrated to the great Head of the church, and they would not seek for human approbation by any means which will not be well pleasing in his sight.

2. The institution is designed to be permanent. . . .

3. The institution is to be entirely for an older class of young ladies . . . whose great desire is to be prepared to use all their talents in behalf of the cause of education, and of the Redeemer's kingdom. . . .

4. The young ladies are to take a part in the domestic work of the family. . . .

What the present generation is beginning to accomplish for the salvation of the world [Mount Holyoke Female Seminary] seeks to preserve and carry forward with increasing rapidity. Whatever of conquest is now gained it seeks to secure forever from the encroachments of the enemy. It seeks to lay the foundation strong, on which, under God, the temple, with all its increasing weight, is to rise, and be sustained, and to secure it from injury and decay. It beholds with painful interest the slow progress of these United States in carrying the blessings of salvation to the two hundred millions, who are the estimated proportion of the inhabitants of this benighted world to be converted to God through our instrumentality. And as it attempts in vain to calculate the time when the work shall be accomplished, it would fain increase its progress a hundred fold, by training up the children in the way they should go. . . .

This enterprise, thus far, has been under the care of a kind Providence. It has not been carried forward by might, nor by power; but in every step of its progress the good hand of God has been upon it. Let all its friends bring in the tithes and the offerings, and let them commit the disposing of the whole to Him who can accomplish the work which his own hands have commenced,. and he will pour out upon this institution, and the cause with which it is connected, and upon the children and youth of our country, and of the world, a blessing, that there shall not be room enough to receive it.

WILLIAM HOLMES MCGUFFEY

A native of the American frontier, William Holmes McGuffey (1800–73) was a product of that rough-hewn culture but later became one of its most important designers for change.

Anna McGuffey encouraged her children to learn, and when a Presbyterian minister, William Wick, offered instruction six miles away, her husband and she sent young William to live with the Wick family during the winter months. Three weeks short of his fourteenth birthday, William McGuffey began teaching school under a formal contract with forty-eight pupils.

Wise enough to recognize how little he knew, McGuffey enrolled for further studies with another Presbyterian minister, Thomas Hughes, at his Old Stony Academy in Darlington, Pennsylvania. By 1820, McGuffey had prepared himself to enter Washington College, now Washington and Jefferson College. His six years there were interrupted by his need to earn money for tuition, which he did by again teaching school wherever he could obtain a position.

In the winter of 1826, while conducting classes in Paris, Kentucky, he met the Reverend Robert H. Bishop, newly appointed president of Miami University at Oxford, Ohio. Bishop offered McGuffey a position as professor of ancient languages, even though the young student-and-teacher had yet to receive his degree.

For ten years, McGuffey taught at Miami. During this time he was ordained to the Presbyterian ministry and proceeded to make a name for himself as a preacher of considerable effectiveness. The fact that he was also a college professor—a breed not generally well received in frontier pulpits—seems not to have been a disadvantage in McGuffey's case.

At this time McGuffey also began his work on behalf of public education, joining with notable persons in Cincinnati—the center of culture in the West—to promote teacher education and the improvement of pedagogical materials. From 1830 on, he had been collecting stories suitable for various ages, and testing these stories by reading aloud to groups of children gathered on his porch. In 1833, he contracted with Truman and Smith, a Cincinnati publishing company, to edit a series of reading textbooks with spelling lists. *The Eclectic First Reader for Young Children* was published in 1836, along with the *Second Reader*. The *Third* and *Fourth* followed in 1837. Not until the 1857 edition were they known as *McGuffey's Readers*.

McGuffey's idea was by no means original with him. John Amos Comenius had published his illustrated reader two hundred years earlier. Nearer to his own time, McGuffey knew of "similar children's textbooks" published in New York, Boston, and Philadelphia, where Benezet had issued his spelling book and primer in the mid-eighteenth century. In fact, in 1838, McGuffey and his publishers were sued by an Eastern firm for "over-imitation," a polite term for plagiarism. Yet, as the word *Eclectic* signifies, McGuffey never claimed originality; his books were compilations of the best stories available.

The publishing of these books is a landmark in American education. The artwork, text, and vocabulary words that appeared in each lesson, or story, kept the child's attention and made the books popular. Through them McGuffey became the teacher of millions; through them he also ministered to the masses long before radio or television broadcasting existed. For McGuffey made it clear, in the preface as well as in the contents of his books, that his purpose was to teach the truths of the Bible. The preface to the *Fourth Reader* contains this paragraph:

> From no source has the author drawn more copiously, in his selections, than from the sacred Scriptures. For this, he certainly apprehends no censure. In a Christian country, that man is to be pitied, who at this day, can honestly object to imbuing the minds of youth with the language and spirit of the Word of God.[5]

McGuffey's assumption of unified purpose in "a Christian country," of course forms a marked contrast with today's reality in America's public schools.

From Miami University, McGuffey's distinguished academic career continued to the presidency of two colleges and on to the University of Virginia at Charlottesville, where for twenty-eight years he was professor of psychology and philosophy.

A selection from the *First Reader* follows. "The Sun is Up" includes a detailed line drawing of a boy at the edge of the woods facing the rising sun. Also included is an excerpt from one of the few speeches or sermons McGuffey prepared for publication. As a rule he shunned the use of notes or a prepared text; but in October 1835, addressing the annual meeting of the Western Literary Institute in Cincinnati, McGuffey wrote down his "Lecture on the Relative Duties of Parents and Teachers."

"The Eclectic First Reader for Young Children" (Excerpt)

Lesson X
The Sun is Up

See, the sun is up. The sun gives us light. It makes the trees and the grass grow.

The sun rises in the east and sets in the west. When the sun rises, it is day.

This little boy was up at five. He saw the sun rise, and heard the sweet songs of birds on every bush.

Do you know who made the sun?

God made it.

God made the moon and all the stars. How good God is to us; he gives us all we have, and keeps us alive.

We should love God.

God sees and knows all things, for God is every where. He sees me when I rise from my bed, when I go out to walk and play. And when I lie down to sleep at night, he keeps me from harm.

Though I do not see the wind, yet it blows round me on all sides: so God is with me at all times, and yet I see him not.

If God is with me, and knows all that I do, he must hear what I say. O, let me not, then, speak bad words; for if I do, God will not love me.

"The Relative Duties of Parents and Teachers"[6] (Excerpt)

FELLOW-CITIZENS: The time has gone by in which doubts were entertained by the intelligent, as to the necessity and practicability of *general* education. . . .

But this cannot be effected without effort, and united effort. There must be concert between the people and their legislators; between those who are already educated, and those who have yet to acquire their education; between the instructors of youth and the parents of the children.

The object of the present lecture is to point out some of the respective and relative duties of teachers and parents; in order that they may the more successfully co-operate in their mutual work of

291

training, to intelligence and virtue, the future citizens of our happy republic.

1st. There must be an increase of teachers. Not more than thirty pupils ought ordinarily to be committed to the care of a single instructor, at any one time. This ratio must, when all our youth shall be in the schools, augment the number of teachers beyond that of any other profession, or even mechanical employment, in the whole land.

It is the duty, therefore, of our young men, of liberal education, to fill up the ranks of this most respectable (and, we trust, soon to be respected) of all professions, the profession of teaching. It is the duty of those already engaged in this profession, resolutely to decline all offers of patronage that would involve the necessity of dividing their attention between a greater number of pupils than they can thoroughly instruct. And, as interest and duty are, in the moral government of God, inseparably connected, those who engage in the business of instruction, with a capable facility, cannot fail of employment, and a competent support. . . .

2d. The faithful and competent teacher never fails to secure the confidence, respect, and even affection of his pupils. He is as he ought to be, esteemed "in place of a parent." He is thought to be infallible. He ought therefore to be correct. He is esteemed as possessing the whole cyclopedia of knowledge. He ought, therefore, to be a man of extensive acquaintance with the principles of science. He is thought by the confiding pupil, to be incapable of any measure, or even intention, at variance with honest views of promoting the best interests of those entrusted to his care. And he ought, accordingly, to enlist all his energies in promoting the solid improvement and moral growth, of every mind submitted to his influence. . . .

We, fellow-teachers, must mold the opinion of society, especially on all subjects connected with education. I say must because, from the nature of the case we cannot avoid it, if we would. The future opinions, plans, and enterprises of our pupils, on these subjects, will be not only tinged, but characterized, if not created by our influence upon their forming minds. All that they shall hereafter think, will in great measure, be the results of what we have previously thought, and inculcated. With us rest the tremendous responsibility of laying the foundation of a nation's literature; and of saying what shall be its future character, for morality and religion.

The foundation can be laid but ONCE. The character of the superstructure, does not depend so much upon those who shall complete the edifice, as upon us, who are called to lay the corner stone. Let us then, divest ourselves of all selfish views; of every narrow prejudice; of every local preference; and of the whole class of temporary expedients, and come up to the work with a zeal, a devotedness, and perseverance worthy of so good a cause. . . .

3d. Parents commit to us their richest treasures, their dearest hopes. In this they are too exclusive; but their fault cannot lessen our responsibility. It rather increases it. We have the formation of character committed to us. The intellectual habits of our pupils will be very much as we form them. Their modes of thought— their principles of taste—their habitude of feeling, will all take their complexion, if not their character, from our methods of training the mind. Who then can enter the classroom without trembling? Where is the spirit stout enough to try experiments upon an immortal mind? No man is fit to teach who does not understand human nature. Nor will an empirical knowledge of the mind suffice. Principles and experiment must go together. Theory, without practice, will be mischievous; and practice without theory must, of course, be at random.

We owe it, then, to our pupils, and to their parents, thoroughly to understand what we profess to teach. For who can communicate intelligibly to another, that which he himself does not clearly comprehend? That man is a swindler of the worst description, who "procures, upon false pretences," the intellectual wealth of the community, and submits to, he cares not what, venturous process, for his own paltry and sordid gain. The fraudulent merchant destroys but the fortunes of those whom he plunders. But the incompetent teacher ruins the immortal mind, which is of more value than all temporal riches.

Nor is it enough once to have understood what we profess to teach. We must constantly review our studies. . . . We should be master of our subject—familiar with its details—clear in our explanations—rapid in our mental movements—glowing in our conceptions of truth—impassioned in our endeavors to produce the same results on the minds of our pupils. . . . Let us then be honest with ourselves; honest with our pupils; honest with their parents; and honest with the public. Let us not drive a pupil too fast, and thus destroy the vigor and energy of his mental action. Let us not check the natural activity of his thought; and thus induce a habit of mental moping, alike unfriendly to accuracy and despatch, whether in acquisition or execution. Let us not flatter our patrons, that their children are capable of professions, for which nature never intended them. Let us be careful never to inculcate any doubtful principle of morality or religion; or to recommend, by precept or example, any wrong, or even equivocal sentiment or feeling.

We may, nay we must, have our own speculative opinions— hypotheses in morals, which we have not yet been able either to verify or disprove by inductive experience. But, in this state, fellow-teachers, let them never once be named in our schools; nor let them begin to influence our conduct as practical teachers. The intellectual and moral character of our pupils is too valuable, to be made the subject of rash and hazardous experiment.

The Christian religion, is the religion of our country. From it are derived our prevalent notions of the character of God, the great moral governor of the universe. On its doctrines are founded the peculiarities of our free institutions. From its sanctions are derived the obligations to veracity imposed in the administration of justice. In its revelations are found the only certain grounds of hope in reference to that, else unknown future, which lies beyond the horizon of time. It alone places a guard over the conscience, which never slumbers, and whose eye cannot be evaded by any address of the delinquent. Its maxims, its precepts, its sentiments, and even its very spirit, have become so incorporated with the mind and soul of civilization, and all refinement, that it cannot be eradicated, or even opposed, without imminent hazard of all that is beautiful, lovely, and valuable in the arts, in science, and in society.

Let us then, fellow-teachers, avoid, on the one hand, the inculcation of all sectarian peculiarities in religion: and on the other, let us beware of incurring the charge, (which will not fail to be made,) of being enemies to our country's quiet, by teaching to our pupils the crude notions, and revolutionary principles of modern infidelity. It is, at best, but an unsustained hypothesis.

4th. The duties that remain to be noticed, in the fourth place, as incumbent on teachers, in relation to the parents of those who are their pupils, are, if possible, more important than any that have yet been noticed. Teachers ought to know best how to do that which is required of them—but parents are, or ought to be, the better judges, as to what is to be done. We, fellow-teachers, are the servants of the public. We have a deep interest, as has been shown, in the results of our own labors in their effects upon public prosperity and national character. But, much as we love, and ought to love those committed to our care, they are but our pupils, not our children. This last relation is one which can be constituted only by the author of our being. All attempts, artificially to form it, must end in comparative defeat. None but the natural parent, can feel that natural affection, which is adequate to the duties of properly educating an immortal mind. . . .

The second general division of our subject, is the duties incumbent on parents, in the business of education.

And here, as in the first division of this discourse, I have the pleasure to rank with those whom I address. I have long been a teacher, and expect to remain in the profession for life. But I am also a parent, who has children to educate, and may therefore be supposed to feel, in some degree at least, the importance of those duties which I venture to urge upon my fellow-citizens.

As, in the preceding remarks, the duties of teachers have been shown to be subordinate to those of parents; so, in what is to follow, I wish the paramount importance of the parent's interests, and the parent's duties to be kept distinctly before us. We who are parents are the employers—teachers our assistants, in the all responsible business of training up the future governors of this republic, who are to give character to the world, and to form characters for eternity.

1. In the first place, we must provide suitable accommodations for our schools. Children cannot learn when uncomfortable. And they cannot be comfortable, either in cold weather, or in hot, unless the school-house, or recitation room, be such as can be

both warmed and ventilated, as occasion may require. How much time, and money, and that which is more valuable than both time and money, I mean mind, is wasted; simply for the want of suitable buildings for schools? Nor is mere convenience, of itself, sufficient. Children are creatures of association and habit; and much depends upon the cheerfulness and taste of that which is connected with their early mental efforts, as to whether they shall become attached to study, and take a delight in thought; or shall contract a disgust for every thing like literature and science. Time was, when the log school-house, with gable-end chimney, clap-board door, and long, narrow windows, papered and greased, was all that could be looked for, in a country that was still a wilderness. But that time is now past. . . .

2. The next duty devolving upon parents, in relation to teachers, is to furnish them with suitable tools, with which to work. They must, we have seen, have comfortable shops—a school-house is the teacher's shop—but this will not avail, unless those shops be furnished. We must furnish or compensate the teachers for furnishing uniform sets of suitable class books. As we value the improvement of our children, then we ought not only to permit, but to encourage the instructors whom we employ, to introduce as rigid a system of classification, and as great a uniformity of books, into the schools, as possible. But still more than books, and classifying is needed to furnish a school-room. Our teachers must have maps and globes, and a variety of apparatus, suitable to illustrate these branches of knowledge, which we expect our children to learn. But the compensation which we ordinarily allow them, is not sufficient to warrant, or enable them to procure these articles, at their own cost. We must furnish them; and in doing so, we shall be the gainers. Our children will learn more rapidly; understand more clearly what they do learn; and retain with more permanency, and greater accuracy, the principles of those practical sciences, which even a school apparatus is sufficient to illustrate.

3. But, to keep up the figure of a shop—it is not enough that our teachers have tools—they must also have stock, or the raw material upon which these tools are to be employed, and their skill expended. This material, parents are to furnish; and it is of vast importance, to success in the result, that it be of the right kind.

Children receive their characters from the preponderant impressions to which they are habitually exposed. Thus their characters will be formed within the domestic circle. Teachers can do but little to alter the tendencies of that almost uninterrupted influence exerted upon young minds by the example of parents, domestics, and friends. Nay, it has before been shown, that it was not the province of the teacher, to oppose, what must be presumed to be the deliberate arrangement of the family circle, in relation to children. Teachers must not only take children as they are; but must permit them to remain as they were, in the respects just noticed. For where is the parent, that will patiently permit any teacher to obliterate those impressions; or change those characteristics; or to interfere with the formation of those habits, in his children, which he has been so solicitous to secure? . . .

We, then, who are parents, must from the constitution of society, form and sustain, the character, intellectual and moral, of those who reside under our roof. The teacher cannot do it without our aid; nor ought he to be permitted to do it without our aid; nor ought he to be permitted to do it without our co-operation. We must lay the foundation; he may help us to build. We must furnish the materials; he may fit and adjust them; but only under our direction and supervision. The teacher may, and will exert an incalculable influence upon the minds of his pupils; and through them on society. But parents are responsible for a great part even of that—because it will be modified by their superior, and [antecedent] influence. . . .

4. The last class of duties, devolving on parents in relation to teachers must be briefly discussed, for the present. . . . And that is, fellow-citizens, we must ourselves be the prominent and persevering teachers of our children, during the whole period, in which their characters are forming. We must subordinate every other concern to that. We must not leave it to hired help. We must not permit either business or pleasure, or even other duties, (none can be paramount,) to interfere with this class of obligations. We must not allow any man to dictate to us in the course which we pursue; nor must we ever lose sight of the actual engagements which employ our children from day to day.

We must here, as in other business, superintend at least, the whole concern, or it will not succeed. Let us decide what our children are to learn—procure for them suitable accommodations, books and apparatus—employ, for their benefit, the ablest instructors—and then keep our eye constantly upon them, their progress, and their instruction—encourage their despondency—repress their waywardness—show an interest in their studies, or we may be assured they will not. In a word, let us post up, every day, the whole concern, that we may have it under our eye, and let all concerned know that it is so. . . .

Fellow-citizens, my thoughts, on this subject, are now before you. . . . Let parents come up to the work as they ought. Let them provide suitable houses, suitable books, suitable apparatus, and suitable instructors for the benefit of their children; and all this within reach of their own homes. And let them be careful to cherish in their children those traits of character, that will make them at once active, and docile, respectful and persevering. And, in addition to all this, let them, as they would discharge the high responsibility that heaven has laid upon them, accompany their children through all their studies, and in person, superintend the whole process of their mental, moral, and religious training. . . .

PART VIII
THE DEIFICATION
OF DEMOCRACY

*T*he easiest way of becoming acquainted with the modes of thinking, the rules of conduct, and the prevailing manners of any people, is to examine what sort of education they give their children; how they treat them at home, and what they are taught in their places of worship.

St. John de Crevecoeur
Letters from an American Farmer, 1782

THE DEIFICATION
OF DEMOCRACY

What John Amos Comenius did not foresee—what few Christian educators other than Jonathan Edwards could have predicted—was that a day would come when mere knowledge would replace "the fear of the Lord." Few could imagine that a day would come when understanding would be measured quite apart from the presence or absence of moral virtue; when culture would determine the relativity of its own system of values. As the United States of America developed its new democratic republic, there seemed little possibility that a day would come when the democracy so treasured would hold a higher priority than obedience to the Lord God by whose sovereign providence that democracy had been permitted.

Certainly, the founders of America's colleges and schools had intended something far different, far more explicitly Christian. In fact, the overseers of Harvard College invited Comenius to become its second president, an offer he declined. Had he chosen to accept the position, he would have been reassured by the mission statement of the college that students read in their 1642 handbook:

> Let every student be plainly instructed and earnestly pressed to consider well the main end of his life and studies is, to know God and Jesus Christ which is eternal life. And therefore to lay Christ in the bottom as the only foundation of all sound knowledge and learning.

Over the next two centuries, from the Massachusetts Bay theocracy to the schools and colleges of the Northwest Territory and beyond, strong religious forces imposed commonly agreed moral standards upon all upstanding citizens, including teachers and students—moral standards derived from Scripture, whose violation carried with it the certain penalty of social ostracism. Whatever atheism or irreligion might have been advocated privately, socially acceptable behavior prescribed otherwise.

Even if not established by law, the unstated fact was that Protestant Christianity in some form—Congregational, Anglican, Baptist, Quaker, Moravian, Lutheran, Presbyterian—was the unofficial religion of the English colonies, with the sole exception of Maryland, which was a Roman Catholic haven. It was taken for granted, therefore, that schools existed for the purpose of inculcating these religiously-ordained moral precepts; understood also that, as a result, educators such as Anthony Benezet, Mary Lyon, and William Holmes McGuffey would be at the forefront of any needed moral or social reform.

So, during the American Revolution, when Samuel Phillips, Jr., founded his academy at Andover, he stipulated his expectations of any teacher: "He shall instruct [his pupils] in the several relations they sustain to God, their parents, the public, and their neighbors, and all their whole course of education one continued lecture on all that is great and good.'"

In Philadelphia, before the War of Revolution had been won, the Quaker Benezet led in founding both a school for girls and a school for black slave children. He wrote, in 1782,

> The advantage of endeavoring to promote the education of our youth, on its right basis, viz. a true estimate of human life, and the amendment of the heart, whence obedience and love to God, benignity to men, and a tender regard for the whole creation would necessarily flow, must be obvious to every feeling mind.

Nearly a half-century later, in 1828, at the founding of Flushing Institute by the Episcopal priest William Augustus Muhlenberg, the Bible was declared to be "the subject of systematic instruction" so that "the pupil must be made to perceive that the law of God is the law of the school."

Such an environment did not simply develop in a vacuum. This philosophy of education complemented what Lawrence A. Cremin later identified as "the united front" derived from "a sameness of views" consistently held by professing Christian families, churches, schools, and voluntary organizations that, together, formed an evangelical *paideia*—a total immersion in Christian orthodoxy and its living representation in cultural and civic piety.[2]

But "the united front" was not unbreachable by secularism and unbelief. By the end of the eighteenth century, agnosticism and irreligion rampaged throughout the new nation, seemingly encouraged by godlessness in the church-related but increasingly apostate colleges. By 1782, the Presbyterian College of New Jersey at Princeton claimed only two professing Christians in its student body. Similarly at Yale, in 1795, according to Lyman Beecher, then a student there, "the College was in a most ungodly state. The college church was almost extinct. Most of the students were skeptical, and rowdies were plenty. Wine and liquors were kept in many rooms; intemperance, profanity, gambling, and licentiousness were common."[3]

That same year, however, Timothy Dwight, a grandson of Jonathan Edwards, became president of Yale and set about to transform the college from "a sink of moral and spiritual pollution" into an evangelical lighthouse. By 1802, revival had converted as many as one-third of the students at Yale.[4] Among these was formed "the Illinois Band," a prayer group committed to missionary service, kindling concern for evangelization endeavors to such exotic places as the Sandwich Islands, now Hawaii, where a family named Dole is remembered as having "come to do good and ended up doing well." Other missionaries to the Northwest Territory— Indiana, Michigan, Illinois—began schools and colleges, such as Illinois College, founded in 1829.

Such student fervor was by no means localized in New Haven; other colleges in New England—Amherst, Williams, Dartmouth, but not Harvard—also experienced spiritual renewal at this same time. Throughout the nation, including distant parts of the frontier, this "Second Awakening" burned.

There were also significant effects upon education directly traceable to the Second Awakening. Voluntary agencies came into being for the specific purpose of producing literate and informed Christians, the better to effect necessary social reforms such as the abolition of slavery and, eventually, women's suffrage. The list is impressive: The American Society for Educating Pious Youth for the Gospel Ministry (1815), American Bible Society (1816), American Sunday-School Union (1824), American Tract

Society (1825), American Home Missionary Society (1826), the American Anti-Slavery Society (1833), and American and Foreign Anti-Slavery Society (1840). Together these organizations, as well as many denominational groups, made possible the education of preachers and then provided them with abundant literature, making necessary the education of their congregations.

As we have already noted, it is well documented that, in many villages and towns, a Sunday school existed before any common or public school was founded. In fact, the purposes of the Sunday school in America—as in England, where Robert Raikes began Sunday school in 1780—was not exclusively for Christian indoctrination; rather, the intention was that rudimentary teaching of reading and writing would be enhanced by using the Bible and other religious literature. Where the Sunday school thrived, it subsequently expanded to occupy other days of the week and with a wider curriculum; so the common school grew out of the evangelical Sunday school movement.

The fact that the church, rather than any political party, occupied the center of antislavery and abolitionist movements—as it was at the center of some campaigns for asserting women's rights to equality of opportunity in education—does not mean that the Christian *paideia* swept away all opposition; nor did the evangelical hegemony eradicate sin and create in America the Christian nation that some pseudohistorians proclaim. What did develop, however, was the formation of a cultural bias toward Christian principles, a "value system" clearly delineated by its Protestant predisposition toward a common standard of morality determined by Christian leaders: clergy, teachers, journalists, politicians, in whose hands the evangelical *paideia* became America's civil religion.

But any nation's civil religion—as the corrupt established churches of Europe demonstrate—is merely a blunted orthodoxy, more patriotic than prophetic in calling for loyalty to the ruling powers rather than repentance; more cultural that Christ-centered in calling for conventional morality rather than submission to His Lordship. Indeed, it was partly the ease with which nineteenth-century Christians assumed their beliefs to be the norm that dulled the sharp-edged thrust of orthodoxy and twisted it into the heresy of deifying democracy.

By the beginning of the nineteenth century, other forces were already at work in America—a spirit of self-reliance rather than the reality of human depravity and need for redemption; a spirit of rationalism rather than submission to the Lordship of Jesus Christ. In America, for instance, the Unitarian sect denied the special power of Jesus Christ's death and the reality of a physical resurrection. But heresy did not stop there; it led on to the greater scandal—embarrassing even to Unitarian clergy—of Ralph Waldo Emerson's declaration that the divinity of Jesus was "a noxious exaggeration."[5] For Emerson, Jesus was but one of many equally admirable examples to follow. The fact that Emerson issued his challenge to orthodoxy at Harvard Divinity School's graduation ceremonies suggests that his choice of location and audience was no coincidence.

Emerson's uncomfortable doctrine eventually found public acceptance throughout New England's Unitarian churches and colleges, many of which were already no longer committed to their founders' Christian orthodoxy and Trinitarian beliefs. Little by little, then with rapid acceleration, institutions founded by Congregationalists, Baptists, Presbyterians, Anglicans, and other denominations fell prey either to Unitarianism or to a secular dismissal of all religious concern.

From New England, a defection from orthodoxy spread throughout the nation. Today most of the schools, colleges, universities, and seminaries founded a century and more ago by believers in Jesus Christ and dedicated to the purpose of educating young people for Christian service no longer hold to the purpose entrusted to them. Governing boards, administrators, faculty, and students at such institutions no longer adhere to the message proclaimed by inscriptions, such as that on the cornerstone of the chapel at Davidson College in North Carolina, reading, "Other foundation can no man lay than that is laid, which is Jesus Christ" (1 Corinthians 3:11).

In spite of this defection, the vestiges at least of evangelicalism's "united front" may actually have been prolonged by the rise of the common or public school. In 1842, Henry Barnard, founder of the common school system in both Connecticut and Rhode Island, and later the first Federal Commissioner of Education, issued this call: "Every schoolhouse should be a temple, consecrated in prayer to the physical, intellectual, and moral culture of every child in the community, and be associated in every heart with the earliest and strongest impressions of truth, justice, patriotism, and religion."

The mere fact that the majority of a community's children sat under the same tutelage in reading, 'riting, 'rithmetic, *and* religiously-prescribed moral expectations meant that a culture's values were indelibly stamped upon most citizens. Similarly, in 1847 Horace Mann asserted the importance of Bible reading in the public schools of Massachusetts. Even though such reading was to be without comment from the teacher, the hearing of the words themselves, Mann argued, would be effective enough in teaching the standards of good citizenship.

This was the framework of civic piety and cultural convention; behind this facade of *paideia* and civil religion stood nothing like a structure of faith and obedience to the God revealed in Holy Scripture and in the Person of Jesus Christ. But, one can argue, the Word of God was able to speak for itself in effectiveness no one could limit or measure.

In that same year of 1847, Horace Bushnell, a minister in Hartford, Connecticut, published a book called *Christian Nurture.* Bushnell claimed that innate depravity had been falsely taught, that a child is the product of his or her home environment. That environment, Bushnell wrote, ought so to nurture the child that no other course than the Christian way seems natural and with the result that "the child is to grow up a Christian."

Moreover, Bushnell saw the common school not necessarily as a sectarian enterprise owned by the Protestant majority, but as an American and *therefore* a Christian institution.

But all such efforts to retain an aura of Protestant, if not evangelical, influence through the agency of the common or public schools were doomed to political and economic reaction. Chief among the factors principally responsible for the change in schooling from its evangelical "united front" to an increasing secularism were immigration, the expansion of the nation westward, and the democratization of American culture.

The tide of immigrants throughout the 1840s and later brought to America fresh waves of Europeans, many of whom were devoutly or nominally Roman Catholic. Their arrival appeared threatening to many Protestant Americans. As a consequence, religious bigotry flourished, and chauvinistic parties such as the "Know Nothing" or "Native American" sprang up, opposed to giving the Catholic immigrant equal rights to the benefits of America's supposedly free society—including equal rights to public education.

Among more openhearted and openminded Americans, their Protestant hegemony and homogeny were being altered by a necessary pluralism that took into account the rights of new citizens from every sort of religious tradition. Now the foresight of the Founding Fathers in so constructing the First Amendment to the Constitution would be tested in the crucible not of the churches but of the schools. It was a test most Americans faced with great reluctance.

In this era of intense anti-Roman Catholic feeling, Horace Bushnell was himself a member of a so-called Christian Alliance committed to opposing any Roman Catholic attempts at attaining equality of opportunity; yet Bushnell could declare that "we must be willing to stretch our forebearance and charity even to Romanists themselves, when we clearly find the spirit of Jesus in their life."

Bushnell's voice of qualified tolerance was lost, however, in the roar of animosity toward Catholics. When Roman Catholic bishops, such as John Hughes of New York, petitioned for a share of public funds for Catholic parochial schools, a Protestant outcry against Romanist infiltration of America's democratic system seemed not to hear its own ironic echoes. Subsequently, the Roman Church abandoned its efforts to obtain tax funds and, in 1884, made mandatory the establishing of a parish school near each church, to be supported by that parish. With this came an order compelling Roman Catholic parents to send their children only to parochial schools; so the Roman Catholic hierarchy struck back at an inhospitable "democracy."

Some Roman Catholic parents chose not to obey this edict; but they were sufficiently loyal both to their church and to the

United States Constitution to object when a local public school insisted on reading aloud the King James Version of the Bible, rather than the church's approved Douai-Reims Version. In the nineteenth century, generally, such objections by a minority were ignored, without fear of litigation; yet when the post-World War II Supreme Court began hearing and acting upon cases involving religious issues and the public schools, those past excesses of a biased Protestant majority came back to haunt mid-twentieth century American evangelicals.

The influx of immigrants and the grudging acceptance of pluralism their presence demanded from the Protestant majority help define the whole matter of westward expansion. As families of whatever religious persuasion settled beyond the Eastern seaboard, beyond the Cumberland Gap, across the wide Missouri, their isolatedness and privation made difficult any establishment of formal schooling. Every able-bodied member of the family was needed to work for the survival of all.

So, even when schools could be founded and maintained, school terms and attendance were often curtailed by weather or work. Parents also demanded that the limited time available be spent on practical skills—the Three R's, preferably. The Fourth R, religion, could be taught—if at all—at home or at church. There was an urgency to this business of getting a useful education; spiritual concerns, seemingly less pressing than learning how to add and subtract or how to read the almanac, must take a back seat.

Thus the schools of the American West were, almost from their inception, more preoccupied with secular matters than were their Eastern counterparts. But, as the response to Catherine Beecher's call for equal educational rights for females indicated, the West was also less inclined to waste one-half its human resources by ignoring the education of girls as well as boys.

The East was not slow, however, in following the West toward a secularistic curriculum. Here again, the question of pluralism was being raised. As Horace Mann's influence spread from Massachusetts to wherever public schools were being formed, so too his argument carried against the teaching of religion in any public school. His fundamental point seemed to contradict the democratic notion that "the majority rules."

Instead, Mann saw the possibility of a new majority exerting its claims every time an election was held. The danger was such disruption over majoritarian struggles would overpower the school's ability to lead students to find truth wherever it might lead them. Better, Horace Mann concluded, to have schools with no religion taught at all than to have schools embroiled in religious controversy.

Still, Mann wished to have the Bible read aloud in public schools, although without comment or interpretation. His intention was clear, to introduce the moral effect of the Bible without the squabblings of its adherents. Surely in the climate of a Christian *paideia,* Mann could not have imagined that a Supreme Court case could be made against Bible reading on the grounds that it affronts the religious belief or unbelief of a single child and his family.

Many Americans agreed with him; but not all. The 1847 General Assembly of the Presbyterian Church, USA, declared that, since Presbyterians could no longer "safely rely" on the public schools to provide a satisfactory religious education, every Presbyterian congregation should commit itself "to establish within its bounds one or more primary schools, under the care of the session of the church, in which together with the usual branches of secular learning, the truths and duties of our holy religion shall be assiduously inculcated."

That same year of 1847 also saw the formation of what is today the Missouri Synod of the Lutheran Church. Wanting Christian schooling for the children of each congregation, the fledgling Synod imposed a mandate with the intention of making such schooling distinctively Lutheran and distinctively German, in order to retain their ethnic heritage. Thus the Synod set up its own training school for pastors and teachers; the Synod also began a publishing firm to produce curriculum materials—catechisms, primers, and a hymnal. We know these enterprises today as Concordia Theological Seminary and Concordia Publishing House, both in St. Louis.

So was planted the second crop of Christian schools in America. The first planting had come by edict in the enactment of the Massachusetts Law of 1647, the "ye old deluder, Satan" law. The second planting came exactly two centuries later as a reaction against the threat to the "united front" and "sameness of views," brought on by the incursion of secularism and a concession to pluralism in the newly-arrived public schools, interpreted then—as is often the case today—as hostile to Christian principles.

But, after only two decades, this new crop of Christian schools fell victim to the blight known as the Civil War. During the years 1861–65 and after, few Christian academies and denominational schools could survive the financial straits brought about by the war. Into the vacuum created by the demise of these schools came the free "common school" and the public high school. Begun in Boston in 1821, as a means of teaching immigrant youths the English language, the public high school took root during Reconstruction, particularly in the more democratically assertive Western states. As more and more communities established their public high schools, enrollment in private schools declined even further. In one hundred years, enrollment percentages reversed themselves: Whereas in the 1830s, 90 percent of schoolchildren attended private schools, by the 1930s, only 10 percent of schoolchildren attended private schools.

By the late years of the nineteenth century and the early decades of the twentieth, two forces had accelerated this groundswell away from private, mostly religious, schooling toward public schooling: an increasing democratization of society at large and a decreasing respect for the authority of Scripture in the mainstream churches of America.

Pressed by a growing sense that *democracy* must be the highest principle and that a "melting pot" of uniform experience could best be cultivated in the institution of public schooling, private academies found themselves facing accusations of promoting an undemocratic—therefore unpatriotic—elitism. Furthermore, among the shapers of public schooling itself the opinion was forming that the schools must not encourage religious convictions, which seemed possible only if religion could be extirpated altogether. Gone were the calls of McGuffey—and even of Horace Mann—for religious instruction. By 1929, Luther B. Weigle, Dean Emeritus of Yale Divinity School, wrote

> The principle of religious freedom which insures the separation of church and state is precious. It touches bed rock in its truth. It is a guarantee of our liberties. But the principle of

the separation of church and state must not be construed so as to render the state a fosterer of non-religion or atheism. Yet that is precisely what we are doing in America today.[6]

Pressed also by disciples of European theologians, their "higher criticism" of the Bible, and their scientific naturalism to explain all religious phenomena, mainline seminaries, colleges, schools, and churches revised their theology accordingly. To these "modernists," the notion of humanity's universal sinful condition and the need of each individual for personal salvation through faith in Jesus Christ could now be exchanged for a new tenet, social salvation through John Dewey's "progressive education." In Dewey's view, experience became the ethical criterion, eliminating the concern for moral absolutes, dismissing the idea of a personal God to whom each individual is accountable.

As a concession, therefore, to both declining enrollment and declining commitment to orthodox doctrine, schools that once proclaimed their fidelity to the gospel of Jesus Christ found themselves needing to accommodate to the spirit of the times.

How did these developments come about? The arguments of the four thinkers we are about to read help to answer that question. Evangelical readers of a book pertaining to Christian thought on education may well question the rationale for including the next four authors: Horace Mann, Ralph Waldo Emerson, Horace Bushnell, and John Dewey.

We must, however, inspect their writings for the following reasons. First, there can be no questioning the impact these thinkers and writers have had upon American education, mapping its direction by their utterances. Second, whereas none of them would have accepted comfortably their own association with evangelicalism —two were accused of heresy even by liberal churches and the other two often expressed attitudes antagonistic toward Christianity— nonetheless much of what they held affects the cause of Christian schooling today. Lastly, as with many famous writers, their names are better known than their work. No doubt, few evangelicals who condemn Mann and Emerson, Bushnell and Dewey, have ever read anything they wrote. In reading their philosophies, we become aware of the faulty thinking that would influence the modernist trend in twentieth century education.

HORACE MANN

Horace Mann (1796–1859) is considered the principal founder of the public school system. After graduating from Brown University in 1819, Mann studied law and was admitted to the bar in 1823. He began his political career as a Massachusetts legislator and senator, during which time he was instrumental in the passing of laws affecting both humanitarian and educational concerns.

Although Massachusetts had pioneered the enacting of compulsory school laws, no uniform system of schooling existed until 1837, when Horace Mann resigned from the Massachusetts senate to become secretary of the newly appointed state Board of Education. For twelve years, Mann directed the development of a public network of schools throughout the Commonwealth of Massachusetts. His philosophy of education was democratic, egalitarian, non-sectarian, and insistent upon a professionally trained administration and staff accountable to local authorities in turn responsible to maintain state-prescribed standards.

In setting up such a system, one of Mann's paramount concerns was to keep the public classroom free from religious controversy. Mann himself was neither irreligious nor personally opposed to the teachings of Christianity. But, before all else, he was a democrat unswervingly committed to preserving the public school from any dominant religious dogma.

Mann's public statements about God and "the religion of the Bible," as he called it, were always favorable. His ideal, expressed in his 1848 report to the Board of Education (from which excerpts follow), was to allow the Bible to "do what it is allowed to do in no other system,—*to speak for itself.*"[7] He commended public Bible reading in the schools of Massachusetts.

But Mann also knew that the ideal was not the reality, that "the religion of the Bible" and institutionalized Christianity, with its internal disputes over liturgy, sacraments, rites, doctrines, and offices were often radically different from each other. He feared that an earnest Christian of one denomination or another would use the position of teacher and the captive audience of pupils to teach sectarian views. Worse, he feared that conflicting dogmatic opinions by two or more Christians with opposing views would be forced upon students, with confusing and disquieting results.

Mann contended "one sect may have ascendency today; another tommorow," and the students would be caught between confusing and warring viewpoints.

Furthermore, Mann argued with persistent logic, an already-poisoned political situation will worsen, with the corruption of gerrymandering demagoguery, and fraud turning religion in the schools into cause for scandal.

> Will not town limits and school district lines be altered, to restore an unsuccessful or to defeat a successful party? Will not fiery zealots move from place to place, to turn the theological scale, as it is said is sometimes now done to turn a political one? And will not the godless make a merchandise of religion by being bribed to do the same thing? Can aught be conceived more deplorable, more fatal to the interests of the young than this?[8]

Finally, Mann warned that the consequences of teaching religious education would lead to "such strifes and persecutions on the question of total depravity as to make all men depraved at any rate; and such contests about the nature and the number of persons in the Godhead in heaven, as to make little children atheists on earth."

Thus Horace Mann determined that all Bible reading in the public schools of Massachusetts must be without comment, without theological interpretation, without personal application. This was Mann's mid-nineteenth century formula for religious neutrality, preserving—he believed—both freedom *of* religion and freedom *from* religion.

In 1848, Mann resigned as secretary of the Massachusetts Board to assume the seat in the House of Representatives left vacant by the death of former president John Quincy Adams. In Washington, D.C., Mann became an outspoken opponent of slavery, a stance that may have cost him the governorship of Massachusetts in the 1852 election he lost.

The following year, he accepted appointment as the first president of Antioch College, in Yellow Springs, Ohio. There until his death Horace Mann contributed to creating the traditions of this socially, politically, and educationally radical institution. Because of these *avant garde* connections, Horace Mann is often cited today as a patron saint—not of the religious neutrality he advocated for public education—but of the elimination of any religious influence whatever. This distortion does a disservice to history and to the character of Horace Mann.

"Report to the Massachusetts Board of Education, 1848"⁹ (Excerpt)

Moral Education

Moral education is a primal necessity of social existence. The unrestrained passions of men are not only homicidal, but suicidal; and a community without a conscience would soon extinguish itself. Even with a natural conscience, how often has evil triumphed over good! From the beginning of time, wrong has followed right, as the shadow the substance. . . .

But to all doubters, disbelievers, or despairers in human progress, it may still be said, there is one experiment which has never yet been tried. It is an experiment, which, even before its inception, offers the highest authority for its ultimate success. Its formula is intelligible to all; and it is as legible as though written in starry letters on an azure sky. It is expressed in these few and simple words: "Train up a child in the way he should go; and when he is old, he will not depart from it." This declaration is positive. If the conditions are complied with, it makes no provision for a failure. Though pertaining to morals, yet, if the terms of the direction are observed, there is no more reason to doubt the result than there would be in an optical or chemical experiment.

But this experiment has never yet been tried. Education has never yet been brought to bear with one-hundredth part of its potential force upon the natures of children, and, through them, upon the character of men and of the race. In all the attempts to reform mankind which have hitherto been made, whether by changing the frame of government, by aggravating or softening the severity of the penal code, or by substituting a government-created for a God-created religion,—in all these attempts, the infantile and youthful mind, its amenability to influences, and the enduring and self-operating character of the influences it receives, have been almost wholly unrecognized. . . .

So far as human instrumentalities are concerned, we have abundant means for surrounding every child in the State with preservative and moral influences as extensive and as efficient as those under which the present industrious, worthy, and virtuous members of the community were reared. And as to all those things

314

in regard to which we are directly dependent upon the divine favor, have we not the promise, explicit and unconditional, that the men SHALL NOT depart from the way in which they should go, if the children are trained up in it? It has been overlooked that this promise is not restricted to parents, but seems to be addressed indiscriminately to all, whether parents, communities, states, or mankind . . .

Religious Education

But it will be said that this grand result in practical morals is a consummation of blessedness that can never be attained without religion, and that no community will ever be religious without a religious education. Both these propositions I regard as eternal and immutable truths. Devoid of religious principles and religious affections, the race can never fall so low but that it may sink still lower; animated and sanctified by them, it can never rise so high but that it may ascend still higher. And is it not at least as presumptuous to expect that mankind will attain to the knowledge of truth, without being instructed in truth, and without that general expansion and development of faculty which will enable them to recognize and comprehend truth in any other department of human interest as in the department of religion? . . .

That our public schools are not theological seminaries, is admitted. That they are debarred by law from inculcating the peculiar and distinctive doctrines of any one religious denomination among us, is claimed; and that they are also prohibited from ever teaching that what they do teach is the whole of religion, or all that is essential to religion or to salvation, is equally certain. But our system earnestly inculcates all Christian morals; it founds its morals on the basis of religion; it welcomes the religion of the Bible; and, in receiving the Bible, it allows it to do what it is allowed to do in no other system,—*to speak for itself.* But here it stops, not because it claims to have compassed all truth, but because it disclaims to act as an umpire between hostile religious opinions.

The very terms "public school" and "common school" bear upon their face that they are schools which the children of the entire community may attend. Every man not on the pauper-list is taxed for their support; but he is not taxed to support them as special religious institutions: if he were, it would satisfy at once the largest definition of a religious establishment. But he is taxed . . . to support schools, because they are the most effective means of developing and training those powers and faculties in a child, by which, when he becomes a man, he may understand what his highest interests and his highest duties are, and may be in fact, and not in name only, a free agent. The elements of a political education are not bestowed upon any school child for the purpose of making him vote with this or that political party when he becomes of age, but for the purpose of enabling him to choose for himself with which party he will vote. So the religious education which a child receives at school is not imparted to him for the purpose of making him join this or that denomination when he arrives at years of discretion, but for the purpose of enabling him to judge for himself, according to the dictates of his own reason and conscience, what his religious obligations are, and whither they lead. . . .

In a social and political sense, it is a *free* school-system. It knows no distinction of rich and poor, of bond and free, or between those, who, in the imperfect light of this world, are seeking, through different avenues, to reach the gate of heaven. Without money and without price, it throws open its doors, and spreads the table of its bounty, for all the children of the State. Like the sun, it shines not only upon the good, but upon the evil, that they may become good; and, like the rain, its blessings descend not only upon the just, but upon the unjust, that their injustice may depart from them, and be known no more.

RALPH WALDO EMERSON

T he son of a Unitarian minister, Ralph Waldo Emerson (1803-82) attended Boston Latin School and Harvard College, graduating in 1821. For three years he taught school, but enrolled at Harvard Divinity School after he felt a call to the ministry. "I deliberately dedicate my time, talents, and my hopes to the Church," he wrote of his call.

He was licensed to preach in 1826 and ordained in 1829 as pastor of Boston's Second Church. His wife Ellen died in 1831, and the following year Emerson showed the first signs of his independent strain of thinking. He refused to celebrate Holy Communion as a ritual, according to prescribed form. The rites of the church, he felt, had gained pre-eminence over the truth they professed to declare. Religious formality was now in the saddle, with "truth only a horse for Christianity."[10] In the furor Emerson resigned his pastorate and demitted his ordination.

From then on, he became a man of letters: an essayist, lecturer, and poet. His most famous, if not his most acclaimed, poem is "Concord Bridge," written for the occasion of the fiftieth anniversary of the skirmish that opened the Revolutionary War. Perhaps its most famous lines are: "Here once, th' embattled farmers stood, / And fired the shot heard 'round the world."

Influenced alike by European romanticists and Oriental mystics, Emerson developed his theories of transcendentalism. The "Over-Soul," made known through nature and the intuitive powers of "Reason" became Emerson's depiction of God. In 1836, he published the essay "Nature," glorifying the natural universe as a metaphor for human perfectability. In August of the next year, Emerson delivered the Phi Beta Kappa Address to open the academic year at Harvard. His remarks, entitled "The American Scholar," were called "our intellectual Declaration of Independence"[11] by Oliver Wendell Holmes; excerpts appear below.

From such high praise, Emerson fell to scathing condemnation the following year. Invited by the 1838 graduating class—and against the wishes of the administration—Emerson appeared at Harvard Divinity School. The Unitarian clergy, suspicious of this troublesome former colleague, realized their worst fears when the guest speaker proceeded to flaunt his heresies from their highest platform.

Jesus Christ, he said, was no more than a prophet; the miracles, a monstrous invention of His overweening followers; the idea that God's revelation of truth has been "given and done" is "an injury to faith." Perhaps today's Unitarians and liberal Protestants would find little quarrel with Emerson, but in 1838, Harvard's Unitarians were still near enough to their former Trinitarian orthodoxy to feel betrayed. They heaped their outrage upon Emerson in newspapers and sermons for months to come. For the next two decades, Emerson was *persona non grata* at Harvard and in any Unitarian pulpit.

He turned to publishing briefer essays, aphorisms, and pithy sayings culled from his journals and occasionally delivered at lyceums and other public lectures. As poet and philosopher, Emerson influenced and continues to influence many whose skepticism cannot accept a supernatural yet personal God. The 1960s' catch-phrase "Do your own thing" is an echo of Emerson's self-reliance; America's abiding preoccupation with Eastern religion is an echo of Emerson's fascination with Hindu mysticism. As mentor to Henry David Thoreau and inspiration for Walt Whitman, Emerson became the catalyst for the American cult of "rugged individualism" and for the pantheistic assertion that God can be found exclusively in nature.

"The American Scholar," The Phi Beta Kappa Address at Harvard[12] (Excerpt)

I greet you on the recommencement of our literary year. Our anniversary is one of hope, and, perhaps, not enough of labor. We do not meet for games of strength or skill, for the recitation of histories, tragedies, and odes, like the ancient Greeks; for parliaments of love and poesy, like the Troubadours; nor for the advancement of science, like our contemporaries in British and European capitals. Thus far, our holiday has been simply a sign of the survival of the love of letters amongst a people too busy to give to letters any more. As such it is precious as the sign of an indestructible instinct.

In this hope, I accept the topic which not only usage but the nature of our association seem to prescribe to this day—the AMERICAN SCHOLAR. Year by year we come up hither to read one more chapter of his biography. Let us inquire what light new days and events have thrown on his character and his hopes. . . . In the right state he is *Man Thinking.* In the degenerate state, when the victim of society, he tends to become a mere thinker, or still worse, the parrot of other men's thinking. . . . Let us see him in his school, and consider him in reference to the main influences he receives.

I. The first in time and the first in importance of the influences upon the mind is that of nature. . . . So much of nature as he is ignorant of, so much of his own mind does he not yet possess. And, in fine, the ancient precept, "Know thyself," and the modern precept, "Study nature," become at last one maxim.

II. The next great influence into the spirit of the scholar is the mind of the Past,—in whatever form, whether of literature, of art, of institutions, that mind is inscribed. Books are the best type of the influence of the past, and perhaps we shall get at the truth,—learn the amount of this influence more conveniently,— by considering their value alone.

The theory of books is noble. The scholar of the first age received into him the world around; brooded thereon; gave it the new arrangement of his own mind, and uttered it again. It came into him life; it went out from him immortal thoughts. It came to him business; it went from him poetry. . . .

Yet hence arises a mischief. . . . Colleges are built on it. Books are written on it by thinkers, not by Man Thinking; by men of talent, that is, who start wrong, who set out from accepted dogmas, not from their own sight of principles. Meek young men grow up in libraries, believing it their duty to accept the views which Cicero, which Locke, which Bacon, have given; forgetful that Cicero, Locke, and Bacon were only young men in libraries when they wrote these books.

Hence, instead of Man Thinking, we have the bookworm. . . . Books are the best of things, well used; abused, among the worst. What is the right use? What is the one end which all means go to effect? They are for nothing but to inspire. I had better never see a book than to be warped by its attraction clean out of my own orbit, and made a satellite instead of a system. . . .

Books are for the scholar's idle times. When he can read God directly, the hour is too precious to be wasted in other men's transcripts of their readings. . . .

I would not be hurried by any love of system, by any exaggeration of instincts, to underrate the Book. We all know, that as the human body can be nourished by any food, though it were boiled grass and the broth of shoes, so the human mind can be fed by any knowledge. And great and heroic men have existed who had almost no other information than by the printed page. I would say that it needs a strong head to bear that diet. One must be an inventor to read well. . . . There is then creative reading as well as creative writing. . . .

III. Action is with the scholar subordinate, but it is essential. Without it he is not yet man. Without it thought can never ripen into truth. . . .

I have now spoken of the education of the scholar by nature, by books, and by action. It remains to say somewhat of his duties.

They are such as become Man Thinking. They may all be comprised in self-trust. The office of the scholar is to cheer, to raise, and to guide men by showing them facts amidst appearances. . . .

These being his functions, it becomes him to feel all confidence in himself, and to defer never to the popular cry. He and he only knows the world. . . . Let him not quit his belief that a popgun is a popgun, though the ancient and honorable of the earth affirm it to be the crack of doom. In silence, in steadiness, in severe abstraction, let him hold by himself; add observation to observation, patient of neglect, patient of reproach, and bide his own time—happy enough if he can satisfy himself alone that this day he has seen something truly. . . .

In self-trust all the virtues are comprehended. Free should the scholar be—free and brave. . . .

HORACE BUSHNELL

B orn in 1802, Horace Bushnell returned to his alma mater Yale in
1829, intending to pursue postgraduate studies in law while serving as a tutor in the college. But during a college revival in 1831,
Bushnell experienced a spiritual awakening and sense of calling to the
ministry. He switched his studies from law to theology, and in 1833 he
became pastor of the North Church (Congregational) in Hartford, Connecticut. There he remained until illness compelled him to resign in
1859.

In 1847, Bushnell's treatise *Christian Nurture* (excerpts follow) was
written to refute the evangelical teaching of universal and innate depravity, from which even the youngest child must be personally converted. In place of this belief, Bushnell proposed an environment in which
every child is brought up to become what he already is: a Christian.

Bushnell's vision of "Christian" education cannot be dismissed
without considering the breadth of his influence. Bushnell's challenge to
nineteenth century evangelicals struck at their habit—especially in the
Connecticut River valley towns—of depending upon periodic "awaken-
ings" and revivals to convert adults, thereby slighting the needs of their
own children. Bushnell's argument is that Christian parents must expect
neither too little nor too much of their children. They cannot treat their
children as though the child had not, from birth, been the recipient of
Christian training; they cannot, like the ostrich in Lamentations 4:3,
abandon the child to whatever natural forces will work upon him.

Christian parents must provide a Christian upbringing by consciously offering examples and by diligently avoiding "the treatment that
discourages piety." Every element of a child's life as a member of a Christian family must be reached. No person presuming to love God and love
children can be free from this responsibility—just as no Christian educator can afford to ignore Horace Bushnell's *Christian Nurture*.

Bushnell is reputed to be "the father of American liberal theology."
Unlike Emerson, however, whose heretical theology scandalized even
his Unitarian audiences, Bushnell offered a mix of orthodox Christianity
with nineteenth-century liberal thinking. For instance, Bushnell
preached that Jesus Christ was indeed the Son of God—something

Emerson had called a "noxious exaggeration." Bushnell preached that Jesus' death was effective for forgiveness of sins. But Bushnell tempered this seemingly orthodox preaching with a view that religious language is always of poetic nature, including the Bible and the creeds. Because all religious language is suggestible of truth, rather than the definitive expression of truth, one can never expect exactness in what is meant by religious affirmations. So, the atonement operates through moral example instead of Christ's substitutionary sacrifice; the trinity is a human perspective on the Godhead, rather than being the divinely ordained distinctions of three persons in one.

In 1850, Bushnell faced charges of heresy brought by the General Association of Congregational Ministers, but he handily answered his accusers. This victory served to elevate Bushnell among liberal clergy, who saw in his case a model for later evasions of orthodoxy in the name of "modernism."

Christian Nurture (Excerpt)

I.
What Christian Nurture Is

"Bring them up in the nurture and admonition of the Lord." —Ephesians, vi. 4.

There is then some kind of nurture which is of the Lord, deriving a quality and a power from Him, and communicating the same. Being instituted by Him, it will of necessity have a method and a character peculiar to itself, or rather to Him. It will be the Lord's way of education, having aims appropriate to Him, and, if realized in its full intent, terminating in results impossible to be reached by any merely human method.

What then is the true idea of Christian or divine nurture, as distinguished from that which is not Christian? What is its aim? What its method of working? What its powers and instruments? What its contemplated results? Few questions have greater moment; and it is one of the pleasant signs of the times, that the subject involved is beginning to attract new interest, and excite a spirit of inquiry which heretofore has not prevailed in our churches.

In ordinary cases, the better and more instructive way of handling this subject, would be to go directly into the practical methods of parental discipline, and show by what modes of government and instruction we may hope to realize the best results. But unhappily the public mind is preoccupied extensively by a view of the whole subject, which I must regard as a theoretical mistake, and one which will involve, as long as it continues, practical results systematically injurious. This mistaken view it is necessary, if possible, to remove. And accordingly what I have to say will take the form of an argument on the question thus put in issue; though I design to gather round the subject, as I proceed, as much of practical instruction as the mode of the argument will suffer. Assuming then the question above stated, What is the true idea of Christian education?—I answer in the following proposition, which it will be the aim of my argument to establish, viz: *That the child is to grow up a Christian, and never know himself as being otherwise.*

In other words, the aim, effort, and expectation should be, not, as is commonly assumed, that the child is to grow up in sin, to be converted after he comes to a mature age; but that he is to open on the world as one that is spiritually renewed, not remembering the time when he went through a technical experience, but seeming rather to have loved what is good from his earliest years. I do not affirm that every child may, in fact and without exception, be so trained that he certainly will grow up a Christian. The qualifications it may be necessary to add will be given in another place, where they can be stated more intelligibly.

This doctrine is not a novelty, now rashly and for the first time propounded, as some of you may be tempted to suppose. I shall show you, before I have done with the argument, that it is as old as the Christian church, and prevails extensively at the present day in other parts of the world. Neither let your own experience raise a prejudice against it. If you have endeavored to realize the very truth I here affirm, but find that your children do not exhibit the character you have looked for; if they seem to be intractable to religious influences, and sometimes to display an apparent aversion to the very subject of religion itself, you are not of course to conclude that the doctrine I here maintain is untrue or impracticable. You may be unreasonable in your expectations of your children.

Possibly, there may be seeds of holy principle in them, which you do not discover. A child acts out his present feelings, the feelings of the moment, without qualification or disguise. And how, many times, would all you appear, if you were to do the same? Will you expect of them to be better, and more constant and consistent, than yourselves; or will you rather expect them to be children, human children still, living a mixed life, trying out the good and evil of the world, and preparing, as older Christians do, when they have taken a lesson of sorrow and emptiness, to turn again to the true good?

Perhaps they will go through a rough mental struggle, at some future day, and seem, to others and to themselves, there to have entered on a Christian life. And yet it may be true that there was still some root of right principle established in their childhood, which is here only quickened and developed, as when Christians of a mature age are revived in their piety, after a period of spiritual lethargy; for it is conceivable that regenerate character may exist, long before it is fully and formally developed.

But suppose there is really no trace or seed of holy principle in your children, has there been no fault of piety and constancy in your church? no want of Christian sensibility and love to God? no carnal spirit visible to them and to all, and imparting its noxious and poisonous quality to the Christian atmosphere in which they have had their nurture? For it is not for you alone to realize all that is included in the idea of Christian education. It belongs to the church of God, according to the degree of its social power over you and in you and around your children, to bear a part of the responsibility with you.

Then, again, have you nothing to blame in yourselves? no lack of faithfulness? no indiscretion of manner or of temper? no mistake of duty, which, with a better and more cultivated piety, you would have been able to avoid? Have you been so nearly even with your privilege and duty, that you can find no relief but to lay some charge upon God, or comfort yourselves in the conviction that he has appointed the failure you deplore? When God marks out a plan of education, or sets up an aim to direct its efforts, you will see, at once, that he could not base it on a want of piety in you, or on any imperfections that flow from a want of piety. It must be a plan measured by Himself and the fullness of his own gracious intentions.

Besides, you must not assume that we, in this age are the best Christians that have ever lived, or most likely to produce all the fruits of piety. An assumption so pleasing to our vanity is more easily made than verified, but vanity is the weakest as it is the cheapest of all arguments. We have some good points, in which we compare favorably with other Christians, and Christians of other times, but our style of piety is sadly deficient, in many respects, and that to such a degree that we have little cause for self-congratulation. . . .

For some reason, we do not make a Christian atmosphere about us—do not produce the conviction that we are living unto God. There is a marvelous want of savor in our piety. It is a flower of autumn, colored as highly as it need be to the eye, but destitute of fragrance. It is too much to hope that, with such an instrument, we can fulfill the true idea of Christian education. Any such hope were even presumptuous. At the same time, there is no ready way of removing the deficiencies just described, as to recall our churches to their duties in domestic life; those humble, daily, hourly duties, where the spirit we breathe shall be a perpetual element of power and love, bathing the life of childhood. . . .

JOHN DEWEY

The single most dominant figure in American education at the end of the nineteenth and the first half of the twentieth centuries was John Dewey (1859–1952). Born in Burlington, Vermont, Dewey lived almost one hundred years, through a century of astonishing change. The Civil War, the Spanish-American War, World Wars I and II, and the Korean War marched through his lifetime. In the year of Dewey's birth Charles Darwin released *The Origin of Species*; the year before his death J. D. Salinger published *The Catcher in the Rye*. Dewey knew both the steam locomotive and the transcontinental airliner.

Dewey also witnessed and helped to energize the transformation of American public life from a God-conscious accountability to its present secular relativism. By his voluminous writing and his prestige of office, Dewey's educational theories swept aside pedagogical and moral tenets he considered outmoded or unscientific, ushering in their place new doctrines based on scientific observation and the absence of absolute moral standards.

Upon graduating from the University of Vermont in 1879, Dewey taught school for two years, then enrolled for graduate studies at Johns Hopkins University, receiving his doctorate in 1884. After teaching philosophy for ten years, at the universities of Minnesota and Michigan, he arrived at the new University of Chicago in 1894. Founded in 1891 by grants from John D. Rockefeller amounting eventually to more than $75 million and intended by him to become "a Christian university," Rockefeller entrusted the University of Chicago to the Northern Baptist Convention, in whose churches he worshiped.

The Baptists appointed William Rainey Harper and Harry Pratt Judson as president and dean of the faculty, respectively. To whatever degree Rockefeller and these Baptist clergymen-educators may have misunderstood each other's intent, the fact remains that early faculty appointments of Dewey and the social theorist Thorstein Veblen did little to ensure the reality of "a Christian university."

At Chicago, Dewey was made head of the merged departments of philosophy, psychology, and pedagogy. In 1896, he and his wife Alice began the University Laboratory School, where his theories could be practiced and observed. That same year, *The School Journal* solicited, and in 1897 published, statements from Dewey and other educators regarding their educational philosophies. Expanded into book form in 1929, *My Pedagogic Creed* may be the clearest explication of Dewey's complex theories.

Dewey's philosophy and psychology of education reflected his rejection of supernatural revelation by a personal God; he also dismissed any claims that the Bible makes concerning the need for redemption and atonement through Jesus Christ. To Dewey, these Christian claims were outdated and unhelpful in the modern scientific age. Instead, like Emerson—who, for Dewey, was comparable to Plato—nature was the only authentic revelation. In Dewey's view, truth came not from any absolute, immutable Source but only from experience; and, adapting Darwinism to his purpose, Dewey claimed that human experience had evolved the act of thinking as an instrument for survival.

By using thought as a tool ("instrumentalism"), by trial-and-error ("experimentalism"), the human race discovers its own principles: If it works, it's true; if it doesn't work, it's false, said Dewey. Thus borrowing from the pragmatism of William James, Dewey developed his own philosophy of progress, whose purpose in educational terms was personal and communal growth, ever moving forward—although Dewey's writings are most ambiguous as to either direction or destination for such progress.

His disciple, John L. Childs, summed up Dewey's philosophy:

> Since experience is an ongoing process, this view also means that finality and absolute certainty are impossible. Absolute dogma must give place to hypotheses. Truths are the opinions, the beliefs, the hypotheses which have been verified by experience. Since experience is ongoing in nature and conditions do change, absolute finality is not to be had. The ultimate source, authority, and criterion for all belief and conduct are to be found in ordinary human experience.[13]

Rousas John Rushdoony comments:

> It was upon these principles that the professional training of public school teachers was established, and modern educational theory is the direct outcome of these ideas. As against the Calvinist conception of man as sinner, man is good; as against the doctrine of man's responsibility and accountability to God, of life as a stewardship, the non-biblical conception of

natural rights is introduced into education. *The pupil is therefore a person with rights rather than responsibilities. Instead of being accountable to God, parents, teachers, and society, the pupil can assert that God, parents, teachers, and society are responsible to him.* [14]

Dewey was also strongly influenced by the romanticist theories of childhood innocence propagated by Jean Jacques Rousseau and William Wordsworth. Rousseau's *Emile*, published in 1762, sets forth an improbable education for a fictitious youth, free from any taint of adult authority, the ideal "natural man." According to Edwin H. Rian, "Perhaps more than any other book *Emile* undermined the foundations of the religious theory of education."[15] The English poet Wordsworth, believing in "natural piety"—a transcendental religious experience obtained through communing with nature—further believed in the child's innate goodness, which only later became corruptible by adult influences.

By denying the Christian doctrine of original sin, Dewey thereby misconceived the true nature of any child and misconstrued the spirit of egoistic rebellion for benign individualism and independence. Thus, when Dewey urged, "Let the child's nature fulfill its own destiny," he was unconsciously uttering a foregone conclusion concerning the nature of children and mankind. He was denying the consequences of a sinful nature left unregenerate; for such an unregenerate being will never fail to fulfill his own destiny—in rebellion against God.

Dewey would have none of this belief in man's degenerate nature. Unlike Horace Mann, Dewey was no theist, although he claimed affiliation with a Congregationalist church. For him, democracy was the only god. Therefore, when he refers, in *My Pedagogic Creed*, to "the true God" and "the true kingdom of God," Dewey must be understood on his own terms. He is speaking about democracy and a democratic society in which "the teacher is always the prophet."

Democracy and Education, his major work published in 1916, makes this clear. But in an earlier book, his 1900 publication, *The School and Society*, Dewey had declared his optimistic belief in the democratic prospects brought about through education:

> When the school introduces and trains each child of society into membership within such a little community, saturating him with the spirit of service, and providing him with the instruments of effective self-direction, we shall have the deepest and best guaranty of a larger society which is worthy, lovely, and harmonious.

To John Dewey, a signer of the first "Humanist Manifesto" in 1933, the antithesis of his democratic and progressive ideal was the Christian message of sin and salvation. For implicit in such a message are those divisions that separate belief from unbelief—such as the sheep and the goats, the saved and the lost, even if those divisions are known only to the Shepherd and Father. For Dewey, such divisions were incompatible with his vision of the democratic ideal or his secular humanist's solution to human problems, which he found to be the concept of a single human family.

In 1904, Dewey joined Teachers College of Columbia University in New York City, where his "progressive education" became the operative model. From this platform as professor at the most influential institution for pedagogical instruction, as prolific author and editor, as president of the American Philosophical Association and the American Psychological Association, Dewey controlled the machinery of public education for half a century. His method also flooded most private schools.

"My Pedagogic Creed"[16] (Excerpt)

Article I. What Education Is.

I believe that all education proceeds by the participation of the individual in the social consciousness of the race. This process begins unconsciously almost at birth, and is continually shaping the individual's powers, saturating his consciousness, forming his habits, training his ideas, and arousing his feelings and emotions. Through this unconscious education the individual gradually comes to share in the intellectual and moral resources which humanity has succeeded in getting together. He becomes an inheritor of the funded capital of civilization. The most formal and technical education in the world cannot safely depart from this general process. It can only organize it; or differentiate it in some particular direction.

I believe that the only true education comes through the stimulation of the child's powers by the demands of the social situations in which he finds himself. . . . For instance, through the response which is made to the child's instinctive babblings the child comes to know what those babblings mean; they are transformed into articulate language and thus the child is introduced into the consolidated wealth of ideas and emotions which are now summed up in language.

I believe that this educational process has two sides—one psychological and one sociological; and that neither can be sub-ordinated to the other or neglected without evil results following. Of these two sides, the psychological is the basis. . . . Without insight into the psychological structure and activities of the individual, the educative process will, therefore, be haphazard and arbitrary. . . .

I believe that knowledge of social conditions, of the present state of civilization, is necessary in order properly to interpret the child's powers. The child has his own instincts and tendencies, but we do not know what these mean until we can translate them into their social equivalents. . . . In the illustration just used, it is the ability to see in the child's babblings the promise and potency of a future social intercourse and conversation which enables one to deal in the proper way with that instinct. . . .

In sum, I believe that the individual who is to be educated is a social individual and that society is an organic union of individuals. If we eliminate the social factor from the child, we are left only with an abstraction; if we eliminate the individual factor from society, we are left only with an inert and lifeless mass. Education, therefore, must begin with a psychological insight into the child's capacities, interests, and habits. It must be controlled at every point by reference to these same considerations. These powers, interests, and habits must be continually interpreted—we must know what they mean. They must be translated into terms of their social equivalents—into terms of what they are capable of in the way of social service.

Article II. What the School Is.

I believe that the school is primarily a social institution. Education being a social process, the school is simply that form of community life in which all those agencies are concentrated that will be most effective in bringing the child to share in the inherited resources of the race, and to use his own powers for social ends.

I believe that education, therefore, is a process of living and not a preparation for future living.

I believe that the school must represent present life—life as real and vital to the child as that which he carries on in the home, in the neighborhood, or on the play-ground. . . .

I believe that the moral education centers about this conception of the school as a mode of social life, that the best and deepest moral training is precisely that which one gets through having to enter into proper relations with others in a unity of work and thought. . . .

I believe that the teacher's place and work in the school is to be interpreted from this same basis. The teacher is not in the school to impose certain ideas or to form certain habits in the child, but is there as a member of the community to select the influences which shall affect the child and to assist him in properly responding to these influences. . . .

I believe that the teacher's business is simply to determine on the basis of larger experience and riper wisdom, how the discipline of life shall come to the child. . . .

Article III. The Subject-Matter of Education

I believe that the social life of the child is the basis of concentration or correlation, in all his training or growth. The social life gives the unconscious unity and the background of all his efforts and of all his attainments. . . .

I believe that we violate the child's nature and render difficult the best ethical results, by introducing the child too abruptly to a number of special studies, of reading, writing, geography, etc., out of relation to this social life.

I believe, therefore, that the true center of correlation on the school subjects is not science, nor literature, nor history, nor geography, but the child's own social activities. . . .

I believe that there is, therefore, no succession of studies in the ideal school curriculum. If education is life, all life has, from the outset, a scientific aspect; an aspect of art and culture and an aspect of communication. It cannot, therefore, be true that the proper studies for one grade are mere reading and writing, and that at a later grade, reading, or literature, or science, may be introduced. The progress is not in the succession of studies but in the development of new attitudes towards, and new interests in, experience . . . .

Article IV. The Nature of the Method

I believe that the question of method is ultimately reducible to the question of the order of development of the child's powers and interests. The law for presenting and treating material is the law implicit within the child's own nature. . . .

Article V. The School and Social Progress

I believe that education is the fundamental method of social progress and reform. . . .

I believe, finally, that the teacher is engaged, not simply in the training of individuals, but in the formation of the proper social life.

I believe that every teacher should realize the dignity of his calling; that he is a social servant set apart for the maintenance of proper social order and the securing of the right social growth.

I believe that in this way the teacher always is the prophet of the true God and the usherer in of the true kingdom of God.

PART IX
TWENTIETH CENTURY RENEWAL

*T*he purpose of a Christian education would not be merely to make men and women pious Christians. . . . A Christian education would primarily train people to think in Christian categories.

T. S. Eliot
Christianity and Culture, 1940

TWENTIETH CENTURY RENEWAL

H istory rarely conforms precisely to conventional dates for its beginnings and endings. While the twentieth century, chronologically speaking, may have begun on January 1, 1900, in education a whole new era may be said to have started some thirty years earlier in England; in America, perhaps the new era began a decade later, in the 1880s.

When Parliament passed the Education Act of 1870, to eleven centuries of British tradition was added a mandate for schooling for all children, regardless of class or gender, under government auspices. In-home schooling by governesses would continue; "public" schools such as Thomas Arnold's Rugby School or Dulwich School or Winchester School, where boys from aristocratic families had been enrolled in preparation for their eventual role as members of the ruling class, would thereafter become more widely attended. But for the first time, as of 1870, the government would levy taxes specifically for the purpose of maintaining education for the masses.

As a consequence of this legislation, British education shifted its focus from preparing the sons of noblemen for state service to preparing sons and daughters at each level of society—the nobility, professional and merchant class, bureaucrats and civil servants, and working class people—for the industrial empire and its future. Furthermore, as British common schooling developed, it retained a component from the "public" schools—instruction in religious education, under the sponsorship of the established church.

The beginnings of English government schooling opened wide the need for women teachers. Here Charlotte M. Mason, her House of Education, and her voluminous writings made their contribution—a fact seemingly lost to standard works of documentation and popular history. Neither the *Dictionary of National Biography* nor the most recent *Encyclopaedia Brittanica*—nor even the *Encyclopedia of Education*—records her name even once. Yet, as will be shown, Charlotte Mason has had a far more lasting effect on education than these omissions would warrant.

In America, the period following the Civil War also witnessed the rise of common schooling, as pre-War academies found themselves unable to survive both the loss of revenue and the loss of manpower to teach. So, entering the twentieth century, most continuing private schools were but a shadow of what they had been one hundred years earlier. Wracked by financial stress and falling enrollments, many schools founded on religious principles made desperate compromises by which they hoped to survive.

Among these were compromises regarding Christian orthodoxy. In many schools, colleges, and seminaries, the new wave of theological speculation, derived from scientific naturalism and known as modernism, swept aside the claims of the old gospel. Denominations were split by controversy over doctrine and the rights of property: To whom did the church or the campus belong? To the denomination or to those who saw themselves as the faithful and therefore rightful sustainers of the founders' trust?

Thus weakened by theological doubt and ecclesiastical strife, eager not to appear backward about acknowledging the new scientific thinking, many Christian educators made appalling choices to jettison that which had been their trusteeship in faith.

The adoption of modernist theology soon radically altered the nature of many remaining Christian schools. In 1879 and 1881, the evangelist Dwight L. Moody had founded, first, the Northfield Young Ladies' Seminary, then Mount Hermon Boys' School. Both schools were intended by Moody and his supporters to prepare young people whose faith in Jesus Christ had been grounded in Scripture. Indeed, in November 1899, only six weeks before he died, in a sermon at New York City's Fifth Avenue Presbyterian Church, Moody declared,

> Five and twenty years ago in my native village of Northfield [Massachusetts]I planted two Christian schools for the training of boys and maidens in Christian living and consecration as teachers and missionaries of Jesus Christ. I bequeath as my legacy those training schools for Jesus to the churches of

America, and I only ask that visitors to the beautiful native village where my ashes slumber on consecrated Round Top when they go there shall not be pained with the sight of melancholy ruins wrought by cruel neglect, but rather shall be greeted by the spectacle of two great, glorious lighthouses of the Lord, beaming out over the land, over the continent, over the world.[1]

Yet within a decade of Moody's death, Northfield Mount Hermon—as these merged schools are known today—had forsaken the orthodoxy of the founder, as Moody's successors diluted the religious persuasion of the earlier evangelically-minded faculty.

What this means, in plain terms, is that—like colleges a century earlier—most of America's independent schools, begun for purposes similar to Northfield Mount Hermon, have long since chosen to assume that their founders' high view of Scripture is outdated and subject to necessary revisionism. So, while "sacred studies" may still appear in the curriculum guide, the course content bears little resemblance to what Samuel Phillips or D. L. Moody or other believing philanthropists intended.

Could the source of this apostasy lie in the fact that, as T. S. Eliot noted, too many Christians were content to be pious, while too few labored to "think in Christian categories"[2]? While personal piety is commendable, is it sufficient to withstand the shocks to both the spirit and the intellect, when scientism and naturalism attack the very foundation of one's faith?

Perhaps what was needed in the twentieth century was a reawakening of intellectual rigor along with faith; academic scholarship in addition to devotion; a keen mind to complement a loving heart; sound argument along with sound doctrine.

In the same year that Dwight L. Moody died, a child was born who grew to become a pioneer in Christian education, particularly in schooling. His story is like that of Moses, a stammering and reluctant spokesman whom God chose to use to His glory. Two decades later, at age twenty-two, Frank E. Gaebelein was about to complete a year of graduate studies in English at Harvard. His future was uncertain. His father, Arno C. Gaebelein, was a famous Bible expositor and author, but there seemed little likelihood that young Gaebelein would follow that course; he suffered from shyness and a speech hesitancy. Frank Gaebelein had studied the piano from boyhood; perhaps he would attempt a career as a recitalist. Or as one who studied and loved English literature, perhaps he would choose to become a writer.

Instead, two board members of the Stony Brook Assembly, a summer conference ministry on Long Island, New York, invited Frank Gaebelein to meet for lunch in New York City. There they made him an improbable offer, proposing that he head a college preparatory school true to the Scriptures. The full board, interdenominational with strong Presbyterian leadership, had responded to the collapse of formerly Christian schools by seeking to establish a school on the campus of the Stony Brook Assembly that would remain true to an evangelical mission.

Gaebelein had no known preparation for the work he was asked to do; he knew little more about education than his own studies at New York University and Harvard had taught him. But, like Vittorino da Feltre, five centuries earlier, he accepted the challenge to begin a school for boys and live as an example before them. In 1971, almost fifty years later, girls were invited to enroll.

By 1952, Gaebelein had completed thirty years as founding headmaster of The Stony Brook School. That year he spoke at Dallas Theological Seminary during the W. H. Griffith Thomas Lectures. His topic was about the single most significant distinctive in a Christian school: the harmony of learning and living that derives from apprehending truth. The lectures, later repeated at Denver Seminary, subsequently were published by Oxford University Press as *The Pattern of God's Truth*. Gaebelein's thesis could be enunciated in just five words: "*All truth is God's truth.*"[3] His book and his aphorism became a keystone to the movement to reestablish schools committed to God's truth. In the later half of the twentieth century, it would give impetus to an educational renewal emphasizing Christian truth in learning.

What Gaebelein announced in his Dallas lectures, three decades after he arrived as headmaster of a new school, was no mere theory. He had developed a college-preparatory curriculum, the centerpiece of which was the Bible, taught with rigor and integrity. From the student's growing familiarity with the Word of God could flow the necessary connectedness and correlation that binds truth into a seamless web. As a practicing artist, Gaebelein was particularly keen on ridding his students of any dichotomy between "sacred" and "secular" truth. He protested against cheap and tawdry "religious" art, preferring even the truthful bawdiness of a Veronese to the sentimental banality of Sallman's "Head of Christ."

But Gaebelein also knew that pedagogical good intentions are not sufficient; a school is only as strong as its best teachers. "The integration of faith and learning" can best be exemplified in the life of a teacher who knows and lives by the Scriptures while, at the same time, exulting in the joys and discoveries of one's art or science. So Gaebelein wrote of the need to create schools whose teachers know and convey truth by the way they live.

Over a long lifetime, until his death in 1983, Frank Gaebelein stood for the highest standards in schooling, in art, and in biblical scholarship; but he was also concerned that evangelical Christians not isolate themselves from the world's problems. In fact, after forty-one years as head of The Stony Brook School he resigned to become co-editor of *Christianity Today*, where he helped evangelical America turn from a scornful attitude toward "the social gospel" to a more precise understanding of what the Scriptures, in fact, teach about faith and works, faith and compassion.

Of course, there were other schools true to their spiritual heritage. In particular, most of the schools founded by Dutch immigrants remained faithful to their founding vision and mission. Beginning with the *Canons of Dordt*, the influence of Dutch Calvinism continues to be felt, especially in certain pockets of America.

Dutch pioneers carried with them the highest regard for education: from the founding of New Amsterdam's Collegiate School, in 1628; and Rutgers University, originally Queen's College, in 1770; through the great mid-nineteenth century migrations to Massachusetts, New Jersey, Michigan, and Iowa; and on to later resettlements in Florida, Southern California, and Washington State. They had a passion for learning whose equal might be compared only to that of Eastern European Jews. Certainly, no other Christian community—not even the several Lutheran groups—had equalled the Dutch in constructing a system of parent-controlled schools in which a philosophy of education in accord with Reformed theological tenets was so carefully upheld and scrutinized.

But the Netherlanders who were among the earliest to settle in America also suffered divisions among themselves. First, the question of retaining the authority of the church's hierarchy in Holland over colonial churches had to be answered; then, after New Amsterdam became New York, the question of using English rather than Dutch as the language for worship. Finally, differences in theology led to schism in Holland; from this division within the state church in the homeland eventually sprang up the Christian Reformed Church. Persecution followed, sending two waves of immigrants to North America in 1847 and 1848. These industrious Christians, desiring an educated *domine* or minister, began their own training school in 1876, in Grand Rapids, Michigan, the forerunner to Calvin College and Seminary. Since the latter part of the nineteenth century, Christian Reformed parents have supported local Christian day schools for their children. For instance, in northern New Jersey, Eastern Christian School claims a lineage that began in the 1890s.

A rigorously developed philosophy upholds these schools. From Abraham Kuyper, Holland's believing politician, theologian, and founder of Amsterdam's Free University, the Christian Reformed schools and colleges have sought to inculcate a rationale for learning that places ultimate truth at the center of knowledge. Such truth can only be perceived by coming to know the Author of Truth.

Another means of expression depends upon the metaphor of the *weltanschauung*, the world-and-life view. Here each human being participates in seeing the world, often unconciously, from a chosen vantage point or perspective. For the believing Christian, such a perspective must start with acknowledging the existence of God, the sovereignty of God, the providence of God, and the human race's accountability to God for redemption through faith in Jesus Christ. All of reality, understood through these lenses, appears quite different from what it seems to the person whose worldview is other than biblical.

A school in the Reformed tradition that is true to these principles will also be quite different from a merely evangelical or fundamentalist school in the role retained for parent involvement, in the school's attitude toward culture and its potential for redemption, as well as in its steadfast understanding of covenant theology.

In his speech cited on page 363, Henry Zylstra, late professor and chairman of the English department at Calvin College, represents the historic linkage between Reformed theology and its practice in North American schools.

CHARLOTTE M. MASON

Little is known about the childhood of Charlotte Mason (1842–1923), this Englishwoman whose books have been instrumental in the revival of "home schooling" in North America. She was apparently orphaned while in her teenage years and obtained her formal education through the help of family friends.

Upon completing a teacher's training course in London, in 1861, Charlotte Mason spent a dozen years teaching in an English infant school. Then for five years she held a position on the faculty of the Bishop Otter Teacher Training College in Chichester, teaching methodology. A new law, the Education Act of 1870, had opened the way for universal schooling in Great Britain, and the demand for teachers was strong.

Mason left her post to turn toward writing. In 1886, the first in a series of six books on education was published, called *Home Education*. In it, Mason advocated practical measures by which parents could teach their own young children at home—not to the exclusion of formal schooling in groups taught by someone other than the parent but to augment and enhance what might otherwise be left wanting in school.

Her book became enormously popular, largely because of its simple and practical terms. From its readership developed the Parents National Education Union, with distinguished leaders among clergy and other educators. Publication of a monthly magazine, *The Parents' Review*, followed, and in 1892, Charlotte Mason founded her own training college, the House of Education, primarily for governesses, at Ambleside, in the Lake District. From four students to thirteen to fifty, the House of Education grew. A laboratory school in which to test Mason's principles enrolled local children at no tuition.

Mason produced five more books containing essays, addresses, and reviews of others' educational theories: *Parents and Children, School Education, Ourselves, Formation of Character,* and *A Philosophy of Education,* published just before her death. Fittingly, she is buried near the family plot of Thomas Arnold, headmaster of Rugby School, whom she much admired, and W. E. Forster, who had influenced the passing of the Education Act of 1870.

Charlotte Mason appears to have been a devout Christian in the Anglican tradition. She held that "the knowledge of God is the principal knowledge and the chief end of education." She did not, however, accept the doctrine of innate depravity, always preferring to think of children as persons who "are not born either good or bad, but with possibilities for good and evil."

In the latter decades of the twentieth century, as the home school movement expanded, the reputation and writings of Charlotte Mason have been revived to bulwark parents' choices of refusing to enroll their children in schools in preference for teaching them at home. Mason herself might not have been so strong an advocate as are those who claim her. A note in each of her books reads, "The 'Home Education' Series is so called from the title of the first volume, and not as dealing, wholly or principally, with 'Home' as opposed to 'School' education."

The passage cited below is a chapter from *School Education*, written in 1904, published in 1907.

School Education[4] (Excerpt)

Some Unconsidered Aspects of Religious Education

Authority in Religious Education. I should like to preface my remarks on Religious Education by saying that there is not the slightest pretense that they are exhaustive. My treatment has for its object the indication of practical lines for religious education, and I very earnestly hope that the reader will find I have left out things I ought to have said, or said things I ought not to have said.

Let us first consider how the principle of authority bears on religious teaching. The sense of duty, more or less illuminated, or more or less benighted, is always relative to a ruler with whom it rests to say "Thou shalt" or "Thou shalt not." It is brought home, too, to most of us who are set in authority, that we ourselves are acting under a higher, and finally, under the highest rule. A child cannot have a lasting sense of duty until he is brought into contact with a supreme Authority, who is the source of law, and the pleasing of whom converts duty into joy. In these days of latitudinarian attitude, there is perhaps no part of religious teaching more important than to train children in the sense of the immediate presence and continual going forth of the supreme Authority. "Thou are about my path and about my bed and spiest out all my ways" should be a thought, not of fear, but of very great comfort to every child. This constant recognition of authority excites the twofold response of docility and of reverence. It is said that the children of our day are marked by wilfulness and a certain flippancy and want of reverence; if this is so, and in so far as it is so, it is because children are brought up without the consciousness of their relation to God, whom we are taught to call "Our Father." This divine name reminds us that authority is lodged in the Author of our being, and is tender, pitiful, preventive, strong to care for and wise to govern; as we see it feebly shown forth even in the best of human fathers.

Questions in the Air. But there are questions in the air about the authenticity of the Scriptures and what not, and we are all more or less at the mercy of words; and, because the so-called higher criticism finds much to question as to the verbal accuracy of passages of the Scriptures, we get a dim idea that the divine authority itself is in question. One part of the work of this Union [Parents National Education Union] is, no doubt, to strengthen the hands of parents by comforting them with the sense of the higher Power behind theirs and always supporting them in the exercise of the deputed powers they hold as heads of families. There is another notion in the air which tells against the recognition of authority, and that is, the greatly increased respect for individual personality and for the right of each individual to develop on the lines of his own character. But it is a mistake to suppose that the exercise of authority runs counter to any individual development that is not on morally wrong lines.

How Authority Works. The supreme authority (and all deputed authority) works precisely as does a good and just national government, whose business it is to defend the liberties of the subject at all points, even by checking, repressing, and punishing the licence which interferes with the rights of others and with the true liberty of the transgressor. The law (that is, the utterance of authority) is for the punishment of evil-doers, but for the praise of them that do well; and the association of harshness, punishment, force, arbitrary dealings, with the idea of authority, human and divine, is an example of the confusion of thought to which most of our errors in conduct are traceable. It is not authority which punishes: the penalties which follow us through life, of which those in the family are a faint foretaste are the inevitable consequences of broken law, whether moral or physical, and from which authority, strong and benign, exists to save us by prevention, and, if needs be, by lesser and corrective penalties.

It seems to me that reading and teaching on the following subjects, for example, might help to focus thought on a subject of vital importance:—our relation to the supreme authority, not a relation of choice, but as inevitable as the family relationships into which we are born; the duty of loyalty and the shame of infidelity; the duty of reverence; the duty of docility to indications of the divine will; scriptural revelations of God, . . . how the sense of the divine authority may be imparted in the home; how reverence for holy things may be taught . . .—Indeed, the subject is capable of great amplification, and suggests trains of thought very important in these days.

The Habits of the Religious Life. The next point we must set ourselves to consider is the laying down of lines of habit in the religious life. We need not enter again into the psychological reasons for the compelling power of habit. My present purpose is to consider how far this power can be employed in the religious development of a child. Let us consider the subject as it bears upon habits of thought and of attitude, of life and of speech; though indeed all these are one, for every act and attitude is begotten of a thought, however unaware we may be of thinking.

Habits of the Thought of God. It is said of the wicked that "God is not in all their thoughts." Of the child it should be said that God is in all his thoughts; happy-making, joyous thoughts, restful and dutiful thoughts, thoughts of loving and giving and serving, the wealth of beautiful thoughts with which every child's heart overflows. We are inclined to think that a child is a little morbid and precocious when he asks questions and has imaginings about things divine, and we do our best to divert him. What he needs is to be guided into true, happy thinking; every day should bring him "new thoughts of God, new hopes of heaven." He understands things divine better than we do, because his ideas have not been shaped to a conventional standard; and thoughts of God are to him an escape into the infinite from the worrying limitations, the perception of the prison bars, which are among the bitter pangs of childhood. To keep a child in this habit of the thought of God—so that to lose it, for even a little while, is like coming home after an absence and finding his mother out—is a very delicate part of a parent's work.

Reverent Attitudes. The importance of reverent attitudes is a little apt to be overlooked in these days. We are, before all things, sincere, and are afraid to insist upon "mere forms," feeling it best to leave the child to the natural expression of his own emotions. Here perhaps we are wrong, as it is just as true to say that the form gives birth to the feeling as that the feeling should give birth to the form. Children should be taught to take time, to be reverent at grace before meals, at family prayers, at their own prayers, in church, when they are old enough to attend. Perhaps some of us may remember standing daily by our mother's knee in reverent attitude to recite the Apostles' Creed, and the recollection of the reverence expressed in that early act remains with one through a lifetime. "Because of the angels" should be a thought to repress unbecoming behavior in children. It is a mistake to suppose that the forms of reverence need be tiresome to them. They love little ceremonies, and to be taught to kneel nicely while saying their short prayers would help them to a feeling of reverence in after life. In connection with children's behavior in church, the sentiment and forms of reverence cannot be expected if they are taken to church too young, or to too long services, or are expected to maintain their attention throughout. If children must be taken to long services, they should be allowed the resource of a Sunday picture-book, and told that the hymns and the "Our Father," for example, are the parts of the service for them. But in these days of bright short services especially adapted for children the difficulty need not arise.

Regularity in Devotions. The habit of regularity in children's devotions is very important. The mother cannot always be present, but I have known children far more punctual in their devotions when away from their mother, because they knew it to be her wish, than if she were there to remind them. . . . It is a great thing for all of us to get the habit of "saying our prayers" at a given time and in a given place, which comes to be to us as a holy place. The chair, or the bedside, or the little prayer-table, or, best of all, the mother's knee, plays no small part in framing the soul to a habit of devotion. . . .

The Habit of Reading the Bible. The habit of hearing, and later, of reading the Bible is one to establish at an early age. We are met with a difficulty—that the Bible is, in fact, a library containing passages and, indeed, whole books which are not for the edification of children; and many parents fall back upon little collections of texts for morning and evening use. But I doubt the wisdom of this plan. We may believe that the narrative teaching of the Scriptures is far more helpful to children, anyway, than the stimulating moral and spiritual texts picked out for them in little devotional books.

Children Formalists by Nature. But while pressing the importance of habits of prayer and devotional reading, it should be remembered that children are little formalists by nature, and that they should not be encouraged in long readings or long prayers with a notion of any merit in such exercises.

The Habit of Praise. Perhaps we do not attach enough importance to the habit of praise in our children's devotions. Praise and thanksgiving come freely from the young heart; gladness is natural and holy, and music is a delight. The singing of hymns at home and of the hymns and canticles in church should be a special delight; and the habit of soft and reverent singing, of offering our very best in praise, should be carefully formed. Hymns with a story, such as: "A little ship was on the sea," "I think when I read that sweet story of old," "Hushed was the evening hymn," are perhaps the best for little children.

Children should be trained in the habits of attention and real devotion during short services or parts of services. The habit of finding their places in the prayer-book and following the service is interesting and aids attention, but perhaps it would be well to tell children, of even ten or eleven, that during the litany, for example, they might occupy themselves by saying over silently hymns that they know.

Habit of Sunday-keeping. The habit of Sunday observances, not rigid, not dull, and yet peculiar to the day, is especially important. Sunday stories, Sunday hymns, Sunday walks, Sunday talks, Sunday painting, Sunday knitting even, Sunday card-games, should all be special to the day,—quiet, glad, serene. The people who clamor for a Sunday that shall be as other days little know how healing to the jaded brain is the change of thought and occupation the seventh day brings with it. There is hardly a more precious inheritance to be handed on than that of the traditional English Sunday, stripped of its austerities, we hope, but keeping its character of quiet gladness and communion with Nature as well as with God. . . .

Inspiring Ideas of the Religious Life. The most important part of our subject remains to be considered—the inspiring ideas we propose to give children in the things of the divine life. This is a matter we are a little apt to leave to chance; but when we consider the vitalizing power of an idea, and how a single great idea changes the current of a life, it becomes us to consider very carefully what ideas of the things of God we may most fitly offer children, and how these may be most invitingly presented. It is a very sad fact that many children get their first ideas of God in the nursery, and that these are of a Being on the watch for their transgressions and always ready to chastise. It is hard to estimate the alienation which these first ideas of the divine Father set up in the hearts of His little children. Another danger is, lest the things of the divine life should be made too familiar and hackneyed, that the name of our blessed Lord should be used without reverence; and that children should get the notion that the Lord God exists for their uses, and not they, for His service.

The Fatherhood of God. Perhaps the first vitalizing idea to give children is that of the tender Fatherhood of God; that they live and move and have their being within the divine embrace. Let children grow up in this joyful assurance, and, in the days to come, infidelity to this closest of all relationships will be as shameful a thing in their eyes as it was in the eyes of the Christian Church during the age of faith.

The Kingship of Christ. Next, perhaps, the idea of Christ their King is fitted to touch springs of conduct and to rouse the enthusiasm of loyalty in children, who have it in them, as we all know, to bestow heroic devotion on that which they find heroic. Perhaps we do not make enough of this principle of hero-worship in human nature in our teaching of religion. We are inclined to make our religious aims subjective rather than objective. We are tempted to look upon Christianity as a "scheme of salvation" designed and carried out for our benefit; whereas the very essence of Christianity is passionate devotion to an altogether adorable Person.

Charlotte M. Mason, *School Education.* Used by permission of Charlotte Mason Research & Supply Co., P.O. Box 172, Stanton, N.J. 08885. All six volumes of Miss Mason's classic series on education and parenting have been reprinted; for information on obtaining this series as well as a quarterly magazine that promotes her Christian philosophy of education, write Charlotte Mason Research & Supply, P.O. Box 172, Stanton, NJ 08885.

FRANK E. GAEBELEIN

Frank E. Gaebelein's work at The Stony Brook School represents a story of one successful venture in stemming the tide of anti-Christian forces that assailed and largely captured American education during the early decades of the twentieth century. His story thus is worthy of close attention by every Christian educator.

While the public school system largely adopted the philosophy of John Dewey, many private church-related schools, colleges, universities, and seminaries were falling under the influence of a similarly anti-supernaturalistic theology called modernism. At the center of this liberal theology was a diminished view of any need for Jesus Christ's atonement and a demythologized rendering of the Bible—its authenticity and authority seemed to lie in tatters. Clearly, the time for a renewed commitment to orthodox Christian doctrine seemed long past.

In 1907, a number of evangelical ministers, looking for an alternative to the increasing modernism at the summer conferences they had been supporting, purchased property at Stony Brook on Long Island, some fifty miles east of New York City. Headed by the Reverend John F. Carson, soon to be elected moderator of the General Assembly of the Presbyterian Church, U.S.A., their venture became the Stony Brook Assembly, which held Bible conferences and youth camps through 1957.

After the turmoil of World War I had passed, Carson began looking for the fulfillment of a second aspiration, the beginnings of a college-preparatory school for boys. The Eastern boarding school, with its traditions going back to the Renaissance, had long been a source of intellectual and spiritual preparation. However, few of the old American schools any longer professed to teach the integrity of Scripture and the Lordship of Jesus Christ. Carson was determined to found a school committed to renewing these evangelical principles.

In spring 1921 Frank Ely Gaebelein (1899–1983), about to complete his graduate studies at Harvard, was appointed headmaster. With no more training than his brief experience as a second lieutenant drilling fellow college students during World War I, and with no firsthand knowledge of independent boarding schools, Gaebelein accepted the challenge of heading a new school as yet without either faculty or students.

He spent the academic year 1921–22 developing a school out of an idea, shared by the founders: that Christian faith is no hindrance to scholarship; that, since God's Word is truth, the study of the Bible must be central to any curriculum. But to give flesh-and-blood to the Stony Brook vision, Gaebelein determined from the beginning that the *sine qua non* of Christian schooling must be this: *No Christian school without a unitedly believing Christian faculty.*

On September 13, 1922, The Stony Brook School held inaugural ceremonies with a student body of only twenty-seven boys and nine teachers. For forty-one years, Frank Gaebelein served as headmaster, watching the school grow in size and influence. During those years he formulated his philosophy for Christian schooling, expressed in his two most important books, *Christian Education in a Democracy*, published in 1951, and *The Pattern of God's Truth: Problems of Integration in Christian Education*, published in 1954.

An accomplished pianist, Gaebelein also wrote and lectured on the arts; a posthumous collection of writings is called *The Christian, the Arts, and Truth*. For several years following his retirement from Stony Brook, he was co-editor of *Christianity Today*. As a Bible scholar, he participated in editing the New Scofield Reference Bible and served as chairman of the English style committee for the New International Version. At his death in 1983, he was general editor of the commentary series based on the NIV.

A man of broad vision, compassion, and encouragement, he was never jealous of others who imitated the Stony Brook model. In fact, in an early address Gaebelein expressed the hope that "the success of The Stony Brook School will stimulate the organization of many another institution of similar aims and ideals. There cannot be too many such."[5]

The Pattern of God's Truth[6] (Excerpt)

Chapter One
Integration and Truth

"Sanctify them through the truth: thy word is truth."

John 17:17

1. By Way of Introduction

One April morning early in the first century, a Roman procurator said three words that have echoed through the ages. As the Man Christ Jesus stood before him, Pontius Pilate asked, "What is truth?"

There was nothing original about the procurator's question; for centuries the sages and philosophers had been asking it. Nor was there anything final about it; ever since that day in Jerusalem it has, in one form or another, been in the minds and on the lips of philosophers, scientists, artists, poets, teachers, and thoughtful men of every sort. It is the age-old query, the perennial question of the human spirit.

In the lectures before us we are to deal with the answer to that question in relation to one of the chief responsibilities committed to the Christian church—the responsibility for education, the nurture and training of youth in the truth of God and in that fear of the Lord which is the beginning of wisdom. You will understand me, then, when I say that the preparation of these pages has been accompanied by a special sense of obligation. More than that, it has brought with it a burden of humility. Even thirty years spent by one man in a corner of the vast field of Christian education, so much of which needs still to be explored, do not justify an attitude savoring in any way of the oracular. As James Stalker of Aberdeen said in beginning a series of addresses on preaching, "It is with no sense of having attained that I am to speak to you; for I always seem to myself to be beginning to learn my trade . . ."

At the same time, I should affirm that what I have to say expresses personal conviction. For there are some things of which Christians are sure. These things are the great verities of the faith. Christianity is a revealed religion, not a human invention. Therefore, convictions respecting it are initially based on faith. Yet there is a sense in which the convictions of faith become more fully our own, as we practice and learn them in the laboratory of daily life and work. It is out of such convictions, first believed and then matured by experience of what happens in the field of education when God's truth is either honored or ignored, as the case may be, that these lectures have grown.

2. The Relevance of the Subject

The Pattern of God's Truth: Problems of Integration in Christian Education. Perhaps some are wondering what a subject like this has to do with seminary students and faculty or, for that matter, with the general Christian reader. "Must every minister or missionary, theological student or professor," the question is asked, "really be concerned with Christian education? Even more, should all Christians be interested in it?" The Bible answers "Yes." For it takes only a glance at the hundreds of listings of such words as "child" and "children" that are to be found in a concordance to demonstrate the fact that the Bible has a great deal to say about youth. Some day a thoughtful student of Christian education will make a thorough study of every reference in the Bible to children and will go on to develop inductively the principles of child training set forth in the Word of God. The result of such an investigation may turn out to be a major contribution to Christian thought.

. . . Whatever else a pastor does, he deals in some way with youth. There are children in all congregations, if not in every home. Churches have Sunday Schools. Young people from churches go to school, and their attitudes and response to their ministers reflect something of the teaching they are receiving. In missionary work, teaching goes hand in hand with evangelizing. And beyond all this is the fact that both home and community are constantly exercising an informal though often decisive influence upon youth. Among the most effective of all teachers are fathers and mothers, brothers, sisters, and friends. In short, teaching, in one form or another, is always going on and is as inescapable as life itself. One of the commonest misconceptions of education is that which limits it to the four walls of the schoolroom or, to broaden the figure, to the acreage of the campus. In reality, however, education is a continuing process as broad as experience itself, and one in which all who have contact with youth share, either consciously or unconsciously. Therefore, it follows that a ministry not interested in education is only half a ministry, and that we who are called to be ambassadors for Christ cannot but be deeply concerned with something so vitally linked to our cause as Christian education.

3. The Problem of Integration

From this brief view of the relevance of our subject, we turn to its analysis. At first glance, there seem to be two separate things before us: "God's truth" and the matter of "integration." In reality, however, the two are closely linked. God's truth is of universal scope. This being the case, every aspect of education must be brought into relation to it. So the problem of integration arises— the word, we are reminded, means "the bringing together of parts into the whole." Our aim will be to point the way to a solution of this problem by showing how in some vital particulars Christian education can achieve integration into the all-embracing truth of God.

It was Josiah Royce who said that every idea has both internal meaning and external meaning. The principle may be applied to Christian education. Using "external" not in its connotation of "superficial" but rather in its denotation of something outside and beyond us, we see that the external meaning of Christian education has to do with God's truth. That is to say, it is objectively true. Whether or not we know it or understand it, believe it, or teach it, it remains His truth. And as we come to knowledge of it, we find that it is nothing less than the context of everything that we know or ever can know. In the words of John Henry Newman, "Religious truth is not only a portion but a condition of general knowledge." As for the internal meaning of Christian education, it is something quite different. It relates to the inner workings of education, to all of its courses and every one of its policies. And in addition it also has to do with the integration of these things with its external meaning.

At this point, an analogy will help us [to understand integration of internal and external meaning]. Consider astronomy. It has to do not just with the solar system but also with the whole vast stellar universe, pointing, as does all creation, to the eternal power and Godhead of Him who made all things. This is its external meaning, its context. But then there is the astronomer, discovering step by step from the vantage point of this little earth one truth after another relating to the well-nigh infinite context of his science. As he follows the principles and techniques of astronomy and as he uses them to think truly about astronomy—that is, in accordance with the external reality of the universe—what he discovers takes its place as part of the spacious external realm to which it belongs.

So with integration in Christian education. It is the living union of its subject matter, administration, and even of its personnel, with the eternal and infinite pattern of God's truth. This . . . is the heart of integration and the crux of the problem.

For problem it is; let us make no mistake about that. In fact, it is not the slightest exaggeration to say that this matter of integration, or uniting the parts into a living whole, is the problem of problems, not only in Christian education but also in all other education as well. Behind every perplexity, difficulty, and dilemma with which our schools and colleges are faced is this central one: How to achieve this unity? How to put together the diverse fragments that make up the raw material of education? These are questions that are being asked by secular educators with the insistence of those who have let go their moorings and are drifting upon uncharted seas. "There is nothing," says Professor Kandel of Columbia, "that so clearly illustrates the uncertainty and instability of American education as the perennial addiction to defining its aims, objectives, and goals"; and Dr. Scott Buchanan makes this frank admission: "We do not know what we ought to learn in education. We have not been able to discern the pattern in our knowledges which would make them one knowledge." Or, as the authors of the Harvard Report on *General Education in a Free Society* declare, "the search continues and must continue for some over-all logic, some strong, not easily broken frame within which both college and school may fulfill their at once diversifying and uniting task."

And so it must. An education that has deliberately departed from God and His Word will continue to search, "ever learning and never able to come to knowledge of the truth," to use Paul's words to Timothy. This is why secular education today, including much of our public-school system, is still centrifugal, despite the vain efforts being made to base it on values derived solely from a sociological and naturalistic setting. Having turned its back upon God and His Word and having thus given up its external meaning, secular education is powerless to put together its internal meaning.

Christian education is different. With all its inadequacies, failures, and difficulties, it has something to which to tie itself. For it, too, integration is a problem, but a problem of quite another kind than for secular education. Christian education does not need to keep looking for the integrating factor; it already has this factor. We who believe the Bible to be the inspired Word of God and who take seriously such truths as the creation of the universe by the living God, the lost condition of man, the atonement, justification by faith, the reality of the resurrection, and the fellowship of believers in the Church know the answer to the secularist's vain search. The problem with which these lectures have to do, therefore, is not so much one of discovery as it is one of application.

At this point, we who are committed to the Christian view of education need to examine our hearts, lest there be anything of pride within us. If for us the unifying factor is the historic faith revealed in Scripture, we can only be very humble about it. Only by the grace of God are we what we are. There is nothing new, and certainly nothing original, in our position, for the faith which we hold has in the past served as the frame of reference for American education. It takes but a glance at the history of our oldest colleges and schools to show that they were founded, without exception, upon the Biblical position and that this position was for them a most practical and vivifying principle. For example, Harvard was founded in 1636 for training the Gospel ministry; its charter of 1650 said that the university had been established "to educate the English and Indian youth in knowledge and godliness," and it had for its motto *Christo et Ecclesiae.* Sixty-five years later, Yale was founded by those who feared Harvard was becoming unorthodox. The purpose of Columbia, begun in 1754, was "to engage the children to know God in Jesus Christ." But the roll could be called of William and Mary, Princeton, Dartmouth, Rutgers, along with other of our older colleges, and similar religious purposes would be revealed. So also with the denominational colleges and especially the women's colleges like Vassar, Smith, Wellesley, and Mt. Holyoke.

Let us remember these things, lest in some lapse into boasting we say of ourselves: "We are the people. We alone have a corner upon truth. We only of all men have discovered the unifying factor of education." No, we have done nothing of the kind. The most we can claim is that we have recovered it, and this by the grace of God. But why claim anything for ourselves? . . .

4. A *Venture in Self-criticism*

Does this mean, then, that we have all the answers? On the contrary, it means nothing of the kind. Granted that we have returned to the only true unifying principle, there remains for us the whole broad realm of application. So our problems multiply. And "problems" mean knots to be untied, needs to be met, errors to be corrected. They point to unrealized aims, and at the same time look toward solutions.

But though we shall be occupied with some of the hard places in Christian education, the achievements of those schools and colleges committed to the Gospel and to the Word of God must not be forgotten. These achievements are already large and make up an impressive chapter in the history of American education. Among them are such things as the remarkable growth of Christian schools and colleges in America in the last thirty years, the rise of the Christian dayschool movement, the coming of age educationally of the Bible institute and Bible college, the foundation and growth of new theological seminaries, the revitalization in many places of the Sunday School, and the development of additional agencies of Christian education, such as the Daily Vacation Bible School, Child Evangelism, Young Life Campaign, and the Inter-Varsity Christian Fellowship.

We are not concerned, however, with expounding that chapter. On the contrary, the choice of the subject before us has grown out of the conviction that, great as the achievements of evangelical Christian education have been, there is much ground to be occupied and some serious error, in both practice and theory, to be corrected. In other words, we are embarking on a venture in constructive thinking, coupled with self-criticism.

That self-criticism is necessary is evident. The time has come, after decades of growth upon the part of Christian education—growth which continues unabated—for us to have the maturity to look within; to measure ourselves by the criteria of truth set forth in the Word of God and apprehended through other sources as well; and, having thus seen some of our problems, to work bravely and honestly toward their solution. . . .

Let us face the fact. When it comes to the application of the noble principles upon which it is built, Christian education in

America has much to learn. We have had a great deal to say about God-centered, Christ-oriented, Bible-based education. But in actual practice we are not doing nearly enough of it. The old Negro spiritual, "Everybody talkin' 'bout heav'n ain't goin' there," might be paraphrased somewhat as follows: "Everybody talkin' 'bout Christian education ain't doin' it." This is not to say, of course, that we are not to any extent practicing Christian education. That is too extreme a judgment. Nevertheless, in respect to a thorough-going integration of Christ and the Bible with the whole institution, with all departments of study, with all kinds of student activities, with all phases of administration, there remains much land to be taken.

The trouble is that a good many Christian institutions are unconsciously deceiving themselves. Not even the theological seminary is exempt from criticism at this point. For it is a fact that in many a seminary the Bible has what amounts to a secondary place; though the program contains plenty of courses about the Bible—its criticism, interpretation, and languages—the student learns too little of the Word of God itself in its plain and forthright power. Therefore, it is entirely possible for students to go to some seminaries and come out knowing much about higher criticism, dialectic theology, the philosophy of religion, sociology, worship programs, and the like, and yet have only a bowing acquaintance with great portions of Scripture. As for many evangelical schools and colleges, because they have daily chapel services, Bible departments, and flourishing student activities of a Christian nature, they conclude that they are Christ-centered, Bible-based institutions, when in reality they have not yet grown up to that stature. There is no originality in the latter judgment. Others have been clear-sighted in recognizing the fact.

For example, Professor Gordon Clark of Butler University speaks of the Christian college, where such good things as "giving out tracts . . . holding fervent prayer meetings, going out on gospel teams, opening classes with prayer" are the accepted practice; "yet the actual instruction is no more Christian than in a respectable secular school . . . The program is merely a pagan education with a chocolate covering of Christianity. And the pill, not the coating, works . . . the students are deceived into thinking that they have received a Christian education when as a matter of fact their training has been neither Christian nor an education . . . Christianity, far from being a Bible-department religion, has a right to control the instruction in all departments. The general principles of Scripture apply to all subjects, and in some subjects the Scriptures supply rather detailed principles, so that every course of instruction is altered by a conscious adoption of Christian principles."

These are plain words and perhaps some concession should be made for the fact that their writer may have overdrawn the picture. Yet the fact that the situation described exists to some degree cannot be blinked.

Dr. Edwin H. Rian puts it somewhat more temperately but at the same time incisively. "A Christian theory of education," he writes, "is an exposition of the idea that Christianity is a world and life view and not simply a series of unrelated doctrines. Christianity includes all of life.

It is well for us to realize that there are still others who share this view. While both Professor Clark and Dr. Rian are evangelicals, there are other [liberal] groups who recognize the challenge of an all-embracing religious frame of reference. . . . [They have published] a reasoned presentation of a definite point of view . . . , something still to be done on any comparable scale by evangelicals. The acknowledgment of these things is, then, a needed corrective to the provincialism into which we, in our zeal for our view, sometimes lapse. Nor does this acknowledgment dull the edge of our faith or compromise in any way our conviction that in the great doctrines of Scripture we have the true integrating factor of Christian education. It is simply an incentive for us to set to work and apply to every aspect of our schools the comprehensive pattern of God's truth.

5. God's Truth and Its Implications

The time has now come to step aside from the near view of the problem and see the direction in which we are going. Reflection upon the nature of our unifying principle will light up our road. To say that we hold Christ and the Bible as central to education demands that we do some hard thinking about God's truth, which is the over-all context of our problem.

For one thing, it leads us into a consideration of truth and its nature. None of us will deny to Christ a personal identification with truth. Pilate's question, "What is truth?" had already been answered in the upper room when our Lord said, "I am the way, the truth, and the life." But Christ's identification with truth does not depend only on that affirmation; it rests rather on every word He spoke and every act He performed. The reason those three brief years He spent in teaching men, ministering to their needs, and finally dying for them outweigh in influence all the writings of all the philosophers is that in Him men saw once and for all the truth. And if Christ Himself is truth incarnate, let us not forget that He also identified truth with the Scriptures, when He prayed to His Father in behalf of His own, "Sanctify them through the truth: Thy word is truth." This was no theoretical statement. On the contrary, our Lord's habitual use of Scripture leaves no doubt of the fact that for Him the written Word was truth indeed.

To Christian orthodoxy these facts are elementary. But their broad implications are not so obvious. Truth, though it comprehends finite things, is greater than all it comprehends; its only limitation is the acceptance of its opposite, which is error. And though it includes the finite, it has also its infinite dimensions, because it inheres in the very nature of God Himself. For Christian education, therefore, to adopt as its unifying principle Christ and the Bible means nothing short of the recognition that *all truth is God's truth*. It is no accident that St. Paul, setting before the Philippian church a charter for Christian thought, wrote: "Finally, brethren, whatsoever things are true . . . think of these things." He knew that Christian truth embraces all truth, and that nothing true is outside the scope of Christianity.

Now the next step is where many have faltered. In all candor it must be admitted that much education called Christian has failed to see that this comprehensive fact of all truth being God's truth breaks down, on the one hand, the division of knowledge between secular and religious; and brings, on the other hand, every area of life and thought "into captivity to the obedience of Christ," to use the great Pauline phrase. To put it bluntly, we have been too prone to set up a false dichotomy in our thinking and thus in our education. We have rightly enthroned the Word of God as the ultimate criterion of truth; we have rightly given pre-eminence to the Lord Jesus Christ as the incarnation of the

God of all truth. But at the same time we have fallen into the error of failing to see as clearly as we should that there are areas of truth not fully explicated in Scripture and that these, too, are part of God's truth. Thus we have made the misleading distinction between sacred and secular, forgetting that, as Cervantes said in one of those flashes of wisdom that punctuate the strange doings of Don Quixote, "Where the truth is, in so far as it is truth, there God is."

We are now at a place where we must think with particular care. We must do this because lack of clarity at this point may lead to the charge of elevating truth in relation to mundane things to an equality with revealed truth. As a matter of fact, however, such a conclusion does not necessarily follow from the premise that all truth is God's truth. It is perfectly possible to recognize the diverse importance of different aspects of truth without in any way denying its indissoluble nature. We do indeed give the primacy to that spiritual truth revealed in the Bible and incarnate in Christ. That does not mean, however, that those aspects of truth discoverable by man in the realm of mathematics, chemistry, or geography, are any whit less God's truth than the truth as it is in Christ. The difference is clearly a question of subject matter. In the latter case, the subject matter is of a different importance from the former; truth about Christ pertains to salvation, that about physics does not. To be sincerely mistaken regarding scientific truth is one thing; to be mistaken, even sincerely, regarding such truth as the Person and the work of the Lord Jesus Christ is another thing. But all the time there is the unity of all truth under God, and that unity we deny in education at the peril of habituating ourselves to the fragmentary kind of learning found on some avowedly Christian campuses today.

The call, then, is for a wholly Christian world view on the part of our education. We must recognize, for example, that we need teachers who see their subjects, whether scientific, historical, mathematical, literary, or artistic, as included within the pattern of God's truth. It is one thing to take for ourselves the premise that all truth is God's truth. It is another thing to build upon this premise an effective educational practice that shows the student the unity of truth and that brings alive in his heart and mind the grand concept of a Christ who "is the image of the invisible God," by whom "all things were created," who "is before all things," and by whom "all things consist," or hold together.

If this is our position, if we actually mean to stand upon this ground, then we are driven to some searching conclusions. Let us not hesitate to state them simply and directly, leaving our conscience to make whatever application is needed. Once more, then, we set down the premise: All truth is God's truth. Whereupon we must conclude that Christian education has a holy obligation to stand for and honor the truth wherever it is found. With Justin Martyr, we must declare: "All that has been well said belongs to us Christians." To be sure, revealed truth, as stated in the Word of God and known through Christ, is of higher importance than natural truth. But the latter is also within the pattern of God's truth. Thus it follows that for any of us, orthodox though our beliefs may be, to try to support revealed truth either by denying any other aspect of truth or by suppressing or distorting it is an offense against the very nature of God, as well as a lapse into the immoral doctrine that the end justifies the means.

What has just been said is especially relevant to preaching. Every preacher of the Bible ought constantly to ask himself questions like this? "Is my exegesis true?" "Is this sermon of mine, no matter how clever and effective, really presenting what Scripture actually says?" Many an attractive and highly praised sermon is based on an irresponsible exegesis. And who has not heard some time-worn illustration told from the pulpit not only as true but as a personal experience of the preacher, when it is nothing of the kind? . . .

The solemn fact is that truth is holy; inherent in the nature of God Himself, it is ever sacred. No man who tampers with it is guiltless. The Bible closes with an unmistakable emphasis upon truth. When John on Patmos sees heaven open, he identifies the returning King by the Name, "Faithful and True." . . . as we go on to struggle with some hard problems, let us do so with a zealous regard for the truth, realizing in deep humility that we may indeed fail to apprehend it in all its sacred perfection, but trusting also that the God of all truth will show us the way to His greater glory in our Christian education.

Excerpted from *The Pattern of God's Truth*, by Frank E. Gaebelein.
Copyright 1954 by Oxford University Press, Inc. Reprinted by permission.

HENRY ZYLSTRA

A graduate of Calvin College, Henry Zylstra (1909–56) completed his post-graduate studies at Harvard University, receiving a Ph.D. in comparative literature. In 1941, he began teaching English at Calvin College, with an interruption for military service from 1943 to 1947. At Calvin he earned distinction as a Ford Foundation and Fulbright scholar, while serving as English department chairman until his sudden death in 1956. A posthumous collection of his writings was published as *Testament of Vision*.

A favorite speaker among audiences of the National Union of Christian Schools (now Christian Schools International), Zylstra set a standard for the Reformed scholar who is thoroughly engaged by university-level studies but never loses sight of the enduring significance of elementary and secondary schooling in the name of Jesus Christ. The address that follows was presented to an audience of Christian elementary and secondary teachers and administrators. It exemplifies the Reformed understanding of the wholeness that must characterize the school that claims to be Christian.

"Christian Education"[7] (Excerpt)

My subject tonight is *Christian Education*. Perhaps I ought first of all to give you in a single sentence what it is I mean to say. It is this: Christian education must be both education and Christian if it is to justify itself and successfully meet the secular challenge. That is the thrust of what I have to say. Our schools must be schools—that for one thing. And then they must be Christian— that for another thing. And in making these two points I shall want to insist, of course, that they must be both at once.

I speak of these obvious considerations again, because it is easy to have the school without the Christian. All we should have to do then is a fairly competent job of handling the curriculum as it is done in any good school, and do it in what we might call a Christian atmosphere, and so justify ourselves. That would be easy. It would be easy, further, to have the Christian without the school, that is, to make what we call the "devotional" element the principal thing, and to pay little more than lip service to the subjects of the curriculum. Either of these would be easy. What is hard is to have the Christian and the school in vital and vigorous interdependence with each other all the while. But that is precisely what we are trying for, and what we must have, if our schools are to solve the problem which secular, neutral, or public education cannot solve.

Our schools must be schools. . . . It is well, I think, to be reminding ourselves constantly that ours is an educational enterprise. It is not, at least not primarily, an evangelical enterprise. We call this work of our schools kingdom work, and rightly so, and the kingdom of Christ is, of course, a spiritual kingdom, and it is most certainly the business of our schools to train our boys and girls, our young men and women, for responsible citizenship in it. But to say that it is the function of our schools to train for citizenship in a spiritual kingdom is not to say that the schools ought so much as possible to be churches. . . . It is at church and not at school that the offer of salvation is presented, the word of truth is preached, the communion of the saints is exercised in the sacrament. These things, and more, are proper to the church as church. They stand high in our hearts, higher than anything else. We think them the most important things. In this we are right. However, it is by no means an implication of this that we can think of the schools as Christian and important only insofar as they extend into the week-days the offices of the church.

There are Christians, though usually not Reformed Christians, or at least not mature Reformed Christians, who cannot get very excited about Christian schools as schools. They are so eager for the honor of what they call the religious and the spiritual in life, that they hesitate to think anything else of much importance. Such Christians are as likely as not to be comparatively indifferent to the curriculum, to the cultural subject matters. We understand such Christians feel something of the attraction of the same idea, perhaps, in ourselves. The Christian, after all, finds himself called to the Christian life in the midst of the world. When regeneration, conversion, sanctification begin to operate in him, he finds himself, particularly in some times and places, estranged, opposed to the culture, the whole complex of life, that presses in upon him from all sides. It bears down upon him mercilessly from every quarter, from the business, the social, the political, the military, the scientific, and aesthetic worlds. We therefore understand the Christian who is inclined, especially at first, to apply his faith in negative ways, and to look upon science, and culture, and history, and the rest as things alien to his religion. There is, I say, something appealing about it that those who seem sometimes to be the most saintly among us, who prize a close walk with God in mystical communion with Christ, should not only by-pass culture, but even attack it as a worldly idol.

Such Christians are rightly aware of an antithesis between Christian and world. They see the line of it running between Cain and Abel, between Noah and those drowned in the flood, between Abraham and Lot, Jacob and Esau, Israel and the peoples around her, between Christ and [his] persecutors, and they hear their Master saying, "My kingdom is not of this world. Not as the world giveth, give I unto thee." And this antithesis such Christians are as likely as not to interpret as an antithesis of Christian versus culture, Christian versus learning, Christian versus science, Christian versus reason, Christian versus literature and art, and so, wittingly or unwittingly, Christian versus school. In the end religion becomes something isolated from life, and in the name of religion the school as school is sacrificed to something not a school: be it a Biblical institute, an evangelical agency, a center for religious instruction, a place of worship, or a missionary enterprise.

We understand, I say, and are sympathetic. All the same, it is not our view of either Christianity or education. We, too, insist on the primacy of the religious, the spiritual, in life. Ours is also the conviction that regeneration, that the choice for Christ, that the turning from sin and self to God and his kingdom, that this is the primary thing, without which indeed nothing else matters, from which everything else issues. We, too, have our special revelation: Christ, and Bible, and church, and sacrament, and worship, and soul, and we refuse resolutely, of course, to identify these with any natural or mundane thing. They are spiritual, they are the one thing needful, the pearl without price.

But we are Calvinists. Our Christian conviction is a Reformed conviction. And it is part of that conviction that the religious and spiritual cannot exist in a void, in isolation from life. It is part of the Reformed conviction that the spiritual in us requires human fulfillment, human embodiment. It is part of the Reformed conviction that the religious in us is part and parcel of the rest of us. We maintain that, so far from identifying science, and nature, and culture, and literature, and history with the world, and so expressing the antithesis of Christian and world in ignoring them, we must know, judge and appropriate these all, and express the antithesis of Christian and world through them. . . . We are not liberals, identifying the task of the church with, and losing the Gospel message in, a preoccupation with cultural concerns. We are not monastic. We neither retire into monasteries, nor into small scale social orders of our own. As a matter of fact, ours is not the facile dualism between church on the one hand, and practical life on the other, the practical life construed then as a way of making some money to continue the work of the church. For us something stands between the church and practical life, and this something is the school. Motivated by Christian conviction, it can, if it is a school, keep religion from becoming a disembodied ghost, and can keep practical life from becoming an irreligious, secularized, and commercialized thing. We take the Calvinist challenge seriously, namely, that the Christian must bring the whole range of life—science and art and society and government—under the sway of Christian principle and purpose as an expression of the kingly rule of Christ.

I repeat: the schools must be schools. It is the very strength of the Reformed profession of Christianity not solely in the isolatedly religious but in the religious commanding the naturally and culturally human. It is as human beings that we are Christians, in our human nature expressing itself in a natural environment, expressing itself also in cultural activity of all kinds, and, further, in a particular historical situation here on earth. Our being called to be saints does not exempt us from being human, nor exempt us from cultural activity, nor exempt us from social and political obligation, nor render reason superfluous, nor permit an indifference to art and literature, nor lift us out of history. On the contrary, it is in and through these things that our moral and religious choice for the spiritual kingdom of Christ becomes concrete, real, and meaningful. And that is why our schools must be schools, our education.

You know that the public schools often designate this as the function of their education: to train for responsible citizenship. They mean, in our democracy. We have that same duty, of course, but we think it is best performed when we denominate the purpose of education, as, yes, responsible citizenship, indeed, but in the spiritual kingdom of Christ. Our responsibility in society inevitably issues from that.

But then our schools must be schools. If it is at church that we make our choice for Christ, it is at school that we keep making that choice always more humanly and culturally and practically significant. Citizenship in the kingdom requires this kind of education. Else we should be dwarfed, stunted, meager, and only partially-conscious Christians. The question after all is not one of how little we can get by with and still be essentially Christians. The question in education is one of how strong, how aware, how full, how rich we make this profession. And, as I say, we have no choice, since we are the kind of creatures that we are, but to do this in our human nature, in our natural environment, by means of cultural activity, in a particular moment of history, and always in reference to a spiritual kingdom. The materials our schools as schools must use, therefore, are not ecclesiastical, or devotional, or always primarily Biblical materials. Our schools are not in this sense Bible schools. We ought not to regret this or proceed unconfidently, as though the cultural curricula of our schools are regrettably necessary for practical reasons, but a kind of interference really or at best addenda to the religious work. Nor ought we even so one-sidedly to prize, shall I say the *devotional* element at school, the religious atmosphere, as we say, the chapel exercises and such, that we suppose the distinctive part of the school inhered in these, and the rest were neutral or religiously indifferent.

You will understand me at this point, I take it. I think that devotional exercises, Bible reading, prayer, meditation, the service of song, and Biblical study seriously pursued, pursued also with evangelical emphasis, and not merely as so much scientific data—I think that these are very precious. Without them a school could hardly be designated Christian. But my point now is that they do not constitute the school a school: for this precious devotional element is just as proper to the home, to Christian industry, Christian recreation, places of Christian mercy, and the like. Understand me further in this insistence of mine that the schools must be schools. I honor the teacher who, when she has reason to suppose that a pupil or student is not a Christian, drops whatever she is doing, her arithmetic, or geography, or history lesson, to press the Gospel message upon him. That teacher has her values in the right order. She puts first things first. So much is absolutely true. But we ought not to go on to infer from this that a Christian school is a Christian school because it offers such wonderful opportunities for church or missionary work. It is a precious by-product. It is a true description of our schools to say of them that they come up out of the church, are supported by Christian parents, conducted under Christian auspices, taught by Christian men and women, include in their curriculum more than the public schools by virtue of Bible study, church history, and doctrine, and are carried on in an atmosphere of worship guaranteed by devotional exercises. Every one of these things is important. No school could be effectively Christian without them. And yet the essence of the distinctive in our schools lies not in these important circumstances but in the character of the education itself.

Our schools must be schools. They must subject the Christian student to as thorough a discipline as he is capable of in the natural, cultural, historical, and spiritual life of man. It is as human beings that we are Christians. All that is human concerns us. That gets us into all the subjects of the curriculum. It involves us in the whole of reality. Unawareness of any part of it, the failure to appropriate any part of it, to know it, and to judge it, and to refer it to a spiritual kingdom for justification, this by so much impoverishes our human expression of our Christian choice.

Now this humanness of ours in which we must be educated, through which we must express both our opposition to the spirit of the world and our choice for the kingdom of Christ, includes a lot. It includes, for instance, that part of us which we share with inor-

ganic and organic nature. We are chemical and physical and biological in part, and so is our environment. Thence the natural
sciences in our curriculum. We have, further, a nervous organization, akin to that of an animal, and yet differing from it, and so we
learn psychology. And at that point the uniqueness of the human
creature among created beings asserts itself rapidly. We are conscious. We have mind. We can think. We are moral. We can
make choices. We have creative freedom. We can make things
out of things, expressive of higher things. You will remember that
second chapter of Genesis: "And God formed every beast of the
field, and every fowl of the air, and brought them unto Adam, to
see what he would call them." There lies the human uniqueness,
the gift of reason, the expressiveness of language. And it is in this
area of our humanity that most of the subjects lie: science, government, history, mathematics, literature, social studies, and the rest.
There are the materials proper of school education. By means of
these, religious man enters into scientific man, aesthetic man, social man, practical man, and the rest. All of these are involved in
the shaping and maturing of the Christian choice for God. These
are the main business of the school as school.

And it is the teaching and learning of these that must be
Christian. That is my other point. For insisting that the schools
must be schools I do not mean to imply that ordinary academic
competence is all that is required. No, no, the education as education must be Christian. The quality of it, the character of it, the
soul of it—that must be Christian. In this lies the distinctiveness
of our schools.

The fact is that education is a human affair. It represents a
human awareness of reality and a human appropriation of it. And
this is a further fact: whatever is human is religious. The religious
in us is as natural and as real to us as the moral, or the rational, as
the scientific and aesthetic, as the biological and psychological, as
the social and historical. This religious in us, I say, is a part of our
being a creature; it is, I say, natural to us. And this continues so in
spite of the pervasive presence of sin. . . .

To be human is to be scientific, yes, and practical, and rational, and moral, and social, and artistic, but to be human further is
to be religious also. And this religious in man is not just another

369

facet of himself, just another side to his nature, just another part of the whole. It is the condition of all the rest and the justification of all the rest. This is inevitably and inescapably so for all men. No man is religiously neutral in his knowledge of and his appropriation of reality. The preamble to the Decalogue does not read, "Thou shalt serve a God," as though there were any choice about that. It is a natural reality, even now, that we shall serve a God. No, the preamble to the Decalogue and the foundation stone of our Christian schools is this: "I am the Lord Thy God . . . Thou shalt have no other gods before me." Belief is a basis of all learning, faith is inevitable in man, men are fundamentally dogmatic. All this I know is rank heresy to the secular mind, but it is the secular challenge I am trying to answer. And the answer I think very satisfactory is this answer: Christian schools in which the God behind the reality there explored is the one true God.

You see, though, that this makes of Christian education a much harder thing than that other method of conducting curricular affairs secularly and neutrally and then bringing in the distinctively religious by way of chapel exercises and the devotional element. It is hard work to prove the spirits whether they be of God. It is hard work to be in the world, really in it, I mean, fully aware, that is, of the religious and prophetic tensions and pressures of it, the ultimate loyalties and allegiances of the various cultures in it, the religio-moral choices of men in the past that make the cultural challenge of the present what it is; I say, it is hard work to be in the world that way, and then not be of it. And yet this proving or testing or trying of the spirits whether they be of God, this being in the world and yet not of it, this, precisely this, is almost the whole business of liberal education in our schools. That is really what we are always busy with in the classroom. That makes our schools distinctive. . . .

Christian teachers, Christian friends: it is so easy in the name of Christianity to turn one's back to art, to science, to politics, to social problems, to historical tensions and pressures, in one word, to culture, if you will. . . . [But realize] that the true discernment of the God behind the culture, the assumption underlying the thought, the dogma beneath the action, the soul in the body of the thing, are precisely what it is the business of our schools as schools to disclose and to judge. In that lies the strengthening of the moral sinews of our young Christians. It is so that their choice for Christ and God can become a meaningful human choice. Christianity versus culture: no, it is the fundamentalist heresy. Culture alone: indeed not; it is the liberal heresy. Christianity through culture: the religious in man governing, shaping, determining the scientific, artistic, social in him, precisely; it is the Reformed truth.

But if this kind of education is to be accomplished in our schools, then it is an implication of Christian education that it be not merely general education but also liberal. By this I mean that our passion should be not so much to try to get everything in that has cropped up on the face of the earth, as to get everything in which exhibits alternative gods, alternative moral choices, alternative beings and principles of cultural vindication. Our education, in other words, must be liberal in that it ministers to the freedom of moral choice. For us that means that it ministers to the choice for Christ already made before we come to school, reinforcing it all the while and making it always anew and always more consciously and more maturely. Devotional exercise plus vocational training is not Christian education! I do not think this is possible if the sum total of our education consists of shop, home economics, typing, stenography, hair-dressing, pile-driving, bookkeeping, accounting, mechanical drawing, and similar vocational skills. I have no objection to the inclusion of these in the schools, provided they are not regarded as adequate substitutes for what are called the humanities, sciences, and social studies. For if this sense that I speak of, the sense of the religious in man, and the religious in every cultural product, and the religious in the various cultures and epochs of history is to be borne in upon us, we shall have to be shaped and disciplined in the spiritual history of man, that inheritance in which and over against which we choose for Christ and against the world. An educated person will then know, for instance, how a Greek looked at reality and to what god he appealed for its vindication, and how a medieval Catholic looked at it, and how a renaissance humanist looked at it, and how an eighteenth-century deist, and a romantic pantheist, and a modern naturalist. It is only so that the student will learn that all things human are religious, that human culture, while inevitable, is not in itself enough in that it requires religious justification. And it is so that the Christian student will be taught and confirmed in his conviction that the religion of Christianity is the only adequate religion. . . .

As to that secular challenge, I can, happily, be very brief about that now. Very brief, for it issues from what I have said already. You know that it is the going theory of secular education in public schools that education must be neutral. I do not say that the advocates of secular education, of public education, deny that man is fundamentally religious. They probably acknowledge that he is, some of them at least. But they are forced from their position to take the stand that this religious claim cannot be allowed in public schools. They must leave it, therefore, to private, and personal, and individual choice of the student, and deal with the curriculum, as they say, neutrally, that is, without exhibiting a religious allegiance or loyalty. This is the Achilles' heel, the vulnerable spot, of public education. I do not gloat over their predicament; far be it from me. These schools are necessary in such a society as ours, and we require a society to live in also, and so we are too involved in their predicament not to share even a sort of responsibility for it. Predicament it is, though. Professor Trueblood said of it: "In our democracy we proceed on the assumption that it is illegal to teach the faith on which it rests." That, in a word, is the predicament our idea of Christian schools avoids. We hold that the education being a human enterprise is inevitably religious, that except it be religious it is not education, at least not moral education, and that the alleged neutrality of the public schools must—if their education is to be real education—turn out to be a mere allegation. Our answer to the secular challenge is this answer: Being neutral is impossible for man as man, certainly impossible in so fundamentally human a thing as education. It is this answer: We believe in order that we may know, for belief is the condition of knowledge. As for those secularists who maintain that the thing to do in education is to adopt scientific method, to adopt an hypothesis and then refuse to adhere to it until the facts make it impossible to disbelieve it, we say that this is making doubt and skepticism the basis of knowledge. And is not to be so objective and neutral as it sounds. It is a protestation made in the name of a god, the god of scientific method. That, too, when you come to examine it closely, is a profession of faith. The god is false. We know whom we have believed, and in His name we appropriate the whole of His reality in our schools.

First printed in *Testament of Vision*, by Henry Zylstra, published by William B. Eerdmans Publishing Co. in 1961. Used by permission of the publisher.

PART X
LOOKING BACK,
LOOKING AHEAD

A mere department of religion may be relatively insignificant. The teaching of the Bible is good, but it is only a beginning. What is far more important is the penetration of the central Christian convictions into the teaching of physics and chemistry and English and anthropology and history and sociology and philosophy. . . . The penetration of total life which we seek will come best by men who have both conviction and intellectual humility, and the gift of passing these on to their students.

D. Elton Trueblood
Lecture at Jamestown (N. D.) College, 1957

LOOKING BACK, LOOKING AHEAD

T his book is being compiled as the final decade of the twentieth century reaches its midpoint. If the Lord Jesus delays His return, what will be the keys to continuing in His service by doing the work of Christian schooling? Merely to speculate is futile, but to rely on the past as a mirror of the future may be useful.

What, then, have Christian educators learned from the past that will equip us better for the future?

First, we must be armed in anticipation of legislation and judicial action that may threaten our freedom to operate schools as we wish.

The earnestness with which Reformed and evangelical Christians maintained their schools in the early part of the twentieth century set the tone for combative political and juridical action. For although the Constitution of the United States does not mention the word *education,* interpreting the laws of this nation became a twentieth-century feature of decisions by the United States Supreme Court.

A few instances can be cited. For the purposes of this book, we consider first whose implications have been lasting for Christian schools in particular.

In 1922, the state of Oregon passed its Compulsory Education Act, arguing that private—especially religiously-oriented—education is narrow, provincial, and anti-democratic. Legislation had therefore been enacted to require attendance at public schools, leaving parents with no alternative for their children's schooling. A Roman Catholic order of teaching nuns, the Society of Sisters of the Holy Names of Jesus and Mary, sued the state and carried the case to the Supreme Court.

In 1925, the Supreme Court rendered its decision, *Pierce v. Society of Sisters,* ruling that Oregon and its then-governor, Walter M. Pierce, were in violation of the Fourteenth Amendment of the

United States Constitution. The majority opinion, written by Justice James Clark McReynolds, declared that:

> The fundamental theory of liberty upon which all governments in this Union repose excludes any general power of the state to standardize its children by forcing them to accept instruction from public teachers only. The child is not the mere creature of the state; those who nurture him and direct his destiny have the right, coupled with the high duty, to recognize and prepare him for additional obligations.

Obviously this precedent continues in force, although in many communities and states the ignorance and antagonism of opponents of Christian schooling periodically make litigation and costly trials necessary to reassert the Supreme Court's 1925 opinion.

Subsequently, other Supreme Court decisions began to draw more clearly the distinction between freedom of religious expression and practice within a private school and freedom from religious expression and practice in the public schools. These decisions began in 1947 with *Everson v. Board of Education*, which reiterated Thomas Jefferson's "wall of separation between Church and State." They include the notorious 1948 case, *McCollum v. Board of Education*, eliminating released-time programs for religious instruction in public school facilities; *Engel v. Vitale* (1962), striking down the New York State Board of Regents' prayer in public schools; *Abington School District v. Schempp* and *Murray v. Curlett*, both 1963, ending the practice in public schools of Bible reading without comment—although *Abington* actually encouraged the study of religion.

This latter case brought to the fore Madalyn Murray O'Hair as leader of the movement to eliminate the last remnants of religious awareness from the public schools. Her ongoing efforts—including her campaign to erase "In God We Trust" from American coins—while flamboyant, have not been entirely successful, largely because of the countervaling force of yet another Supreme Court opinion.

The least well-known of these school decisions, *Zorach v. Clauson*, rendered in 1952, also concerned released-time programs but those conducted voluntarily and off public school premises.

The court held that such a program in no way violated the Constitution's First Amendment. How, then, does this decision pertain to Christian schools? In a telling paragraph, the court stated:

> We are a religious people whose institutions presuppose a Supreme Being. We guarantee the freedom of worship as one chooses. We make room for as wide a variety of beliefs and creeds as the spiritual needs of men deem necessary. We sponsor an attitude on the part of government that shows no partiality to any one group and that lets each flourish according to the zeal of its adherents and the appeals of its dogma

Given these conditions, the Court went on,

> When the state encourages religious instruction or cooperates with religious authorities by adjusting the schedule of public events to sectarian needs, it follows the best of our traditions. For it then respects the religious nature of our people and accommodates the public service to their spiritual needs.

The Court continued, declaring that to hold that the state may not encourage religious instruction

> would be to find in the Constitution a requirement that the government show a callous indifference to religious groups. That would be preferring those who believe in no religion over those who do believe. . . . But we find no constitutional requirement which makes it necessary for government to be hostile to religion and to throw its weight against efforts to widen the effective scope of religious influence.

The opinion's most significant statement then followed, with italics here added:

> *The government must be neutral* when it comes to competition between sects. It may not thrust any sect upon any person. It may not make a religious observance compulsory. It may not coerce anyone to attend church, to observe a religious holiday, or to take religious instruction. But it can close its doors or suspend its operations as to those who want to repair to their religious sanctuary for worship or instruction. No more than that is undertaken here.[1]

379

Thus the lines were drawn. The state must remain neutral in public matters of religion, neither promoting nor forbidding the practice of religion among any of its citizens; not advancing any religion nor impeding any religion; doing no more than guaranteeing the freedom to worship as one chooses. But at the same time, the Court clearly held that, because "we are a religious people," no citizen has the right to presume the absence of religious sentiment in this country.

Unfortunately, few antagonists of religion in general, of Christianity in particular, understand the Supreme Court's opinion in *Zorach v. Clauson.* Thus, everywhere the mistaken assumption holds that the Supreme Court, once and for all, ordained that all public institutions be rid of any and all religious consciousness. The fact, of course, is that court ruled precisely opposite and the decision leaves ample room for the free—not coerced—expression of religious belief.

However, in extreme and ironic instances, some private schools with erstwhile religious—indeed, Christian—traditions of their own have found it expedient to act as if they would rather err on the side of ignoring religious faith than offend someone who chooses to be offended. In so doing, they sacrifice the very independence their charters grant.

Christian schools must assert without compromise their inherent liberty to appoint only believers to govern, administer, teach, and coach. To dilute this distinctive is to open the door to some eventual charge of arbitrary discrimination, based on the fact that an exception once made creates a precedent to be followed.

One more decision must be cited, however painfully; it too impinges on Christian schooling. The 1954 *Brown v. Board of Education* decision overturned *Plessy v. Ferguson* (1896) and its "separate but equal" provisions, declaring unconstitutional all such measures that would preserve racial segregation in public schools. Almost from its first announcement, the movement to educate children in schools committed to the Lordship of Jesus Christ received a blow, as opponents to racial integration sought to establish private academies under allegedly religious auspices. In many communities, "Christian school" meant nothing more than "white flight" and "No niggers need apply!"[2]

Approaching the end of the the twentieth century, such schools are fewer and fewer, although some remain with only the least possible number of token black students or other minority representation.

To date, the Supreme Court has yet to hear a case in which any plaintiff is appealing for a judgment against a Christian school based on a "lifestyle" or sexual preference issue. Given the clear indications of which direction the power of political correctness and cultural diversity will lead, one cannot suppose that such a case is more than a short time in the future. Indeed, it is to be expected that, in the name of democracy and tolerance, legislation will be enacted to deprive persons and institutions of current rights under law, unless they conform to new standards of cultural acceptability.

For Christian schools, the ultimate imposition will be the loss of tax-exempt status, depriving donors of the right to claim tax deductions for contributions to a school. Of course, when such an imposition falls on Christian schools, it will also affect every other Christian institution—college and seminary, church and mission agency.

In direct consequence of Supreme Court decisions already rendered—whether for positive or negative reasons—the attitudes they have engendered, and a fresh understanding of the nature of God's truth mediated through formal learning, many Christians have recently awakened to their children's need for elementary and secondary schooling in an unashamedly Christian context. For some parents, this has meant educating their children at home; for others, it has meant finding the means to pay tuitions and fees while still being taxed in support of public education. In search of tax and other relief, several initiatives such as the 1993 Proposition 174 in California, offering $2,600 or one-half the State's per pupil appropriation, have been placed before the electorate. Each has been ardently opposed by advocates of public schooling.

In spite of this financial burden, the closing decades of the twentieth century have seen a wave of Christian schools attracting a steadily increasing student enrollment. At the same time, public school enrollment—already affected by a decline in births and in the numbers of school-age children—has fallen; this has resulted in diminished population-based funding for public schools. This economic reality has alarmed public schooling advocates. But even more alarming to supporters of public schooling is the probability that they must share in future decisions regarding the education of American children with Christian school proponents.

For those leading the resurgent Christian school movement, such growth in enrollment carries with it great promise for the present and succeeding generations of school children. But this growth also carries the inherent dangers of eagerness without experience, shallow enthusiasm without wisdom, knowledge, or understanding. Such growth is often accompanied by a basic ignorance of the history and development of Christian schooling, sometimes springing from a fundamental mistrust of the intellect as an instrument with which to serve God.

Furthermore, in the past, some Christians have tried to conduct their schools in isolation from the fellowship or counsel of veteran educators, as if the knowledge possessed by novices had left them sufficient unto themselves. Christian schooling is a sphere of service within the Church of Jesus Christ; a Christian educator is one organ of the Body of Christ. A board member, an administrator, a teacher in a Christian school can no more exist in a vacuum than an infant can survive without nourishment.

If Christian schools are to be—until the Lord's return—the training ground for subsequent generations of Christian leaders, such schools must not neglect to teach their students what it means to love the Lord our God with heart, soul, strength, and mind; what it means to love God not merely emotionally, devotionally, and with physical energy, but also intelligently and intellectually, rationally and articulately. Teachers must use both knowledge and understanding to communicate the wisdom of God, which alone is truth.

Furthermore, those who govern, administer, teach, and support the work of these schools must recognize that the Lord of the universe can be glorified by nothing less than the best work of our hands. Excellence of effort and excellence in result are never attained without excellence in prayer, planning, and preparation. Defining and achieving excellence are part of discipleship; they are the evidences of good stewardship.

The selections chosen to represent Christian thought on education at the end of this century and for the beginning of the next reach back to a reminder of World War II and the martyrdom of an unacknowledged saint; to a challenge to do the work of Christian schooling in a manner that is "as Christian as possible"; and forward to a renewed call for wholeness; and to an affirmation of intent to enter into a covenant for excellence.

SIMONE WEIL

S imone Weil (1909–43), born in Paris of agnostic and non-obser-
vant Jewish parents, could quote passages from the French classics
at age six; she received her undergraduate degree with distinction
at age fifteen. Her professors recognized her genius, describing her gift as
"a power of thought which was rare."

Although she acquired all the necessary credentials to qualify as a
schoolteacher, Simone Weil found greater interest in working toward
social reforms—helping the unemployed, involving herself in the Spanish Civil War, seeking to improve working conditions in the Renault
automobile plant. She carried on all these activities in spite of fragile
health and debilitating headaches.

When World War II erupted, she left Paris for the south of France.
There Weil became acquainted with a Dominican priest, J. M. Perrin,
and was introduced by him to serious consideration of the claims of
Christ. Her inclination toward mysticism prevented her from accepting
any system of doctrine, but she clearly understood what divine compulsion she was under to believe. Her long letter to Father Perrin, which
she called her "Spiritual Autobiography," written in May 1942, outlines
her tortuous pilgrimage.

In the summer of 1942, Simone Weil and her parents arrived in
New York, but in November she was commissioned to work for the
French government-in-exile and so returned to London. There she assisted the Resistance movement, identifying so closely with her countrymen living under the German occupation that she refused to eat any
more than the meager rations available in Occupied France. As a result
of her self-imposed deprivation, she died in an English sanitarium on
August 29, 1943.

Her collection of essays and letters have been published in English
under the title *Waiting on God*. The Greek sense of the word for "waiting," which is *hypomene*, connotes a desperate clinging, as if hanging on
until the blood vessels under one's fingernails have burst. This was Simone Weil's commitment in faith.

Her work, exemplified in the essay that follows, shows a highly
developed sense of what biblical Christians understand to be "the inte-

gration of faith and learning." To Simone Weil, learning, or what she calls "school studies," must be seen as a lower means to a higher end: "the love of God." Weil argues that a concentrated mind is necessary for a student to persevere through prayer in waiting on God. School studies offer that discipline of concentration, which, in turn, enables the believer to wait attentively for God to speak. So, she writes, "Every school exercise, thought of in this way, is like a sacrament."

Is she idealistic and impractical? Perhaps. But this woman of profound faith challenges us to abandon ourselves utterly to the God she came to know in Jesus Christ.

"Reflections on the Right Use of School Studies with a View to the Love of God"[3] (Excerpt)

The key to a Christian conception of studies is the realization that prayer consists of attention. It is the orientation of all the attention of which the soul is capable toward God. The quality of the attention counts for much in the quality of the prayer. Warmth of heart cannot make up for it.

The highest part of the attention only makes contact with God, when prayer is intense and pure enough for such a contact to be established; but the whole attention is turned toward God.

Of course school exercises only develop a lower kind of attention. Nevertheless, they are extremely effective in increasing the power of attention that will be available at the time of prayer, on condition that they are carried out with a view to this purpose and this purpose alone.

Although people seem to be unaware of it today, the development of the faculty of attention forms the real object and almost the sole interest of studies. Most school tasks have a certain intrinsic interest as well, but such an interest is secondary. All tasks that really call upon the power of attention are interesting for the same reason and to an almost equal degree.

School children and students who love God should never say: "For my part I like mathematics"; "I like French"; "I like Greek." They should learn to like all these subjects, because all of them develop that faculty of attention which, directed toward God, is the very substance of prayer.

If we have no aptitude or natural taste for geometry, this does not mean that our faculty for attention will not be developed by wrestling with a problem or studying a theorem. On the contrary it is almost an advantage. . . .

Students must . . . work without any wish to gain good marks, to pass examinations, to win school successes; without any reference to their natural abilities and tastes; applying themselves equally to all their tasks, with the idea that each one will help to form in them the habit of that attention which is the substance of prayer. When we set out to do a piece of work, it is necessary to wish to do it correctly, because such a wish is indispensable in any true effort. . . .

The second condition is to take great pains to examine squarely and to contemplate attentively and slowly each school task in which we have failed, seeing how unpleasing and second rate it is, without seeking any excuse or overlooking any mistake or any of our tutor's corrections, trying to get down to the origin of each fault. . . .

Above all it is thus that we can acquire the virtue of humility, and that is a far more precious treasure than all academic progress. From this point of view it is perhaps even more useful to contemplate our stupidity than our sin. Consciousness of sin gives us the feeling that we are evil, and a kind of pride sometimes finds a place in it. When we force ourselves to fix the gaze, not only of our eyes but of our souls, upon a school exercise in which we have failed through sheer stupidity, a sense of our mediocrity is borne in upon us with irresistible evidence. No knowledge is more to be desired. If we can arrive at knowing this truth with all our souls we shall be well established on the right foundation.

If these two conditions are perfectly carried out there is no doubt that school studies are quite as good a road to sanctity as any other.

To carry out the second, it is enough to wish to do so. This is not the case with the first. In order really to pay attention, it is necessary to know how to set about it.

Most often attention is confused with a kind of muscular effort. If one says to one's pupils: "Now you must pay attention," one sees them contracting their brows, holding their breath, stiffening their muscles. If after two minutes they are asked what they have been paying attention to, they cannot reply. They have been concentrating on nothing. They have not been paying attention. They have been contracting their muscles.

We often expend this kind of muscular effort on our studies. As it ends by making us tired, we have the impression that we have been working. That is an illusion. Tiredness has nothing to do with work. Work itself is the useful effort, whether it is tiring or not. This kind of muscular effort in work is entirely barren, even if it is made with the best of intentions. Good intentions in such cases are among those that pave the way to hell. Studies conducted in such a way can sometimes succeed academically from the point of view of gaining marks and passing examinations, but that is in spite of the effort and thanks to natural gifts; moreover such studies are never of any use.

Will power, the kind that, if need be, makes us set our teeth and endure suffering, is the principal weapon of the apprentice engaged in manual work. But, contrary to the usual belief, it has practically no place in study. The intelligence can only be led by desire. For there to be desire, there must be pleasure and joy in the work. The intelligence only grows and bears fruit in joy. The joy of learning is as indispensable in study as breathing is in running. Where it is lacking there are no real students, but only poor caricatures of apprentices who, at the end of their apprenticeship, will not even have a trade.

It is the part played by joy in our studies that makes of them a preparation for spiritual life, for desire directed toward God is the only power capable of raising the soul. Or rather, it is God alone who comes down and possesses the soul, but desire alone draws God down. He only comes to those who ask him to come; and he cannot refuse to come to those who implore him long, often, and ardently.

Attention is an effort, the greatest of all efforts perhaps, but it is a negative effort. Of itself, it does not involve tiredness. When we become tired, attention is scarcely possible any more, unless we have already had a good deal of practice. It is better to stop working altogether, to seek some relaxation, and then a little later to return to the task; we have to press on and loosen up alternately, just as we breathe in and out.

Twenty minutes of concentrated, untired attention is infinitely better than three hours of the kind of frowning application that leads us to say with a sense of duty done: "I have worked well!"

But, in spite of all appearances, it is also far more difficult. Something in our soul has a far more violent repugnance for true attention than the flesh has for bodily fatigue. This something is much more closely connected with evil than is the flesh. That is why every time that we really concentrate our attention, we destroy the evil in ourselves. If we concentrate with this intention, a quarter of an hour of attention is better than a great many good works.

Attention consists of suspending our thought, leaving it detached, empty, and ready to be penetrated by the object; it means holding in our minds, within reach of this thought, but on a lower level and not in contact with it, the diverse knowledge we have acquired which we are forced to make use of. Our thought should be in relation to all particular and already formulated thoughts, as a man on a mountain who, as he looks forward, sees also below him, without actually looking at them, a great many forests and plains. Above all our thought should be empty, waiting, not seeking anything, but ready to receive in its naked truth the object that is to penetrate it. . . .

We do not obtain the most precious gifts by going in search of them but by waiting for them. Man cannot discover them by his own powers, and if he sets out to seek for them he will find in their place counterfeits of which he will be unable to discern the falsity.

The solution of a geometry problem does not in itself constitute a precious gift, but the same law applies to it because it is the image of something precious. Being a little fragment of particular truth, it is a pure image of the unique, eternal, and living Truth, the very Truth that once in a human voice declared: "I am the Truth."

Every school exercise, thought of in this way, is like a sacrament.

In every school exercise there is a special way of waiting upon truth, setting our hearts upon it, yet not allowing ourselves to go out in search of it. There is a way of giving our attention to the data of a problem in geometry without trying to find the solution or to the words of a Latin or Greek text without trying to arrive at the meaning, a way of waiting, when we are writing, for the right word to come of itself at the end of our pen, while we merely reject all inadequate words.

Our first duty toward school children and students is to make known this method to them, not only in a general way but in the particular form that bears on each exercise. It is not only the duty of those who teach them but also of their spiritual guides. . . .

Happy then are those who pass their adolescence and youth in developing this power of attention. No doubt they are no nearer to goodness than their brothers working in fields and factories. They are near in a different way. Peasants and workmen possess a nearness to God of incomparable savor which is found in the depths of poverty, in the absence of social consideration and in the endurance of long drawn-out sufferings. If, however, we consider the occupations in themselves, studies are nearer to God because of the attention which is their soul. Whoever goes through years of study without developing this attention within himself has lost a great treasure. . . .

So it comes about that, paradoxical as it may seem, a Latin prose or a geometry problem, even though they are done wrong, may be of great service one day, provided we devote the right kind of effort to them. Should the occasion arise, they can one day make us better able to give someone in affliction exactly the help required to save him, at the supreme moment of his need.

For an adolescent, capable of grasping this truth and generous enough to desire this fruit above all others, studies could have their fullest spiritual effect, quite apart from any particular religious belief. . . .

PETER K. HAILE

Peter K. Haile, born in 1925 in Tiger Kloof, South Africa, to missionary parents, studied English literature at Oxford University's Jesus College. He ran cross country with teammate Roger Bannister (who soon would run a mile in less than four minutes) and was active in the Christian Union, along with two other notables, James Packer and James Houston. As president of the Christian Union, he invited a young curate at All Souls' Church, London, John Stott, to preach his first university sermons.

After receiving his master's degree in 1951, Peter Haile was sent to North America to represent Britain's Inter-Varsity Fellowship to Canadian and American university students. Invited to remain, he was appointed the New England representative for InterVarsity. In 1954, he married a colleague, Jane Hollingsworth, a noted Bible teacher whose active ministry continued until her death in 1993.

In 1961, Frank E. Gaebelein invited Peter Haile to join the faculty of The Stony Brook School, where Haile remained until 1990. He served as English and Bible teacher, chaplain, and assistant headmaster. He is currently associate pastor of the Three Village Church, East Setauket, New York.

His greatest contributions to Stony Brook were his example of servanthood—friend to friend, colleague to colleague, adult to adolescent—and his call for an unremitting pursuit of excellence in the smallest details that constitute the work of a school. Having himself once been a boy a long way from home, he was especially compassionate toward teenagers—day students as well as boarders—in need of a surrogate parent.

Peter Haile served as chairman of the board of Latin America Mission and of Fellowship of Christians in Universities and Schools (FOCUS). The excerpt from his article "Why I Believe in Schools That Are as Christian as Possible" appeared in the *Latin American Mission Evangelist,* and reflects a keen understanding on the impact of truly Christian schools.

". . . Schools That Are as Christian as Possible"[4] (Excerpt)

What kind of schools do we want to see our children influenced by? And what kind of schools do we want our money to be invested in? As a concerned Christian, my answer must be, "Schools that are as Christian as possible."

I like to put it in this comparative way—"as Christian as possible"—because a person becomes a Christian by putting his trust in Jesus Christ and so being "born again."

But it is different with an institution. The "Christianness" of an institution can be measured only by the degree of Christian thinking and behavior in it from day to day.

Don't tell me a school is Christian because it has a Biblically orthodox "Platform of Principles," or because it was founded by the board of trustees of a Christian missionary society. No, the only way we can talk about a school—or any other institution—being Christian or non-Christian is in comparative terms—in terms of its being "more Christian" or "less Christian" in its thinking and behavior.

What then do we mean by "schools that are as Christian as possible"?

First of all, I would like to see strong faith in the hearts of the teachers—teachers who believe in God as a real Person—powerful, active, and able to change human hearts. They must believe in Him deeply enough to leave issues in His hands. When we try to cajole or coerce children into becoming Christians, we show that we don't really believe in God and in the reality of His persuasive Spirit.

This has an important carry-over into the area of teaching the Bible. Proper Bible teaching concentrates on getting the student to read the Bible thoughtfully and intelligently, and then to evaluate it for himself.

In our Bible classes at The Stony Brook School we study nothing but the text of Scripture itself, without condensing it or summarizing it or analyzing it or presenting apologies for it. We read it and re-read it and then set our students to write about it. In this way, we try to honor the intrinsic power and integrity of God's Word and to demonstrate our belief in the fact that it is the Word of the living God, who Himself speaks through it.

One year, I had the fascinating experience of teaching the Bible to students from many kinds of homes—devoutly Christian, nominally Christian, totally nonreligious, Jewish, professedly agnostic, and one Muslim home.

Before the year was half out, the Muslim student had come to me and said, "You have made me love the Bible the way I love the Koran." And later he came and said, "My religion teaches me I must believe in Mohammed or else I'll be lost. The Bible teaches me I must believe in Jesus or else I'll be lost. I don't want to be lost." During that summer, I had a letter from his home in a Middle Eastern country, and he said, "I'm continuing to read the Bible, and I hope I can finish it."

In our Bible class during the year, we have had significant discussions on lying, stealing, gossip, abortion, marriage, sexuality, homosexuality, divorce, attitudes toward parents, drunkenness, obedience to authority, civil disobedience, race relations, competitiveness, trade unionism, strikes, money, gluttony, and the occult. Every discussion arose spontaneously from the reading of the text. Each year some students come quietly to know and love Jesus Christ.

Besides calling for strong day-to-day faith on the part of teachers, Christian thinking and behavior in a school also demands the hourly demonstration of Christian love. This means, first of all, the full acceptance of each student, however disrespectful, deceptive, unkempt, thoughtless, irresponsible or unattractive he may be.

It also means acceptance of students whether they do or don't believe in the Christian Gospel. We must never feel or show toward a non-Christian student an attitude different from the one we show toward a Christian student. As teachers and administrators, we should be so secure in Jesus Christ that all our defensiveness has gone and we are free to be as open to the skeptic and the doubter as to the believer.

True Christian love also means that we don't threaten students, because threats imply that love is conditional—and Christian love never is. If I say to a student, "You do this, or else . . . !" he subconsciously assumes that if he doesn't do it, I will change my attitude toward him. The only way we can come anywhere near enforcing discipline and administering punishment—as we must—without conveying a change of attitude is by laying down beforehand—and as objectively as possible—what the rules are and what we will have to do if they are broken, and then simply and calmly following through on what we've said when the occasion arises.

Christian love also listens—I mean not only listens, but really hears. One of the most frequent statements I hear from students is that they cannot talk to their parents because their parents don't listen to them. As soon as they say something, it is met with a value judgment, shutting off further discussion.

This is not God's way. His ear is always open to what we have to say, however inane and unreasonable it may be. And to be Christian, we've got to be like Him. . . .

Christian thinking and behavior is always concerned with excellence, whether it's in personal relationships and societal structures, or in art, literature and scientific inquiry.

A man once said to me, "Don't you find that your striving for academic excellence at Stony Brook militates against your spiritual emphasis?" I suppose what he was really asking was whether putting such a high priority on trying to improve academics didn't lessen the amount of time we could spend on prayer meetings and other "spiritual" activities. But, personally, I don't see how we can separate our devotional duty to God from our academic duty to Him. He sees us as whole people; how we study, play games, do chores, spend money, practice the piano, join in fellowship, or study the Bible are all one. All must be done unto Him and for His glory—and His standards are high.

Truly Christian thinking and behavior does its best to guard against falling into a little subculture of its own that leads to smugness and complacency. We should constantly reach out to the world of ideas beyond us to learn what we can from the great deposit of God's truth given by common grace to past and present generations. We should constantly guard against the danger of being boxed in to a little world of familiar clichés, and unexplored ideas.

I want to see schools where there is no gossip, where teachers' rooms aren't sanctuaries where all the Biblical teaching against talebearing is forgotten or ignored.

I want to see schools where there's the kind of love that reproves and rebukes gently but firmly. . . .

I want to see schools in which teachers and administrators don't *use* God—either to preserve a party line or just simply to get their own way. One of the chief complaints that young people have about their supposedly Christian parents and teachers is that they use their Christianity to get things done their way.

Not only do we sometimes try to justify our own incompetence, sloppiness, mediocrity, highhandedness and arbitrariness, but we also impose on others our preferences in purely cultural matters by intimating that to question these things or complain about them would somehow be to question or complain against the Lord. Let's remember that Jesus had a particularly vehement hatred for the kind of religion that used God to preserve its own vested interests.

I want to see schools where young people are helped in the awesome and inescapable business of making choices for themselves. I want to see schools where they are educated, not indoctrinated.

The fact that there can be schools like these is why I want schools that are as Christian as possible.

KENNETH O. GANGEL

Born in 1935 in Paterson, New Jersey, Kenneth Gangel was sent by his mother to Stony Brook School in seventh and eighth grades. The experience was painful; he suffered acute homesickness and did not do well in his studies. Although Headmaster Frank Gaebelein tried to encourage him to stay on, midway through the eighth grade Gangel chose to leave Stony Brook and return home for the rest of his schooling.

In 1991, Gangel revisited Stony Brook School for the first time. Addressing students and faculty, Gangel revealed to them his own adolescent sense of failure and purposelessness; but he also encouraged them to realize how God can shape a life and hone the gifts of someone willing to submit to His purposes.

Gangel would receive his undergraduate training from Taylor University and his theological training from Grace, Fuller, and Concordia seminaries. He was awarded a Ph.D. from the University of Missouri, and after teaching and serving in administration at Calvary Bible College for nine years, in 1970 he became the founding director of the School of Christian Education at Trinity Evangelical Divinity School, near Chicago. In 1974, he accepted the presidency of Miami Christian College (now Trinity College of Miami). He has been at Dallas Theological Seminary since 1982, first as chairman of the Christian education department and now as vice president for academic affairs and academic dean.

Gangel has developed a practical philosophy of Christian education effective for elementary and secondary schools, undergraduate colleges, and graduate seminaries; his work also extends to churches and families. His great distinctive is the clarity with which he articulates and illustrates his ideas, making him a most effective communicator in the many conferences and conventions at which he speaks. His several books include *Understanding Teaching, Toward a Harmony of Faith and Learning, Christian Education: Its History and Philosophy* (coauthored with Warren E. Benson), and *Building a Christian Family*.

The selection that follows is one of the four lectures given during the 1978 W. H. Griffith Thomas Memorial Lectures at Dallas Theological Seminary.

"Integrating Faith and Learning: Principles and Process"[5] (Excerpt)

On September 20, 1912, the great Christian apologist, J. Gresham Machen, addressed the convocation exercises at the opening of Princeton Theological Seminary's one hundred and first year. The address still stands as one of the great classics on what is now called "the integration of faith and learning." Perhaps Machen tipped his hand that day regarding the caliber of his address when he added these words in the very first line: "One of the greatest of the problems that have agitated the Church is the problem of the relation between knowledge and piety, between culture and Christianity." The gauntlet was laid, the banner was raised, and more than six decades later Christian educators are still attempting to practice what Machen said in that hour.

And yet most educators are able to talk about the integration of faith and learning better than they can practice it. Indeed, in some quarters it becomes almost a symbol, a term to be uttered but not demonstrated. Invariably it is a rallying cry which will bring nods of approval from the faithful multipled hundreds of teachers in Christian classrooms at all levels of education as they continue to grope for evasive implementations of the ideal.

The phrase, "integration of truth" refers to *the teaching of all subjects as a part of the total truth of God, thereby enabling the student to see the unity of natural and special revelation.* Though this may seem simple, it requires a lifetime of effort and the best possible education a teacher can bring to his task in order to achieve what Machen challenged educators to do that September evening.

Principles for Integrating Faith and Learning

The cardinal essential for the achievement of the integration of truth in the Christian classroom is *a commitment to the authority of the Bible.* Gaebelein identifies several reasons why the Word of God "must be central in Christian education":

1. The sheer, unapproachable greatness of the written Word of God . . . to take as the center of the curriculum the one book among all the other great books to which alone the superlative "greatest" can without challenge be uniquely applied—this is nei-

ther narrow nor naive. Rather it is simply good judgment to center on the best rather than the second best.

2. Its authority as the inspired, inerrant Word of God.

3. Its indispensable critical function. In a day of debased values and satisfaction with the second or even third rate, education requires a standard and point of reference by which the cheapened standards of our day may be judged.

4. It relates to the all-important matter of knowing and finding the truth.

Quite obviously any one of Gaebelein's points could be expanded into a full treatise of theological and pedagogical implications. The essential issue here, however, centers on the word *authority*. It is one thing to verbalize a commitment to the inspiration of Scripture; it is quite another to accept the inerrant authority of Scripture as the centerpiece for contemporary education.

And that leads to a second principle: The integration of faith and learning demands *a recognition of the contemporaneity of the Bible and the Holy Spirit*. Here the authoritative and inerrant Bible is related to the student's life where he is. To borrow an idea from Korzybski, the great general semanticist, the "here and now" depends greatly on the "then and there." The Bible, as God's special written revelation, is an accurate and absolute record of the "then and there," which in most cases continues to the "here and now." But the Bible alone is insufficient to develop a distinctively evangelical view of the teaching-learning process. The educator must also recognize the role of the Holy Spirit in interpreting God's truth in accordance with the words of the Lord Jesus who said to His disciples, "When He, the Spirit of Truth, comes, He will guide you into all truth" (John 16:13 ff.).

A third principle for the integrative process is *a clear understanding of the nature, source, discovery, and dissemination of truth*. How can one deal with this vast conceptualization without a full epistemological essay? The classic banner many have raised a thousand times continues to fly over the castle: All truth is God's truth. But what does it mean to say that all truth is God's truth? Simply that wherever truth is found, if it is genuine truth, it is ultimately traceable back to the God of the Bible. And since the God of the Bible is also the God of creation, the true relationship between natural and special revelation begins to emerge at the junction of a Christian epistemology. Another reference from [my] former mentor speaks eloquently to the subject:

> Now Christian education, if it is faithful to its deepest commitment, must renounce once and for all the false separation between secular and sacred truth. It must see that truth in science, and history, in mathematics, art, literature, and music belongs just as much to God as truth in religion. While it recognizes the primacy of the spiritual truth revealed in the Bible and incarnate in Christ, it acknowledges that all truth, wherever it is found, is of God. For Christian education there can be no discontinuity in truth, but every aspect of truth must find its unity in the God of all truth.

Let it be said that the thinking Christian does not fear research and experimentation. He understands that since all truth is God's, the more honest effort put forth by man, regenerate or unregenerate, must ultimately result in an uncovering of more of God's truth. Such is the design of common grace.

A fourth principle on which the integrative process is based has to do with *designing a curriculum which is totally constructed on the centrality of special revelation.*

. . . When properly implemented, such a Christian curriculum designed around the centrality of special revelation produces a student who is able, at the end of his educational pattern, to demonstrate commensurate levels of wisdom, witness, holiness, and churchmanship as representative ideals. At the end of his secondary educational experience the student in the Christian institution ought to demonstrate a maturity level in these and similar virtues which is parallel with the educational pattern he has achieved at that point.

. . . A fifth principle dealing with the integration of truth in Christian education is *a demand for the development of a Christian world and life view.* There is no dichotomy between the sacred and secular for the thinking Christian. And the teacher who understands what Christian education is all about will work courageously at developing an internalization of God's truth, not just a cognitive knowledge.

Some have feared that the development of a Christian world and life view will produce a spirit of "worldliness" about the Christian or about Christian education. To be sure, history shows that such a danger is ever present. On the other hand, the New Testament shows that the demand of the task is worth the risk.

. . . A sixth principle demands that *bibliocentric education extend to all areas of student life.* Just as there is no divorce of the sacred and secular in the genuinely Christian life, so there is no divorce between faith and learning, for faith is related to every other activity on the distinctively Christian campus. The student who is able to memorize Bible verses for personal evangelism or offer a profound explanation of the Westminster Shorter Catechism is not a positive product of the system unless that knowledge affects his life in the dormitory, on the football field, and in relationships with his parents at home. The Christian school which speaks openly of its integration of faith and learning has the accompanying responsibility to demonstrate how that philosophical posture is implemented in the lives of students at all times and in all places.

Practicing the Integration of Faith and Learning

How can faith and learning actually be integrated? That is the constant and legitimate cry of all who earnestly yearn to treat Christian learning as a sacred trust. The following are six suggestions for this integration process.

First, *the teacher who would integrate faith and learning must constantly be about the all-important task of theological sieve-building.* . . . Each student may be thought of as having a funnel in his mind and life into which there will be poured during the years of his education a great deal of information—some good, but much of it bad. Some educators in educational institutions within the Christian world have opted to close off the top of the funnel not allowing information to enter which is not consonant with what the institution or the educator wishes the student to hear.

. . . The alternative is to build into the funnel what may be called a theological sieve. Insofar as a certain student at a given level of education understands and internalizes the absolute truth of God and makes it his own through the applicatory power of the

Holy Spirit, to that extent he is able to cope cognitively and affectively with other kinds of information which bombard his mental processes.

When such information makes it through the filtering system it can be tucked away for use in the reservoir of truth for faith and life. When, however, it is shown by the theological sieve to be inconsistent with biblical teaching, it is labeled "untruth" and the computer spits it out the rejection valve.

. . . This is made possible by a second suggestion: *Every teacher must be at least an amateur theologian.* The word *amateur* is used here not in a sense of inadequacy or inability, but to suggest that a person who has specialized in mathematics or science should not be expected to write scholarly criticisms on theological subjects nor to make his living by teaching theology. He is an amateur. But just like many amateur golfers and tennis players, he might be very good at his avocation. Indeed, the better he is at his theological pursuits, the more effective he will be at his vocation in the teaching of whatever subject matter he calls his specialty.

The implication for boards and administrators of Christian schools is quite clear: Teachers at any level of Christian education who have not had a respectable exposure to formal study of Bible and theology should not be hired. . . .

A third suggestion is that *teachers must help students "get it all together" in a Christian world and life view.* This is simply the implementation stage of principle number five enunciated above. Holistic Christian thinking does not just happen but is deliberately designed by the effective Christian teacher. . . .

Fourth, the practice of integration can only go forward if *teachers stop confusing the integration of truth with classroom devotions.* Indeed, chapel and classroom devotions . . . are praiseworthy. But they are not to be compared in value to the total awareness created in the mind of the student by the alert teacher who facilitates the informal experiencing of truth by digging fertile furrows across the minds of his students. Classroom devotions may be worship and worship is important but the integration of faith and learning is truth-searching in depth.

A fifth step in the process of integration is the procedure of *learning to walk a carefully balanced line between openmindedness and unchallengeable doctrine.* Christian teachers . . . tend to err in one of two extremes with respect to classroom attitude toward truth. Quite obviously, one extreme is an unwarranted dogmatism which offers regimented indoctrination as a religious sop to a student who really comes for rational inquiry and learning. . . .

But the other extreme is also dangerous, namely, an open-mindedness which does not lead the student to consider that one or two alternatives of interpretation may be better than others because they are more biblical. Note the qualifying phrase—they could only be better *because they are more biblical,* not because they are more closely related to the teacher's point of view. There is a world of difference between having an inspired Bible and an inspired interpretation of that Bible. As James has warned, "Not many of you should act as teacher, my brothers, because you know that we who teach will be judged more strictly" (James 3:1).

Sixth, it may be helpful to remember that *the task of integration should be approached with reverence, relevance, and relaxation.* Sometimes teachers try too hard, as Gaebelein suggests regarding the subject matter in mathematics. To be sure, integration of faith and learning will not automatically fall into place. Learning unrelated to life is as dead as faith without works. The end of the integrative process is to develop Christian minds, and to have a Christian mind is to think "Christianly."

Kenneth O. Gangel, "Integrating Faith and Learning: Principles and Process," *Bibliotheca Sacra,* April–June 1978. Used by permission of *Bibliotheca Sacra,* 3903 Swiss Ave., Dallas TX 75204.

JOHN H. WESTERHOFF III

As an Episcopal priest, scholar, teacher, and writer, John Wester-hoff III has been responsible for reawakening his own church and other mainline denominations to the need for a genuine Christian education inside and outside the church. In some respects, he is the twentieth century's Horace Bushnell, calling for the Christian nurture of our youth.

Born in Paterson, New Jersey, Westerhoff attended Harvard Divinity School and Columbia University, earning doctorates in both theology and education. Ordained in 1958 in the United Church of Christ, he served pastorates in Maine and Massachusetts. He became an Episcopal priest in 1978.

Early in his pastoral experience, John Westerhoff observed the easy-going nature of much of what passed for Christian education. The consequences, he knew, would be disastrous as uninstructed and uncommitted people passed by a church that made too few demands of them. The title of a later book stated the problem directly: *Will Our Children Have Faith?* He argued that they will not unless we provide the example of faith and the substance of faith, which are the best means by which to inculcate the truth we profess to believe.

Convinced that the mid-twentieth century American church's casual approach to teaching was seriously flawed, John Westerhoff undertook to revolutionize the programs called Christian education, both within the local parish and beyond. His strategy for change took him to Duke Divinity School, where he has influenced a generation of Christian educators. As editor of the professional journal *Religious Education* and author of more than two dozen books, he has helped to shape Christian education for its defining task of faith formation.

Westerhoff views the development of faith, typically, in four stages:

1. *Experienced faith,* whereby a young child observes benefits of love, trust, and acceptance transmitted by someone who attributes these graces to Christian faith.

2. *Affiliative faith,* in which an older child seeks to identify with action that draws that child into a community of faith; for instance, participation in worship or church-sponsored fellowship.

3. *Searching faith,* characterized by doubt and/or critical opinions about institutional religion and those who practice it; often rejecting some aspects of earlier evidence of faith in favor of new—or sometimes—no manifestation of religious interests.

4. *Owned faith,* the personal value of which derives from the fact that it is real, not merely a cultural or family tradition, and calls for committed action.[6]

Westerhoff is no ivory-tower pedant. During his years at Duke, he served as an associate rector at the nearby Chapel of the Cross, Chapel Hill, North Carolina; today he is director of the Institute for Pastoral Studies, based at St. Bartholomew's Episcopal Church in Atlanta, Georgia.

Westerhoff's task to reform Christian education is by no means complete, but it is farther advanced as a result of his vision and work.

"Hidden Curriculum in the Classroom"[7] (Excerpt)

Ten years of experience in the parish during the fifties and sixties led me to an intuitive conclusion: there were serious foundational difficulties with the church's dominant understandings and practices of Christian education, namely, the instruction by volunteers of children and youth in a Sunday church school. Thus began my thirty-five year search for an alternative.

Today many of my early controversial convictions are common-place assumptions: Christianity is fundamentally a way of life, and therefore, faith (how we perceive life and our lives) and character (our sense of identity and how we are disposed to behave) are more important goals for Christian education than biblical knowledge and theological doctrine, moral decision making and value clarification; quality adult education is the key to faithful education with children and youth; education is not to be limited to the church school, but must include every aspect of parish and family life; how we live with children and youth is more important than what we do to/for them; and the list goes on.

Now at sixty I have an understanding of the church's educational ministry that is much broader and inclusive than in my early, developing years. My work has become focused on trying to address the consequences of an early phrase by the third century theologian, Tertullian: "Christians are made (fashioned) not born!" When asked how Christians are fashioned, the early church answered through catechesis. "Catechesis" is a Greek word which literally means to echo. When the Christians used it they meant to echo the Word, and the Word was a person, Jesus. Catechesis was the process by which Christ-like persons, persons with Christ's faith and character, were fashioned. Of course, catechesis could not be a determinative process; rather it was a process of influence which persons were always free to accept or reject.

As I have reflected on the process of catechesis, I have concluded that it can best be described as three deliberate or intentional, systematic or interrelated, sustained or life-long processes: formation, education, and instruction.

Formation includes the participation in and the practice of the Christian life of faith. Formation is a conforming (nurturing) and transforming (converting) process. Further, it is a natural process known as enculturation or socialization, about which we are intentional. And it is the primary means by which faith and character are fashioned; therefore, it is the focal point of catechesis.

Education involves critical reflection on every aspect of our life of faith in the light of the Gospel. It is a reforming process that assumes and necessitates growth and change. Education, in this sense, needs to be a natural part of our personal and communal lives. Without faithful education or critical reflection as believers in Jesus Christ and members of His church, we would be unable to engage in the faithful formation of Christ-like persons and communities.

Instruction focuses on the acquisition of knowledge, such as the contents of the Scriptures and skills, such as the interpretation of the Scriptures. It is an informing process that is essential to faithful education and therefore to faithful formation.

Having established that catechesis includes formation, education, and instruction, I intend to focus the rest of this article on formation, in this case on formation as it is engaged in the classroom. Recall that formation describes a natural process, one that occurs whether or not we are conscious of it. When we are not intentional about formation, it becomes a "hidden curriculum," indicative of what our students really learn regardless of what we desire to teach.

While having other necessary and important goals and objectives, the school needs to engage mindfully in the formation of Christian faith and character in the lives of both students and teachers. To accomplish this end, it will be necessary to reflect critically on what we participate in and practice in the school in light of our understandings of Christian faith and character. Of course, formation in the home, the church, and the school needs to be consistent if we are to achieve our aim.

As we engage in this endeavor, I suggest that we need to explore eight aspects of our life in the school. . . . Of course, we need first to establish a common understanding of Christian faith, how Christians are to perceive life and their lives, and Christian character, how Christians are to be disposed to live, that is, the virtues they are to manifest in their lives. Let's look briefly at each of these aspects of life in a school.

Environment. We shape our environment, and then it influences our lives. From the moment students enter a classroom, perceptions are being formed. Further, the furniture in the room and how it is arranged will influence behavior. (Does the arrangement set the teacher apart as authority or does the circle of chairs welcome and include everyone?) What students see, touch, taste, smell, and hear is important to their learning. . . .

Ritual Participation. Rituals are repetitive symbolic actions, that is, words and deeds point beyond themselves and participate in that to which they point, giving them particular power and influence. Classroom life is filled with rituals. Some are liturgical rituals, that is, they express and make present the Christian sacred story in the context of prayer and worship. But there are many others, such as games played and awards given. For example, many games, while fun and supportive to learning, also form persons to be competitive when cooperation is the Christian virtue. Further, when we give awards based on deserving, we work against the good news that God gives us what we need and not what we deserve. And when persons earn awards for their works we negate the faith perception that grace is free and all we have is gift from God, which we are responsible to share with others.

Ordering Time. There are many ways to order time in the classroom. Every curriculum resource orders time. The most important means for ordering time, if we will to fashion Christians, is the church's sacred narrative as it is expressed in the church year. Further, we need to be particularly careful that the ecclesial calendar, which often serves the church's institutional needs rather than its story, and the Hallmark card calendar with its Valentine's Day, Mother's Day, St. Patrick's Day, Halloween, July Fourth, and birthdays, are avoided, for both work against the formation of Christian faith and character. For example, why would the church celebrate birthdays? Are not our . . . rebirth day[s] and our death days (our resurrection day) more important from a Christian point of view?

Organization of Life. How we ask our students to spend their time, talents, and treasures influences how they live. Do we encourage tithing as a minimum standard for Christians? Are we good stewards of the many resources used in class? When we have fundraising projects are we raising money for our own benefit or the benefit of others? Further, how do we influence our students to spend their time, talent, and treasures outside of class? How much time is spent in prayer, service, and study as preparation for class?

Interactions. How we interact and how we are encouraged and discouraged to interact with each other forms us. Are girls and women treated differently than boys and men? Do we encourage students to share and help each other learn? For example, we cannot shape persons to understand themselves as intra-dependent communal beings if every student has his/her own box of crayons or if there is a lot of independent study in which students are encouraged to progress at their own rate of speed. Students learn to treat others fairly, to be sensitive to each other's needs, and to be present to each other in helpful ways by being treated that way by their teachers. Further, if our teaching methods encourage passivity, we cannot expect our students to be active in society.

Role Models. The persons we present as role models communicate to others the ways we wish them to live. Teachers are natural role models and therefore need to reflect upon their lives to be sure they are sharing the good news in both words and example. Further, in our society role models are typically athletes and entertainers. When we present such persons, even if they are Christian athletes and entertainers, we suggest that this is the best way to live out the Christian life. Further, the people we often think most of are those who began their lives in poverty and became rich and famous, but the Christian saints were typically those who began rich and became poor. How do we make persons who are downwardly mobile role models for our lives?

Discipline. Discipline has to do with what we practice regularly. If Christian character is comprised of character traits, such as being completely dependent upon God, as having as our only end for life an ever deepening and loving relationship with God, as having our motives as pure as our acts, as being self critical of how we live, as being generous, patient, and a reconciler, and as being willing to risk everything to do God's will (see Matt. 5:1–11), then such behaviors need to be practiced in class. Further, in terms of teaching methods, do students practice coloring in coloring books? If they do, are they learning to stay within the lines and be other-directed persons rather than being inner-directed and creative persons, that is, persons created in the image of God?

Language. How we talk influences how we live. For example, if we say, "I can't do that for you," rather than "I will not do that for you," we learn/teach how to be victims rather than responsible moral decision makers. When a child asks for something, if we respond, "We can't afford it," even if that is true, we do not teach him/her to use as criteria for buying something whether or not it is God's will. We need to talk more about how little we have a right to keep and [how] much we have a need to give away. Further, we need to consider how much the possessive dominates our conversation. We typically talk about having families, homes, cars, occupations, salaries. We act as if we possess things and people. And then we worry if we do not have any friends, forgetting that we cannot have, that is, possess, a friend. The issue is: are we being a friend. . . .

407

These are a few brief examples of things to consider if we are to be serious about the formation of Christian faith and character. Nevertheless, a faithful school must strive to turn its hidden, covert curriculum into a mindful, overt curriculum so that while it engages in instruction and education, it also consciously attempts to fashion persons who embody the Christian life of faith.

D. BRUCE LOCKERBIE

Born in Canada in 1935, D. Bruce Lockerbie attended a series of public schools there and in the United States—ten in all—before receiving his high school diploma in Brooklyn, New York. He completed both undergraduate and graduate work at New York University, receiving an M.A. in American studies. During his studies he also became a middle distance runner, winning national championships in both Canada and the United States.

But his heart was in teaching, not athletics. After teaching English at Wheaton (Illinois) College, he became an instructor at The Stony Brook School, where he served thirty-four years as in many positions, including Bible and English teacher, choral music conductor, track and cross-country coach, and the dean of faculty. During this time he enjoyed a mentoring relationship with the school's headmaster who had recruited him, Frank E. Gaebelein.

For the past thirty years Lockerbie also has served as an educational consultant to schools, colleges, seminaries, and churches. In 1987 he founded the Frank E. Gaebelein Memorial Conference on Christian Schooling, which calls leaders in Christian schooling to annual conferences to discuss trends, issues, and problems in Christian schooling. In 1993 the conference adopted "A Covenant for Excellence," a document of beliefs and standards for Christian school board members, administrators, and teachers. The document, drafted by Lockerbie and signed by those in attendance at the conference, has been circulated and signed by several hundred more educators who wish to affirm their intention to seek even higher standards of professional excellence in education.

The document follows. It represents the desire of teachers and leaders to remain committed to excellence in Christian schooling. For further information about the covenant or the Gaebelein Memorial Conference, inquiries may be addressed to D. Bruce Lockerbie, Stewardship Consulting Services, Post Office Box 26, Stony Brook, New York 11790–0026

A Covenant for Excellence⁸

*As colleagues in Christian schooling, we hereby
solemnly declare and affirm this Covenant for
Excellence in our calling as Christian educators:*

Whereas, we acknowledge that we are sinners redeemed by the grace of God through faith in Jesus Christ; and

Whereas, we have submitted ourselves to the Lordship of Jesus Christ and to the authority of Holy Scripture as God's Word; and

Whereas, God's Word declares that the fear of the Lord is the beginning of godly wisdom, knowledge, and understanding; and

Whereas, God's Word commands us to make disciples of all persons everywhere, especially our own children, by the training and instruction of the Lord;

Therefore, we affirm that

—godly *wisdom* comes only by special revelation through the Person of Christ, Holy Scripture, and the whole counsel of God given by the Holy Spirit through the Church;

—godly *knowledge* comes by general revelation through formal and informal study and contemplation of nature and human nature, in pursuit of an academic curriculum, and in work and play;

—godly *understanding* comes only when the whole of life's experience passes through the lens of a biblical world-view, meaning that all truth is framed by biblical reality and everything that is ultimately of God is true.

We further affirm that

—God who is perfect and holy commands of us service that aspires to be both perfect and holy, therefore excellent;

—lacking in ourselves the capacity to fulfill this command, we are nonetheless summoned to know and strive after the highest attainment of our gifts, while humbly ascribing only to God all glory for our lowly efforts;

—to keep back anything that would honor God is sin; to endeavor to achieve less than our best is sin; to commend ourselves for doing what is only our duty is sin; to judge others whose achievement is either more or less than our own is sin;

—for these our sins of omission and commission, we most earnestly repent.

We further affirm that

—the goal of achieving excellence in any sphere of human service to God is essential to the good stewardship of our gifts and calling;

—both the example of Holy Scripture and the work of God in history commend the founding and sustaining of schools honoring to the Lord Jesus Christ by the excellence of their stewardship;

—both objective and subjective standards of excellence exist for measuring the quality of our schools and our work in them;

—these standards of excellence reflect both biblical virtues and cultural values compatible with Scripture;

—among the biblical virtues are the objective spiritual qualities of Christian living enumerated by St. Paul as exemplary of the life transformed and the mind renewed [Romans 12:1–15:13]: humility, sobriety, proportion, love, honor for one another, zeal, joy, hope, patience, faithfulness in prayer, generosity, hospitality, forgiveness, sympathy, harmony, peaceable behavior, absence of vengefulness, submission to authority, justice, good citizenship, fiscal responsibility, non-judgmental spirit, absence of legalism and license, mutual acceptance—all evidences of the powerful work of the Holy Spirit;

—among those cultural values acknowledged by our society and compatible with Scripture are these subjective temporal qualities, exemplary of academic, artistic, athletic, and social attainment, such as personal or communal recognition for scholastic honors, artistic originality, athletic skill and sportsmanship, social maturity and responsibility, and altruistic deeds;

—among other cultural values acknowledged by our society and compatible with Scripture are excellence of professional skills in teaching and administering, business practice and financial management, maintenance of resources, and valid recognition by one's peers of work worthy of commendation.

Therefore, be it resolved by all those undersigned that the schools we found or sustain be institutions where

—governing boards, administrators, teachers, staff, and supporters recognize the holistic and interdependent nature of our work together, as set forth in St. Paul's analogy for the Body of Christ;

411

—governing boards, administrators, teachers, staff, and supporters all recognize and act upon their distinct and separate roles and responsibilities in our schools;

—as those called to hone the intellect and shape the will of our students to imitate "the mind of Christ," our calling may be recognized and respected for its own unique contribution to the Body of Christ.

Be it further resolved by all those undersigned that our students

—be stimulated, challenged, and encouraged to make the best possible use of the intellectual, aesthetic, physical, social, and spiritual gifts given to them;

—be offered every opportunity to excel in academic studies, athletic competition, artistic performance, and social growth, while keeping before them their need for spiritual maturity in proportion to their age and experience in faith;

—be provided with examples of excellence worthy of emulation, not only by their teachers and by their own participation in learning, testing, exhibition, competition at the highest appropriate levels, but also by the finest quality of human endeavor by guests invited to our schools or by visits to lectures, concerts, exhibits at museums or galleries, theatrical productions, and sporting events;

—become inculcated by biblical virtues leading to excellence, taught by example and precept in the living and teaching of those who govern, administer, teach, serve, and support;

—be taught only those cultural values leading to excellence that are compatible with Scripture, such as intellectual integrity or athletic courage, and fostered as corollaries to biblical virtues;

—be urged to recognize the grace of God apparent throughout the whole human race and in every nation and culture;

—be pointed toward every possible adult field of service worthy of God's call and their gifts, fully assured that God is no respector of the hierarchy, favor, nationality or gender of persons.

Finally, let it be our covenant together to
examine our work daily against the highest
standard of our Lord's excellent example of
teaching; let us also follow the injunction
of St. Paul, who urges,

". . . whatever is true, noble, right, pure, lovely, admirable—if anything is excellent or praiseworthy—think about such things."

[Philippians 4:8]

Signed to affirm in the presence of these witnesses, June 30, 1993:

NOTES

Preface

1. Kenneth O. Gangel, Keynote Address, The Frank E. Gaebelein Memorial Conference on Christian Schooling, Eastern College, St. Davids, Penn. (June 18, 1988). See also "Introduction," *Christian Education Journal* IX: (Autumn 1988) 7.

2. Kenneth Smitherman, "ACSI Pastors' Survey," *Advocate* (April–May 1991), 4–5.

3. Fred R. Wilson, "The Dramatic Growth of Christian Schools," *Christian Education Journal* 9: (Autumn 1988) 11–29.

4. *Peterson's Choose a Christian College: A Guide to Academically Challenging Colleges Committed to a Christ-Centered Campus Life* (Princeton: Peterson's Guide and Christian College Coalition, 1992).

PART 2:
The First Five Centuries

1. "The Second Apology," *The Fathers of the Church*, ed. Thomas B. Falls (New York: Christian Heritage, 1948), 133–34.

2. An excerpt from "Prescription Against Heretics" begins on page 71.

3. "Panegyric on St. Basil," *Nicene and Post-Nicene Fathers*, ed. Philip Schaff, vol. VII. (Grand Rapids: Eerdmans, 1979), 395.

4. Augustine of Hippo, "The Usefulness of Belief," *Augustine: Earlier Writings*, The Library of Christian Classics, vol. VI, ed. John A. S. Burleigh (Philadelphia: Westminster, 1953), 284–323.

5. An excerpt from "On Christian Doctrine" begins on page 78.

6. Frank E. Gaebelein, *The Pattern of God's Truth* (New York: Oxford, 1954), 20.

7. "Epistle to the Corinthians," *Treasury of Early Christianity*, ed. Anne Fremantle (New York: Viking, 1953), 27.

8. Donald P. Hustad, "Introduction to Worship Leaders' Edition," *The Worshiping Church: A Hymnal* (Carol Stream, Ill.: Hope, 1990), viii; see also Hustad, "Worship and Congregational Song in 2000 A.D.," The Worshiping Church: A Hymnal, xi.

9. Etheria is sometimes called Egeria, Aetheria, or Silvia. Marion J. Hatchett, *Sanctifying Life, Time and Space: An Introduction to Liturgical Study* (New York: Seabury, 1976), 53.

10. *The Book of Common Prayer and Administration of the Sacraments and Other Rites and Ceremonies of the Church according to the Use of the Episcopal Church* (New York: The Church Hymnal Corporation and Seabury, 1979), 52.

11. *The Hymnal 1940 Companion* (Worcester, Mass.: Hefferman, 1949), 236.

12. Ibid.

13. Ibid., 545.

14. Augustine of Hippo, *Confessions*, Book 9 (Garden City, N.Y.: Doubleday, 1960), vii.

15. *Book of Common Prayer*, 52–53.

16. *Hymnal Companion*, 16–17, 535; see also *The Hymnal 1982* (New York: The Church Hymnal Corporation, 1985), 82.

17. *Hymnal Companion*, 65–66, 435; see also *The Hymnal 1940*, 86; *The Hymnal 1982*, 216.

18. *The Apostolic Fathers*, ed. J. B. Lightfoot and J. R. Harmer (Grand Rapids: Baker, 1984), 232–33; see also Hustad, *The Worshiping Church*, xii.

19. *Book of Common Prayer*, 333–34.

20. Ibid., 59.

21. Fremantle, *Treasury of Early Christianity*, 29–34.

22. *The Fathers of the Church*, ed. Schaff, 33–34, 40.

23. Fremantle, *Treasury of Early Christianity*, 338.

24. Ibid., 327.

25. *Book of Common Prayer*, 327–28.

26. D. Bruce Lockerbie, *The Apostles' Creed* (Wheaton, Ill.: Victor, 1977), 17–18.

27. *Book of Common Prayer*, 96.

28. *The Fathers of the Church*, 133–34.

29. *Stromateis* (Grand Rapids: Eerdmans, 1951), 305.

30. *The Ante-Nicene Fathers*, ed. Alexander Roberts and James Donaldson, vol. 2 (Grand Rapids: Eerdmans, 1975), 222–34.

31. "Apologeticus," Chapter 1; quoted in *The New Schaff-Herzog Encyclopedia of Religious Knowledge*, ed. Samuel Macauley Jackson, vol. 11 (Grand Rapids: Baker, 1977), 306.

32. *Readings in Christian Humanism*, ed. Joseph M. Shaw, R. W. Franklin, Harris Kaasa, and Charles W. Buzicky. (Minneapolis: Augsburg, 1982), 88–89, 91–92.

33. Fremantle, *Treasury of Early Christianity*, 66–69.

34. Fremantle, 70–78.

35. *The Ante-Nicene Fathers*, Roberts and Donaldson, 7: 393.

36. *The New Schaff-Herzog Encyclopedia*, 3: 285.

37. Ibid., 290.

38. Ibid., 291.

39. Ibid., 2:519–97.

40. Ibid., 6:189–91.

PART 3:
Popes, Princes, and Pedagogues, 500–1400

1. *Pastoral Care*, trans. and annotated Henry Davis (New York: Newman, 1978), 20–25.

2. Bede, *Opera Historica* (Cambridge, Mass.: Harvard Univ., 1954), 383.

3. Ibid., 11.

4. As quoted in Andrew Fleming West, *Alcuin and the Rise of Christian Schools* (New York: Scribners, 1892), 54.

5. Ibid., 37.

6. Ibid., 52.

7. Ibid., 106.

8. Ibid., 49.

9. Ellwood P. Cubberley, *Readings in the History of Education* (Boston: Houghton Mifflin, 1920), 106–11.

10. Ibid., 97

11. Ibid., 94.

12. Ibid., 94.

13. *Anselm of Canterbury*, ed. and trans. Jasper Hopkins and Herbert Richardson. Vol. 1. (New York: Edwin Mellen, 1974), 89–93.

14. Arthur O. Norton, *Readings in the History of Education: Mediaeval Universities.* (Cambridge, Mass.: Harvard Univ., 1909), 15.

15. Ibid., 17.

16. Ibid., 26.

17. *Basic Writings of Saint Thomas Aquinas*, ed. Anton C. Pegis. Vol. 1 (New York: Random, 1945), 5–6.

18. Ecclesiasticus 3:22. Ecclesiasticus is from the Apocrypha, a collection of books accepted by the Roman Cathoic Church as canonical. The Protestant church does not recognize the Apocrypha as part of the Holy Scriptures.

19. Ecclesiasticus 3:25. Part of the Apocrypha.

20. *The Medieval University*, ed. Helene Wieruszowski. (Princeton, N.J.: Nostrand, 1966), 146–147.

PART 4:
Christian Humanism and the Protestant Reformation

1. D. Bruce Lockerbie, "Reclaiming Christian Humanism," *Thinking and Acting Like a Christian* (Portland, Ore.: Multnomah, 1989), 83–95. See also *The Christian, the Arts, and Truth*, ed. D. Bruce Lockerbie. (Portland: Multnomah, 1985), 13–17.

2. "Protestation of 1529," *The Oxford Dictionary of the Christian Church*, ed. Frank L. Cross (London: Oxford, 1958), 1280.

3. William Boyd, *The History of Western Education* (New York: Barnes and Noble, 1969), 198.

4. William H. Woodward, *Vittorino da Feltre and Other Humanist Educators* (New York: Teachers College, 1964), 20–67.

5. Thomas á Kempis, *The Imitation of Christ*, trans. William C. Creasy. (Macon, Ga.: Mercer Univ., 1989), 3–6.

6. Nicholas of Cusa, *Of Learned Ignorance*, trans. Germain Heron. (New Haven, Conn.: Yale Univ., 1954), 160–65.

7. E. Harris Harbison, *The Christian Scholar in the Age of the Reformation.* (New York: Scribners, 1956), 109.

8. *The Collected Works of Erasmus*, vol. 26, trans. Beert C. Verstraete (Toronto: Univ. of Toronto, 1985), 295–346. Reprinted by permission of Teacher College Press © 1964 from William H. Woodward, ed., *Desiderius Erasmus Concerning the Aim and Method of Education.*

9. Boyd, *The History of Western Education*, 188.

10. Ellwood P. Cubberley, *Readings in the History of Education* (Boston: Houghton Mifflin, 1920), 273.

11. *The Library of Christian Classics*, vols. 20 and 21 (Philadelphia: Westminster, 1960), 241–44.

PART 5:
The Roots of Modern Universal Schooling

1. C. S. Lewis, *English Literature in the Sixteenth Century* (London: Oxford, 1954), 274–75.

2. *The Schoolmaster*, ed. Lawrence V. Ryan. (Ithaca, N.Y.: Cornell Univ., 1967).

3. John Edward Sadler, *J. A. Comenius and the Concept of Universal Education*, (New York: Barnes and Noble, 1966), 51.

4. *The Portable Milton*, ed. Douglas Bush (New York: Viking, 1955), 135–50.

5. *The Educational Writings of John Locke*, ed. James L. Axtell. (Cambridge: Cambridge Univ., 1968), 258–62.

6. *The Works of Hannah More.* (New York: Harper, 1838), 130. All statements by More and the excerpt from "Strictures on the Modern System of Female Education" 311–12) come from this early nineteenth century work.

PART 6:
The American Experience, 1620–1750

1. *Puritan Manifesto*, ed. W. H. Frere (New York: Church Historical Society, 1954), 5–39.

2. *The Puritans*, ed. Michael L. Lasser (New York: Holt, Rinehart and Winston, 1969), 8.

3. Ellwood P. Cubberley, *Readings in the History of Education* (Boston: Houghton Mifflin, 1920), 292–94. The excerpts from "Rules of Harvard College" and "New England's First Fruit" originally were printed in old middle English; the spellings and punctuation have been updated to current English style.

4. *The Puritans*, Lasser, 23–24.

5. Ibid., 61–62.

6. Richard Hofstadter, *Anti-Intellectualism in American Life* (New York: Knopf, 1963), 98.

7. Ibid., 70.

8. *The Puritans*, Lasser, 54.

9. *Documentary History of Religion in America to the Civil War*, ed. Edwin Gaustad. (Grand Rapids: Eerdmans, 1982), 214–20.

PART 7:
American Reformers: 1750–1900

1. George S. Brookes, *Friend Anthony Benezet* (Philadelphia: Univ. of Pennsylvania, 1937), 31.

2. Ibid., 46–47.

3. Ibid., 49.

4. *Letters on the Equality of the Sexes and Other Essays*, ed. Elizabeth Ann Bartlett. (New Haven: Yale, 1988), 112–20.

5. Quoted in John H. Westerhoff III, *McGuffey and His Readers: Piety, Morality, and Education in Nineteenth Century America* (Nashville: Abingdon, 1978), 61.

6. Ibid., 171–93.

PART 8:
The Deification of Democracy

1. James McLachlan, *American Boarding Schools* (New York: Scribner's, 1970), 38.

2. Lawrence Cremin, *American Education: The National Experience 1783–1876* (New York: Harper & Row, 1980), 60.

3. Quoted in William Warren Sweet, *The Story of Religion in America* (New York: Harper, 1950), 223–24.

4. Ibid., 226.

5. *The Selected Writings of Ralph Waldo Emerson* (New York: Modern Library, 1950), 73.

6. Frank E. Gaebelein, *Christian Education in a Democracy* (New York: Oxford, 1951), 6.

7. See p. 325.

8. Ellwood P. Cubberley, *Readings in the History of Education* (Boston: Houghton Mifflin, 1920), 575–76.

9. *An American Primer*, ed. Daniel J. Boorstin. (Chicago: Univ. of Chicago, 1966), 351–54.

10. *Selections from Ralph Waldo Emerson*, ed. Stephen E. Whicher. (Boston: Houghton Mifflin, 1957), 10.

11. *An American Primer*, 300.

12. *Selections*, Whicher, 63–80.

13. John L. Childs, "The Meaning of the Term: Experimentalism," *Frontiers of Democracy*; cited by Edwin H. Rian, *Christianity and American Education* (San Antonio: Naylor, 1949), 71.

14. Rousas John Rushdoony, *The Messianic Character of American Education* (Nutley, N.J.: Craig, 1968), 23.

15. Rian, *Christianity and American Education*, 30.

16. *An American Primer*, ed. Boorstin, 609–19.

PART 9:
Twentieth Century Renewal

1. Richard K. Curtis, *They Called Him Mister Moody* (Garden City, N.Y.: Doubleday, 1962), 297–98.

2. T. S. Eliot, *Christianity and Culture: The Idea of a Christian Society* (New York: Harcourt Brace, 1940), 22.

3. Frank Gaebelein, *The Pattern of God's Truth* New York: Oxford Univ. Press, 1954) 20; see p. 372.

4. Charlotte M. Mason, *School Education* (Wheaton, Ill.: Tyndale, 1989), 137–45. Now out of print; however, all six volumes of Miss Mason's classic series on education and parenting have been reprinted by Charlotte Mason Research & Supply Co. For information on obtaining this series, write Charlotte Mason Research & Supply. P.O. Box 172, Stanton, NJ 08885.

5. D. Bruce Lockerbie, *The Way They Should Go* (New York: Oxford, 1972), Introduction, n. p.

6. Gaebelein, *The Pattern of God's Truth*, 3–26.

7. Henry Zylstra, *Testament of Vision* (Grand Rapids: Eerdmans, 1958), 138–49.

PART 10:
Looking Back, Looking Ahead

1. William O. Douglas, Zorach v. Clauson, (1952)

2. D. Bruce Lockerbie, *Who Educates Your Child?* (New York: Doubleday, 1980), 119–20.

3. Simone Weil, *Waiting for God* (London: Collins, 1969), 66–76.

4. Peter K. Haile, "Why I Believe in Schools That Are as Christian as Possible," *Latin America Mission Evangelist* (October–December, 1977), 4–5. Reprinted by permission of author.

5. Kenneth O. Gangel, "Integrating Faith and Learning: Principles and Process," *Bibliotheca Sacra*, 135: (April–June 1978), 99–108.

6. See John H. Westerhoff III, *Will Our Children Have Faith?* (San Francisco: Harper, 1985).

7. John H. Westerhoff III, "Hidden Curriculum in the Classroom, *Church Teachers*, September–October 1993, 45–47. Reprinted by permission of author.

8. *Saluting Christian Schools,* 5 (Summer, 1993): 3–4.

SELECTED
BIBLIOGRAPHY

Anselm. *Anselm of Canterbury*, ed. and trans. Jasper Hopkins and Herbert Richardson. Toronto and New York (Edwin Mellen), 1974.

Aquinas, Thomas. *Basic Writings of Saint Thomas Aquinas*. New York: Random House, 1945.

Ascham, Roger. *The Schoolmaster*, ed. Lawrence V. Ryan. Ithaca, New York: Cornell Univ., 1967.

Augustine of Hippo. *On Christian Doctrine*, trans. D. W. Robertson, Jr. Indianapolis: Bobbs-Merrill, 1958.

Barnes, Gilbert H. and Dwight L. Barnard, eds. *Letters of Theodore Dwight Weld, Angelina Grimké Weld and Sarah Grimké*. New York: Appleton-Century, 1934.

Bartlett, Elizabeth Ann, ed. *Letters on the Equality of the Sexes and Other Essays*. New Haven, Conn.: Yale Univ., 1988.

Boorstin, Daniel J., ed. *An American Primer*. New York: New American Library, 1968.

Brookes, George S. *Friend Anthony Benezet*. Philadelphia: Univ. Pennsylvania, 1937.

Bushnell, Horace. *Christian Nurture*. New York: Scribner's, 1914.

Calvin, John. *Institutes of the Christian Religion*. Vols. 20 and 21 of *The Library of Christian Classics*. Philadelphia: Westminster, 1960.

Cubberley, Ellwood P. *A Brief History of Education*. Boston: Houghton Mifflin, 1920.

_____. *Readings in the History of Education*. Boston: Houghton Mifflin, 1920.

Cusa, Nicholas of. *Of Learned Ignorance*, trans. Germain Heron. New Haven, Conn.: Yale Univ., 1954.

Dewey, John. *My Pedagogic Creed*. New York: Macmillan, 1929.

Elyot, Sir Thomas. *The Book of the Governor*. New York: Dent, 1956.

Erasmus, Desiderius. *The Collected Works of Erasmus*. Toronto: Univ. of Toronto, 1985.

Fremantle, Anne, ed. *A Treasury of Early Christianity*. New York: New American Library, 1953.

Gaebelein, Frank E. *Christian Education in a Democracy*. New York: Oxford, 1951.

————. *The Pattern of God's Truth: Problems of Integration in Christian Education.* New York: Oxford, 1954.

————. *The Christian, the Arts, and Truth: Regaining the Vision of Greatness,* ed. D. Bruce Lockerbie. Portland, Ore.: Multnomah, 1985.

Gaustad, Edwin, ed. *Documentary History of Religion in America to the Civil War.* Grand Rapids: Eerdmans, 1982.

Goodsell, Willystine. *Pioneers of Women's Education in the United States: Emma Willard, Catherine Beecher, Mary Lyon.* New York: McGraw-Hill, 1931.

Gregory the Great. *Pastoral Care,* trans. and annotated, Henry Davis, New York: Newman, 1978.

Harbison, E. Harris. *The Christian Scholar in the Age of the Reformation.* New York: Scribner's, 1956.

Kienel, Paul A. *The Christian School.* Wheaton, Ill.: Victor, 1974.

Lasser, Michael L. *The Puritans.* New York: Holt, Rinehart & Winston, 1969.

Locke, John. *The Educational Writings of John Locke,* ed. James L. Axtell. Cambridge: Cambridge Univ., 1968.

Lockerbie, D. Bruce. *The Way They Should Go.* New York: Oxford Univ., 1972.

————. *The Apostles' Creed: Do You Really Believe It?* Wheaton: Victor, 1977.

————. *Who Educates Your Child? A Book for Parents.* Grand Rapids: Zondervan, 1981.

————. "Protestant Education: History and Issues," *Encyclopedia of Educational Research,* 5th ed. New York: Free Press, 1982.

————. *Thinking and Acting Like a Christian.* Portland: Multnomah, 1989.

————. "Christian Education," *New Twentieth-Century Encyclopedia of Religious Knowledge,* 2d ed. Grand Rapids: Baker, 1991.

Lowrie, Roy W., Jr. *Inside the Christian School.* Whittier, Calif.: ACSI, 1980.

Norton, Arthur O. *Readings in the History of Education.* Cambridge, Mass.: Mediaeval Universities (Harvard), 1909.

Painter, F. V. N. *Luther on Education.* St. Louis: Concordia, 1928.

Rian, Edwin H. *Christianity and American Education.* San Antonio, Tex.: Naylor, 1949.

Roberts, Alexander and James Donaldson, eds. *The Ante-Nicene Fathers.* Grand Rapids: Eerdmans, 1975.

Rushdoony, Rousas John. *The Messianic Character of American Education.* Nutley, N.J.: Craig, 1968.

Sadler, John Edward. *J. A. Comenius and the Concept of Universal Education.* New York: Barnes and Noble, 1966.

Schaff, Philip, ed. *Nicene and Post-Nicene Fathers.* Grand Rapids: Eerdmans, 1979.

Shaw, Joseph, et al., eds. *Readings in Christian Humanism.* Minneapolis: Augsburg, 1982.

Sklar, Kathryn Kish. *Catherine Beecher: A Study in American Domesticity.* New Haven: Yale, 1973.

Spinka, Matthew, ed. *Advocates of Reform from Wyclif to Erasmus.* Vol. 14 of *The Library of Christian Classics.* Philadelphia: Westminster, 1953.

_____. *John Amos Comenius: That Incomparable Moravian.* New York: Russell and Russell, 1967.

Sweet, William Warren. *The Story of Religion in America.* New York: Harper, 1950.

Thorndike, Lynn, ed. *University Records and Life in the Middle Ages.* New York: Columbia Univ., 1944.

Vaux, Roberts. *Memoirs of the Life of Anthony Benezet.* Philadelphia: York, 1817.

Weil, Simone. *Waiting on God.* Trans. Emma Crawford. London: Fontana, 1969.

Westerhoff, John H. III. *McGuffey and His Readers: Piety, Morality, and Education in Nineteenth-Century America.* Nashville: Abingdon, 1978.

_____. *Will Our Children Have Faith?* San Francisco: Harper, 1985.

Wieruszowski, Helene, ed. *The Medieval University: Masters, Students, Learning.* Princeton, N.J.: Nostrand, 1966.

Woodward, William Harrison. *Desiderius Erasmus Concerning the Aim and Method of Education.* New York: Teachers College, 1964.

_____. *Vittorino da Feltre and Other Humanist Educators.* New York: Teachers College, 1964.

Zylstra, Henry. *Testament of Vision.* Grand Rapids: Eerdmans, 1958.

INDEX
OF SUBJECTS

INDEX
OF PERSONS

435

INDEX
OF SCRIPTURE

Moody Press, a ministry of the Moody Bible Institute,
is designed for education, evangelization, and edification.
If we may assist you in knowing more about Christ
and the Christian life, please write us without obligation:
Moody Press, c/o MLM, Chicago, Illinois 60610.